T0353352

Information Technology Risk Management and Compliance in Modern Organizations

Manish Gupta
State University of New York, Buffalo, USA

Raj Sharman
State University of New York, Buffalo, USA

John Walp
M&T Bank Corporation, USA

Pavankumar Mulgund
State University of New York, Buffalo, USA

A volume in the Advances in
Information Security, Privacy, and
Ethics (AISPE) Book Series

IGI Global
DISSEMINATOR OF KNOWLEDGE

Published in the United States of America by
    IGI Global
    Business Science Reference (an imprint of IGI Global)
    701 E. Chocolate Avenue
    Hershey PA, USA 17033
    Tel: 717-533-8845
    Fax: 717-533-8661
    E-mail: cust@igi-global.com
    Web site: http://www.igi-global.com

Library of Congress Cataloging-in-Publication Data

Names: Gupta, Manish, 1978- editor. | Sharman, Raj, editor. | Walp, John,
  1967- editor.
Title: Information technology risk management and compliance in modern
  organizations / Manish Gupta, Raj Sharman, John Walp, and Pavankumar
  Mulgund, editors.
Description: Hershey : Business Science Reference, [2018]
Identifiers: LCCN 2017006893| ISBN 9781522526049 (hardcover) | ISBN
  9781522526056 (ebook)
Subjects: LCSH: Business enterprises--Computer networks--Security measures. |
  Information technology--Security measures. | Data protection. | Computer
  security. | Risk management.
Classification: LCC HF5548.37 .I545 2017 | DDC 658.4/78--dc23 LC record available at https://
lccn.loc.gov/2017006893

This book is published in the IGI Global book series Advances in Information Security, Privacy, and Ethics (AISPE) (ISSN: 1948-9730; eISSN: 1948-9749)

British Cataloguing in Publication Data
A Cataloguing in Publication record for this book is available from the British Library.

All work contributed to this book is new, previously-unpublished material.
The views expressed in this book are those of the authors, but not necessarily of the publisher.

For electronic access to this publication, please contact: eresources@igi-global.com.

Advances in Information Security, Privacy, and Ethics (AISPE) Book Series

ISSN:1948-9730
EISSN:1948-9749

Editor-in-Chief: Manish Gupta, State University of New York, USA

MISSION

As digital technologies become more pervasive in everyday life and the Internet is utilized in ever increasing ways by both private and public entities, concern over digital threats becomes more prevalent.

The **Advances in Information Security, Privacy, & Ethics (AISPE) Book Series** provides cutting-edge research on the protection and misuse of information and technology across various industries and settings. Comprised of scholarly research on topics such as identity management, cryptography, system security, authentication, and data protection, this book series is ideal for reference by IT professionals, academicians, and upper-level students.

COVERAGE

- Device Fingerprinting
- Global Privacy Concerns
- Information Security Standards
- Tracking Cookies
- Telecommunications Regulations
- Risk Management
- Internet Governance
- Cookies
- Security Classifications
- Network Security Services

IGI Global is currently accepting manuscripts for publication within this series. To submit a proposal for a volume in this series, please contact our Acquisition Editors at Acquisitions@igi-global.com or visit: http://www.igi-global.com/publish/.

Titles in this Series

For a list of additional titles in this series, please visit:
http://www.igi-global.com/book-series/advances-information-security-privacy-ethics/37157

Detecting and Mitigating Robotic Cyber Security Risks
Raghavendra Kumar (LNCT Group of College, India) Prasant Kumar Pattnaik (KIIT University, India) and Priyanka Pandey (LNCT Group of College,India)
Information Science Reference • ©2017 • 384pp • H/C (ISBN: 9781522521549) • US $210.00

Advanced Image-Based Spam Detection and Filtering Techniques
Sunita Vikrant Dhavale (Defense Institute of Advanced Technology (DIAT), Pune, India)
Information Science Reference • ©2017 • 213pp • H/C (ISBN: 9781683180135) • US $175.00

Privacy and Security Policies in Big Data
Sharvari Tamane (MGM's Jawaharlal Nehru Engineering College, India) Vijender Kumar Solanki (Institute of Technology and Science Ghaziabad, India) and Nilanjan Dey (Techno India College of Technology, India)
Information Science Reference • ©2017 • 305pp • H/C (ISBN: 9781522524861) • US $210.00

Securing Government Information and Data in Developing Countries
Saleem Zoughbi (UN APCICT, UN ESCAP, South Korea)
Information Science Reference • ©2017 • 307pp • H/C (ISBN: 9781522517030) • US $160.00

Security Breaches and Threat Prevention in the Internet of Things
N. Jeyanthi (VIT University, India) and R. Thandeeswaran (VIT University, India)
Information Science Reference • ©2017 • 276pp • H/C (ISBN: 9781522522966) • US $180.00

Decentralized Computing Using Blockchain Technologies and Smart Contracts ...
S. Asharaf (Indian Institute of Information Technology and Management, Kerala, India) and S. Adarsh (Indian Institute of Information Technology and Management, Kerala, India)
Information Science Reference • ©2017 • 128pp • H/C (ISBN: 9781522521938) • US $120.00

Cybersecurity Breaches and Issues Surrounding Online Threat Protection
Michelle Moore (George Mason University, USA)
Information Science Reference • ©2017 • 408pp • H/C (ISBN: 9781522519416) • US $195.00

For an enitre list of titles in this series, please visit:
http://www.igi-global.com/book-series/advances-information-security-privacy-ethics/37157

701 East Chocolate Avenue, Hershey, PA 17033, USA
Tel: 717-533-8845 x100 • Fax: 717-533-8661
E-Mail: cust@igi-global.com • www.igi-global.com

Editorial Advisory Board

Table of Contents

Preface xv

Section 1
Frameworks and Methodologies

Chapter 1
An Analytical Study of Methodologies and Tools for Enterprise Information
Security Risk Management 1
Jaya Bhattacharjee, Jadavpur University, India
Anirban Sengupta, Jadavpur University, India
Mridul Sankar Barik, Jadavpur University, India
Chandan Mazumdar, Jadavpur University, India

Chapter 2
A Step-by-Step Procedural Methodology for Improving an Organization's IT
Risk Management System 21
Shanmugapriya Loganathan, Excelok Technologies, Singapore

Chapter 3
Strengthening IT Governance With COBIT 5 48
Gaurav Chaudhari, Independent Researcher, Egypt
Pavankumar Mulgund, University at Buffalo, USA

Section 2
Regulatory and Compliance Risks

Chapter 4
Implications of HIPAA and Subsequent Regulations on Information
Technology 71
Payod Soni, University at Buffalo, USA

Chapter 5
Navigating Through Choppy Waters of PCI DSS Compliance 99
    Amrita Nanda, University at Buffalo, USA
    Priyal Popat, University at Buffalo, USA
    Deepak Vimalkumar, University at Buffalo, USA

Section 3
Human and Social Risks

Chapter 6
Fortifying Corporate Human Wall: A Literature Review of Security
Awareness and Training..142
    Anandharaman Pattabiraman, University at Buffalo, USA
    Sridhar Srinivasan, University at Buffalo, USA
    Kaushik Swaminathan, University at Buffalo, USA
    Manish Gupta, University at Buffalo, USA

Chapter 7
A Tale of Policies and Breaches: Analytical Approach to Construct Social
Media Policy 176
    Neha Singh, University at Buffalo, USA
    Tanya Mittal, University at Buffalo, USA
    Manish Gupta, University at Buffalo, USA

Section 4
Technology Risks

Chapter 8
Information Technology Outsourcing Risk Factors and Provider Selection 214
    Salim Lahmiri, ESCA School of Management, Morocco

Chapter 9
Impact of Technology Innovation: A Study on Cloud Risk Mitigation.............229
    Niranjali Suresh, University at Buffalo, USA
    Manish Gupta, University at Buffalo, USA

Chapter 10
Swimming Upstream in Turbulent Waters: Auditing Agile Development 268
    Priyadarsini Kannan Krishnamachariar, State University of New York,
        Buffalo, USA
    Manish Gupta, State University of New York, Buffalo, USA

Chapter 11

Do Privacy Concerns Affect Information Seeking via Smartphones?...............301

Mohamed Abdelhamid, University at Buffalo, USA
Srikanth Venkatesan, University at Buffalo, USA
Joana Gaia, University at Buffalo, USA
Raj Sharman, University at Buffalo, USA

Compilation of References 315

About the Contributors 356

Index 359

Detailed Table of Contents

Preface xv

Section 1
Frameworks and Methodologies

Chapter 1
An Analytical Study of Methodologies and Tools for Enterprise Information
Security Risk Management 1

Jaya Bhattacharjee, Jadavpur University, India
Anirban Sengupta, Jadavpur University, India
Mridul Sankar Barik, Jadavpur University, India
Chandan Mazumdar, Jadavpur University, India

An enterprise is characterized by its business processes and supporting ICT infrastructure. Securing these entities is of utmost importance for the survival of an enterprise and continuity of its business operations. In order to secure them, it is important to first detect the risks that can be realized to cause harm to those entities. Over the years, several kinds of security risk analysis methodologies have been proposed. They cater to different categories of enterprise entities and consider varying levels of detail during risk analysis. An enterprise often finds it difficult to select a particular method that will best suit its purpose. This paper attempts to address this problem by presenting a detailed study of existing risk analysis methodologies. The study classifies them into specific categories and performs comparative analyses considering different parameters addressed by the methodologies, including asset type, vulnerabilities, threats, and security controls.

Chapter 2
A Step-by-Step Procedural Methodology for Improving an Organization's IT
Risk Management System 21

Shanmugapriya Loganathan, Excelok Technologies, Singapore

Risks in IT are described as a form of threat in context with data security, network transfer, system scheduled processes, critical applications, and business procedures.

IT risk management is broadly defined as the process of managing IT risks, and must be executed on a regular basis. It is neither a product nor a purchase, but a policy of an organization implements to protect its business systems. Managing IT risk plays a vital role in administering any business in today's world. Irrespective of the business, deep knowledge of IT risk leads to increased data security, reduced business cost, and greater compliance. This chapter deals with methodologies to improve risk management in an IT organization, their impact, and some examples.

Chapter 3
Strengthening IT Governance With COBIT 5 48
    Gaurav Chaudhari, Independent Researcher, Egypt
    Pavankumar Mulgund, University at Buffalo, USA

This paper aims to explore the importance of COBIT 5 as a framework, in ensuring the effective "Governance of Enterprise Information Technology (GEIT)", and to promote the understanding of the five COBIT 5 principles. A comprehensive literature review has also been performed taking into account a total of 56 research papers published in the last decade on COBIT. The data collected from these research papers was analyzed in order to identify various trends- commonalities, differences, themes, and the nature of study. The research papers have been categorized first on basis of their scope and secondly on their nature (empirical, conceptual or descriptive). Towards the end of the paper, we have provided an overview of our findings on the strengths and weaknesses of the research papers studied, and have made suggestions for future research.

Section 2
Regulatory and Compliance Risks

Chapter 4
Implications of HIPAA and Subsequent Regulations on Information
Technology...71
    Payod Soni, University at Buffalo, USA

Abysmal state of policies governing the health plan providers lead to a huge discontent amongst the public in regards to their health plan besides privacy and security of their medical records. Anyone with access to the patient's medical records could potentially share it with parties like health plan providers or the employers. To address the privacy and the security of patient's medical records, Congress enacted HIPAA in 1996. Chapter starts with discussing the need for HIPAA. Subsequently, we discuss HIPAA at considerable depth. Significant additions and changes were made in subsequent acts and amendments due to pressing policy needs and to address various loopholes. The chapter provides a chronological recount of HIPAA since its introduction. Once the reader develops a complete understanding of HIPAA regulation, we shift our focus to the compliance to HIPAA. We delve deeper into implications of HIPAA on healthcare organizations and the information technology world.

Chapter 5

Navigating Through Choppy Waters of PCI DSS Compliance 99
Amrita Nanda, University at Buffalo, USA
Priyal Popat, University at Buffalo, USA
Deepak Vimalkumar, University at Buffalo, USA

PCI Data Security Standard is increasingly becoming one of the major compliance requirements all organizations are concerned about. This chapter taking a holistic approach, provides an overview of various components of PCI DSS. We discuss various versions of PCI DSS and the industries affected by this standard, the scope and requirements to comply and hesitation on part of most companies to imbibe it. We also look at the high-profile credit card breaches which have occurred recently and their impact on concerned industries. Additionally, we focus on the challenges faced by financial institutions to effectively meet PCI DSS requirements. Based on our analysis of different requirements of PCI DSS, challenges faced by organizations and recent security breaches of companies which were PCI DSS complaint at the time of breach, we propose recommendations to help organizations secure their cardholder data beyond the achieved compliance in place.

Section 3
Human and Social Risks

Chapter 6

Fortifying Corporate Human Wall: A Literature Review of Security
Awareness and Training...142
Anandharaman Pattabiraman, University at Buffalo, USA
Sridhar Srinivasan, University at Buffalo, USA
Kaushik Swaminathan, University at Buffalo, USA
Manish Gupta, University at Buffalo, USA

It has been very evident from data breaches from last few years that attackers are increasingly targeting the path of least resistance to compromise the security of organizations. Cyber security threats that exploit human behavior are becoming sophisticated and difficult to prevent against. At the same time humans are the countermeasures that can adapt swiftly to changing risk landscape than technological and procedural countermeasures. Organizations are implementing and enhancing their security awareness and training programs in an attempt to ensure that risks from human elements, which pose the greatest risks, are mitigated. The chapter conducts a thorough literature review in the area of security awareness and training and presents a classification scheme and a conceptual research model to provide insights into the existing body of knowledge in the area. Trends and analyses are also presented from the reviewed papers, which can be of importance to organizations in improving their security awareness programs. The insights from the study can be leveraged to build a strong human wall against both internal and external threats that are fast evolving and causing tremendous amount of loss.

Chapter 7

A Tale of Policies and Breaches: Analytical Approach to Construct Social Media Policy 176

Neha Singh, University at Buffalo, USA
Tanya Mittal, University at Buffalo, USA
Manish Gupta, University at Buffalo, USA

While the use of social media offers great opportunities to interact with customers and business partners, there are significant risks associated with this technology if a clear strategy has not been defined to address both the risks and the benefits that come along with it. The best approach for an organization to effectively utilize the benefits of this technology is to engage all relevant stakeholders and establish a strategy that addresses the pertinent issues. The organization needs to have in place relevant policies so as to be able to achieve it. To be able to identify the most frequent risks and their source, we captured breach data from various sources. In the chapter, we analyzed that the most important source of risk that can occur due to use of social media for a company is from its own workforce and an employee might find various ways of doing so.

Section 4
Technology Risks

Chapter 8

Information Technology Outsourcing Risk Factors and Provider Selection 214

Salim Lahmiri, ESCA School of Management, Morocco

Information technology outsourcing has become a major issue in business and received a large attention from both business managers and scholars. Indeed, it helps a business company to reduce it costs and to maintain its competitiveness. The purpose of this chapter is to introduce the utility of information technology outsourcing for the enterprise and to review some recent works in outsourcing risk factors identification and provider selection. Finally, drawbacks of information technology outsourcing will be presented along with future research directions.

Chapter 9
Impact of Technology Innovation: A Study on Cloud Risk Mitigation.............229
    Niranjali Suresh, University at Buffalo, USA
    Manish Gupta, University at Buffalo, USA

Cloud enables computing as a utility by offering convenient, on-demand network access to a centralized pool of configurable computing resources that can be rapidly deployed with great efficiency and minimal management overhead. In order to realize the benefits of the innovative cloud computing paradigm, companies must overcome heightened risks and security threats associated with it. Security and privacy in cloud is complex owing to newer dimensions in problem scope such as multi-tenant architectures and shared infrastructure, elasticity, measured services, viability etc. In this paper, we survey existing literature on cloud security issues and risks which then guides us to provide a section on auditing based to address the identified risks. We also provide a discourse on risk assessment frameworks to highlight benefits using such structured methods for understanding risks. The main contribution of the paper is investigation of current innovations in cloud computing that are targeted towards assisting in effective management of aforementioned risks and security issues. The compilation of discussed solutions has been developed to cater to specific cloud security, compliance and privacy requirements across industries by cloud service providers, software-as-a-service (SaaS) application vendors and advisory firms.

Chapter 10
Swimming Upstream in Turbulent Waters: Auditing Agile Development 268
    Priyadarsini Kannan Krishnamachariar, State University of New York,
        Buffalo, USA
    Manish Gupta, State University of New York, Buffalo, USA

Agile approach is a pragmatic fashion of software development, wherein the requirements are flexible to the changing needs of the customers, fast paced markets and the iterations of software are implemented and delivered based on business priorities. A risky or experimental project where the project requirements are not clear/not defined well in advance, are the most suitable candidates for adopting agile approach, as agile enables us to work with calculated risks during development, aiming to reduce the risks. The value of any implementation is realized only if it delivers benefits to organization and users, which could be assured by effective auditing of the implementation by understanding the implications of agile approach and figuring out right audit techniques and processes. Many organizations already have well established audit functions and matured IT Audit procedures for auditing traditional SDLC waterfall processes. Yet the methods for auditing software development based on agile approach requires a different attitude and audit techniques that goes well with the proactive nature of agile approach. This paper aims to present risk based audit approach on the agile implementation of software development, how risk identification and assessment can be merged along with the phases of software development and the ways by which agile techniques can be effectively utilized as tools for audit.

Chapter 11

Do Privacy Concerns Affect Information Seeking via Smartphones?...............301
Mohamed Abdelhamid, University at Buffalo, USA
Srikanth Venkatesan, University at Buffalo, USA
Joana Gaia, University at Buffalo, USA
Raj Sharman, University at Buffalo, USA

The innovation and evolution of technologies in smartphone industry has enabled users to efficiently achieve many tasks including utilizing search engines for instant information retrieval anytime and anywhere. Nonetheless, some users choose not to use these smartphone features including search engines to seek information. This study explores the factors that impact the likelihood of information seeking via smartphones. Privacy concern was found to be one of the main factors influencing the likelihood of seeking information. Android users were more likely to seek information compared to iPhone users, possibly due to the differences in the features of the operating systems of these phones. Motivation to seek information captured by technology ownership increases the likelihood of information seeking. The diversity of social network connections also plays a significant in information seeking behavior of the users.

Compilation of References 315

About the Contributors 356

Index 359

Preface

Last decade has witnessed an unprecedented and exponential growth in reliance on IT by companies of all sizes. IT has emerged as critical business enabler from a mere support function. This trend has catapulted the strategic importance of managing technology risks to a standing agenda item on the board of directors' conventions (Deloitte, 2016). Companies are increasingly putting efforts on identifying, assessing and managing risks to their IT systems, infrastructure and processes as they directly impact business operations and objectives (Morales, 2014; Jackson, 2012). Understanding of risks and controls around IT has also significantly improved as a result of that. There are many existing and newer regulatory requirements that have emerged in response to that in an attempt to provide consistent, structured and auditable frameworks for managing risks. In a recent survey (Deloitte, 2016), it was also found that "Compliance with new and existing regulation was a clear leader regarding focus with over 70% indicating this was a top priority for their executive. Many organizations still do not feel fully equipped to respond to the regulatory challenge, especially those with a global and multi-product footprint" (p. 3). The survey also highlighted that there is a widening gap between actual risk exposure and established risk appetite because the exposure has been increasing at a steady and consistent rate due to increasing reliance on IT to support business goals, but this appetite hasn't been updated to reflect that. This gap clearly underscores the importance of IT risk management and compliance in organizations.

With the evolving threats and advancing technology, newer and innovative methods are needed to counter the resulting risks to IT effectively. This progress has also led the emergence of a new field of profession – GRC (governance, risk, and compliance). The Open Compliance & Ethics Group (OECG, 2016) defines GRC as:

GRC is a system of people, processes, and technology that enables an organization to understand and prioritize stakeholder expectations; set business objectives congruent with values and risks; achieve objectives while optimizing risk profile and protecting value; operate within legal, contractual, internal, social and ethical boundaries; provide relevant, reliable and timely information to appropriate stakeholders; and enable the measurement of the performance and effectiveness of the system.

Recent research has shown that ineffective technology risk practices adversely impact the financial performance of companies (Teilans et al., 2011; Gill, 2012). The impact to financial bottom-line has been attributed to several factors including reputational damage, disruption in business continuity (Farah, 2011) and loss of data (Carcary, 2013). At the same time, there have been studies that show that managed technology risks lead to additional business opportunities and greater return on IT investments (Bakshi, 2012). These findings have given the field of IT Risk management a huge impetus leading to executive management and board of directors making decisions on investing in proving IT risk management practices (Debreceny, 2013). Internal audit and external audit had traditionally been relied upon to provide services for risk identification, risk assessment and control implementation (Ibrahim, 2014; Heroux & Fortin, 2013). But in recent years to provide more dedicated and focused approach to risk management, companies have instituted internal governance group to aid with proactive and effective technology risk management, including efforts towards managing compliance with regulatory requirements and with established frameworks. This governance group, usually, has direct lines with c-level executives such as chief operating officer and chief risk officer, which leads to the much-needed influence for carrying out their duties.

The risks to IT which can impact the strategic and operational support to business goals have many sources such as technology risks, human and social risks and compliance risks. The book is organized into four sections: Framework and Methodologies, Regulatory and Compliance risks, human and social risks and technology risks. The chapters in the book are organized around these high-level themes.

FRAMEWORKS AND METHODOLOGIES

There are several risk management frameworks and methodologies that companies have been using to gain visibility into technology risks they face and to manage them effectively. These frameworks, while based on similar approaches, tend to cater to different categories of enterprise entities and consider varying levels of detail during risk analysis. For any enterprise, it often becomes challenging to adopt one overarching framework for management of all types of technology risks. This problem is more pronounced in today's environment with the growing complexity of IT implementations and increasing reliance of business on IT. Chapter 1, titled

"An Analytical Study of Methodologies and Tools for Enterprise Security Risk Management" written by Jaya Bhattacharjee, Anirban Sengupta, Mridul Sankar Barik and Chandan Mazumdar attempts to address this problem by presenting a detailed study of existing risk analysis methodologies. The chapter classifies them into specific categories and performs comparative analyses utilizing some parameters addressed by the methodologies, including asset type, vulnerabilities, threats, and security controls.

While we see a comparison and analysis of most prevalent information security risk management frameworks in Chapter 1, there is often the need to revisit the evolving requirements and threat landscape to adapt and combine these frameworks for an organization's needs. 'One size fits all' is not always applicable in technology risk management area on account of various factors such cultural inclinations, business priorities, etc., that mandate a different approach. Along those lines, Chapter 2 ("A Step-by-Step Procedural Methodology for Improving an Organization's IT Risk Management System") by Shanmugapriya Loganathan presents methodologies to improve risk management in an IT organization. The chapter discusses their specific impacts, while also illustrating them with examples. The author asserts that irrespective of the business, deep knowledge of IT risk leads to increased data security, reduced business cost, and greater compliance.

One of the most common frameworks that are in use today for the management of IT risks and overall IT governance is COBIT 5 by ISACA. In Chapter 3, titled "Strengthening IT Governance Using COBIT 5 Framework," authors Gaurav Chaudhari and Pavankumar Mulgund explore the importance of COBIT 5 as a framework, in ensuring the effective "Governance of Enterprise Information Technology (GEIT)," and to promote the understanding of the five COBIT 5 principles. The authors conduct a comprehensive literature review on COBIT. They conducted an incisive review of 56 research papers on COBIT that have been published in the last decade. They categorized the research papers by their scope and their nature (empirical, conceptual or descriptive). This study illustrates the importance of COBIT in research for last decade while also highlighting contributions of those studies.

REGULATORY AND COMPLIANCE RISKS

Regulatory and compliance risks play a major role in any organization's efforts around information security and technology risk management. There are many sector-based, state-based and federal regulations that companies are required to be in compliance with. The risk of not being in compliance with regulations usually takes priority regarding resource allocations and other managerial action. Healthcare industry traditionally has been challenged with lack of a robust and comprehensive set of regulations for security and privacy of sensitive information. The major regulation currently governing the protection of privacy of patient data is the Health Insurance Portability and Accountability Act (HIPAA) of 1996. To track this evolution and present the current state, Chapter 4 titled "Implications of HIPAA and Subsequent Regulations on Information Technology" by Payod Soni and Banashri Pavankumar discusses the state of the pre-HIPAA era and the impact HIPAA when it was introduced in 1996. To illustrate the tenets and provisions of HIPAA, the authors discuss HIPAA's first draft in detail while presenting various significant additions and changes that were made in subsequent acts and amendments due to pressing policy needs and to address various loopholes. This includes discussion of Health Information Technology for Economic and Clinical Health (HITECH) Act of 2009, the Enforcement Rule and the Final Omnibus Rule, which helps present the current state of HIPAA laws. The chapter also analyzes the costs to a non-HIPAA compliant organization in case of a breach of data and impact of HIPAA on the patients.

Payment Card Industry (PCI) Data Security Standard (DSS) is increasingly becoming one of the major compliance requirements for many companies that handle credit card related data. Chapter 5, titled "Navigating Through Choppy Waters of PCI DSS Compliance," authored by Amrita Nanda, Priyal Popat, and Deepak Vimal Kumar, provides an overview of various components of PCI DSS, discusses the history of PCI DSS and investigates recent high-profile credit card breaches and their impact on concerned industries. The chapter illustrates that while companies face many challenges to effectively meet requirements put forth by PCI DSS, the data breaches highlight the fact the compliance is not enough to adequately protect the covered information. Authors, based on their analyses, propose recommendations to help organizations secure their cardholder data that go beyond the efforts to achieve compliance.

HUMAN AND SOCIAL RISKS

Data breaches from last few years provide testimony to the fact that attackers are increasingly targeting the path of least resistance to compromise the security of organizations. Cyber security threats that exploit human behavior are becoming sophisticated and difficult to prevent against. At the same time, humans can adapt swiftly to changing risk landscape than technological and procedural countermeasures. Organizations are implementing and enhancing their security awareness and training programs in an attempt to ensure that risks from human elements, which pose the greatest risks, are mitigated. In Chapter 6, "Fortifying Corporate Human Wall," authors Anandharaman Pattabiraman, Sridhar Srinivasan, Kaushik Swaminathan and Manish Gupta conduct a thorough literature review in the area of security awareness and training and present a classification scheme and a conceptual research model to provide insights into the existing body of knowledge in the area. Trends and analyses are also presented in the chapter from the reviewed papers, which can be of importance to organizations in improving their security awareness programs. The insights from the chapter can be leveraged to build a strong human wall against both internal and external threats that are fast evolving and causing a tremendous amount of loss.

The use of social media is becoming a dominant factor for enterprises and individuals and has far-ranging implications. While this emerging technology in the field of communication offers great opportunities to interact with customers and business partners, there are significant risks associated with this technology if a clear strategy has not been defined to address both the risks and the benefits that come along with it. The best approach for an organization to effectively utilize the benefits of this technology is to engage all relevant stakeholders and establish a strategy that addresses the pertinent issues. The organization needs to have in place relevant policies so as to be able to achieve it. To identify the most frequent risk and its source, the authors analyzed breach data captured from various sources. In Chapter 7, "A Tale of Policies and Breaches: Analytical Approach to Construct Social Media Policy," based on the analysis of breach data, authors Neha Singh, Tanya Mittal and Manish Gupta found that the most important source of risk that can occur due to use of social media for a company is from its workforce and an employee might find various ways of doing so. Authors conclude by asserting that apart from just defining efficient policies, the organization should be able to enforce them, have proper management and continuous "social media awareness" training sessions for its employees.

TECHNOLOGY RISKS

Outsourcing for a long time now has been considered as a business strategy to reduce costs, gain better focus with core and competitive activities while enabling access to talent and better products (Belcourt, 2006). However, significant research has been done on risks with outsourcing arrangements. Chapter 8 ("Information Technology Outsourcing Risk Factors and Provider Selection") by Salim Lahmiri introduces the utility of information technology outsourcing for the enterprise and reviews recent trends in outsourcing risk factors identification and provider selection to provide specific risks of information technology outsourcing.

Companies have been adopting cloud in last few years at an unprecedented rate. While initially there was concerns and skepticism, companies had gotten over them when cloud deployments withstood the test of time. Even today, however, to realize the benefits of the innovative cloud-computing paradigm, companies must overcome heightened risks and security threats associated with it. There have been a few areas that have been tremendously helping companies get more comfortable with cloud adoption such as auditing frameworks for the cloud, specific risk assessment methodologies for cloud and cloud providers' own pace with the innovations in their offerings to mitigate the risks. In Chapter 9, "Impact of Technology Innovation: A Study on Cloud Risk Mitigation," Niranjali Suresh and Manish Gupta cover these three areas and investigate of current innovations in cloud computing that are targeted towards assisting in the effective management of aforementioned risks and security issues.

The agile approach is a pragmatic fashion of software development, wherein the requirements are flexible to the changing needs of the customers, fast-paced markets and the iterations of software are implemented and delivered based on business priorities. The agile approach provides various benefits in implementing risky, small and medium sized projects where requirements are uncertain while managing business and project risks. Many organizations are used to perform an audit on traditional SDLC waterfall processes, and the matured IS audit processes are in practice. The methods for auditing software development based on agile approach requires a different approach and audit techniques tailored to unique proactive nature of the agile approach. Chapter 10, "Swimming Upstream in Turbulent Waters: Auditing Agile Development," by Priyadarsini Kannan Krishnamachariar and Manish Gupta, presents a risk-based audit approach on the agile implementation of software development demonstrating how risk identification and assessment can be merged along with the phases of software development and how the ways agile techniques can be effectively utilized as tools for audit.

In last few years, the smartphones have become the primary device that has enabled a large number of people around the world to connect, compute and transact with the world. Smartphones have ushered a new decade of connectivity that the world has not seen before. This proliferation has led to many security and privacy concerns arising from emerging technologies that track mobile usage. Chapter 11 ("Impact of SNS Diversity and Privacy Concerns on Information Seeking Through Smartphones"), Mohamed Abdelhamid, Srikanth Venkatesan, Joana Monteiro and Raj Sharman investigates the factors that impact the likelihood of seeking information via smartphones. The study finds that the diversity of social networking sites and privacy concerns are two main factors influencing the likelihood of seeking information.

REFERENCES

Bakshi, S. (2012). Risk IT framework for IT risk management: A case study of National Stock Exchange of India Limited. *COBIT Focus*, *1*, 5–10.

Belcourt, M. (2006, June). Outsourcing — The benefits and the risks. *Human Resource Management Review*, *16*(2), 269–279. doi:10.1016/j.hrmr.2006.03.011

Carcary, M. (2013). IT risk management: A capability maturity model perspective. *Electronic Journal Information Systems Evaluation*, *16*, 3–13.

Debreceny, R. (2013). Research on IT governance, risk, and value: Challenges and Opportunities. *Journal of Information Systems*, *27*(1), 129–135. doi:10.2308/isys-10339

Deloitte. (2016). *2016 EMEA Financial Services IT Risk Management Survey*. Retrieved online on January 30, 2017, from https://www2.deloitte.com/content/dam/Deloitte/ch/Documents/risk/ch-en-it-risk-management-survey-16.pdf

Farah, B. (2011). A maturity model for the management of information technology risk. International Journal of Technology. *Knowledge in Society*, *7*(1), 13–25.

Gill, M. (2012). IT risk is business risk. *COBIT Focus*, *2*, 10–11.

Heroux, S., & Fortin, A. (2013). The internal audit function in information technology governance: A holistic perspective. *Journal of Information Systems*, *27*(1), 189–217. doi:10.2308/isys-50331

Ibrahim, N. (2014). IT Audit 101. *Internal Auditor*, *71*(3), 19–21.

Jackson, R. (2012). Facing IT risk head - on. *Internal Auditor*, *69*(4), 36–42.

Morales, J. (2014). 6 Tips for implementing IT governance with COBIT 5. *COBIT Focus, 3*, 7-8. Retrieved online on January 30, 2017 from http://www.isaca.org

OCEG. (2016). *GRC capability model: Red Book 2.0*. Retrieved from http://www.oceg.com

Teilans, A., Romanovs, A., Merkuryer, Y., Kleins, A., Dorogovs, P., & Krastas, O. (2011). Functional modelling of IT risks assessment support system. *Economics & Management*, *16*, 1061–1068.

Section 1
Frameworks and Methodologies

Chapter 1

An Analytical Study of Methodologies and Tools for Enterprise Information Security Risk Management

Jaya Bhattacharjee
Jadavpur University, India

Mridul Sankar Barik
Jadavpur University, India

Anirban Sengupta
Jadavpur University, India

Chandan Mazumdar
Jadavpur University, India

ABSTRACT

An enterprise is characterized by its business processes and supporting ICT infrastructure. Securing these entities is of utmost importance for the survival of an enterprise and continuity of its business operations. In order to secure them, it is important to first detect the risks that can be realized to cause harm to those entities. Over the years, several kinds of security risk analysis methodologies have been proposed. They cater to different categories of enterprise entities and consider varying levels of detail during risk analysis. An enterprise often finds it difficult to select a particular method that will best suit its purpose. This paper attempts to address this problem by presenting a detailed study of existing risk analysis methodologies. The study classifies them into specific categories and performs comparative analyses considering different parameters addressed by the methodologies, including asset type, vulnerabilities, threats, and security controls.

DOI: 10.4018/978-1-5225-2604-9.ch001

INTRODUCTION

An enterprise can be defined as an organization (Industry/Govt./Academic) created for business or service ventures. The term encompasses a wide range, from a large corporation or government department to a small office / home office (SOHO). From Information Security point of view, an enterprise is characterized by its business goals, business processes, information assets, personnel, organizational structure, site (physical and virtual) and ICT infrastructure. Protection of each of these entities is of utmost importance for the survival of an enterprise and continuity of its business operations.

Usually, the business processes and ICT infrastructure (hardware, software and network assets) of an enterprise contain several weaknesses, or *vulnerabilities* (ISO/IEC, 2014), that may arise owing to improper configuration, erroneous workflows, incorrect usage, etc. *Threats* (ISO/IEC, 2014) abound in the physical and virtual worlds whose sole objective is the exploitation of vulnerabilities to breach security parameters of enterprise assets and business processes.

Information Security Risk is defined as the probability that threat(s) will exploit vulnerabilities to cause harm to enterprise assets (ISO/IEC, 2011). It refers to the effect of uncertainty on information security objectives of an enterprise. The primary objective of an information security programme is the protection of enterprise resources by managing the identified risks. *Information Security Risk Management* comprises of a set of coordinated activities to direct and control an enterprise with regard to risk (ISO/FDIS, 2009). ISO 31000 (ISO/FDIS, 2009) lists seven phases for managing risk: establishing the context, risk identification, risk analysis, risk evaluation, risk treatment, communication and consultation, monitoring and review. These are illustrated in Figure 1. As is obvious, the risk management phases are cyclic in nature and need to be applied continuously during the life-cycle of an enterprise information system.

Among the components of risk management, risk identification, risk analysis and risk evaluation are of utmost importance, and are together referred to as *Information Security Risk Assessment* (ISO/FDIS, 2009). The quantity, complexity and dynamic nature of enterprise assets and their inter-relationships pose serious challenges to the process of risk assessment.

Over the years, several manual, as well as, automated methods and tools have been proposed / developed for assessing information security risks. Some of them are qualitative in nature and categorize assets based on subjective values, like low-, medium- and high-risk. CORAS (Hogganvik & Stølen, 2006), Information Systems Security Risk Management (ISSRM) (Mayer & Heymans, 2007) and Facilitated Risk Analysis and Assessment Process (FRAAP) (Peltier, 2010) are some examples of

Figure 1. Risk management process

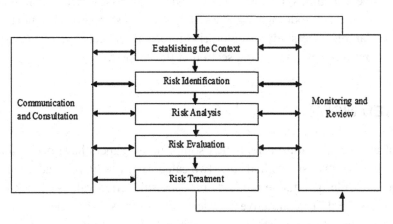

qualitative approaches. On the other hand, there are some methodologies that compute quantitative risk values on an integer point-scale to indicate the intensity of risk. Examples include COBRA (COBRA, 2003), Value-at-risk (VaR) approach (Wang, Chaudhury, & Rao, 2008), Sun et. al. methodology using Dempster-Shafer theory of belief functions (Sun, Srivastava, & Mock, 2006), etc. There is a third category of risk assessment methodologies that combine quantitative and qualitative elements to derive risk values. Examples of such methods are OCTAVE (Alberts & Dorofee, 2001), Ten-Step Process (Peltier, 2010) and Risk-Matrix technique (Peltier, 2010).

Besides, several standards propose specific techniques for conducting security risk assessment. The popular ones are ISO 31000 (ISO/FDIS, 2009), ISO/IEC 31010 (IEC/ FDIS, 2009), ISO/IEC 27005 (ISO/IEC, 2011) and NIST SP 800-30 (Stoneburner, Goguen & Feringa, 2002). These standards collate information from existing risk assessment techniques and suggest approaches for designing and implementing a comprehensive security risk management programme.

This chapter contains a systematic study of various information security risk management (primarily, risk assessment) methodologies and tools. It classifies the techniques into specific categories and performs comparative analyses considering different parameters addressed by them, including asset type, vulnerabilities, threats, and security controls. This study will help to put the risk assessment methodologies in perspective and identify their benefits and constraints. This will enable an enterprise to select the methodology that best suits its purpose.

Rest of this chapter is organized as follows. The next section discusses the existing survey papers of risk analysis. The following section explains the logic behind the classification of risk assessment methodologies in this chapter. This is followed by three sections describing, respectively, several supporting asset-based risk assessment methods, business process-based risk assessment techniques, and risk management methodologies suggested by security standards. The next section presents a sample case study of enterprise information security risk assessment. This is followed by the concluding section of the chapter.

RELATED WORK

Study of existing literature reveals that some survey papers have been published that classify risk analysis methods into two categories: *qualitative* and *quantitative* techniques. While qualitative methods produce subjective values of risk ("low", "medium", or "high"), quantitative techniques express risk on a numeric point-scale. We describe some of the existing survey works in this section.

Ghazouani et. al. (Ghazouani, Faris, Medromi and Sayouti, 2014) and Shukla and Kumar (Shukla and Kumar, 2012) studied risk analysis methods based on their activities, inputs and outputs.

Behnia et. al. (Behnia, Rashid and Chaudhry, 2012), besides classifying risk analysis methods, also discussed their strengths and weaknesses. The authors assigned scores to each method based on their popularity as is evident by their relative number of citations. In another related survey, Lee (Lee, 2014) discussed the advantages and disadvantages of specific risk analysis methods like Analytic Hierarchy Process (Suh and Han, 2003), Neural networks technique (Zhao, Liu and Zhang, 2009), and Fuzzy logic method (Chujiao and Guoyuan, 2006).

In a recent work, Agrawal (Agrawal, 2015) analyzed existing risk analysis methods in terms of their parameters and the relationships among them. However, very few methods (two quantitative and two qualitative methods) were considered for the study.

Thus, it is obvious that the existing survey papers have mostly studied risk analyses methods considering the nature of their outcome. Hence, they have ended up classifying them as either quantitative or qualitative methods. However, it is difficult for an enterprise to choose a suitable risk analysis method if the decision has to be based entirely on the nature of the outcome (qualitative or quantitative) of the method. It would be helpful if the enterprise could associate a particular method with the specific categories of assets whose risk can be measured by that method. Moreover, it may be important for some enterprises to understand whether a particular method considers explicit values of vulnerabilities, threats and control effectiveness while computing risk. These aspects reflect the amount of detail that a method addresses, and the level of preparedness that is necessary on the part of the enterprise before implementing the method. On one hand, this helps in performing an accurate cost-benefit analysis while selecting a risk analysis method; while, on the other, it helps in training and preparing personnel, who will be involved in the process, much before the actual implementation.

This chapter presents a comprehensive study and classification of existing risk analyses methodologies that attempts to address the shortcomings of existing surveys as detailed above.

CLASSIFICATION OF EXISTING RISK MANAGEMENT / ASSESSMENT METHODOLOGIES

The assets of an enterprise are generally classified into two categories: primary and supporting assets (ISO/IEC, 2011). Since, the primary activities of an enterprise revolve around its business processes and information assets, these are referred to as *primary assets*. There are several other types of assets that provide support to an enterprise for carrying out business activities and processing its information assets. These are termed as *supporting assets* and comprise of hardware, software, network assets, personnel, site and organization (ISO/IEC, 2011). Interestingly, analysis of existing risk assessment methodologies reveal that while some of them address asset-based risks, others are concerned with risks to business processes. Additionally, there are several standards that describe the activities and best practices for implementing an effective risk management programme.

Based on the above, we have classified the existing risk management / assessment techniques into the following three categories: risk assessment for supporting assets, risk assessment for business processes, and risk management methodologies suggested by standards. These have been detailed in subsequent sections. Besides, the chapter also presents comparative analyses of the risk assessment methods considering common parameters like Assets, Threats, Vulnerabilities and Security Controls.

METHODOLOGIES FOR ASSESSING RISKS TO SUPPORTING ASSETS

A large number of existing risk assessment tools and techniques belong to this category. Some of the more popular ones are discussed in this section.

The OCTAVE method (Alberts & Dorofee, 2001) defines the essential components of a context-driven information security risk analysis. This method follows a three-phase approach, and allows an organization to make information-protection decisions, based on the risks to confidentiality, integrity and availability of critical information technology assets. A team is established within an organization to perform risk analysis. In the first phase, asset-based threat profiles are constructed. The team identifies the critical assets of the organization and their security requirements. The threats to each asset are determined in the form of an asset-based threat profile. During the second phase, the infrastructure vulnerabilities, corresponding to the threats, are identified. The third and final phase analyses risks and prepares a protection strategy to address those risks. OCTAVE is a non-linear and iterative risk analysis method. Due to its iterative nature, it has many feedback loops.

There are two variants of OCTAVE: OCTAVE-S and OCTAVE Allegro. OCTAVE-S (Alberts, 2005) caters to the needs of small manufacturing organizations. It is performed by an analysis team with a working knowledge of important information-related assets, security requirements, threats, and security practices of the organization. On the other hand, OCTAVE Allegro (Richard, 2007) performs a broad assessment of an organization's operational risk environment, with no need for an extensive knowledge of the risk assessment components. It focuses primarily on information assets in the context of how they are used, stored, transported and processed, and how they are exposed to threats and vulnerabilities. Based on an organization's requirements, OCTAVE method has been customized; none of its variants formally represent risk and its parameters.

COBRA (COBRA, 2003) consists of a range of risk analysis, consultative and security review tools. It incorporates both qualitative and quantitative approaches to risk analysis, and essentially uses expert system principles with an extensive knowledge base. The degree of risk is computed based on system threat, vulnerabilities and exposure. However, the computational technique, that is employed to compute the degree of risk, is not apparent.

ISRAM (Karabacaka & Sogukpinarb, 2005) method was developed to analyze risks to complex information systems and allowed the participation of enterprise managers and staff. The method consists of seven steps. Step 1 attempts to create an awareness of the problem and emphasizes the needs of structured risk analysis. Step 2 identifies the factors that cause risks. Weights are assigned to the probability of occurrence and consequence of the factors considering the values of assets, strength of existing countermeasures, and the levels of vulnerabilities. In Step 3, factors are converted into survey questions. Answers to these questions are solicited from stakeholders. A risk table is prepared in Step 4 considering the values obtained in previous steps. In Step 5, the risk table is distributed among the staff for obtaining feedback. A single risk value is computed in Step 6, which is finally evaluated in Step 7. Thus, ISRAM is a quantitative method that does not follow the conventional approach of risk analysis.

CORAS method graphically represents the risks to an asset (Hogganvik & Stølen, 2006). The risk is modeled in a structured way, using a risk graph to represent security events, their causes, and consequences (Braendeland, Refsdal & Stolen, 2010). A risk graph is divided into two parts - one part represents the target of analysis, while the other part describes the assumptions made for the estimation of the risk values. It is a semi-formal model and differs from traditional risk assessment techniques. Loss is estimated by multiplying the impact with the probability of occurrence of threats. Due to its simplicity, it can be easily implemented by organizations. However, it cannot provide precise risk assessment results.

An information security risk analysis using the Dempster-Shafer theory of belief functions was developed (Sun, Srivastava, & Mock, 2006). A structured approach is undertaken for computing risk to an Information System (IS). IS security risk is defined in terms of the plausibility that an information resource is not adequately protected. It incorporates the impact of threats and counter-measures on information system security. In this method, risks to the individual assets are aggregated to determine overall organizational risk.

A modeling language was proposed by Mayer and Heymans (Mayer & Heymans, 2007) for Information Systems Security Risk Management (ISSRM). It considers the three basic components of risk, namely asset, threat and vulnerability. It defines the risk, cause of risk, impact, threat and vulnerability. In this model, risk is perceived as a composition of cause and impact. However, it does not suggest any specific methodology for assessing risks.

The Ten Step Process (Peltier, 2010) enumerates ten specific steps for risk assessment. The steps include the Development of Scope Statement, Assembling a Competent Team, Identification of Threats, Prioritization of Threats, Prioritization of Loss Impact, Calculation of Risk Factor, Identification of Safeguards, Cost-Benefit Analysis, Ranking of Safeguards based on priority, and Preparation of Risk Analysis Report. However, this methodology does not explicitly consider vulnerabilities.

The Facilitated Risk Analysis and Assessment Process (FRAAP) (Peltier, 2010) is a qualitative risk assessment methodology that identifies risks in terms of their effects on the business processes or the mission of an enterprise. It does not attempt to obtain specific numbers for the likelihood of occurrence of threats or loss estimates. Instead, it focuses on identifying the risk-prone areas, and determining appropriate controls to mitigate risks. An expert acts as the facilitator during the entire process. Since FRAAP relies heavily on inputs from an expert, it too suffers from the disadvantage that most qualitative methodologies suffer from, i.e. lack of consistency in risk values.

CRAMM (Yazar, 2002) is a comprehensive collection of tools for risk assessment. It includes tools for asset dependency modeling, business impact assessment, identification and assessment of threats and vulnerabilities, assessment of levels of risks, and identification of security controls based on the results of risk assessment. In CRAMM, risk assessment is done for groups of assets (data, application software and physical assets). It is a matrix-based semi-quantitative approach suitable for large organizations, like government departments. This method consists of the following phases: Asset Identification and Valuation, Threat and Vulnerability Assessment, and Counter-measure Selection and Recommendation. CRAMM suggests two types of approaches for risk assessment – "full" and "rapid". In full risk assessment, the threats and vulnerabilities are identified by posing questions to the support personnel. The answers are used to calculate the levels of threats to, and vulnerabilities within, the assets. While threats are computed on a 5-point scale (Very Low, Low, Medium, High and Very High), vulnerability values follow a 3-point scale of measurement (Low, Medium and High). The rapid approach can be employed when an organization possesses a comprehensive knowledge of its threats and vulnerabilities.

Value at Risk (VaR) approach (Wang, Chaudhury, & Rao, 2008) is suitable for financial and insurance sectors. Security incidents are classified into two types: High-Frequency-Low-Impact incidents and Low-Frequency-High-Impact incidents. Using extreme value analysis, risks to information systems are quantified; these are then used to identify appropriate security solutions. Qi et. al. (Qi, Liu, Zhang & Yuan, 2010) introduced a technique for dynamic risk assessment. It uses a risk quantification model and a VaR-based risk measure. The maximum loss, which may occur owing to a threat, is measured; this is used to compute "daily loss". It has been shown that "daily loss" follows a Poisson distribution.

Lo and Chen (Lo & Chen, 2012) proposed a risk assessment method based on inter-dependencies of security controls. Controls are grouped into seventeen families; the families have been further grouped into three areas. Risk is determined for each control family by considering the likelihood of occurrence of threats and their impacts.

Bayesian Attack Graphs have also been used for security risk assessment (Poolsappasit, Dewri, & Ray, 2012). Cause-consequence relationships between different network states are considered during computation of likelihood of occurrences of threats. The method also considers the common vulnerability scoring system for assessing exploits. Feng et. al. (Feng, Wang, & Li, 2013) proposed a Bayesian network-based risk analysis method. It considers the different propagation paths of vulnerabilities to determine risks and select relevant controls.

Kotzanikolaou et. al. (Kotzanikolaou, Theoharidou, & Gritzalis, 2011) developed a risk assessment method that considers the dependencies among critical infrastructure. This method analyzes the possible cumulative effects of a single security incident on multiple critical infrastructures.

Bhattacharjee et. al. (Bhattacharjee, Sengupta & Mazumdar, 2013) proposed a formal asset-based risk assessment methodology that models all critical elements of enterprise information systems. It derives two types of risk values – consolidated risk factor that presents a summary value, and detailed risk factor that enumerates the elements contributing to the risks. This method mathematically models all risk elements, including exploitability of vulnerabilities, and dependencies between assets, vulnerabilities, and threats.

Alese et. al. (Alese, 2014) proposed a method for analyzing complex systems and identifying sources of risks. It calculates the value of risk impact on a 5-point scale. A tool has also been developed based on this method. The tool generates assessment reports containing risk description, impact cost and mitigation cost.

Fu, S. et al. (Fu, 2015) developed an information security risk assessment methodology based on fuzzy set and entropy theory. It considers basic elements like asset impact, threat frequency and severity of vulnerability. Relative importance of risk factors is measured by using entropy theory.

Network risk modeling using attack graphs was proposed by Dai et. al. (Dai, Hu, Zheng & Wu, 2015). It examines vulnerabilities and the relationships among them. It helps to identify the root-causes of risks. Attack paths are analyzed to determine the implicit dependencies among vulnerabilities; this information is used to assess network risks.

A formal model and risk assessment method was developed for security-critical real time embedded systems (RTES) by Zhuang et.al. (Ni, Zhuang, Gu & Huo, 2016). Z notation was used to model RTES. The risk assessment process consists of three steps: establishment of risk context, assessment of risks, and treatment of risks. Risk to the RTES is analyzed based on its likelihood and impact.

A comparative summary of supporting asset-based risk assessment methodologies is given in Table 1.

METHODOLOGIES FOR ASSESSING RISKS TO BUSINESS PROCESSES

Some methodologies have been developed to identify and/or assess risks to enterprise business processes. These are discussed in this section.

Lambert et. al. (Lambert, Jennings & Joshi, 2006) proposed a method to identify risks to an enterprise based on business process model. In this method, business process is represented with the help of input, control, output and mechanism. Risks to each of these components are identified and consolidated to determine the overall risks to the business process.

Shedden et. al. (Shedden, Smith & Ahmad, 2010) considered non-technical elements of information systems for identifying risk. They considered risks pertaining to asset leakage, user-created assets and critical knowledge of users. However, the authors have not proposed any formal methodology for computation of risk values.

Jakoubi et. al. (Jakoubi, Tjoa, Goluch, & Kitzler, 2010) presented a technique for risk-aware business process management. It consists of five distinct phases: Perform

Table 1. Comparison of methodologies for assessing security risks to supporting assets

Risk Assessment Method	Considers Asset value and their Dependencies?	Considers Vulnerability values and their Dependencies?	Considers Threat Evaluation?	Considers security control implementation status?
OCTAVE, OCTAVE-S and OCTAVE Allegro (2004 -2007)	No	No	Yes	No
COBRA	Considers asset value	Considers severity of vulnerability	Considers likelihood of occurrence of threat	No
ISRAM, 2005	Considers asset value	Considers severity of vulnerability	Yes	Yes
CORAS (2006 -2010)	No	Yes	Yes	No
Sun, Srivastava, and Mock, 2006	No	No	Considers impact of threat	Considers impact of counter-measure
ISSRM by Mayer and Heymans, 2007	No	No	No	No
Ten Step Process, 2010	No	No	No	Yes
Facilitated Risk Analysis and Assessment Process (FRAAP), 2010	No	No	No	Yes
CRAMM, 2011	Yes	No	No	Yes
Wang, Chaudhury and Rao, 2008	No	No	Considers impact of threat	No
Wenjing Qi, Xue Liu, Jian Zhang, Weihua Yuan, 2010	Considers asset value	Considers vulnerabilities within information system	Considers threats to information system	No
Chi Chun Lo and Wan Jia Chen, 2012	No	Considers vulnerabilities that can be exploited by threats	Considers likelihood and impact of threat	Considers security control areas
Nayot Poolsappasit, Rinku Dewri and Indrajit Ray, 2012	No	Considers common vulnerability scoring system	Considers likelihood of occurrence of threat	No
Nan Feng, Harry Jiannan Wang and Minqiang Li, 2013	No	Yes	No	No
Kotzanikolaou et al. 2013	Considers dependencies among critical infrastructure	No	Yes	No
Bhattacharjee et. al. 2013	Yes	Yes	Yes	Yes
Alese B. K et al. 2014	No	No	Considers threat impact	Yes
Sha Fu et al., 2015	Considers asset impact	Considers severity of vulnerability	Considers threat frequency	No
Fangfang Dai et al, 2015	No	Yes	Yes	No
A formal model and risk assessment method for RTES, 2016	Yes	No	Yes	Yes

Program Management, Determine As-Is Situation, Re-engineer Processes, Implement Processes and Review and Evaluate. However, the methodology is mostly verbose and does not suggest any quantitative or formal technique for the computation of risks to business processes.

Khanmohammadi and Houmb (Khanmohammadi & Houmb, 2010) proposed a business process based risk assessment methodology that focuses on business goals rather than assets. Businesses and their control processes are identified during the initial phase. Vulnerabilities within processes, and their corresponding threats, are analyzed. Finally, risk is computed considering the degree of exposure of vulnerabilities, effects of installed security controls, threat levels and process value.

MEHARI (MEthod for Harmonized Analysis of RIsk), a method for analyzing business process-specific risks, was developed by CLUSIF, France (MEHARI, 2010; Mihailescu, 2012). The method first identifies threats and computes their likelihood values on a 4-point scale. Threat is defined by an event type, an accompanying description of the circumstances and relevant participants. The impacts of risks are estimated considering existing security measures. Finally, risk treatment options are suggested, taking into consideration the values of threat likelihood and risk impact.

Tjoa et. al. (Tjoa, 2011) proposed a formal model that considers relations between threats, detection mechanisms, safeguards, recovery measures and their effects on business processes. Business process is represented by a set of resources, activities and their attributes. Threats to the attributes of different elements of business processes are identified and their preventive, blocking and reactive measures are recommended.

In (Spagnoletti, 2011), business processes are examined to identify business-specific security risk factors and to address the strategic, organizational and managerial issues of enterprises pertaining to risk management. Table 2 lists the business related risk factors. In another related work (Ahmed & Matulevicius, 2013), security risk patterns within business processes are identified and used for suggesting security

Table 2. Business-related risk analysis factors

Strategic level	(a) The competition intensity
	(b) The compliance with legal and governance frameworks
Organizational level	(a) The level of procedure formalization
	(b) The control system performance
Customer Relationship level	(a) The customer variety
	(b) The channel variety
Value Chain Configuration	(a) The IT integration
	(b) The inter cyber process relations

solutions. This method may help non-security experts in addressing security concerns during business process definition.

Bhattacharjee et. al. (Bhattacharjee, Sengupta & Mazumdar, 2016). proposed a method to quantitatively compute security risks that exist owing to vulnerabilities within the basic structure of business processes. These risks are independent of the underlying assets of an enterprise. This includes both internal as well as external risks. For example, lack of training on use of privileged access rights (internal risk) could lead to users divulging their credentials, thus leading to serious security breaches. Again, high attrition of personnel owing to better opportunities elsewhere (external risk) could seriously jeopardize enterprise operations. The method also provides a formal definition of business process based on tasks and their flow relations.

Alizadeh and Zannone (Alizade & Zannone, 2016) proposed a process model to define the activities and procedures of an organization. They used a risk-based auditing framework to analyze process execution. The framework identifies processes non-conformities and corresponding severity values. Finally, risk is computed based on the likelihood of occurrences of an event and severity values.

A comparative summary of business process-based risk assessment methodologies is shown in Table 3.

RISK MANAGEMENT METHODOLOGIES SUGGESTED BY STANDARDS

Besides tools and methodologies, numerous standards have been published that recommend best practices for implementing an effective security risk management programme. Some of the widely accepted standards for risk management are discussed in this section.

The International Organization for Standardization (ISO) has published a set of standards for risk management. ISO 31000 (ISO/FDIS, 2009) provides generic guidelines for risk management and can be applied to assess any type of risk. Systematic techniques for risk assessment are stated in IEC/FDIS 31010:2009 (IEC/FDIS, 2009). However, it does not specify the criteria for identifying risks to a particular application. ISO/IEC 27005:2011 (ISO/IEC, 2011) provides comprehensive guidelines for the implementation of a risk management programme. In addition it specifies two types of risk assessment approaches: high-level assessment and detailed assessment. High-level risk assessment provides an overview of information security risks. While in the detailed approach, an in-depth identification of risks is carried out based on the valuation of assets, threats to those assets and vulnerabilities.

Table 3. Comparison of methodologies for assessing security risks to business processes

Risk Assessment Method	Considers Business Process and their Values?	Considers Vulnerability values?	Considers Threat Evaluation?	Considers security control implementation status?
Lambert method, 2006	No	No	No	No
Shedden, Smith and Ahmad, 2010	No	No	No	No
Jakoubi S. et al method for risk-aware business process management	No	No	No	No
Khanmohammadi and Houmb, 2010	Considers business process value	Considers degree of exposure of vulnerabilities	Considers threat levels	Considers effect of installed security controls
MEHARI, 2010	Consider Business Process	Considers intrinsic and contextual vulnerabilities	Yes	Yes
Tjoa et al., 2011	No	No	Considers relations between threats	No
A Business Aware Information Security Risk Analysis Method, 2011	No	No	No	No
Securing business processes using security risk-oriented patterns, 2013	No	No	No	No
Bhattacharjee et. al. 2016	Yes	Yes	Yes	Yes
Risk-based Analysis of Business Process Executions, 2016	Yes	Yes	Yes	No

Risk IT framework based on COBIT standard (ISACA, 2009) provides guidelines for enterprises to identify, govern and manage IT risks effectively. This framework helps to identify the business risks related to use of IT.

NIST SP 800-30 (Stoneburner, Goguen & Feringa, 2002) risk management guide for information technology systems recommends that risk management should be integrated with System Development Life-Cycle (SDLC). During the initiation phase of SDLC, risks need to be identified. These may be used to analyze security of the IT system. Risk assessment results should be used to identify appropriate controls for eliminating risks. The risk assessment methodology suggested by NIST SP 800-30 comprises of nine steps: System Characterization, Threat Identification, Vulnerability Identification, Control Analysis, Likelihood Determination, Impact Analysis, Risk Determination, Control Recommendation and Results Documentation. In the system characterization phase, scope and boundaries of the risk assessment are defined. In Steps 2 and 3, sources of threats and vulnerabilities are identified, respectively. Then, based on likelihood of occurrence of threats and their corresponding impacts, risks to the system are determined.

It is important to note that, in essence, standards suggest means for designing, implementing and maintaining risk management programmes within enterprises. These need to be adopted, along with appropriate risk assessment methodologies (discussed in earlier sections), for effectively managing risk in an enterprise.

DISCUSSION

Thus, over the years, various kinds of security risk assessment techniques have been designed and implemented. While, some of them are generic in nature, others have been designed to meet the specific needs of particular types of enterprises (bank, healthcare, etc.). Moreover, some of these approaches are qualitative in nature (ISO/IEC, 2011); they usually express the amount of risk as "low", "medium", or "high". While, there are other approaches that quantify risk parameters and express the final risk value on a numeric point-scale (IEC/FDIS, 2009). A third category of risk assessment techniques exist that combine elements of both of these approaches (IEC/FDIS, 2009).

Both qualitative and quantitative techniques have their pros and cons. The former methods are easy to implement, less costly and their outcome is easily interpretable. However, they lack in accuracy and depend on the expertise of risk analysts, who may have biased opinions. Moreover, the results may seem inconsistent when computed for different enterprises and/or involving different experts.

On the other hand, quantitative techniques provide accurate, unbiased results that are consistent over time and space. However, accuracy of results depends on the model used at the time of assessment and availability of historical data. Besides, quantitative methods are generally more costly than qualitative ones.

We now describe a case study for risk value computation that may be used as a guideline for performing risk assessment. A bank-loan management process has been used for this illustration. The values of all parameters have been considered on a 5-point scale whose interpretation is given in Table 4.

Confidentiality (C), Integrity (I) and Availability (A) values of the Primary Asset (Loan Management Process) and a Supporting Asset (Server) are shown in Table 5.

Table 4. Values of security parameters and their meaning

Parameter Value	Interpretation
1	Very Low
2	Low
3	Medium
4	High
5	Very High

Table 5. C, I, A values of primary and supporting assets

Asset	C	I	A
Loan Management Process	3	4	4
Server	5	5	4

Threats to the assets, their Likelihood of Occurrences (LOC), corresponding vulnerabilities and their Severity (Sev) values are shown in Table 6.

Risk (R) can be computed as a function of C, I, A, LOC and Sev values.

Thus, $R \equiv f(C, I, A, LOC, Sev)$

Let us assume that a particular risk assessment methodology generates risk values as shown in Table 7.

The security measures that can be deployed for mitigating the identified risks need to be specified. A sample set of measures is shown in Table 8.

Table 6. Threats to primary and supporting assets

Asset	Threat	Likelihood of Occurrence	Vulnerability	Severity
Loan Management Process	Corruption of data	3	Lack of training of concerned personnel may lead to incorrect execution of tasks	4
Server	Error in use	5	Lack of care at disposal	2

Table 7. Risk values

Asset	Risk Value
Loan Management Process	3
Server	3

Table 8. Security measures for mitigating risks

Asset	Security Measures
Loan Management Process	Conduct information security awareness programs; Organize the information security-training program periodically
Server	Media Disposal Procedure; Media Handling Policy

CONCLUSION

The chapter presents a survey of risk assessment methodologies and tools. These have been classified into three categories: risk assessment methods for supporting assets, risk assessment methods for business processes and risk management processes suggested by standards. In addition, comparative analyses of different risk assessment methodologies have been included in the chapter. It will help different enterprises to select a risk assessment methodology as per their requirement. A case study for risk value computation has been provided that may guide users for carrying out risk assessment.

REFERENCES

Agrawal, V. (2015). A Comparative Study on Information Security Risk Analysis Methods. *International Journal of Computers*. DOI: 10.17706/jcp.12.1.57-67

Ahmed, N., & Matulevicius, R. (2013). Securing business processes using security risk-oriented patterns. *International Journal of Computer Standards & Interfaces*, *36*(4), 723–733. doi:10.1016/j.csi.2013.12.007

Alberts, C. (2005). *OCTAVE-S Implementation Guide, Version 1*. Software Engineering Institute, Carnegie Mellon University. Retrieved August 12, 2015, from http://repository.cmu.edu/cgi/viewcontent.cgi?article=1478&context=sei

Alberts, C., & Dorofee, A. (2001). *OCTAVE Criteria, Version 2.0*. Software Engineering Institute, Carnegie Mellon University. Retrieved August 12, 2015, from http://repository.cmu.edu/cgi/viewcontent.cgi?article=1217&context=sei

Alese, B. K. (2014). Evaluation of Information Security Risks Using Hybrid Assessment Model. *Proceedings of the 9th International Conference for Internet Technology and Secured Transactions (ICITST-2014)*, 387 - 395. doi:10.1109/ICITST.2014.7038843

Alizadeh, M., & Zannone, N. (2016). Risk-based Analysis of Business Process Executions. *Proceedings of the 6th ACM Conference on Data and Application Security and Privacy (CODASPY'16)*, 130-132. doi:10.1145/2857705.2857742

Behnia, A., Rashid, R. A., & Chaudhry, J. A. (2012). A Survey of Information Security Risk Analysis Methods. *Journal of Smart Computing Review*, *2*(1), 79–94. doi:10.6029/smartcr.2012.01.007

Bhattacharjee, J., Sengupta, A., & Mazumdar, C. (2013). A Formal Methodology for Enterprise Information Security Risk Assessment. *Proceedings of the CRiSIS'13, 8th International Conference on Risks and Security of Internet and Systems*, 1-9. doi:10.1109/CRiSIS.2013.6766354

Bhattacharjee, J., Sengupta, A., & Mazumdar, C. (2016). A Quantitative Methodology for Security Risk Assessment of Enterprise Business Processes. *Proceedings of the 2nd International Conference on Information Systems Security and Privacy (ICISSP 2016)*, 388-399. doi:10.5220/0005739703880399

Braendeland, G., Refsdal, A., & Stolen, K. (2010). Modular Analysis and Modeling of Risk Scenarios with Dependencies. *International Journal of Systems and Software, 83*(10), 1995–2013. doi:10.1016/j.jss.2010.05.069

Chujiao, W. & Guoyuan, L. (2006). The Model of Network Security Risk Assess Based on Fuzzy Algorithm and Hierarchy. *Journal of Wuhan University (Natural Science Edition), 5*, 24.

COBRA. (2003). *Introduction to Security Risk Analysis*. Retrieved August 12, 2015, from http://www.security-risk-analysis.com/

Dai, F., Hu, Y., Zheng, K., & Wu, B. (2015). Exploring risk flow attack graph for security risk assessment. *International Journal of IET Information Security, 9*(6), 344–353. doi:10.1049/iet-ifs.2014.0272

Feng, N., Wang, H. J., & Li, M. (2013). A security risk analysis model for information systems: Causal relationships of risk factors and vulnerability propagation analysis. *International Journal of Information Sciences., 256*, 57–73. doi:10.1016/j.ins.2013.02.036

Fu, S., Liu, Z., Sun, G., Zhou, H., & Liu, W. (2015). Study on Security Risk Assessment for Information System Based on Fuzzy Set and Entropy Theory. *International Journal of Software Engineering, 9*(4), 818–827. doi:10.3923/jse.2015.818.827

Ghazouani, M., Faris, S., Medromi, H., & Sayouti, A. (2014). Information Security Risk Assessment - A Practical Approach with a Mathematical Formulation of Risk. International Journal of Computer Applications, 103(8).

Hogganvik, I., & Stølen, K. (2006). Lecture Notes in Computer Science: Vol. 4199. A Graphical Approach to Risk Identification, Motivated by Empirical Investigations. Springer. doi:10.1007/11880240_40

IEC/FDIS. (2009). *Risk management — Risk assessment techniques. IEC/FDIS 31010*. Final Draft.

ISACA. (2009). *The Risk IT frameworks, Principles Process Details Management Guidelines Maturity Models. Risk IT based on COBIT.* ISACA.

ISO/FDIS ISO TMBWG on risk management. (2009). *Risk Management - Principles and guidelines, ISO/FDIS 31000:2009, ISO/FDIS.*

ISO/IEC JTC 1 IT SC 27. (2011). *Information technology – Security techniques - Information security risk management, ISO/IEC 27005:2011, ISO/IEC.*

ISO/IEC JTC 1 IT SC 27. (2014). *Information technology – Security techniques - Information security management systems – Overview and vocabulary, ISO/IEC 27000:2014, ISO/IEC.*

Jakoubi, S., Tjoa, S., Goluch, S., & Kitzler, G. (2010). Risk-Aware Business Process Management—Establishing the Link Between Business and Security. In *Book of Complex Intelligent Systems and Their Applications.* Springer Science+Business Media.

Karabacaka, B., & Sogukpinarb, I. (2005). ISRAM: Information security risk analysis method. *International Journal of Computers & Security, 24*(2), 147–159. doi:10.1016/j.cose.2004.07.004

Khanmohammadi, K., & Houmb, S. H. (2010). Business Process-based Information Security Risk Assessment. *Proceedings of the 4th International Conference on Network and System Security,* 199-206.

Kotzanikolaou, P., Theoharidou, M., & Gritzalis, D. (2013). Interdependencies between Critical Infrastructures: Analyzing the Risk of Cascading Effects. *Proceedings of the CRITIS 2011,* 104–115. doi:10.1007/978-3-642-41476-3_9

Lambert, J. H., Jennings, R. K., & Joshi, N. N. (2006). Integration of Risk Identification with Business Process Models. *International Journal of Systems Engineering, 9*(3), 187–198. doi:10.1002/sys.20054

Lee, M. C. (2014). Information Security Risk Analysis Methods and Research Trends: AHP and Fuzzy Comprehensive Method. *International Journal of Computer Science & Information Technology, 6*(1). doi:10.5121/ijcsit.2014.6103

Lo, C., & Chen, W. (2012). A hybrid information security risk assessment procedure considering interdependences between controls. *International Journal of Expert Systems with Applications, 39*(1), 247–257. doi:10.1016/j.eswa.2011.07.015

Mayer, N., & Heymans, P. (2007). Design of a Modeling Language for Information System Security Risk Management. *Proceedings of the First International Conference on Research Challenges in Information Science.*

MEHARI. (2010). *Risk analysis and treatment Guide.* Available at: http://46.227.81.250/fr/production/ouvrages/pdf/MEHARI-2010-Risk-Analysis-and-Treatment-Guide.pdf

Mihailescu, V. L. (2012). Risk analysis and risk management using MEHARI. *International Journal of Applied Business Information Systems., 3*(4), 143–162.

Ni, S., Zhuang, Y., Gu, J., & Huo, Y. (2016). A formal model and risk assessment method for security-critical real-time embedded systems. *International Journal of Computers & Security, 58*, 199–215. doi:10.1016/j.cose.2016.01.005

Peltier, T. R. (2010). *Information Security Risk Analysis* (3rd ed.). Auerbach Publications.

Poolsappasit, N., Dewri, R., & Ray, I. (2012). Dynamic Security Risk Management Using Bayesian Attack Graphs. *International Journal of IEEE Transactions on Dependable and Secure Computing, 9*(1), 61–74. doi:10.1109/TDSC.2011.34

Qi, W., Liu, X., Zhang, J., & Yuan, W. (2010). Dynamic Assessment and VaR-based Quantification of Information Security Risk. *Proceedings of the 2nd International Conference on e-Business and Information System Security (EBISS 10)*, 1 – 4. Doi:10.1109/EBISS.2010.5473537

Richard, A. (2007). *Introducing OCTAVE Allegro: Improving the Information Security Risk Assessment Process.* Software Engineering Institute Technical Report CMU/SEI-2007-TR-012 ESC-TR-2007-012. Retrieved from ftp://ftp.sei.cmu.edu/pub/documents/07.reports/07tr012.pdf

Shedden, P., Smith, W., & Ahmad, A. (2010). Information Security Risk Assessment: Towards a Business Practice Perspective. *Proceedings of the 8th Australian Information Security Management Conference.*

Shukla, N., & Kumar, S (2012). A Comparative Study on Information Security Risk Analysis Practices. *International Journal of Computer Applications.*

Spagnoletti, P. (Ed.). (2011). Information Technology and Innovation Trends in Organizations: A Business Aware Information Security Risk Analysis Method. Physica-Verlag. Doi:10.1007/978-3-7908-2632-6_51

Stoneburner, G., Goguen, A., & Feringa, A. (2002). *Risk Management Guide for Information Technology Systems, NIST Special Publication 800-30.* Gaithersburg, MD: NIST.

Suh, B., & Han, I. (2003). The IS risk analysis based on a business model. *International Journal of Information Management, 41*(2), 149–158. doi:10.1016/S0378-7206(03)00044-2

Sun, B. L., Srivastava, R. P., & Mock, T. J. (2006). An Information Systems Security Risk Assessment Model under Dempster-Shafer Theory of Belief Functions. *International Journal of Management Information Systems, 22*(4), 109–142. doi:10.2753/MIS0742-1222220405

Tjoa, S. (2011). A Formal Approach Enabling Risk-Aware Business Process Modeling and Simulation. *International Journal of IEEE Transactions On Services Computing, IEEE., 4*(2), 153–166. doi:10.1109/TSC.2010.17

Wang, J., Chaudhury, A., & Rao, H. R. (2008). A Value-at-Risk Approach to Information Security Investment. *International Journal of Information Systems Research, 19*(1), 106–120. doi:10.1287/isre.1070.0143

Yazar, Z. (2002). *Qualitative Risk Analysis and Management Tool – CRAMM, (GSEC, Version 1.3)*. SANS Institute.

Zhao, D. M., Liu, J. X., & Zhang, Z. H. (2009). Method of risk evaluation of information security based on neural networks. *Proceedings of the International Conference on Machine Learning and Cybernetics*, 1127-1132. Doi:10.1109/ICMLC.2009.5212464

Chapter 2
A Step–by–Step Procedural Methodology for Improving an Organization's IT Risk Management System

Shanmugapriya Loganathan
Excelok Technologies, Singapore

ABSTRACT

Risks in IT are described as a form of threat in context with data security, network transfer, system scheduled processes, critical applications, and business procedures. IT risk management is broadly defined as the process of managing IT risks, and must be executed on a regular basis. It is neither a product nor a purchase, but a policy of an organization implements to protect its business systems. Managing IT risk plays a vital role in administering any business in today's world. Irrespective of the business, deep knowledge of IT risk leads to increased data security, reduced business cost, and greater compliance. This chapter deals with methodologies to improve risk management in an IT organization, their impact, and some examples.

NTRODUCTION

The basic concept of an information system is to support the objectives and mission of the organization. All organizations are exhibited to risks, many of which affect the organization in an obstructive manner. Risks are nothing but uncertainties about what will happen in the future. The more number of uncertainty leads to a higher number of risks. To support the organization, IT professionals should help management to perceive and manage these risks.

DOI: 10.4018/978-1-5225-2604-9.ch002

Managing risks is not an easy task. Completely mitigating all risk is impossible, due to threats, vulnerabilities, and limited resources, threats and vulnerabilities. Therefore, IT professionals should have a methodological approach to support them in allocating resources and articulating, together with technical and business managers, the possible outcomes of various IT-related threats to their objectives.

This methodological approach must be cost effective, accurate, and repeatable, and minimize risks to a justifiable and reasonable level. Risk management is not new. There are many approaches and techniques available for managing IT risks.

This chapter explores risk management with respect to information technology systems, and answers the following questions:

- What is risk in information technology systems?
- What is the importance of understanding risk?
- Why is monitoring risk processes crucial?
- What is risk management?
- How is risk managed efficiently?
- What are the risk management methodologies for improving IT risk management systems?

BACKGROUND

Risk

Risk refers to a prospective warning about a given situation that will incur losses, disrupt service, and lead to system failures such as defects, thereby provoke maltreat to the organization. Its future outcomes and consequences are uncertain by nature, and can be expressed in the form of its possibility of occurrence and the likelihood of consequences.

The impact of the risk is its ability to affect the goals of an organization. Risk cannot be avoided in every situation. It is available in human lives, organizations, and institutions, irrespective of their environments. Risks are acceptable to certain extents, depending upon those impacts and outcomes. Some are adverse by default, and some are neutral. Hence, in simple terms, risk is described as uncertainty of consequences.

Importance of Understanding Risk

Being aware of risk, and in particular of the specific uncertainties related to a system, would empower the system owner to safeguard assets such as information systems in proportion to their organizational value. All organizations have a restricted number of resources, so risk cannot be diminished to zero. Hence, understanding risk, especially the measure of risk, enables organizations to give most important consideration to the resources they lack.

Risk Process Monitor

Today, companies face different types of risks, based on operations, policies, safety, and technical issues. The biggest challenge for most companies is to establish a repeated process to identify, plan, analyze, and solve risk associated with business activities. It is highly challenging to run a business successfully in this competitive world. Added challenges arise in dealing with different cultures, people, and diverse regulatory frameworks. Organizations whose people think that managing IT risks is completely the job of the IT staff are in even more challenging situations.

Planning tasks to do when things go wrong is equally important to prevent it. Hence, it is important for the organization to understand the risk involved in processes, strategies, and business environments, to arrive at proactive actions that need to be done before any disaster occurs. This actually paves the way for the organization to turn crisis into opportunity. Failure to develop an IT risk management plan sets up the organization up for security breaches, disasters-in-the-making, and financial losses for management. Therefore, it is crucial for any organization to repeatedly monitor the risk process, to provide security in its business environment.

Risk Management

Risk management is the practice of the fundamental ideologies of risk management, to manage risks in an organization with respect to the corresponding fields. It may also be defined as a strategy for managing uncertainty by setting better methodological approaches.

Risk Management in IT

IT risk management is part of a huge risk management system in an enterprise. This encloses not only the negatives and uncertainties of an organization's service and operations can not only erode the objectives and values of the organization, but also benefit its risky proceedings and ventures.

From the perspective of an IT organization, risk management is the activity of understanding and reacting to components that cause failures in confidentiality, service integrity, and accessibility of an information system. IT risk is harmful to the process and its related activities, as a result of an intentional or unintentional event that negatively impacts the organization's objectives. Risk is a function of the probability of a prescribed threat exploiting a particular prospective vulnerability, whose resulting impact will be the harmful event that befalls the organization.

Effective Risk Management

To apply risk management efficiently, it is important to develop a risk management culture that supports the organization's goals, vision, and mission. Limitations are set and communicated, relating to agreed-upon risk procedures and consequences. Uncertainty associated with future events and consequences governs risk management, implying that all planning embraces a certain form of risk management. This also clearly implies that all people at all levels, who can give some details and information about the risk and impacts associated with it, must take care of risk management. Risk management is all about making correct decisions, in accordance with the organization's objectives, by relating them to the individual level, the management level, and functional areas. It helps with decision making by bringing together science-based evidence, proofs, and other factors; organization governance; and the control structures needed to assist in responsible risk taking, due diligence, accountability, and innovation. The main reason for any organization to manage risk is to secure its vision and assets. Therefore, it is important to manage the organization's risks.

RISK MANAGEMENT METHODOLOGY

Figure 1 shows the process that helps management to minimize uncertain events by achieving balance between actual and operational cost, which in turn protects the organization systems and data that assist the business mission.

Figure 1. Risk management methodology

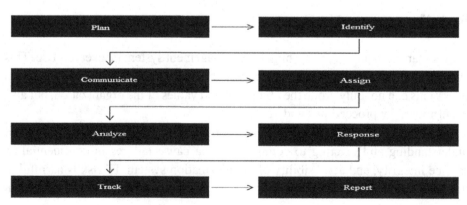

- **Plan**: Deciding phase in which the methods and activities pertaining to risk management are formed.
- **Identify**: Determining phase that points out the risks that could affect system, project, or organization growth.
- **Communicate**: Phase that helps to share the information about risks and efforts, so that they will not surprise stakeholders, customers, or management later.
- **Assign**: Ownership phase that assigns a person to each risk, who has the responsibility for improving system efficiency by optimizing the associated risk.
- **Analyze**: Informative phase gathers the complete details about the risk, which helps to articulate consequences, likelihood, and risk responses.
- **Responses**: Execution phase that supports understanding, prioritizing, and focusing on the risk, to enhance opportunities by minimizing the threats.
- **Track**: Integration phase that helps to unite the identified and associated risks, to ensure the execution of the plan and evaluate the potency of threat reduction.
- **Report**: Log phase that informs the team about the risk details, such as cause and effect, current scenario, action taken, and progress with regard to bookkeeping purposes, for future reference.

Risk Management Planning

The risk management process starts with the planning phase, the primary focus of which is to identify the risks. Detailed information about the risk is helpful in preparing the risk management planning documents. Risk mitigation on the most complex projects can be easily completed if the risks are identified in an early stage, and the planning documents capture the details. However, the scope of risk mitigation is smaller during the planning phase, due to the lack of available detailed information and definition. Development of a detailed risk management plan document for the identified project is crucial, with only limited support tools in hand. Risk planning pinpoints potential uncertainties that could cause harm to the project, analyzes how frequently and similarly they are likely to occur, and describes the necessary actions to take to avoid the risks and reduce those that could not be resolved completely.

When a risk actually happens on the project, it is very late to take any possible actions to mitigate it. That is why planning for risks from the project initiation phase, and working on them throughout the project, is important.

The risk management plan describes how to handle risk in the project. It documents the risk description, risk type, how to assess and mitigate the risk, its impact, and the person responsible for doing it and updating the risk planning activities regularly.

It is vital to create guidelines to assist in figuring out the complexity of potential risk impact. The impact describes the harm the risk would cause to the project. Project impact is classified from minimal to worst or from low to high. The risk management plan also provides supporting measures to identify the possibility of occurrence of the risk as given in the Table 1.

Risk Identification

Risk identification is the first step in the process of determining the risks that may affect the project. Identification of risks also contributes more to documenting the characteristics of the risk. Risk identification is a repetitive process. A few people from the project team or the risk management team carry out the first process, followed by a second process performed by the entire team with the primary stakeholders. To achieve an unbiased analysis, persons not involved in the project can perform a last iteration. Finally, create the effective risk responses and implement them as soon as the uncertainties are identified.

Classification of Risk Identification

Risk identification can be classified by either top-down or bottom-up approaches, or both. Top-down risk identification assigns a furious beginning to the assessment, and starts with an overall view of the schedule, but needs an understanding of the project's scope and the organization's mission and objectives. Implications of other processes must be reviewed to identify potential risks all through the project.

Alternatively, bottom-up identification includes a procedural and complete detail about the project management, project team, and technical deliverables. This method

Table 1. Risk management planning

Risk Ref No	Description	Risk Occurrence	Assessment	Impact	Mitigation plan	Action	Person-In-Charge
1004	Plugin Error	Technical	Input validation	No output	System	Immediate	Vicky

Risk Ref No is the unique identification for the risk.
Description provides the explanation about the risk.
Risk Type identifies the type of risk. Ex: service interruption, domain accessibility etc.
Assessment estimates the measure of risk in the scale of low-medium-high, and its priorities.
Impact gives information about the possible outcomes.
Mitigation plan describes the set of plans to reduce the risk.
Action describes all the actions taken to resolve the risk.
Person-In-Charge identifies who is responsible for each action.

should review all phases of the project right from requirements to deliverables and project interfaces, in order to identify risk scope and its areas.

Key questions that would assist in identifying risks are:

How, why, where, and when are the risks likely to occur in a way that would obstruct achieving the project goals?

How can the risks associated with the project priorities cause failure to meet the scope of the project?

What are the risks associated with priorities related to project deliverables, measured in terms of low- to high-scale?

Who might participate in the risk situation?

Why does the definition (scope) not meet the execution (outcomes), and how would that increase the level of risk?

Risk Breakdown Structure

The Risk Breakdown Structure (RBS) helps to understand when a project is exposed to threat/vulnerability (i.e., risks). The RBS can also provide management with detailed information to enable a better understanding of the potentially recurring risks, and the impact that could give rise to problems that affect project status as given in Figure 2.

The Risk Breakdown Structure provides a means for management to organize the risks addressed. The RBS could be defined as an "orderly organized representation of the identified project risks exhibited by risk category.

Tools to Identify Risk

The risk identification process is elaborated upon using checklists of possible uncertainties, and evaluating the frequency with which those events might occur on the project. Some organizations develop risk checklists based on prior experience from

Figure 2. Risk breakdown structure

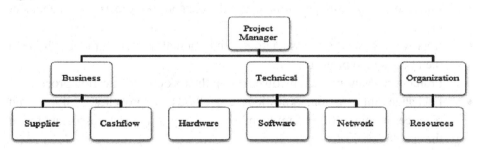

past projects. These checklists are useful to the project manager and team, both in identifying independent risks on the checklist, and amplifying the thinking capability of the team. The previous experience of the team, overall project experience in the company, and experts in the organization can be precious resources for identifying possible risk on the project.

At each stage of the project, identify risks by acknowledging the project's risk factors. A risk factor is a situation that would allow one or more potential risks to arise in the project. A risk factor alone does not affect the project, schedule, product, and resource target. However, it improves the probability that something might happen that will cause harm to the project.

Involve experts from different parts of the organization in collecting information about the internal risks that arose in previous projects. Audit reports, documentation, research results, and relevant reports support the expertise of the group in identifying risk.

Risk Communication

The very basic objective of risk communication is to provide appropriate, meaningful, and precise information, in terms clearly and understandably aimed at a specific audience. It may not settle all differences between parties, but certainly it will lead to better understanding of those differences. It will result in more widely recognized and accepted risk management decisions. Effective risk communication must have objectives that strengthen and retain trust and confidence. It should elicit a higher degree of consent and assistance from all interested parties, for the risk management options being recommended.

The aim of risk communication is to:

- Increase recognition and understanding of the definite issues under the project team's consideration during the risk analysis process.
- Promote stability and clarity in making and executing risk management decisions.
- Provide a detailed understanding of the proposed risk management decisions.
- Enhance the overall performance and efficiency of the risk management process.
- Improve the working associations and mutual respect among all team members on the project.
- Promote relevant parties' involvement in the risk communication process.
- Exchange information, knowledge, methods, approaches, values, and practices among all the team members, relating to the risks associated with the specific project.

Characteristics of Risk Communication

Factors such as what to communicate, and to whom, determine risk communication messages, which may include the following details:

The Nature of the Risk

- The importance and role of the threat of concern.
- The measure and extremity of the risk.
- The seriousness of the situation and its priority.
- Likelihood the scale of the risk may become lower or higher.
- The possibility of exposure to the threat.
- The administration of exposure.
- The quantity of exposure that comprises a significant hazard.
- The parties at higher risk.

The Nature of the Benefits

- The existing or expected benefits related to each risk.
- Identification of the stability of the risks and benefits.
- Location of the balance points of the risk and benefits.
- The importance and measure of the benefits.

Uncertainties in Risk Assessment

- The tools used to analyze the risk.
- The significance of the risk.
- The inaccuracies of the available data.
- The estimated assumptions of the inadequate data.
- The ways that the severity of the assumptions changes the estimates.
- The changes in the evaluated information that affect risk management decisions.

Risk Management Options

- The actions performed to mitigate or manage the risk.
- The justification for adopting a specific risk management decision.
- The accuracy and benefits of a specific decision.
- The cost involved in managing the risk, and the sponsor.
- The risks that exist even after a risk management decision is implemented.

Principles of Risk Communication

- **Know the Targeted Team Member**s: In constructing risk communication messages, in addition to knowing what the team members have in common, it is important to identify them specifically as groups or as individuals, to understand their concerns and to open communication with them.

- **Assign Project Specific Experts in Communication** Successful risk communication needs expertise in conveying information to all, in an understanding and useful way. People with in-depth knowledge of the specific project can elaborate on details about risk and impacts. Therefore, project-specific expert communication should begin as early as possible.

- **Include Credible Sources of Information**: The credibility of the information is more likely to influence the stakeholders about the risk. The credibility of the source is determined by factors such as expertise, competence, trustworthiness, and lack of bias. The factual expert track records play a vital role. Effective communication must acknowledge current issues with added content, and approaches that are timely. Timely conveying of information is most important, as most controversies focus on the question, "Why didn't you inform us earlier?" instead of on the risk itself.

- **Share Responsibilities**: All project members involved in the risk communication process (e.g., manager, stakeholder, developer, and tester) have joint responsibilities. As a result, communication will impact all, even though their individual roles may vary. Since in-depth knowledge about the project plays the basis for decision making, all members involved in the communication process should know the project details, basic principles, supporting and factual data of the risk assessment, and the pertained policies behind the resulting risk management decisions.

- **Emphasize Accuracy and Transparency**: In order to accept the risk analysis process and its impacts, the process must be accurate and transparent. While respecting authorized concerns to save confidentiality, transparency in the process of risk analysis should consist of possessing the overall process open and accessible for inspection by the team. Productive two-way communication between managers, team members, and stakeholders is an effective part of risk management, and a key to achieving accuracy and transparency.

- **Examine Risk in the Context of Benefits Associated with the Project**: The interpretation of risk addresses the concerns of the stakeholders and project team. Comparing the risk with another issue in the same or in a different project helps to explore the risk in context of the benefits associated with the project.

Risk Assignment

Risks are assigned to calculate their results and impacts. If risk is not assigned to resources or tasks, it will continue to exist in a risk register, and the probability of its impact and its measures will not be shown.

Classifications of Risk Assignment

- **Comprehensive Risk Assignments**: Comprehensive risk assignments are those risk assignments that have a probability of affecting the whole project, and are not restricted to specific resources and tasks. For example, risk pertaining to achieved scope and organizational risks are considered comprehensive risks.
- **Confined Risk Assignment**: Confined risk assignments are those that have a probability of affecting only specific resources and tasks. A confined risk assignment can impact more than one task or resource. For example, technical issues and resource sharing are assigned as confined risks.

Every risk assignment consists of the following information:

- Risks are assigned to resources and tasks.
- Risks are assigned by their probability of occurrence. The probability can be described per resource and task by default, and expectation of resolution in certain duration units.
- Every risk has a different impact. Impacts could be related to schedule, non-schedule, and cost. The result of impact is related to cost and duration, and depends on the duration and the cost it will increase or decrease.
- The high-risk project calculates risk impact factors for the specific duration and cost. Since the Risk Register for Tasks and Resources displays the result of risk assignment pertaining to cost and duration, issues would be resolved more efficiently.

The moment of risk is described by the start time, most likely time, finish time, and distribution of risk occurrence. Start, most likely time, and finish times are depicted as a percentage of the total task duration that starts with beginning the task. For example:

Distribution: Triangular
Start: 40%

Most likely: 60%

Finish: 100%

Responsibility Assignment Matrix

The Responsibility Assignment Matrix (RAM) describes the roles and responsibilities of the various members of the project team. In spite of the candid features of the information and details included in the RAM, bringing the team members to agreement on people's roles and responsibilities will be time consuming as stated in Table 2.

Following are steps to develop the Responsibility Assignment Matrix, which can support getting members' concern and acceptance with the least time and effort:

- Identify all the members who will actively participate, in order to support the project scope.
- Evolve an absolute list of deliverables of the project.
- Discuss with the team members how they would support the effort to come up with the various project deliverables.

For all of their assignments, discuss the level of their role and responsibility, as well as the specific task they will perform. Also discuss the involvement in cross-functional and cross-departmental activities for their task. If exact members are not yet identified for particular activities, consult with other members, experts who have already done those types of projects.

- **Prepare an Initial Draft of RAM:** Draw a table for the project, and include project's deliverables in the left column, and the members who will support the task in the initial row. In the cells at the intersection of each row and column, include the roles and responsibilities that each person will have, which would actually be based on the earlier discussions with the team members.
- **Review and Approve the Project Draft Chart:** If all the identified team members agree with the chart, ask them to designate their acceptance in writing. If the team members convey concerns about some features, aspects, or details mentioned in their task, demand that they jot down their concerns in a memo or an email.
- **Revise and Address Concerns in the Project Draft Chart:** If most of the team members do not accept the draft chart, revise the chart to mark their problems. After making updates to the draft RAM, insist all the team members review and accept the revised chart, especially when they have already approved the earlier version.

- **Continue the Process Until all the Team Members Approve the Draft Chart:** For high-risk projects, the RAM could be quite big. Keeping the chart updated and consulting with the identified team members throughout the project could be time-consuming. However, possessing a chart with incorrect details will result in duplicated activities and overlooked efforts.

Recommendations to Keep RAM Accurate and Updated All Over the Project

- **Develop a Hierarchy of Charts:** Hierarchy of charts is defined as a series of nested charts. Having more tasks on the same RAM can be troublesome, so develop a hierarchy of charts for larger projects. Develop a high-level chart that includes roles and responsibilities for higher-level structures and components in the project phases and deliverables; then prepare individual charts that identify roles and responsibilities for lower-level deliverables and project work packages.
- **Get Input from Everyone Involved:** Involve the whole team in the chart development work. The project managers would not predict exactly how the team members would perform tasks in their specialized areas, so it is better to ask for their concerns and commitments to their task. People tend to have a higher level of commitment to a plan when they are given ownership and engage in developing it.
- **Keep Risk Assignment Matrix in Written Format:** Though keeping the RAM in written format appears to be a time-consuming task, it will actually save time throughout all other phases of the project. However, placing the chart in writing is compulsory, for these reasons:
  - Possible potential problems in the project might be overlooked if they are kept in the form of pieces of details and separate information.
  - Written form ensures that the whole team has an understanding of their roles and relationships.

Table 2. Responsibility assignment matrix

Code	Title	Project Manager	Team Leader	Team Member A	Project Director	Purchase
1.2	Design Questionnaire	A	S,A	P		
2.4	Pretest		P	S		

P – Primary Responsibility, S- Secondary Responsibility, A-Approval

Risk Analysis

Risk analysis is the assessment of the risks related to a specific event or task. Risk analysis is a segment of risk management used throughout the industry's IT projects, security issues, and any task where risks can be analyzed on a quantitative and a qualitative basis.

Risks are a component of every IT project and business venture. Risk analysis must be executed concurrently and updated to mitigate new potential vulnerabilities. Strategic risk analysis decreases risk probability and future harm to the project.

Qualitative Risk Analysis

Qualitative risk analysis is a risk analysis technique related to discovering the probability of risk occurrences, and the outcome the risk will have if it occurs. All risks have both probability and outcome. Probability is the possibility that a risk will occur, and outcome is the essence of the risk's effect. Outcome affects project elements such as costs, deliverables, and performance. Qualitative risk analysis assesses threats, and establishes methods for risk mitigation and its solutions.

From the initial phase of risk identification, the project team should have an actual list of risks that could possibly affect the project. From the developed list, the project team has to distinguish between those that seem lower and need no further scrutiny, and those that require immediate follow-up with qualitative analysis, quantitative analysis, and risk mitigation and management. This process entails some qualitative assessment of the measure and severity of all the identified risk. Different methods to analyze failures in service, equipment, and systems have also been put into practice, in one form or another, to reduce project risks.

Tools and Techniques for Qualitative Risk Analysis

Risk Probability and Impact:

Risk probability and risk impact may be described in qualitative terms as very high, moderate, low, and very low. *Risk probability* expresses the likelihood that the risk will happen. *Risk impact* is the effect on the goal of the project if the risk event occurs. These two dimensions of risk relate to particular risk actions, not to the overall project. Analysis of risks using probability and impact helps to identify those risks that urgently require management.

34

Risk Probability Impact Rating Matrix

The most frequently used risk tool is shown in Figure 3. It is a two-by-two matrix that enables assigning a risk to one of the four quadrants, based on a qualitative assessment of its relative impact (high or low) and the frequency with which it happens (high or low).

Risks mentioned in the upper-right quadrant in Figure 3 require immediate attention. A finer scale of impact and likelihood—for example, very high, high, medium, very low, and low (a five-by-five matrix)—would permit more varied consideration of the attention required.

Low Impact, Low Probability

Negligible risks classified as both low impact and low likelihood of occurrence can generally be eliminated from active analysis. Effective monitoring of these factors can determine decreases in impact or likelihood.

High Impact, High Probability

Risks characterized as high impact and high probability of occurrence often lead to discontinuation of a project, or to its failure if it is continued despite the risks.

Figure 3. Risk probability impact rating Matrix

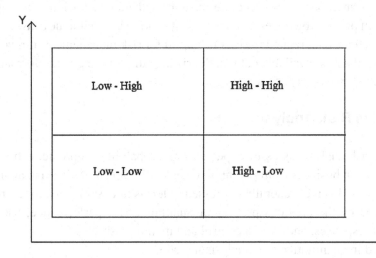

Low Impact, High Probability

Risks characterized as low-impact and high-probability of occurrence happen mainly due to uncertainties in a number of components that independently may be minor risks, but as whole could amount to a sizable risk.

High Impact, Low Probability

By default, high impact, low probability risks are rare events; hence, it is incorrect to allocate probabilities to them based on historical records. Data are not available, and subjective prediction of probabilities is required. However, the objective is to determine management actions to monitor, mitigate, and manage the risks.

Project Assumptions Testing

The following criteria are used to test the identified assumption:

- The stability of the assumption, and the outcomes of the project if the assumption is false.
- Auxiliary assumptions that may be factual must be identified, and their outcome for the project scope is tested in the qualitative risk-analysis process.

Data Precision Ranking

Qualitative risk analysis requires accurate and unbiased information if it is to support achievement of project objectives. Data precision ranking is a technique to assess the degree to which the data related to risks is helpful for risk management. It involves understanding the risk, available data on the risk, quality of the given information, and integrity and reliability of the data.

Quantitative Risk Analysis

Quantitative risk analysis assesses expected risk probability, to predict estimated financial losses in business from potential uncertainties. Quantitative risk analysis assigns a projected value, generally expressed in terms of cost or time, to the risks already ranked by the previous process of qualitative risk performance, used to estimate risk responses, and also to control and monitor risks.

Tools used in quantitative risk analysis include:

- **Probability Distributions:** Probability distributions are usually represented in a graph or table structure, and the probability of a risk occurrence is represented mathematically. These probability distributions assist in the decision-making process by considering the actual probability of a risk happening, and determining the most efficient way to approach each risk.

- **Data Gathering and Representation Techniques:** Data gathering and representation techniques are carried out using a questionnaire to decide the probability of risk occurrence, and the impact of risks according to the experts on that particular subject matter. These experts must possess the in-depth knowledge, effective skills, and sufficient experience to form a realistic view of risk probability and impacts.

- **Sensitivity Analysis:** Sensitivity analysis is defined as analyzing the project to examine how sensitive it is to specific risks, by analyzing the impact and extremity of each risk. Applying the result of sensitivity analysis to any quantitative risk analysis is highly advisable. A sensitivity coefficient is derived from underlying assets: the change in some result with respect to a modification in some input. Even if the probability of the occurrences of a specific risk cannot be determined exactly, sensitivity analysis can be used to determine the variables that have more influence on the event of risk occurrence. Because a vital role of risk analysis is to break down the issue into essential components that can be solved by management, sensitivity analysis is highly helpful in determining the decisions that the manager should make to get the desired outcomes, or to stay away from it. In the absence of hard data, sensitivity analysis is very useful in evaluating the authenticity of risk models.

- **Decision Tree Analysis:** Decision tree analysis appears in the form of a flow diagram, in which each node is represented by a rectangle that contains a description of the risk characteristics and its cost. These rectangles are linked to each other by arrows, each arrow extending to another box that, in turn, represents the percentage probability of risk. These totals are derived by calculation, multiplying the costs of risk by the probability, and summing that value to the initial cost.

- **Tornado Diagrams:** Tornado diagrams are so named because of their funnel shape. They illustrate graphically the cost of project sensitivity and other factors involved in it. Each tornado diagram represents the result of risks, in terms of specific aspects. These aspects are the stages in phases of all projects, and are ordered vertically and headed by a horizontal bar displaying a plus or minus impact on cost.

- **Expected Monetary Value Analysis:**In general terms, the anticipated monetary value is determined by multiplying the probability of occurrence by the cost impact, to get a presumed value for each risk. These are then summed up to acquire the expected monetary value for the project. Expected monetary value is frequently calculated by using decision trees.

- **Modeling and Simulation:** The usual form of modeling and simulation method is Monte Carlo analysis. The system calculates it, by analyzing various scenarios for the schedule of the project, and calculating the impact of specific risk occurrences. It is useful in identifying risks by the consequences they have on the schedule of the project.

- **Expert Judgement:** In the same way a structured interview is conducted, this would usually involve asking project experts to review data of the risk in the manner in which it has been gathered. As a result, these project experts might also identify additional risk areas.

Risk Responses

Risk responses are the evolving of options for risk strategies, and deciding on actions to improve opportunities and minimize threats to the project's scope. A member of that particular team is assigned to take control of each risk response.

Risk Response Strategies

Risk management strategies direct how organizations propose to evaluate, react to, and monitor risk, with risk perceived to be clear and open, and routinely involved in making both technical and operational decisions. As components of organizational risk management strategies, risk response strategies are essential, due to the practical realities that organizations face. These include the necessity of enterprise effectiveness offered by information technology, the shortfall of reliability in available technologies, and the growing consciousness by adversaries of the potential to accomplish their goals for creating harm, by accepting organizational information systems and the domain in which those systems operate. Most senior leaders in organizations are faced with an almost ungovernable dilemma—that is, the information technologies required for organization success may be the same sort of technologies through which adversaries can harm the organization by causing system failure. The risk response strategies that organizations develop and execute give these senior leaders and decision makers' realistic, pragmatic paths for managing this dilemma. Clearly defined and stated risk response strategies support ensuring that senior leaders take responsibility for organizational risk responses, and are finally accountable and responsible for risk decisions, by understanding, acknowledging, and accepting the impact of organization risk.

Risk response strategies include:

- Organizational and individual components accountable for choosing risk response measures and details of effectiveness criteria.
- Formation of thresholds against which the effectiveness of risk response actions and measures can be judged.
- Dependencies of the identified risk response actions and measures on other risk response actions and measures.
- Dependencies of identified risk response actions and measures on other factors, such as execution of other planned tasks or information technology measures.
- Executing a timeline for risk responses.
- Detailed plans and methods for monitoring and calculating the effectiveness of the risk response actions and measures.
- Identifying risk monitoring triggers.
- Selecting interim risk response actions and measures for implementation, if required.

Risk response strategies for implementation include interim actions and measures that organizations choose to implement. A complete risk response strategy provides an organizational method of selecting the basic risk responses in the prescribed risk situation. A decision to undertake risk must be consistent with the organizational tolerance for risk, and requires a well-defined and established organizational path for selecting the methods of risk responses strategies. Organizations are often put in situations where there is higher risk than the designated senior leaders are willing to accept. Some risk acceptance will probably be required.

It may be possible to avoid risk, or to share or transfer risk, and some risk mitigation is likely feasible. Avoiding risk may require selective reengineering of organizational processes, and renouncing some of the benefits accrued by the use of an IT organization, perhaps even those that organizations recognize as necessary benefits. Mitigating risk calls for disbursement of limited resources, and will quickly become cost-ineffective because of the pragmatic practicalities of the degree of mitigation that can actually be accomplished. Ultimately, risk sharing and transfer have impacts as well, some of which are not unacceptable, even if undesirable. The risk response strategies of IT organizations allow senior leaders to develop risk-based decisions in compliance with the goals, scope, and perspectives of the wider organization.

Types of Risk Responses

- **Avoid:** Risk can be avoided by eliminating the root cause of the risk, or implementing the project in another way, while still aiming to accomplish the project's scope. Not all risks can be avoided, and for some, this method may be too expensive and time consuming. However, this must be the first strategy considered.

- **Transfer:** Transferring risk includes identifying another party who desires to take responsibility for controlling it, and who will carry the liability for the risk when it occurs. The goal is to make certain that the risk is owned and controlled by the party best able to work with it efficiently. Risk transfer generally involves a premium payment, whose cost-effectiveness must also be taken into account when deciding whether to acquire a transfer strategy.

- **Mitigate:** Risk mitigation reduces the possibility and/or impact of a harmful risk action to an acceptable threshold. Taking action early to minimize the possibility and/or impact of a risk is often more efficient than trying to recover from the damage after the risk has occurred. Risk mitigation may need resources and time, creating a tradeoff between the cost of doing nothing and the mitigation cost of the risk.

- **Share**: An opportunity to assign risk responsibility to another party provides the best fit for maximizing its likelihood of occurrence and improving the potential benefits if it occurs. Transferring risks and sharing opportunities are the same, in that a third party is used. Those to whom risks are transferred take on the accountability, and those to whom opportunities are assigned should be authorized to share in the potential benefits.

- **Acceptance:** This strategy is embraced when it is impossible or impractical to provide a response to the risk using other strategies, or a response is not guaranteed to be consistent with the significance of the risk. When the project team members decide to adopt a risk, they are consenting to address the risk if and when it does occur. An emergency plan, work action plan, and/or emergency reserve may be developed for that case.

Risk Response Matrix

A Risk Response Matrix is a matrix used, while assessing risk, to describe the different levels of risk as the result of the harm possibility categories and harm extremity categories. This is a simple method to improve visibility of risks and support management in making decisions which is briefly mentioned in Table 3.

Risk Tracking

Risk tracking is the process of monitoring and controlling identified risks, monitoring leftover risks, and identifying new risks, to ensure the implementation of risk plans, and assess their efficiency in risk reduction. Risk tracking records risk measures related

Table 3. Risk response matrix

Risk Event	Response	Contingency Plan	Trigger	Responsible Person
Equipment malfunction	Transfer	Order Replacement	Equipment fails	Krish
UI interface issue	Mitigate	Work around until resolves	Not solved in 18hrss	Gana

to implementing eventuality plans. Risk tracking is a continual process throughout the life of the project. The risks modify as the project grows, new advanced risks develop, or expected risks disappear.

Good risk tracking process provides information that supports making effective decisions ahead of the risk happening. Communicating the risk-tracking details to all project members is needed to periodically evaluate the level of risk in the project.

The aim of risk tracking is to determine if:

- Risk responses are implemented as planned.
- Risk response events are as efficient as expected, or if new responses have to be developed.
- Project speculation is still valid.
- Risk exposure has been updated from its previous state, with new analysis and trends.
- A risk trigger has happened.
- Proper policies and methods are followed.
- Risks not previously identified have occurred.

A risk control includes identifying alternative strategies, executing a contingency plan, taking corrective action, and re-planning the project. The person responsible for risk response must report occasionally to the project manager and the risk team leader about the efficiency of the plan, any unanticipated impacts, and any mid-level correction required mitigating the risk.

Risks can change over the period of a project, which implies that tracking is a vital part of the organization's risk-management process. Having knowledge about advanced risks can modify the results of the project scope by assigning resources to them.

Risk Track Form

By collecting an initial set of prospective risks from project members, the officials responsible for management and the risk response can contribute on a risk track form. Also known as a risk database, this information warehouse enumerates the real-time harms to any project's objectives. As the project team takes on more direct duties, the risk officials can begin to take a daily and a weekly approach to placing information into the database, to gain insight on major decisions as stated in Table 4.

Risk Tracking Tools and Techniques

- **Risk Reassessment:** Risk tracking must identify new risks and reassess risks continually. Assess project risk periodically on a predetermined schedule. Project risk reassessment must be an agenda item at project risk management status meetings. The amount of associated repetition depends on the progress of the project appropriate to its goals. Then it will be important to accomplish additional response planning to monitor and control the risk.
- **Risk Audits:** Risk audits evaluate and document the efficiency of risk responses in working with identified risks and their causes, as well as the efficacy of the risk management process.
- **Variance and Trend Analysis:** The project implementation trends must be revised using performance data. Project variance and other methods of earned

Table 4.

RISK TRACK FORM	

Risk Planning

Risk No:	
Type of Risk:	
Mitigation Plan:	
Contingency Plan:	

Risk Identification

Risk Track Name:	Person In Charge:
Risk Track Code:	Risk Identified Date:
Description:	Risk Materialize Indicator:
Impact:	Diagram attached: Y/N
Cost:	Delay:

Risk Re-Assessment

Date	Description of Change

Final Disposal

Did risk materialize?	
If yes, details about cost, delay and action:	
Comments:	

value analysis and trend analysis are used to track overall project performance. Results from this analysis might determine possible divergence of the project at finalization from targeted duration, cost, and schedule. Variations from the original plan may indicate the possible impact of risks.

- **Technical Performance Measurement:** Technical performance measurement estimates technical achievements during project implementation, in relation to the project risk management plan's schedule of technical accomplishment. Demonstrating more or less functionality than planned at identified milestones will support forecasting the percentage of success in accomplishing the project objectives.

- **Reserve Analysis:** All through the implementation of the project, some risks may occur, with positive or negative consequences for cost and time contingency reserves. Reserve analysis collate the percentage of the contingency reserves remaining to the amount of risk left over during the project duration, in order to confirm whether the balance on reserve is sufficient.

- **Status Meetings:** Project risk tracking management will be a main agenda item at periodic team status meetings. This may take no time or a long time, depending on the risks that have been already identified, their level of priority, and difficulty in responding. Risk tracking management will be easier the more often it is put into practice, and discussions conducted often about risk will make talking about risks, particularly vulnerability, easier and more accurate.

Risk Reporting

Risk reporting is defined as the medium for communicating the value that the risk activity represents to an organization. It authorizes proactive risk management in organizations to identify and escalate problems either as they arise, or before they are perceived, to create a proactive method for managing risks. Reporting must be connected to the application of the whole risk management process, if the framework of the risk management is clearly defined and executed.

It is usual for the organization to submit reports to their management, which show:

- The risk profile of the complete IT organization.
- The updates and modifications in the risk profile since the last submitted report.
- The effective performance of the risk management framework.

In reality, this means that most of the organization needs departments to prepare reports to submit twice a year to an audit and the risk management committee. Some organizations submit only one consolidated report that covers all departments in the organization.

Risk Profile Report

Generally, a risk profile indexes the highest level of risk that represents summarized and strategic risks from all divisions in the organization. It is advisable to preface this with an executive summary that provides commentary and explains:

- What are the most important risks and why.
- How the risks are being controlled.
- Any specific control gaps and how to fill them.

While it is usual to rate risks by the residual risk ranking, often management would like to see the highest possible impact of risk, as scaled by a potential scenario in an organizational system, and to make sure that these risks in specific are controlled.

Risk Report Changes

The risk report changes are either separate from or a component of the risk profile report. The idea is to tell management about changes in the risk profile report since the last report, how the report was done, and why. Normally this is more helpful and crucial than just a basic risk profile report.

The report explains:

- Those risks that have been minimized in risk level or the possible scenario, probably due to control activity.
- Those risks that have been maximized in level or a possible scenario.
- Those risks where important changes have affected risk control efficiency, either positively or negatively.

It is also useful to note emerging risks on the projects watch list.

Risk Management Framework Performance Report

The organization also requires producing reports that describe in detail and define the quantity, quality, measure, and maturity of the risk management system in its

Table 5. Risk management performance report

Risk	Aim	Impact	Risk Indicators	Consequences	Performance	Changes	Management Controls	Person-In-Charge
Deliverables	Supplier issue	Quality and production loss	Late deliverables	Occur frequently	Lack	Meeting with purchase and QA	Analyze and mitigate	Wong

Risk – identified risk, uncertainties
Aim – target of the identified risk
Impact – possible results of the risk
Risk indicator – component which is used to mention the indicate the risk
Consequence – effects of the occurred risk
Performance – show the degree of the production or achievement
Changes – updates that are not stated in the last report
Management Controls – actions taken by the management to control the risk
Person-In-Charge – accountable person to resolve the risk

different divisions and departments. This reporting on risk management framework performance to the organization will authorize management to attest that the organization's risk framework and internal control and compliance methods are operating effectively in all respects.

The report contains:

- The latest risk management plan for all departments and divisions in the organization.
- An explanation of the progress in executing the risk management plan since the latest report.
- A goal and procedural evaluation of the level of risk management maturity, and the update since the latest report.

It is also important to note and explain if there is any decline in performance of the progress that is indicated in Table 5.

CONCLUSION

Each and every organization is unique, but risk management has common practices that could be noticed among many organizations. By following the above method or model, organizations can successfully implement risk management processes and add value to the enterprise.

REFERENCES

Berg, H.-P. (2010). Risk management: Procedures, methods and experiences. *Journal of International Group on Reliability: Theory and &Applications*, 2(17), 79–88.

Committee for Oversight and Assessment of U.S. Department of Energy Project Management, Board on Infrastructure and the Constructed Environment, Division on Engineering and Physical Sciences. (2005). Risk identification and analysis: The owner's role in project risk management. The National Academies Press.

Cooper. (2007). *Risk Management, Reporting and Governance*. Broadleaf Capital International.

Elky, S. (2006). An Introduction to Information System Risk Management. SANS Institute.

Exploration System Mission Directorate. (2007). *Exploration Systems, Risk Management Plan*. ESMD-RMP-04.06 Rev 2 (3-12). NASA.

Halpin, D. W., & Martinez, L.-H. (1999). Real-world Applications of Construction Process Simulation. *Proceedings of the 1999 Winter Simulation Conference*. Available online at http://www.informs-cs.org/wsc99papers/prog99.html

HB 436. (2004). *Handbook Risk Management Guidelines*. Standards Australia International Ltd.

Molenaar, K., Anderson, S., & Schexnader, C. (2010). Guide to Planning Phase: Guidebook on Risk Analysis Tools and Management to Control Transportation Project Cost. The National Academies of Science, Engineering and Medicine.

Parker, D., & Mobey, A. (2004). Action research to explore perceptions of risk in project management. *International Journal of Productivity and Performance Management*, 53(1), 18–32. doi:10.1108/17410400410509932

Portny, S. E. (2013). Venturing with Unknown: Dealing with Risk. In Project Management for Dummies (4th ed.). Academic Press.

Project Management Institute. (2013). A guide to the project management body of knowledge. In PMBOK(R) Guide (5th ed.). Author.

Taylor, J., Jr. (2013). *Risk Management: Keeping track of risk and utilizing risk manager*. Bright Hub Project Management.

Techopedia. (2016). Retrieved from https://www.techopedia.com/definition/25836/it-risk-management

Watt, A. (2014). *Project Management: Risk Management Planning*. BC Open Textbook.

Widerman, R. M. (1992). *Project and program risk management: A guide to managing project risks*. Academic Press.

Wikipedia. (2016). Retrieved information from https://en.wikipedia.org/wiki/Risk_analysis

KEY TERMS AND DEFINITIONS

Data Precision Ranking: Technique to evaluate the accuracy of data in the identified risk.

Decision-Tree-Analysis: Describes the risk characteristics and cost in flow diagram.

Monte Carlo Simulation: Probability assessment algorithm used to obtain numerical results based on random sampling.

Responsibility Assignment Matrix: Description of the member roles in the project.

Risk: The uncertain outcome of an event.

Risk Audit: Examine and document the efficiency of risk responses.

Risk Breakdown Structure: Hierarchical order of representing the identified risks of the project.

Risk Profile Report: Indexing the high level of risks.

Variance and Trend Analysis: Revision of project implementation is done with performance data.

Chapter 3
Strengthening IT Governance With COBIT 5

Gaurav Chaudhari
Independent Researcher, Egypt

Pavankumar Mulgund
University at Buffalo, USA

ABSTRACT

This paper aims to explore the importance of COBIT 5 as a framework, in ensuring the effective "Governance of Enterprise Information Technology (GEIT)", and to promote the understanding of the five COBIT 5 principles. A comprehensive literature review has also been performed taking into account a total of 56 research papers published in the last decade on COBIT. The data collected from these research papers was analyzed in order to identify various trends- commonalities, differences, themes, and the nature of study. The research papers have been categorized first on basis of their scope and secondly on their nature (empirical, conceptual or descriptive). Towards the end of the paper, we have provided an overview of our findings on the strengths and weaknesses of the research papers studied, and have made suggestions for future research.

1. INTRODUCTION_

Information is of vital importance for the existence of all organizations. From the point of time when information is created, to the time it is destroyed, the organization must ensure that it is adequately safeguarded and put to efficient use.

DOI: 10.4018/978-1-5225-2604-9.ch003

Management and protection of information has become a top priority for the organizations more than ever. Information Technology is the key driver that helps the enterprises to manage and make the most out of the information. The executive management is focusing on the following areas now more than ever:-

- Ensuring compliance with the ever increasing list of rules and regulations.
- Leveraging information and IT as a competitive advantage and using them to make business critical decisions.
- Maintaining IT Risk at an acceptable level.
- Optimizing the costs of information technology and services.
- Creating business value by efficient use of IT.
- Improving operational efficiency by reliable use of IT.

Since IT has become a business enabling function from being a support function, it is imperative that the board and management accept IT as a vital part of doing business. And to do the justice to IT that it commands, enterprises would need a framework that can help them to identify the IT best practices, to align the IT objectives to the business objectives, and to ensure effective IT governance and management. This is where COBIT 5 comes to the rescue.

2. EXPLAINING COBIT

COBIT 5 as defined by ISACA is – "A Business Framework for the Governance and Management of Enterprise IT". COBIT 5 is based on five major principles related to IT governance and IT management:-

- Meeting Stakeholder Needs
- Covering the Enterprise End-to-End
- Applying a Single Integrated Framework
- Enabling a Holistic Approach, and
- Separating Governance from Management

Now that we have listed the five COBIT principles, let's delve into each of them and explore how each one of them can help an enterprise.

Figure 1. COBIT 5 Principles

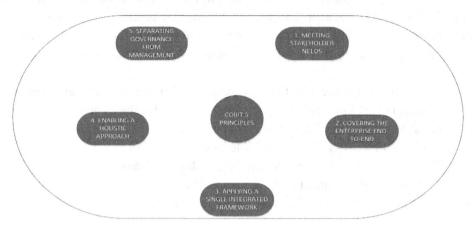

2.1. Principle 1: Meeting Stakeholder Needs

Enterprises strive to create and deliver value for their stakeholders, and try to maintain a balance between the realization of benefits and the optimizing risk and resource usage. The COBIT 5 framework provides multiple processes and enablers to help the organizations in creating business value through IT.

Every organization aims to create value by maximal realization of benefits while trying to optimize the risk and ensuring optimal costs. Thus we can say that governance objective is value creation, through benefits realization, Risk optimization and Resource optimization.

But many a times, since there are multiple stakeholders any enterprise, they get stuck amidst conflicting needs of the stakeholders. Thus arises the need to negotiate and agree upon a defined set of needs, through a careful analysis of all stakeholders' needs. These agreed upon needs then shape and drive the actionable strategy of the enterprise. The COBIT 5 framework goals cascade helps an enterprise to SMART (Specific, Measurable, Attainable, Relevant and Time Bound) and customized goals. These goals can be in the form of overall enterprise goals, or be specific to IT, or just be some form of enablers.

Let us have a look at how these goals cascade down from stakeholder drivers (top-most) to enabler goals (at the bottom). Stakeholder drivers are the factors that influence the stakeholders' needs and can be anything related to a business requirement, regulatory requirement, technological advancement or change in strategy.

The enterprise goals are generic in nature based on stakeholder needs and are generally developed by taking balanced scorecard dimensions into consideration. The success of enterprise goals depends great deal on the success of IT functions as well, thus enterprise goals cascade down to IT related goals. And since it is

Figure 2. Goals Cascade as defined by COBIT 5

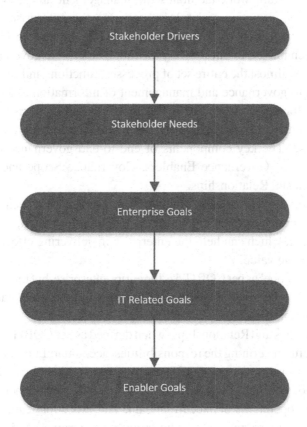

important that the IT related goals are well aligned to Enterprise goals and help the organization progress towards achieving its mission, we need enabler goals.

The goal cascade is important as it aids the organization to define the priorities for various stakeholder needs and in order to assure effective governance of Enterprise IT. The goal cascade helps the enterprise to zero down onto tangible, relevant goals; assigning responsibilities to appropriate personnel; and identifying the importance of enablers.

2.2. Principle 2: Covering the Enterprise End-To-End

Since it is important for an organization's IT objectives to extend its business objective, COBIT 5 provides on this front as well, by integrating governance of IT with the governance of enterprise. COBIT 5 covers all functions and processes, an enterprise might undertake. It treats organizational information and technologies that support it as assets, that need to protected and managed like other assets of the organization.

The COBIT 5 framework facilitates the management and governance of all information and information technology, covering the enterprise end-to-end. It allows for the integration of IT governance (EGIT- Enterprise Governance of Information Technology, to put it nicely) with the enterprise governance practice. And it also covers almost the entire set of processes, functions and activities that are vital requisites to governance and management of information and the associated technologies. Moreover, the ambit of COBIT 5 doesn't stop on the internal IT services of the enterprise, but it also caters to IT services that are external to the parent enterprise. The key components of end-to-end governance as defined by COBIT 5 include – Governance Enablers, Governance Scope and the different Roles, Activities and Relationships.

COBIT 5 defines 'Governance Enablers' as the resources such as principles, processes, structures, practices, frameworks, people, information, IT applications, and infrastructure, which can help the enterprise in delivering effective EGIT and enabling it to create value.

'Governance Scope' as per COBIT 5 is the entire enterprise, but for implementation convenience, it can be modified to provide a zoomed in view of a particular entity or any organizational asset.

'Roles, Activities and Relationships' when defined as per COBIT 5 directions are particularly useful in defining the responsibilities, accountabilities, and interactions between different roles. As per COBIT 5, owners or stakeholders delegate work to governing body, which sets direction for the management to act upon, who in turn instruct the operations or execution team. The execution team reports on the status/progress to the management, who monitor the progress and keep informed the governing body. And in the end, it's the governing body who is accountable for the success/achievement of enterprise goals to the owners/stakeholders.

2.3. Principle 3: Applying a Single Integrated Framework

We all know that there are numerous IT-related standards, frameworks, and good practices that provide guidance of specific set of IT activities and processes. COBIT 5 aims to align with all other relevant standards at a high level, and serve as an umbrella framework that could provide governance and management of enterprise IT, across all IT activities, processes and services.

As already pointed in the introduction, COBIT 5 is a single and integrated framework, that with effective implementation and monitoring can help the enterprise to align with other specific and relevant frameworks or standards as well, and it thus functions as an umbrella framework. It provides an enterprise wide coverage and a simple architecture along with the relevant guidance. Moreover, it is the most enhanced version amongst all ISACA provided frameworks, as it has been developed by integrating previous version of COBIT with Risk IT, ITAF, Val IT and others. Not only this, it has been further aligned to non-ISACA frameworks and standards such as ISO Standards, ITIL, TOGAF. However, organizations still find it difficult to identify the mapping of COBIT with other frameworks. There have been a lot of research on mapping specific processes as defined in all these frameworks to similar processes in COBIT, and also on identifying the best ways to use COBIT in conjunction with others.

COBIT 5 comes with an entire product family that can help the enterprise in successful implementation of the framework. It includes COBIT 5 Enabling Processes, COBIT 5 Enabling Information, Other Enabler Guides, and Professional guides such as- COBIT 5 Implementation Guide, COBIT 5 Guide for Information Security, COBIT 5 Guide for Assurance, COBIT 5 Guide for Risk and other professional guides.

2.4. Principle 4: Enabling a Holistic Approach

COBIT 5 provides a set of enablers that help enterprises to implement a comprehensive, efficient and effective, governance and management system for its IT activities. Enablers help an organization to achieve its objectives. There are seven categories of enablers, as defined in COBIT-5:-

- **Principles, Policies, and Frameworks**: These act as the medium bridging the gap between the as-is and to-be states of the enterprise. They provide the practical, elaborate guidance both for effective governance and daily management of activities.
- **Processes**: Processes define and elaborate upon a set of activities and practices that enable an enterprise to attain its objectives and produce outputs that contribute towards attain IT related goals and enterprise goals.
- **Organizational Structures**: These are the prominent decision making entities that aid the organization in setting direction.
- **Culture, Ethics and Behavior**: The work culture and behavior of employees and other key individuals have a definite impact on the success of the endeavors of the enterprise. However, their impact is usually under estimated or unaccounted for, on the governance and management success.
- **Information**: The information set for an enterprise consists of all the information that the enterprise produces or uses. Information is vital to keep any organization in a healthy state at governance, management or operational levels. Sometimes, information is the main product of the enterprise, and thus commands even more attention.
- **Services, Infrastructure and Applications**: These include all IT related processes, services, infrastructure that are an asset to the enterprise.

- People, Skills and Competencies – People and their skills and competencies are central to the success of any activity, and any decision making process.

It is absolutely essential to have the correct mindset in order to correctly adopting EGIT, and thus enterprises must understand that these enablers are interrelated- they would be ineffective in isolation. Correct understanding of the relationships between these enablers is central to the idea of enabling a holistic approach. All these enablers need inputs from one or the other enablers and create outputs that are beneficial to the other enablers. Thus, it's only worthy to say, that in order to ensure a sound and efficient decision making process, the systematic nature of these enablers be considered and accounted for- analyze all these enablers that are relevant to any requirement, look for the dependencies and address the concerns (if any).

All these COBIT 5 enablers have an associated set of common dimensions, namely – the stakeholders, the goals, the intrinsic quality, the contextual quality and the access and security. While the intrinsic quality refers to the degree to which the enablers function accurately, contextual quality is a measure of the enablers being a good fit for the intended purpose. All enablers have a lifecycle as well- that starts with enabler inception and ends with enabler disposal. The various phases of an enabler life cycle are planning, designing, building or acquiring, operating, evaluating and disposing. COBIT 5 enablers also come with a set of good practices defined for each enabler. This set of good practices play a pivotal role in attaining the goals of that particular enabler. While evaluating the performance of enablers, the metrics should be clearly defined, and accurately measured- check whether the stakeholders' needs are getting addressed, whether the enabler life cycles are adequately managed, and whether the goals are attained.

2.5. Principle 5: Separating Governance from Management

COBIT 5 makes a strong and successful attempt at establishing a clear distinction between governance and management. Governance is about taking measures to ensure that stakeholder requirements are well evaluated to determine a balanced list of objectives, and setting the direction for the organization through decision making, monitoring performance and compliance with the objectives of the enterprise.

Management on the other hand is responsible for planning, conducting, monitoring and controlling the activities with respect to the direction set by the governance body, in order to achieve the laid down objectives.

COBIT 5 advises enterprises to implement various EGIT and IT Management processes in a manner such that, all key aspects are taken care of. Governance team analyses the business needs and directs the management team to act upon it. The Management team Plans (Align, Plan and Organize- APO), Builds (Build, Acquire and Implement- BAI), Runs (Deliver, Service and Support- DSS) and Monitors (Monitor, Evaluate and Assess- MEA) and provides feedback to the governance team, who also monitor the work. This entire set of activity/process lifecycle is known as the 'COBIT 5 Process Reference Model'.

COBIT 5 PRM (Process Reference Model) does a really good job in separating and establishing a boundary between governance and management. As per COBIT 5 model, governance encompasses five key processes, and within each process EDM (Evaluate, Direct and Monitor) activities are defined.

Management on the other hand has four domains in all, and provided complete coverage of IT. These domains as named earlier are "Align, Plan, Organize (APO)", "Build, Acquire and Implement (BAI)", "Deliver, Service and Support (DSS)" and "Monitor, Evaluate and Assess (MEA)".

The COBIT 5 process reference model has its roots in the process model of its predecessor- COBIT 4.1. The earlier model was integrated with Val IT and Risk IT process models to shape up the current version of process reference model.

There are a total of 37 governance and management processes as listed in COBIT 5, however any enterprise is at liberty to choose the processes that are a good fit to its business. Usually larger organizations are more complex and have many processes, while the smaller one may not be covering the entire suite of processes.

Here's a detailed list of all 37 COBIT 5 processes (Tables 1-5).

3. LITERATURE REVIEW

After taking a view of the COBIT 5 framework as described by ISACA, I undertook a literature review exercise, in order to gauge the perception, the usability, the enhancements/modifications and other research that are being pursued on COBIT 5. I started with about 95 papers that were related to COBIT and were published over

Table 1.

PROCESSES FOR GOVERNANCE OF ENTERPRISE IT
Evaluate, Direct and Monitor
EDM01 - Ensure governance Framework Setting and Maintenance
EDM02 - Ensure Benefits Delivery
EDM03 - Ensure Risk Optimization
EDM04 - Ensure Resource Optimization
EDM05 - Ensure Stakeholder Transparency

Table 2. Processes for management of enterprise IT

ALIGN, PLAN AND ORGANIZE (APO)
APO01 - Manage the IT Management Framework
APO02 - Manage Strategy
APO03 - Manage Enterprise Architecture
APO04 - Manage Innovation
APO05 - Manage Porfolio
APO06 - Manage Budget and Costs
APO07 - Manage Human Resources
APO08 - Manage Relationships
APO09 - Manage Service Agreements
APO10 - Manage Suppliers
APO11 - Manage Quality
APO12 - Manage Risk
APO13 - Manage Security

Table 3.

BUILD, ACQUIRE AND IMPLEMENT (BAI)
BAI01 - Manage Programmes and Projects
BAI02 - Manage Requirements Definition
BAI03 - Manage Solution Identification and Build
BAI04 - Manage Availability and Capacity
BAI05 - Manage Organisational Change Enablement
BAI06 - Manage Changes
BAI07 - Manage Change Acceptance & Transitioning
BAI08 - Manage Knowledge
BAI09 - Manage Assets
BAI10 - Manage Configuration
APO11 - Manage Quality
APO12 - Manage Risk
APO13 - Manage Security

a span of 10 years between 2005 and 2014. After going through the description and taking a high level view of the content of these research papers, I dropped about 40 papers as they were not really centered on COBIT, and thus continued my analysis with a set of 56 papers. I then categorized these research papers into four broad categories based on their content. These categories include- COBIT integration with other frameworks, Explaining COBIT, Specific use of COBIT and Studying/Improving COBIT. Now let's have an overview of the content of these research papers.

Table 4.

DELIVER, SERVICE AND SUPPORT (DSS)
DSS01 - Manage Operations
DSS02 - Manage Service Requests and Incidents
DSS03 - Manage Problems
DSS04 - Manage Continuity
DSS05 - Manage Security Services
DSS06 - Manage Business Process Controls

Table 5.

MONITOR, EVALUATE AND ASSESS (MEA)
MEA01 - Monitor, Evaluate and Assess Performance and Compliance
MEA02 - Monitor, Evaluate and Assess the System of Internal Control
MEA03 - Monitor, Evaluate and Assess Compliance with External Requirements

3.1. Literature Review: COBIT Integration With Other Frameworks and Standards

Here's what the research papers mainly talked about:

Hesham and Saad [1] have explained the importance of COBIT framework in providing a simple, integrated approach to IT Governance Assessment. Many others have attempted to integrate specific framework and/or standard to COBIT. For instance, Latifi, Nasiri and Mohsenzadeh [3] have mapped DSS domain of COBIT to eTOM; Rubino and Vitolla [4] have worked on integrating COBIT with COSO; Amid and Moradi [5] tried to blend CMM with COBIT; Pretorious and Solms [14][15], have evaluated complementary use of COBIT and ISO 17799; while several others [2][6][7][8][9][10][11][12][13] have explored the integration of COBIT with multiple frameworks and/or standards such as ITIL v3, ISO/IEC 27002, ISO 270001, ISO 17799, PCIDSS, BS 7799, and Prince2. Some of the papers comment on simultaneous use of COBIT with other frameworks/standards, without necessarily integrating them, while others have focused on framework integration in a specific industry, so as to support the fulfilment of requirements laid down by the applicable laws and regulations. The authors Highlighting the similarities and differences of COBIT with other frameworks/standards, and providing a more comprehensive framework based on the analysis. Few authors have explored the pros and cons of implementing only COBIT, implementing only one of the other frameworks/standards, and implementing COBIT in conjunction with others- for instance Solms [14].

3.2. Literature Review: Explaining COBIT

Many authors perceive COBIT to be a tough to understand and/or implement framework and thus have tried to bring more clarity, through better explanation of the framework. Bartens, de Haes, Eggert, Heilig, Maes, Schulte, and Voß [16] presented a software prototype, to facilitate better understanding of COBIT 5, its components and their relationships to one another. Aliquo Jr. and Fu [17] established a COBIT 5 process capability assessment model (PAM), and explained the planning, execution, and development/communication of results, of the PAM. Kerr and Murthy [18] explored the relationship between COBIT 5 and financial reporting, by conducting a survey of IT Professionals, and evaluating the importance of each COBIT 5 process from the viewpoint of effective internal control over financial reporting. Pasquini and Galie [19] provided insights on evolution of COBIT from version 4.1 to 5, and analyzed the attributes that characterize COBIT 5. Suer [20] explored the use and importance of balanced scored card approach in COBIT. Preittigun, Chantatub and Vatanasakdakul [21] investigated the similarities/differences between COBIT 5 concepts and those discussed in various academic literature over the past decade. Van Haren Publishin [22] provified a detailed description of COBIT enabler models, process model, process maturity model, and their respective implementation strategies. Stekhoven [23] defined active software escrow and identified its benefits with respect to the support it lends to effective implementation of COBIT 5. Oliver and Lainhart [24] examined the business benefits of using COBIT 5. Mataracioglu and Ozkan [25] explained the importance and use of COBIT in information security governance. Radovanović, Radojević, Lučić, and Šarac [27] have explored the benefits of COBIT in IT Auditing, with respect to the control activities, effectiveness measurements and documentation of processes and operations. Campbell [28] has presented a simplified view on COBIT by discussing how COBIT is valuable, what is it and what documents are related to COBIT.

3.3. Literature Review: Specific Use of COBIT

Several authors have used their research prowess in order to examine the use of COBIT framework in a specific setting or for a specific purpose. Othman, Ahmad, Suliman, Arshad, and Maidin [29] carried out a feasibility analysis on use of

COBIT framework in governance of natural disaster management projects by having well-defined governance over processes, the required information and associated technology. Nugroho [30]; and Ribeiro and Gomes [39] portrayed aspects of COBIT 5 that can be used as a reference for governance and management of IT in academic and non-academic activities in an educational institution. Brandas, Stirbu, and Didraga [32] provided an integrated approach model of risk, control and auditing of Accounting Information Systems (AIS), by keeping COBIT 5 as the benchmark. Peña, Vicente, and Ocaña [33] used COBIT in conjunction with EFQM to measure the quality of services and processes. Haes, Grembergen, and Debreceny [34] linked the core elements of COBIT to insights from literature and explored the use of COBIT in future research activities. Wilkin, Campbell, Moore, and Grembergen [35] tried to gauge the value that COBIT can provides in a service oriented approach. Nwafor, Zavarsky, Ruhl and Lindskog [36] explored the usage of COBIT in small to medium sized enterprises in order to more effectively implement user account management. Radovanović, Lučić, Radojević and Šarac [37] identified the benefits of using COBIT 5 in planning and conducting of IT Audits that have a regulatory audit universe. Bernroider and Ivanov [38] explored the feasibility of metrics provided by COBIT to control processes, through a survey of Project Management Professionals and suggested improvements. Mahnic and Zabkar [40] studied the applicability of COBIT in carrying out audits of an Agile Software Development environment. Salle and Rosenthal [42] explored the benefits of COBIT in enhancing the existing Information Technology program of a large MNC.

3.4. Literature Review: Studying/Improving COBIT

Moving on to the next classification, I would say that authors have not only attempted to provide the better explanation of COBIT (as we saw in the section 3.3), but many have actually suggested improvements to the framework, by employing extensive study and research. Several authors (for instance Morimoto [50]; Mangalraj, Singh and Taneja [43]) have identified the scope of COBIT as discussed in various research papers and then compared it with the scope as defined by ISACA. Moeller, Erek, Loeser and Zarnekow [44] explored the sustainability of COBIT 5 Process Reference Model, from a user perspective. Betz [46]; Simonsson and Johnson [54] presented examples in support of the hypothesis that COBIT is inconsistent with the crucial aspects of business process management thinking and that it lacks in providing information on how decision making structures should be implemented. Bakry and Alfantookh [45]; and Marrone, Hoffmann and Kolbe [47] examined the satisfaction with COBIT by plotting it against the implementation level achieved, by employing the data collected through a survey, and made suggestions for improvement. Feltus, Petit and Dubois [48] identified the effective use of RACI chart in COBIT. Svata [49] made recommendations for improvement in COBIT, so as to increase its adoption and adaptation rates. Musa [51]; Tuttle and Vandervelde [52] analyzed and compared the adoption rates of COBIT processes in different industries, and also commenting on relative importance of the different processes, by means of a survey.

4. RESULTS AND TRENDS

I would now present a brief on the history of COBIT as it evolved over the years and would then look at the year wise distribution of the research papers (Figure 3).

Since COBIT started gaining popularity mostly after the introduction of its fourth version, it's only appropriate that most of the research on it also found prominence then, and for the same reason only the papers published in or after 2005 have been incorporated in this study.

I would also like to mention that between the fourth and the fifth versions, there was an enhanced fourth version (COBIT 4.1) which was introduced in May, 2007. To summarize the number of research papers used in this study, with respect to the different COBIT versions, I present this pie-chart (Figure 4).

So we have an equal distribution of papers based on versions 4.1 and 5 (23 each). 10 of the 56 papers studied were based on COBIT 4. Also, let's have a look at the yearly distribution of papers (Figure 5).

Figure 3. Evolution of COBIT framework

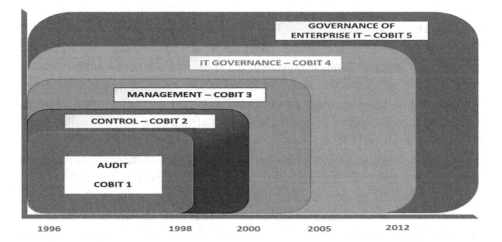

Figure 4. COBIT version wise distribution of research papers

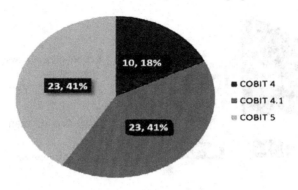

Figure 5. Yearly distribution of research papers

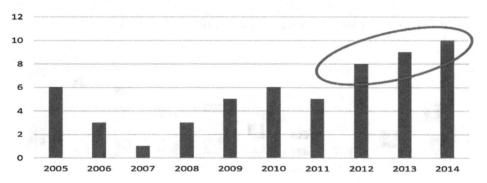

From the distribution, we can derive the following conclusions:-

- The number of research papers generally increase whenever a new version of the framework is introduced, and it shows an upward trend for a few years at least.
- Most of the research papers studied (Approximately 50%) were published after the introduction of COBIT 5, and thus we can say, that with each newer version, the COBIT framework is drawing more and more attention- not only of the industry, but also of the researchers.

After exploring the year wise distribution of research papers, I tried to identify and categorize the papers broadly on basis of their content. The four categorizes that almost all papers fall in are- "Integrating COBIT with other frameworks/standards", "Explaining COBIT", "Studying/Improving COBIT", and "Specific use of COBIT (In a particular setting)". The four categories in fact have an almost equal share of the papers, as seen in the following pie-chart (Figure 6).

Figure 6. Categorization of research papers

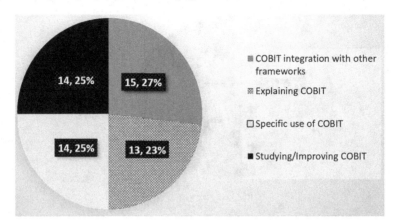

Figure 7. Year wise categorical distribution of research papers

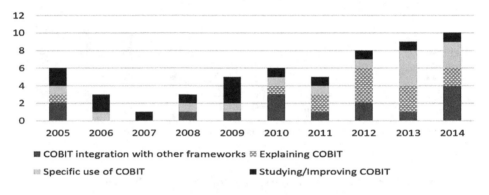

From Figure 7 we can make the following conclusions:-

- Over the years there has been a decline in the number of papers focused on "Studying/Improving COBIT", which is natural as COBIT itself has been improvising with each version.
- The focus is gradually shifting towards explaining COBIT – as it is becoming more holistic and more complex, and also towards exploring the use of COBIT in a specific environmental setting, such as in an academic institution, in small to medium size enterprises, in flood/disaster management or in a country specific setting.
- The only category that has maintained its significance across the decade is "COBIT integration with other frameworks/standards", which is because the introduction of new processes in each version, thus eliciting the need of a remapping to other internationally accepted IT frameworks and/or standards.

Another important classification that I made was on the basis of nature of the research. I classified the papers into three categories- Descriptive Research, Conceptual Research and Empirical Research.

Figure 8 shows us that majority of the research papers (~60%) are descriptive in nature; about a third are conceptual are nature and very few are empirical in nature. Thus we can gauge that there is much more scope of doing empirical studies through industry surveys.

Figure 9 shows us that, only in the case of exploring "Specific Use of COBIT", is there a relative balance amongst the three types of research. In all the other three categories, the distribution is highly skewed in favor of descriptive studies.

Figure 8. Categorization of research papers based on type of research

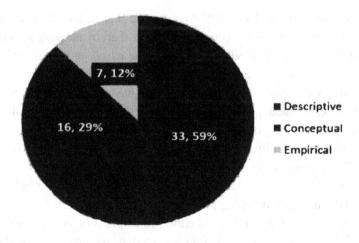

Figure 9. Type of research in each category

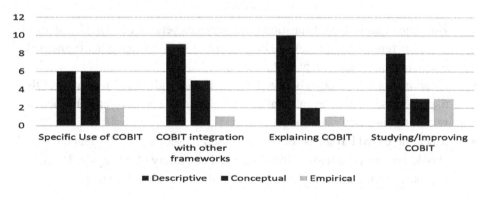

Figure 10. Type of research distribution over the years

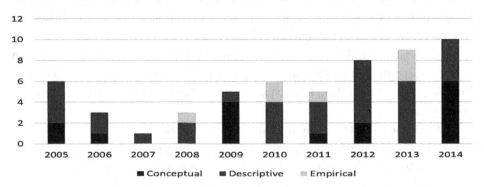

5. CONCLUSION

From the literature review, I was able to conclude that many of these researchers consider COBIT either to be too generic in nature, thereby needing a good amount of customization to suit the needs of the enterprise based on its size, industry, and the existing processes; or they find it to be inadequate by itself in covering the enterprise processes end-to-end. Thereby, there have been multiple attempts by various researchers to clearly explain the COBIT 5 framework with an aim to increase its understanding, and proposing modifications to the framework so as to increase its adoption and adaptability. Although several of the research papers have tried to map COBIT processes to respective processes in other frameworks or standards, these mappings are either too narrow in scope or present a very weak linking as compared to the in-depth mapping provided by ISACA.

Moreover, most of the studies are either conceptual or descriptive in nature. There is definitely a lot of scope for empirical studies, which can gauge the relative performance of COBIT 5 against other frameworks and standards. There are few other areas that can be considered for future research:

- How can organizations transition from previous version of COBIT framework to the current version, or how to implement COBIT 5 when other frameworks/ standards are already in place?
- Establishing a distinction between "Must-Have" and "Good-to-Have" COBIT 5 processes, so that even smaller organizations can leverage the benefits, without going way over budget.
- Since the COBIT framework has increased its scope over the years, research should be undertaken to explore its usage in a variety of settings/industries, as compared to the current focus on financial, accounting domains.

REFERENCES

Abu-Musa, A. (2008). Exploring the importance and implementation of COBIT processes in Saudi organizations: An empirical study. *Information Management & Computer Security, 17*(2), 73–95. doi:10.1108/09685220910963974

Afzali, P., Azmayandeh, E., Nassiri, R., & Shabgahi, G. L. (2010). Effective Governance through Simultaneous Use of COBIT and Val IT. *2010 International Conference on Education and Management Technology.* doi:10.1109/ICEMT.2010.5657549

Aliquo, J. F., Jr., & Fu, Z. (2014). DuPont Drives Continuous Improvement with COBIT 5 Process Assessment Model. *COBIT Focus Journal.*

Amid, A., & Moradi, S. (2013). A Hybrid Evaluation Framework of CMM and COBIT for Improving the Software Development Quality. *Journal of Software Engineering and Applications, 6*(05), 280–288. doi:10.4236/jsea.2013.65035

Haj Bakry, Saad, & Alfantookh. (2012). *IT-governance practices: COBIT.* Academic Press.

Bartens, Y., de Haes, S., Eggert, L., Heilig, L., Maes, K., Frederik, S., & Voß, S. (2014). A Visualization Approach for Reducing the Perceived Complexity of COBIT 5. *9th International Conference, DESRIST 2014.* doi:10.1007/978-3-319-06701-8_34

Bartens, Y., Schulte, F., & Voß, S. (2014). E-Business IT Governance Revisited: An Attempt towards Outlining a Novel Bi-directional Business/IT Alignment in COBIT5. *47th Hawaii International Conference on System Science.* doi:10.1109/HICSS.2014.538

Bernroider, E. W. N., & Ivanov, M. (2010). IT Project management control and the control objectives for IT and related Technology (COBIT) framework. *International Journal of Project Management.*

Betz, C. T. (2011). *ITIL, COBIT and CMMI: Ongoing confusion of process and function.* BP Trends.

Bin-Abbas, H., & Haj Bakry, S. (2014). Assessment of IT Governance in organizations: A simple integrated approach. *Computer in Human Behavior Journal.*

Brandas, C., Stirbu, D., & Didraga, O. (2013). *Integrated approach model of risk, control and auditing of accounting information systems* (Vol. 17). Informatica Economica.

Campbell, P. L. (2005). *A COBIT Primer.* Sandia Report.

De Haes, S., Van Grembergen, W., & Debreceny, R. S. (2013). COBIT 5 and Enterprise Governance of Information Technology: Building Blocks and Research Opportunities. *Journal of Information Systems, 27.*

Elhasnaoui, S., Medromi, H., Faris, S., Iguer, H., & Sayouti, A. (2014). Designing a Multi Agent System Architecture for IT Governance Platform. *International Journal of Advanced Computer Science and Applications.*

Feltus, C., Petit, M., & Dubois, E. (2009). Strengthening Employee's Responsibility to Enhance Governance of IT – COBIT RACI Chart Case Study. *Proceedings of the first ACM workshop on Information security governance.* doi:10.1145/1655168.1655174

Hardy, G. (2006). Using IT governance and COBIT to deliver value with IT and respond to legal, regulatory and compliance challenges. *Information Security Technical Report, 11*(1), 55–61. doi:10.1016/j.istr.2005.12.004

Huang, Z., Zavarsky, P., & Ruhl, R. (2009). An Efficient Framework for IT Controls of Bill 198 (Canada Sarbanes-Oxley) Compliance by Aligning COBIT 4.1, ITIL v3 and ISO/IEC 27002. *2009 International Conference on Computational Science and Engineering.* doi:10.1109/CSE.2009.336

Hussain, S. J., & Siddiqui, M. S. (2005). Quantified Model of COBIT for Corporate IT Governance. *1st International Conference on Information and Communication technologies.* doi:10.1109/ICICT.2005.1598575

Kerr, D. S., & Murthy, U. S. (2013). *The importance of COBIT framework IT processes for effective internal control over financial reporting in organizations: An international survey. Information and Management Journal.*

Latifi, F., Ramin, N., & Mohsenzadeh, M. (2014). Enriched eTOM Framework in Service Deliver Operation through Alignment with some of COBIT5 Strategic Objectives. *International Journal of Digital Information and Wireless Communications, 4*(1), 35–42. doi:10.17781/P001081

Lemus, S. M., Pino, F. J., & Velthius, M. P. (2010). Towards a Model for Information Technology Governance applicable to the Banking Sector. *5th Iberian Conference on Information Systems and Technologies.*

Mahnic, V., & Zabkar, N. (2008). *Using COBIT indicators for measuring scrum-based software development.* 12th WSEAS International Conference on Computers, Heraklion, Greece.

Mangalraj, G., Singh, A., & Taneja, A. (2014). *IT Governance Frameworks and COBIT - A Literature Review.* Academic Press.

Marrone, M., Hoffmann, L., & Kolbe, L. M. (2010). *IT Executives' Perception of COBIT: Satisfaction, Business-IT Alignment and Benefits. 16th Americas Conference on Information Systems*. AMICS.

Mataracioglu, T., & Ozkan, S. (2011). *Governing information security in conjunction with COBIT and ISO 27001*. Researchgate article.

Moeller, B., Erek, K., Loeser, F., & Zarnekow, R. (2013). *How Sustainable is COBIT 5? Insights from Theoretical Analysis and Empirical Survey Data. 19th Americas Conference on Information Systems*. Chicago: AMICS.

Morimoto, S. (2009). Application of COBIT to Security Management. *International Conference on Frontier of Computer Science and Technology*.

Nastase, P., Nastase, F., & Ionescu, C. (2010). *Challenges Generated By the Implementation of the IT Standards COBIT 4.1, ITIL V3 and ISO/IEC 27002 in Enterprises*. Academic Press.

Nugroho, H. (2014). Conceptual Model Of It Governance For Higher Education Based On COBIT 5 Framework. *Journal of Theoretical and Applied Information Technology*.

Nwafor, C. I., Zavarsky, P., Ruhl, R., & Lindskog, D. (2012). A COBIT and NIST-Based Conceptual Framework for Enterprise User Account Lifecycle Management. *World Congress on Internet Security (WorldCIS)*.

Oliver, D., & Lainhart, J. (2011). Delivering Business Benefits With COBIT: An Introduction to COBIT 5. *COBIT Focus Journal*.

Oliver, D., & Lainhart, J. (2012). *COBIT 5: Adding Value Through Effective GEIT: EDPACS: The Edp Audit. Control, And Security Newsletter*.

Othman, M. Ahmad, M. N., Suliman, A. Arshad, N. H., & Maidin, S. S. (2014). COBIT principles to govern flood management. *International Journal of Disaster Risk Reduction*.

Pasquini, A., & Galie, E. (2013). COBIT 5 and the Process Capability Model Improvements Provided for IT Governance Process. *Symposium for Young Researchers*.

Peña, J. J. S., Fernández Vicente, E., & Ocaña, A. M. (2013). ITIL, COBIT and EFQM: Can They Work Together?. *International Journal of Combinatorial Optimization Problems and Informatics, 4*(1).

Pretorius, E., & Solms, B. v. (2005). *Information Security Governance using ISO 17799 and COBIT*. KPMG Study. doi:10.1109/AMS.2008.145

Radovanović, D., Lučić, D., Radojević, T., & Šarac, M. (2011). *Information technology governance – COBIT Model*. MIPRO.

Radovanović, D., Radojević, T., Lučić, D., & Šarac, M. (2010). *IT audit in accordance with COBIT standard*. IEEE xplore.

Ribeiro, J., & Gomes, R. (2009). IT Governance using COBIT implemented in a High Public Educational Institution – A Case Study. *3rd International Conference on European Computing*.

Ridley, G., Young, J., & Carroll, P. (2005). COBIT and its Utilization: A framework from the literature. *Proceedings of the 37th Hawaii International Conference on System Sciences*.

Rubino, M., & Vitolla, F. (2014). Corporate governance and the information system: How a framework for IT governance supports ERM. *Corporate Governance*, *14*(3), 320–338. doi:10.1108/CG-06-2013-0067

Sahibudin, S., Sharifi, M., & Ayat, M. (2008). Combining ITIL, COBIT and ISO/IEC 27002 in Order to Design a Comprehensive IT Framework in Organizations. *Second Asia International Conference on Modelling & Simulation*.

Salle, M., & Rosenthal, S. (2005). Formulating and Implementing an HP IT program strategy using COBITT and HP ITSM. *Proceedings of the 38th Hawaii International Conference on System Sciences*. doi:10.1109/HICSS.2005.276

Shivashankarappa, A. N., Dharmalingam, R., Smalov, L., & Anbazhagan, N. (2012). Implementing it Governance Using Cobit: A Case Study Focusing on Critical Success Factors. *World Congress on Internet Security (WorldCIS-2012)*.

Simonsson, M., & Johnson, P. (2006). Assessment of IT Governance - A Prioritization of COBIT. *Conference on Engineering Systems Research*.

Stekhoven, A. (2012). Active Software Escrow's Usefulness for Companies Embracing COBIT 5. *COBIT Focus Journal*.

Susanto, H., Almunawar, M. N., & Tuan, Y. C. (2011). Information Security Management System Standards: A Comparative Study of the Big Five. *International Journal of Electrical & Computer Sciences*, *11*(5).

Svata, V. (2009). *IS Audit Considerations in Respect of Current Economic Environment*. International Auditing and Assurance Standards Board.

Symons, C. (2006). *COBIT Versus Other Frameworks: A Road Map to Comprehensive IT Governance. Trends Journal.*

Tuttle, B., & Vandervelde, S. D. (2007). An empirical examination of COBIT as an internal control framework for IT. *International Journal of Accounting Information Systems.* doi:10.1016/j.accinf.2007.09.001

Van Haren Publishing. (2012). *COBIT 5 - A Management Guide.* Author.

von Solms, B. (2005). *Information Security governance: COBIT or ISO 17799 or both? Computers & Security Journal.*

Walker, A., McBride, T., Basson, G., & Oakley, R. (2012). ISO/IEC 15504 measurement applied to COBIT process maturity". Benchmarking. *International Journal (Toronto, Ont.), 19*(2), 159–176.

Wilkin, C., Campbell, J., Moore, S., & Van Grembergen, W. (2013). Co-Creating Value from IT in a Contracted Public Sector Service Environment: Perspectives on COBIT and Val IT. *Journal of Information Systems, 27.*

Section 2
Regulatory and Compliance Risks

Chapter 4
Implications of HIPAA and Subsequent Regulations on Information Technology

Payod Soni
University at Buffalo, USA

ABSTRACT

Abysmal state of policies governing the health plan providers lead to a huge discontent amongst the public in regards to their health plan besides privacy and security of their medical records. Anyone with access to the patient's medical records could potentially share it with parties like health plan providers or the employers. To address the privacy and the security of patient's medical records, Congress enacted HIPAA in 1996. Chapter starts with discussing the need for HIPAA. Subsequently, we discuss HIPAA at considerable depth. Significant additions and changes were made in subsequent acts and amendments due to pressing policy needs and to address various loopholes. The chapter provides a chronological recount of HIPAA since its introduction. Once the reader develops a complete understanding of HIPAA regulation, we shift our focus to the compliance to HIPAA. We delve deeper into implications of HIPAA on healthcare organizations and the information technology world.

STATE OF THE FEDERAL HEALTHCARE IN THE US BEFORE HIPAA

The inception of the idea of HIPAA started in the early 90s. Before HIPAA, there was an underlying discontent amongst the Americans about their health coverage. According to ERISA, the states were prohibited to regulate the health insurance

DOI: 10.4018/978-1-5225-2604-9.ch004

of about 60% of the employees who chose the route of self-insurance. There was a growing feeling of anguish in the people who suffered due to the system even after 47 states had rules to regulate the insurance. Few cases surfaced where the employees working in self-insured companies lost their coverage due to terminal illness within their families. People feared to change their jobs because they would not be able to continue their or their family's insurance coverage. Many people who were self-employed were not able to afford insurance premiums without getting a tax benefit, which others got through their employers. There was a lot of discrepancy regarding what health insurance could get people an exemption in their taxes.

There was also an increased fear amongst people to seek medical care due to no laws that prevented the medical records from being disclosed. There were no specific laws that catered to the privacy and security of the medical records with all the focus being on the financial sector. Although each state did have laws that catered to the privacy of the healthcare information, there was a dire need of consensus amongst the various laws and the states to arrive at one common set of standards. This need arose from the fact that there was an increased use of computers and technologies in the medical landscape. Also, there were many players in the healthcare industry much more than when paper-based records were being used. The information needed to be exchanged between a lot many hands than before and the patient's data was much more vulnerable and there was a clear need for one set of standards and laws concerning privacy and security of the patient's medical records.

Meanwhile there was were a lot of cases that came into light which put light on the condition of the ignorance of the privacy and security in the context of the medical records of the patient. Few such cases before the introduction of HIPAA are cited below:

1. An employee of the healthcare department in Tampa, Florida sneaked out a disk containing the information of about 4000 patients who had been tested positive for HIV (as reported by USA Today, October 10, 1996)

2. A woman from Nevada after purchasing a used computer discovered that the system still had the prescriptions of the customers of the pharmacy that previously owned the system. The data that was still there on the system included names, addresses, social security numbers and a list of medicines that the patient had purchased. (as reported by The New York Times, April 4, 1997, and April 12, 1997)

3. A speculator bid $4000 for the patient records of a family practice in South Carolina. Among the businessman's uses of the purchased records was selling them back to the former patients. (as reported by The New York Times, August 14, 1991).

4. A few weeks after an Orlando woman had her doctor perform some routine tests, she received a letter from a drug company promoting a treatment for her high cholesterol. (as reported by Orlando Sentinel, November 30, 1997).

5. A banker who also sat on a county health board gained access to patients' records and identified several people with cancer and called in their mortgages. (See the National Law Journal, May 30, 1994),

6. A physician was diagnosed with AIDS at the hospital in which he practiced medicine. His surgical privileges were suspended. (See Estate of Behringer v. Medical Center at Princeton, 249 N.J. Super. 597).

7. A candidate for Congress nearly saw her campaign derailed when newspapers published the fact that she had sought psychiatric treatment after a suicide attempt. (As reported by The New York Times, October 10, 1992, Section 1, page 25)

8. Consumer Reports found that 40 percent of insurers disclose personal health information to lenders, employers, or marketers without customer permission. "Who's reading your Medical Records," Consumer Reports, October 1994, at 628, paraphrasing Sweeny, Latanya, "Weaving Technology and Policy Together to Maintain Confidentiality," The Journal Of Law Medicine and Ethics (Summer & Fall 1997) Vol. 25, Numbers 2,3.

All these cases confirm to the shoddy state of laws concerning medical records in those days. The personal information, when disclosed can be of serious harm to the patient whose information it is. It also highlighted the risk and the harm the leak incurs to the patient. It stressed the need of protection of the privacy of the patient's medical record. In the pre-HIPAA scenario, this leak could have had significant implications beyond what is obvious, including loss of employment, loss of health insurance and a great deal of humiliation.

Also, the patients did not have any control over their medical information and feared the improper usage of their data in a way that could bring about any or all of the above risks and problems to their path of leading a peaceful life. A survey conducted in 1995 validated the fact by showing that about 80% if the people thought that they did not have any control over their medical information.

In another survey that was conducted in 1999, people when asked about the issue that concerned them the most in the century, 29% of people chose "Loss of Personal Privacy" either the first or the second most important concern.

All these issues caught the eyes of the Congress and it was Sen Nancy Kassebaum (R-KS) and Sen. Edward M. Kennedy (D-MA) who took the onus to introduce the Health Insurance Portability and Accountability Act that aimed to reform the federal healthcare in the United States.

INTRODUCTION TO HIPAA

The Healthcare Insurance Portability and Accountability Act (referred to as HIPAA in the following instances of the chapter) changed the way the healthcare systems in the USA used to function. It should come as no surprise that there are many different players (both big and small) in the healthcare industry. Before the advent of computers and the establishment of HIPAA, patient's healthcare information was usually stored and transferred in the form of paper between different healthcare providers.

With the increased usage of the computers in healthcare, it became clear that there would soon be a requirement to digitize the healthcare data. The providers used approximately 400 different types of electronic formats to transmit the data with possibly different requirements for various transactions. There were efforts to come up with a set of standards, but there was never a consensus on a single set of standards. This lead to an increase in the administrative costs. With this increase of usage and no particular set of standards to follow to protect the information, the privacy concerns also increased. Although there were laws to protect privacy, they catered mainly to the financial aspect of the personal information. There was also a lot of inconsistency in the state laws that dealt with the protection of the information about the healthcare conditions. The US Congress thus enacted HIPAA law (also known as Kennedy-Kassebaum Bill) with two major goals:

1. **Health Insurance Portability**: This part of the HIPAA law enabled the employees to maintain their insurance between two jobs. This part of the law has been successfully implemented because of it being relatively simple and straightforward (HHS.gov).
2. **Accountability**: This portion of the law provides a set of rules and standards for the security and confidentiality of the health information of the patient. It also sets standards for electronic transmission of any data that relates to the patient's health information.

We will now discuss these goals in further detail (HHS.gov).

First, let us understand what does the portability of health insurance means. Portability essentially means the right bestowed upon the employee to retain benefits like pension plans and health insurance when they switch employers. As we saw earlier, before HIPAA, a lot of American workers felt that they could not freely change jobs because they would not be able to afford the loss of their health insurance. This was because the health insurance system in the US is employer based and the workers needed to change their insurance between two jobs.

The Health insurance portability clause in the HIPAA law introduced a new law that the workers have the right to maintain a certain number of health insurance plans and their benefits when they switch jobs or when they retire. This law goes ahead and prohibits any discrimination against the employees and their families based on their health condition, including pre-existing conditions, previous claim history, etc. Thus, the health insurance companies cannot deny the individual's coverage and cannot require the worker to undergo a physical exam and use its result to discriminate against the employee. It ensured that the federal government was responsible for regulation and enforcement of these laws. Health insurance portability the following relevant standards:

1. **Preexisting Conditions**: HIPAA outlined that any insurance provider cannot limit the coverage for preexisting conditions for more than 12 months if the employee switches his employer after this waiting period. It also states that no new restrictions based on the preexisting conditions can be placed if the employee, without any gap of more than sixty-three days, maintains the health insurance. It also excluded pregnant women and newborns from the restrictions based on the new preexisting conditions (Atchinson, B & Fox, D).

2. **Small-Scale Employers**: HIPAA states that any medical insurance company cannot refuse to offer any health plan to businesses that have 2 to 50 employees.

3. **Individual Coverage**: HIPAA specifies that health plan providers should offer coverage plans to people who have had group insurance for minimum eighteen months, and who are ineligible for any other employment-based coverage. It further directs the insurance companies to make such individuals eligible for all the policies that are available in the state, in case the state does not opt to enact these reforms.

4. **Discrimination by Health**: It directs the employers to not exclude an employee or his dependents from coverage, or charge higher premium from them based on the person's medical history (Atchinson, B & Fox, D).

5. **Renewable Plans**: HIPAA also states that the health plan providers are required to renew the plans as long as all the premiums are paid. The only exception to this case is when fraud or misrepresentation by an employer occurs.

The second goal of HIPAA was to policies, procedures, and guidelines to maintain the privacy and the security of the medical records. It brought accountability of the loss of information into the purview of the federal government. It also outlined various civil and criminal offenses relating to the breach of privacy and security of the medical data. It also aimed to start various programs for fraud control and for minimizing the abuse within the healthcare system. It also required that the Department of Health and Human Services draft rules for privacy and security of the healthcare data by creating or defining a set of standards for use and transmission of the healthcare data.

Since the year it has been established, the HIPAA law has undergone many incremental changes which we will see in further sections.

HIPAA law is an exhaustive document and the healthcare IT professionals should be able to understand a few essential items. These elements include the HIPAA Privacy Rule, which defines what a healthcare provider or payer can do with the information collected on patients. Also important is the HIPAA Security Rule that includes the administrative safeguards to protect the patient's medical records by requiring the providers and payers to follow specific business practices.

The safeguards are divided into two main types – physical and technical. The physical safeguards refer to the protection of physical buildings and tangible assets that store the patient's information. The technical safeguards imply the use of technology to prevent unauthorized access to the patient's medical information. Before we proceed any further, it is important to go through a few important terms that are used extensively in HIPAA literature and understand them properly

IMPORTANT TERMS

Below is a list of important terms related to HIPAA along with their definitions.

1.   Covered Entities

Covered entities are defined in the HIPAA rules as (1) health plans, (2) health care clearinghouses, and (3) health care providers who electronically transmit any health information in connection with transactions for which HHS has adopted standards (HIPAA Privacy Rule and its impacts on research. Retrieved from https:// privacyruleandresearch.nih.gov/pr_06.asp). These are the businesses that are required to comply with HIPAA. Covered entities can also be defined as health plans, healthcare clearinghouses and healthcare providers who deal with the transmission of healthcare data during transactions for which the HHS has a set of standards. These transactions generally are related to billing and payment of services or for the health plans. Covered entities can be institutes, organizations or individuals.

Researchers also may come under cover entities if they are also involved in the electronic transmission of data for which HHS has adopted a standard. Eg. Physicians conducting clinical trials or administering experimental drugs to the participants must comply with the HIPAA privacy rule if they are by definition, a covered entity (HIPAA Privacy Rule and its impacts on research. Retrieved from https://privacyruleandresearch.nih.gov/pr_06.asp).

a. **Health Plan**: A plan (whether individual or group), with certain exceptions, which pays for the medical care of the patients is called a health plan. HIPAA includes various kinds of organizations and government programs as health plans.

b. **Health Care Clearinghouses**: An entity (whether public or private) that facilitates the processing of medical information which is received from any other entity in nonstandard format into standardized data elements or vice versa is called a health care clearinghouse. These can include a billing service, community health information system, value-added networks, repricing system, community health management information system, etc.

c. **Health Care Provider**: Someone who is paid for providing health care in the normal course of business. It can be a service provider, medical or health services provider or any organization that bills its customers for health care.

d. **Health Care:** Services that are related to an individual's health and that affect the person's body structure and the function are called health care. They can be preventive, therapeutic, maintenance related, palliative, diagnostic, rehabilitative, counseling etc. Also, the services that sell drugs and medical equipment or any other items based on a prescription come under the jurisdiction of healthcare.

Covered entities could include clinics, doctor's office, hospitals, nursing homes, etc. They also include insurance companies, private and public health plans that pay for healthcare.

2. Hybrid Entity

HIPAA mandates that all covered entities have to follow the guidelines outlined in the Privacy Rule and will be subjected in its entirety to them. However, under the privacy rule, there are means through which many covered entities can avoid the global application of the rule through hybrid entity provision. This provision defines and directs the parts of the covered entity that must comply with the Privacy Rules.

Any entity can choose to be a hybrid entity if it performs covered as well as the noncovered functions as a part of its operation. A covered function may be defined as any function that makes the performing entity either a health plan, a health care provider, or a health care clearing house. To function as a hybrid entity, the entity should clearly distinguish the healthcare components within its organization. Within a hybrid entity, the majority of the rules apply only to the healthcare components although the covered entity retains certain compliance and enforcement obligations.

For example, a university can function as a hybrid entity if it can manage to designate the hospital and other related components as health care components. If this happens, most of the privacy rules will apply only to the healthcare components. However, the PHI disclosures by the hospital to the rest of the university will still be regulated by the HIPAA privacy rules.

Another point to note is that research components that function as healthcare providers but do not take part in the transmission of healthcare data may need not be included in the healthcare components.

However, a hybrid entity is not allowed to include a research component that does not function as healthcare components into its health care component.

3. Protected Health Information

The information that includes a patient's identifiable information about health status, administration of health care, or payment for healthcare that is collected from the patient by the covered entities. It includes the name, phone number, address, zip code (of more than three digits), dates, email address, medical record numbers, medical history, medical conditions, results, social security number, medical record number, license number amongst others.

4. Business Associates

The HIPAA Privacy Rule also protects the PHI when it is handled by an individual or an organization on behalf of a covered entity. Such individual or organization is referred to as Business Associate (HIPAA Privacy Rule and its impacts on research. Retrieved from https://privacyruleandresearch.nih.gov/pr_06.asp).

It can be anyone having any access to patient's information on behalf of the covered entities that require access to the PHI for use or disclosure. Additionally, any IT organization providing solutions or services to the covered entities are also included in the purview of the Business Associates. A business associate is not an employee of the covered entity. They are also required to maintain HIPAA compliance at all levels.

HIPAA Administrative Simplification Rules do not regulate the research activities directly. Hence a researcher or a sponsor does not need to become a business associate. The Privacy Rules requires that a covered entity enters into a contract with their business associates. Once the contract is in place, the laws allow the covered entity to disclose PHI to the business associates after receiving satisfactory assurances. A contract generally does not authorize the business associate to use or disclose the PHI in a manner that would violate the Privacy Rules of HIPAA.

5.   Business Associate Agreement

This agreement is a standard document that clearly specifies the roles and responsibilities of both a business associate and the covered entity. The assurance that the business associates will take due care in implementing safeguards to achieve HIPAA compliance is also captured in the Business Associate Agreement

6.   Electronic Health Records

EHR is an electronic record of the patient's medical information generated in a hospital or a doctor's office. This includes the test results, medical history, demographics amongst others. It is generally managed and consulted by the authorized staff of the covered entities.

7.   HIPAA Audit

It is based on a set of regulations and implementation specifications. The audit is conducted to help understand the current state of the organization's compliance with HIPAA and the corrective steps required to make it HIPAA compliant.

A company is required to perform an evaluation annually at the minimum. This is attributed to the every changing scenario in the technical ecosystem and addition of new components in an organization's infrastructure.

It is also required that along with the covered entities; the third party associates also need to by HIPAA compliant.

8.   Due Diligence

Any organization that even after implementing everything possible in their control to prevent the foreseeable causes is still in violation.

9.   Meaningful Use

This term implies using the EHR to improve the quality, increase the safety, efficiency, and access. Meaningful use compliance results in better healthcare, improved health outcomes, increased efficiency, and research that is more robust. It sets specific standards that the eligible professionals and covered entities must achieve to be eligible for CMS incentive programs.

This meaningful use rule is a part of a set of standards (regulations) which help in creating a private and a secure state of the art electronic health system. On June

18, 2010, the DHHS issued a rule that formulated a process to certify the EHR so that the covered entities that use the EHR can be assured of meaningful use.

The meaningful use strikes a balance between acknowledging the urgency of adopting EHRs to improve the healthcare system and recognizing the challenges that it will pose to healthcare providers.

DHHS is also in the process of establishing a nationwide network of Regional Extension Centers which will help the providers to adopt the qualified EHR and extract meaningful use out of them.

HIPAA Timeline

On August 21, 1996, Healthcare Insurance Portability and Accountability Act was passed as a Law with the following functions (HHS.gov):

1. It established broad guidelines for the insurance markets regarding the underwriting practices.
2. It provided a set of rules to protect an individual who lost his group coverage.
3. It created a set of underwriting requirements for self-insurance health benefit plans under ERISA.
4. It also included a section called "Administrative Simplification", whose sole motive was to standardize the electronic transmission of all healthcare related transactions to reduce the costs and administrative overhead.
5. With administrative simplification, the law also enforced the protection of the patient's personal health information during the digitization of the healthcare data.

This law made the Secretary of Health and Human Services (referred further as HHS) responsible for developing standards and requirements about the storage and the transmission of the patient's health records. All these rules applied to all parties involved in the healthcare space, including the providers and the payers.

Once this law was passed, the HHS started creating the first draft of the HIPAA Privacy and HIPAA Security rules. Let us look at each one of them separately to understand what they are and what their implications on IT are.

HIPAA Privacy Rules

Given that the information now was required to be transmitted electronically to receive payments, it became of utmost importance to protect the privacy of that patients. These set of rules were formulated by HHS after receiving about 52,000+ comments and had the effective compliance date of April 14, 2003, for large plans and 2004 for the smaller plans. It introduced the concept of Protected Health Information (PHI). Here it is also important to understand the concept of de-identified data. The de-identified data must not include names, phone numbers, email address, social security numbers, medical record numbers and the likes.

The crux of these rules was that every individual had the right to know how his medical information was being used by the covered entities. The repercussions of a leak of the patient's PHI can be detrimental for the patient and can also lead to financial and legal trouble to the organization responsible for the leak.

1. **Use and Disclosure**: Under the privacy rules, the patient's PHI can be disclosed only for treatment, payment and healthcare operations without the written consent of the patient. Few other places where the information can be disclosed without permission of the patient are:
    a. Law Enforcement Purpose
    b. Abuse Victims
    c. Public Health Services, etc.
2. **Authorizations**: To use the patient's information for psychotherapy notes, marketing, fund raising and research and other related uses, HIPAA Privacy Rule requires the respective organizations to obtain patient's authorization.
3. **Incidental Disclosure**: Even though enough precautions are taken to avoid sharing patient's PHI with people who are not involved in the patient's care, some minor information may get through to such people when the care is being administered to the patient. This is known as Incidental Disclosure. While the privacy laws do not prohibit the incidental disclosure, they require the CEs and the Business Associates to take steps to minimize it.
4. **Minimum Necessary**: The information that a covered entity or a business associate need to just complete their responsibilities is called minimum necessary. If a business associate or a covered entity comes across the PHI that is not required by them, that information should not be discussed or used.
5. **Privacy Notice**: The privacy rules state that all the organizations that have access to the PHI must provide notice to the patients that include their rights, and how their PHI may be disclosed or used. The patient has the right to:
    a. Access their own medical records.
    b. Ask to correct any inaccurate PHI
    c. Request a restriction to access or disclosure of PHI.
    d. Request how their PHI has been used.
    e. Receive notice on how their PHI may be used or disclosed.
    f. File a complaint if they feel that their privacy has been violated.

6. **Complaints and Enforcements**: All organizations having access to the PHI must have a procedure to address the grievances of the patient. The privacy rules also require all covered entities to have a privacy officer. A privacy officer is responsible for documenting and maintaining the privacy notice. He is also responsible for responding to and remediating the complaints related to breach of privacy.

7. The privacy rules also define the fines that are to be enforced on any organization that is not HIPAA compliant. The range of the fines can be from $100 per violation up to a maximum annual fine of $25,000. With civil fines, there are also criminal penalties associated when a CE knowingly discloses the PHI.

HIPAA Security Rules

Formulated by the HHS, these rules came into picture approximately around two years after the HIPAA Privacy Rules. They had an effective compliance date of April 20, 2005. These rules define how the covered entities and the business associates ensure the integrity, confidentiality, and availability of the electronic PHI (ePHI). The security rules specify three different set of safeguards to protect the ePHI and requires that the organizations comply with them.

1. **Administrative Safeguard**: These are the actions, policies and the procedures that are required to protect the ePHI and manage the conduct of CEs. The Security Rule defines administrative safeguards as "administrative actions, and policies and procedures, to manage the selection, development, implementation, and maintenance of security measures to protect ePHI and to manage the conduct of the covered entity's workforce about the protection of that information. (HHS, 2007)." They include
    a. Appointing a Chief Security Officer to look after all security related functions.
    b. Training the employees on the organization's principles of security and other procedures and policies.
    c. Monitoring the employee's access to the information systems.
    d. Security Awareness and Training
    e. Reporting security incidents.
    f. Coming up with a contingency plan
2. **Physical Safeguards**: These are the measures and the policies that cover the tangible assets and the ePHI that they contain. The Physical Safeguards in the HIPAA Security Rule are "physical measures, policies, and procedures to protect a covered entity's electronic information systems and related buildings

and equipment, from natural and environmental hazards, and unauthorized intrusion (HHS, 2007)." They include

    a.   Restricting the access to the information systems that contain the ePHI to only those who require it.

    b.   Preventing the unauthorized viewing of the ePHI on the workstations.

    c.   Completely removing the ePHI from the computers and workstations before disposing them.

    d.   Backing up the ePHI.

3.   **Technical Safeguards**: These are the technologies, policies and the procedures that are used to control access to ePHI and to protect them. Technical safeguards are "the technology and the policy and procedures for its use that protect electronic protected health information and control access to it. (HHS 2007)" They include

    a.   Implementing proper access control to restrict the viewing of ePHI.

    b.   Provisions to access the ePHI during emergencies.

    c.   Encrypting ePHI during transmission.

    d.   Authentication

    e.   Automated logging off the users after a set period.

Even after implementing and ordering the covered entities and the business associates to comply with the privacy and the security rules, many organizations failed to fully comply with them. Due to this, a new Enforcement Rule was introduced in 2006. The enforcement rule empowered the Department of Health and Human Services to investigate the complaints of non-compliance against the covered entities and to fine the avoidable breaches of ePHI due to not implementing the safeguards specified by the HIPAA Security Rules.

The enforcement rule also gave the power to Department's Office for Civil Rights to press criminal charges against repeated offenders who did not introduce the corrective measures within 30 days of the violation. It also empowered the individuals to pursue legal action against the covered entity if they disclosed their ePHI without the individual's consent if it caused them serious harm.

One of the first entity that was fined $50,000 was the Hospice of North Idaho (HONI) for a potential breach affecting fewer than 500 people.

In 2009, the Health Information Technology for Economic and Clinical Health Act (HITECH) was introduced as a part of the American Recovery and Reinvestment Act of 2009. The ARRA detailed the incentives that related to the healthcare information technology and contained various specific incentives, which were formulated mainly to increase the adoption of the electronic health records (EHR). HITECH had the goal of forcing the covered entities to implement the use of EHR. At the time of enactment, HITECH was touted to be the most important piece of healthcare law to be passed in the last 20 to 30 years. ARRA expected a huge expansion in the exchange of ePHI. Due to this fact, HITECH act further broadened the scope of privacy and security under HIPAA. It also increased the legal liability for noncompliant covered entities. It was with the HITECH Act that the concept of Meaningful Use was introduced. This act set meaningful use of EHR as an important national goal. It also incentivized the use of EHR. The goal was to spread the use of EHR by the healthcare providers to improve the care. Subsequently, meaningful use of EHR by the providers was the only way to get eligible for the CMS incentive programs.

The main components that are included in meaningful use are:

1. Use of certified EHR like e-prescribing.
2. Use of certified EHR for electronic transmission and exchange of health information to improve the health care's quality.
3. Use of certified EHR to provide clinical quality feedback.
4. The meaningful use intended by the US government incentives is categorized as follows:
5. Improve care coordination
6. Increase access to healthcare facilities.
7. Engage patients and their families.
8. Improve population health.
9. Ensure privacy and security

HITECH subsequently also introduced the concept of meaningful use stage 1. This stated that the first steps in achieving meaningful use are to use a certified EHR and to be able to prove that it is being used optimally to meet the requirements of meaningful use. Stage 1 of meaningful use contains 25 measures for eligible providers (EP) and 24 measures for eligible hospitals. These measures have been further divided into a core set and a menu set. The requirement states that all the core measures must be adhered to and EPs must meet five of the ten menu set items, with one of them being a public health objective.

To receive incentives through CMS, it is required that the participants to attest that during a 90 day period, they have used certified EHR and have met the Stage 1 criteria.

HITECH Act focused on the enforcement of HIPAA and related laws. Before the HITECH Act, HIPAA was not rigorously enforced in the health care space. HITECH contained mandatory penalties, which were to be enforced on the violators for willful neglect. Civil penalties increased to about $250,000 with repeat violations extending up to $1.5 million. Furthermore, these penalties also extended to the Business Associates under some conditions. Though HITECH did not allow an individual to bring a cause of action against the provider, it allowed a state attorney to do so on this behalf. It also required the HHS to conduct periodic audits of covered entities and business associates.

One important change that the HITECH Act brought into the view was that now certain HIPAA provisions applied directly to the business associates. These privacy and security requirements were previously imposed on the business associates through contractual requirements. The business associates were now directly under the purview of HIPAA compliance as they were required to comply with the HIPAA Security Rule. It also brought the vendors of the EHR systems under the definition of a business associate. They are also required to report any security or privacy breach of the PHI to the covered entities they are in contract with. The business associates now were also subject to civil and criminal penalties if certain conditions were found missing. To sum up, the business associates now will share responsibilities over the ePHI with the covered entities.

Another important change brought by HITECH was that in the breach notification requirements. It required the HHS to define "unsecured PHI" within 60 days of its enactment. It requires the covered entities, business associates and all organizations that have access to PHI must follow a new notification system. Previously, covered entities were not required to give notice to the individuals whose PHI was inappropriately disclosed, but with this new breach notification requirements, they were required to notify the affected individuals no later than 60 days after the breach. Also, if the breach involved more than 500 individuals, the organization is also supposed to send a notice to US Department of Health and Human Services and the media.

Furthermore, under HITECH there were new rules that governed the access to the electronic health records. In cases where the covered entity had implemented the electronic health record system, HITECH provided the individual, the right to obtain their PHI in electronic format. It also gave the individual the right to authorize someone to access this data on his behalf. Any provider with an established EHR implemented should be prepared to let the patient access his PHI for it to participate in the incentives program outlined by HITECH. Also, in case any provider is unable to provide access to this information, the use of their EHR will not be considered meaningful.

As the HITECH Act was passed, there was a huge hike in demand for skilled workers in the field of healthcare information technology space. The HITECH act also allocated $25.9 billion for the expansion of healthcare IT.

The Final Omnibus Rule for HIPAA was introduced in 2013 and is the latest and the most recent act in the history of HIPAA. While this rule did not introduce any new act, it did fill the gaps in the existing acts and legislations of HIPAA and HITECH. Few examples include specifying the encryption standards that are required to be used to encrypt the ePHI and render it unusable in the event of a breach.

There were a lot of gaps and gray areas that were left out during the introduction of the initial legislations. They were amended as a part of the final omnibus rule. Few important changes were:

1. It made business associates of the covered entities directly liable for compliance with certain Privacy and Security Rules proposed by the HHS.
2. It limited the use of and the disclosure of the PHI for marketing and fund raising and prohibited the selling of PHI without authorization from the individual.
3. It expanded the rights of a patient to receive their electronic copies of their PHI.
4. It allows the patient to instruct their providers to refrain from sharing the information about their treatment when the patient pays out of his pocket.
5. It based the penalties in case of non-compliance on the level of negligence and increased the maximum penalty to $1.5 million per violation (Gamble, M, 2013).
6. It modified the breach notification rule with a requirement to determine the risk of compromise of the breach rather than the harm caused by it. It thus made breach notification necessary in all situations except when the CEs demonstrates a probability that the PHI has been compromised.
7. It provides instructions to the CEs and to the business associates to determine the low probability that the PHI has been compromised. The risk assessment to determine this should consider at least the factors specified below(Gamble, M, 2013):
   a. The nature and extent of PHI involved, including the likelihood of re-identification.
   b. The unauthorized person to whom the disclosure was made.
   c. Whether the PHI was viewed or acquired.
   d. The extent of the risk to the PHI that has been mitigated.
8. It changed what incidents were an exception to the PHI breaches. Previously, if the PHI disclosed a limited set of data that did not contain any date of birth or zip, it was an exception to the definition of a breach. With the final rule, any breach, whether of limited data sets or not, was to be handled similarly.
9. It raised the level breach for unauthorized disclosure of PHI if the PHI was unsecured.

Costs Associated With HIPAA Breach

After studying all the aspects of HIPAA in detail, let us know look at a general set of steps that can occur if an HIPAA violation occurs. It is generally estimated that HIPAA breach costs approximately around $300 per victim (HIPAAJournal.com).

1. **Investigation of the Breach**: An external organization should be allowed to investigate the breach to identify the causes of the breach. It should also ensure that the unauthorized access to the PHI has been blocked.

2. **Remediation Steps**: All of the safeguards that should have been in place must now be installed under the scrutiny of the Office of Civil Rights and the general public.

3. Temporary Operational Changes: A breach considerably increases the administrative burden on the covered entities. The staff of the covered entity should issue notifications, update the website, answer customer queries and implement new safeguards.

4. **Breach Notification**: Letters must be issued to all affected individuals by first class post. Subsequent notifications also need to be sent to them in a timely manner.

5. **Prevention of Identity Theft**: HIPAA requires that the covered entities should provide free credit monitoring and identity theft protection to all the victims for one to two years.

6. **Fines and Penalties**: The office of civil rights issues financial penalties.

7. **Regulatory Fines**: Attorney General assists the OCR in policing the HIPAA Privacy and Security Rules. State AG offices issue fine for HIPAA breaches at a state level.

8. **Loss of Reputation**: Providers should expect a patient churn rate of about 5-6% while it is noticed that about 65% of customers generally consider switching providers once a breach occurs.

Implications of HIPAA on Healthcare Information Technology

The Health Insurance Portability and Accountability Act of 1996 (HIPAA) presents an important challenge to the healthcare system in its evolution from a cottage industry to a new, yet-to-be determined form (Califf R. & Muhlbaier L., 2003). Now that we have looked through the history of the HIPAA act and have understood various parts of the act, it is now important to understand the implications of HIPAA on the healthcare IT industry. With HIPAA becoming so essential in the American healthcare industry and with it promoting the increase in the use of electronic transmissions, it becomes of immense significance to understand the changes that will eventually determine the readiness of the IT industry to enforce HIPAA in its entirety. Although the generally estimated cost of being HIPAA compliant might be considered very high, but when one compares it to the cost of being non-compliant, it is significantly lesser. If an organization dealing with any amount of PHI fails to be HIPAA compliant, there are substantial fines, criminal and civil lawsuits that can be imposed upon them should a breach occur.

An organization cannot ignore the HIPAA regulations and an organization's ignorance is not considered as defense by the Office of Civil Rights of the Department of Health and Human Services (OCR). The fines are issued by the OCR irrespective of whether the violation was a willful neglect or was inadvertent.

Once an organization determines the need of being a HIPAA compliant organization, either as a covered entity or as a business associate, to protect the security and the privacy of the PHI it holds, it is best that the organizations dissect the following four rules (Wang, J., 2013):

1. HIPAA Privacy Rule
2. HIPAA Security Rule
3. HIPAA Enforcement Rule
4. HIPAA Breach Notification Rule

Let us go systematically and look what each of these rules mean for the information technology players. We will also see the implementation specifications in regards to the above four laws.

1. HIPAA Security Rule

As seen before, the HIPAA security rule requires the covered entity to provision appropriate safeguards to protect the confidentiality and the integrity of the PHI it holds. It contains a set of standards that must be applied by any organization that has any access to PHI. It divides the implementation requirements as required and addressable. All the required safeguards are mandatory to be implemented. The addressable safeguards should be implemented in case they are reasonable and appropriate to be implemented. In case there is a doubt, the organizations should implement the addressable safeguards. The organization should make sure that they document their choices. The major two implementation requirements for the security management process require a covered entity to conduct a risk analysis and implement a risk management program (Dwyer S.) that we see in the administrative safeguard section.

Let us now look at other categories of the safeguards:

- **Technical Safeguards**:The technical safeguards addresses the technology that should be used to protect the electronic PHI and safeguard it. Whether at rest or during transmission, it is required that the ePHI must be encrypted to NIST Standards once it is transmitted beyond the organizations firewalled servers. (HIPAA Compliance Checklist. Retrieved from http://www.hipaajournal. com/hipaa-compliance-checklist/) This ensures that in case there is a breach

of data, the encryption renders the data unreadable. Broadly there are five standards that find their way into the technical safeguards:
- ◦ Technologies to implement access control
- ◦ Proper audit control mechanisms
- ◦ Data integrity
- ◦ Effective authentication
- ◦ Security during transmission

Further breaking down the requirements in more technical terms, an organization that has access to any form of PHI should take steps to implement the following (Wang, J., 2013):

- **Access Control (Required)**: Implementing an access control means assigning a unique centrally controlled credentials for each user that uses the system. It also establishes the procedures to release the ePHI in case of emergency. Access control can also be used to track the user identity across the system.
- **Mechanism to Authenticate ePHI (Addressable)**: This mechanism helps an organization to determine an organization to be HIPAA compliant by checking if the ePHI has been modified, destroyed or accessed in an unauthorized way.
- **Tools for Encryption and Decryption of PHI (Addressable)**: This safeguard is related to the devices used by the authorized users. These devices should have the capability to encrypt outgoing ePHI transmission and to decrypt the incoming ePHI.
- **Activity Audit Control (Required):** All the access, modification and destruction of the PHI once it has been accessed should be logged in order to be able to view that at any time. It should be available to audit at any point in time. This helps in understanding the cause in the case of breaches and also helps in formulating preventive steps to avoid breaches. It can also act as a preventive control wherein the logs, if monitored regularly can avoid a major catastrophe.
- **Automatic Logoff (Addressable):** Although this function is addressable function, it helps prevent unauthorized access to the ePHI in case any device that contains the ePHI is left unlocked or unattended. It aims at logging off the authorized personnel from the device after a pre-defined period of inactivity (Wang, J., 2013).
- **Authentication (Required):** The organizations should make sure to implement set of standards or procedures to verify if the individual that requires access to the ePHI is the one who is getting it.

Majority of the breaches in ePHI can result from loss of devices containing unencrypted data and due to transmission of unencrypted and unsecured PHI through open networks. Although the current HIPAA regulations do not require encryption in each and every such circumstances, it is a measure for the data security that should not be ignored or taken lightly. In case data encryption is not implemented, there should be an alternate that should be in place.

If the encrypted data is stolen, it will not result in HIPAA breach of the ePHI. Encryption is also important to prevent theft of data on computer networks by preventing hackers from gaining access.

- **Physical Safeguards**: The physical safeguards addresses the physical access to ePHI irrespective of where it is stored. It could be in a remote center, in cloud or in the servers which are located under the premise of the covered entity. These standards also define the security of the workstations and mobile devices against unauthorized access. Broadly there are four standards that find their way into the physical safeguards (Wang, J., 2013):
  - Facility Access Control
  - Workstation Use
  - Workstation Security
  - Device and Media Control

Further breaking down these four standards, the following things need to be implemented in the area where the PHI is being stored (Wang, J., 2013).

- **Contingency Operations (Addressable)**:The organizations need to establish and implement a set of procedures that allows access to facility to support restoration of lost data within the disaster recovery plan and the emergency mode operations plan in case of emergencies.
- **Facility Security Plan (Addressable)**: The organization should implement proceddures to safeguard the devices and the location where PHI is being stored from unauthorized physical access, theft and tampering.
- **Access Control Procedures (Addressable)**: The organization should also implement safeguards to control an individual's access to the facilities based on what data they require access to and should follow a minimum necessary policy. It should also have policies for visitor control and the likes.
- **Maintenance of Records (Addressable)**: The organization should implement policies and procedures for effective documentation of the repairs of the physical components that are related to security of the premise.
- **Workstation Use (Required)**: The organization is required to implement standards that specify the manner in which certain functions are supposed to

be performed and the physical attributes of the areas surrounding the machine that contains ePHI.

- **Security of Workstation (Required)**: The organization is also supposed to implement physical safeguard measures for all workstations that have access to the PHI to restrict access.
- **Disposal of Device and Media Control (Required)**: The covered entity should also implement policies and procedures to dispose the ePHI and the hardware where it was stored.
- **Media Reuse (Required):** Before the organization reuses the system and the hardware, it should also implement policies on removal of ePHI from that piece of hardware.
- **Accountability (Addressable):** The organizations should maintain a record of the movement of hardware and media that any person was responsible for.
- **Data Backup (Addressable)**: The organizations should also create an, exact copy of ePHI before movement of equipment, when needed.
- **Administrative Safeguards**: These safeguards are the set of standards which bring the privacy and the security rule of HIPAA together. These safeguards are the most important elements of HIPAA compliance and requires a Security Officer and a Privacy Officer to be appointed by the covered entity to put measures to protect ePHI. They are also responsible to govern the employee conduct.

The OCR identifies the risk assessment as one of the most major area of Security rule non compliance. Risk assessment reports are supposed to be checked in detail in the second phase of audits to ensure that the organizations have conducted risk assessment. The report is also checked to be comprehensive and ongoing. Broadly there are nine standards that find their way into the administrative safeguards (Wang, J., 2013):

- Security Management Process
- Assigned Security Responsibility
- Workforce Security
- Information Access Management
- Security Awareness and Training
- Security Incident Procedures
- Contingency Plan
- Evaluation
- Business Associate Contracts and Other Arrangements

Further breaking down these nine standards, the following things need to be implemented in the area where the PHI is being stored (Wang, J., 2013).

- **Risk Analysis (Required)**: The organization is directed to perform extensive risk analysis to see how and where is PHI being used or stored in order to determine potential breach of PHI.
- **Risk Management (Required):** The organization should also implement enough measures and steps to mitigate or transfer the risk in order to reduce these risks to an appropriate level.
- **Sanction Policy (Required)**: The covered entity should have in place, sanction policies for the noncompliant workspace.
- **Activity Review of the Information Systems (Required):** The organization should regularly review and monitor the audit trails, logs etc.
- The organization should appoint designated HIPAA Security and Privacy Officers. (required)
- **Employee Oversight (Addressable)**: The organization should implement procedures to authorize and unauthorized employees to access PHI when they need it. It should also make sure that the employee's access to PHI is revoked on termination of the job.
- **Access to Multiple Organizations (Required)**: The organization should ensure that parent organizations or subcontractors that are not authorized to access it, do not access the PHI.
- **Access to ePHI (Addressable):** The organization should document and implement standards and policies to provide access to ePHI.
- **Security Reminders (Addressable)**: The organization is also responsible for sending periodic updates and reminders about the privacy policy and the security policy to the employees.
- **Malware Protection (Addressable):** The organization should have policies to prevent, detect and report malware attacks.
- **Monitoring the Login (Addressable):** The covered entities should monitor the logins of the individuals accessing the PHI and report discrepancies.
- **Password Management (Addressable)**: The organization should ensure that there are procedures for creating, changing, and protecting passwords.
- **Response and Report (Required):** The organizations should have standards to identify, document and respond to incidents relating to security.
- **Contingency Plans (Required)**: The organizations should ensure that there exists accessible backups of ePHI and procedures to restore the lost data.
- **Contingency Plans Updates and Analysis (Addressable):** The organization is also expected to test and review the contingency plan periodically.

- **Emergency Mode (Required)**: The organization should be ready with a backup plan in order to achieve business continuity while operating in emergency mode.
- **Evaluations (Required)**: There should be constant periodic evaluations that should take place if there is any change in the law or the business.
- **Business Associate Agreements (Required)**: The organizations are mandated to have a contract with the business associates. It has already been explained in details in the previous parts of this chapter.

2. HIPAA Privacy Rule

The HIPAA Privacy Rule governs how ePHI can be used and disclosed. In force since 2003, the Privacy Rule applies to all healthcare organizations, the providers of health plans (including employers), healthcare clearinghouses and – from 2013 – the Business Associates of covered entities. (HIPAA Compliance Checklist. Retrieved from http://www.hipaajournal.com/hipaa-compliance-checklist/) This rule sets standards about how the electronic PHI can be used or disclosed. It applies to all healthcare organizations, health plan providers and their employees, health care clearing houses and the business associates.

The Privacy rule requires that sufficient and suitable safeguards are implemented to protect the privacy of the patient's medical record. Under this rule, the covered entities and the business associates are required to respond to patient requests in 30 days. It also includes Notices of Privacy Practices to let the patient know the circumstances in which their data will be used or shared.

Covered Entities are required to:

1. Train their employees to ensure that they are well versed and aware of what information constitutes as PHI and what information can further be shared or not shared outside an organization.
2. Take appropriate steps to maintain the integrity of the ePHI.
3. Obtain written authorizations from patients before using their health information for marketing, research, etc.

Covered entities are also required to update the authorization forms from time to time to include the disclosure of the immunization records to the schools, include the option to restrict the disclosure of information to health plan providers and also include an option to provide an electronic copy to the patient when they request it (HIPAA Compliance Checklist. Retrieved from http://www.hipaajournal.com/hipaa-compliance-checklist/).

3.   HIPAA Breach Notification Rule

As seen in previous sections, the breach notification rule requires the covered entities and the business associates to notify the patients in case of a breach in their system that contains ePHI. It also requires the covered entities to notify HHS of any such breach and issues a notice to the media. All this should be done if the breach affects more than 500 patients. In case the number of patients affected by the breach are less, the covered entity is supposed to report the breach via the OCR web portal annually.

The notification of breach should include the following information (HIPAA Compliance Checklist. Retrieved from http://www.hipaajournal.com/hipaa-compliance-checklist/):

1.   The nature of ePHI, including the types of personal identifies that have been exposed.
2.   If it is knows, then the identity of the unauthorized person to whom the disclosure has been made.
3.   Whether the ePHI was actually acquired or viewed.
4.   The extent to which the risk of damage has been mitigated.

Breach notifications must be made in no later than 60 days following its discovery. Along with the notification of the breach, the covered entities should also inform the affected individuals of the steps that they can take to protect themselves from any potential harm. The notice should also include the investigations that have happened and the actions that have been taken to prevent any further incidents.

4.   HIPAA Enforcement Rule

This rule governs the investigations that happen when a breach in PHI happens. It enforces penalties on covered entities and its business associates who are responsible for a breach in ePHI that could have been potentially avoided (HIPAA Compliance Checklist. Retrieved from http://www.hipaajournal.com/hipaa-compliance-checklist/) Therefore, it becomes important for organizations that are in possession of PHI to be aware of the potential penalties. Although we have discussed this briefly, let us now delve into the details.

1.   A fine of $100 - $50,000 can be imposed on a violation that occurs due to ignorance.
2.   A violation that occurs even after reasonable vigilance can attract fines of $1000 - $50,000.

3. Violations occurring due to willful neglect that can be corrected in no more than 30 days will attract a fine ranging between $10,000 and $50,000
4. Violations occurring due to willful neglect that can not be corrected in no more than 30 days will attract a maximum fine of $50,000.

The above fines are imposed based on each violation category and also based on the number of records exposed or compromised during a breach. Penalties can easily reach maximum fines of about $1,500,000 per year, per violation category. If the violation is based on willful neglect, there can also be criminal charges pressed against the covered entities. Victims can also file civil lawsuits for damages.

In addition to the above standards and implementations, there are a lot more steps that an IT department of an organization can take to prevent any HIPAA breach. Some of these steps can be:

1. By using secure messaging services while transmission of ePHI.
2. Encrypting the emails that are sent outside the company's firewall. The emails containing the patient's PHI must be archived securely for minimum six years.
3. Using a web content filter to prevent criminals from obtaining password to EMRs.

Implications of HIPAA on Patients

After studying in much detail, the HIPAA law and its implications healthcare providers, it becomes more important to study the implications of HIPAA for the patients. We have detailed the patient side of the story in bits and pieces; this section is set to provide comprehensive knowledge about the patient rights under HIPAA. With the passing HIPAA as a law, the patients were given the necessary power to control the privacy and security for their medical records or identifiable PHI. They were also given various rights to control who can see or use these records and for what purpose. The patient rights are explained in much detail below:

1. The patients have the right to request, see or get a copy of their medical records and other health information. To get this information, the patient has to request the provider and pay for the cost of copying and mailing. Once it is requested, the records should be mailed to the patients within 30 days.
2. The patient also has the right to review the medical records and change any wrong information or add any information that is missing or incomplete. If the patient believes that the information is incorrect, he still has a right to have a disagreement noted in his file, even if the provider believes that the information in question is correct.

3. The patient, by law, can find out about the visibility of his medical records. The patient can:

   a. Know how his information is used and shared by providers or payers – Mostly, a patient's health records may not be used for purposes that are not directly related to their care without their authorization. In such cases, before using the patient's information, the provider or the payer has to send the patient a notice on how his health information can be used. This usually happens during the first visit to the provider or during enrollment in a new health plan. The patient can at any time request another copy of that notice.

   b. Inform providers and health insurance companies about information that he does not want to share with others. The patient can also ask for other kinds of restrictions, but the providers and the payers hold the right to refuse the same if it affects the patient's care. A patient can also ask a provider to not tell the health plan provider about the care and the prescribed drugs if the patient pays for it from his pocket.

   c. Request to be reached somewhere other than his home

Under the privacy regulations, individuals have the right to request restrictions upon the use and disclosure of PHI (45 CFR 164.522). However, covered entities may exercise discretion in honoring such requests. Individuals are limited to the types of uses and disclosures for which they may request a restriction. (Dwyer S)

In case these rights are violated, the patient has the right to file a complaint with either the provider, health insurer or the HHS. While all these rights are made to help the patients, it is equally important for them to know about it for HIPAA to be successfully implemented and to serve its purpose.

REFERENCES

Atchinson, B., & Fox, D. (n.d.). *The Politics Of The Health Insurance Portability And Accountability Act.* Academic Press.

Blackburn, M. (n.d.). *HIPAA, Heal Thyself.* Retrieved from http://pages.jh.edu/jhumag/1104web/hipaa.html

Califf, R., & Muhlbaier, L. (n.d.). *Health Insurance Portability and Accountability Act (HIPAA).* Academic Press.

Clark, K. (n.d.). *How HIPAA Final Rules Affect Health Information Technology Vendors.* Retrieved from http://www.duanemorris.com/articles/static/clark_bilimoria_jmpm_0713.pdf

Dwyer, S. (n.d.). *Health Insurance Portability and Accountability Act.* Academic Press.

Gamble, M. (2013, August 13). *15 Things to Know About the HIPAA Omnibus Final Rule Before Sept. 23.* Retrieved from http://www.beckershospitalreview.com/legal-regulatory-issues/15-things-to-know-about-the-hipaa-omnibus-final-rule-before-sept-23.html

HIPAA and Health Privacy: Myths and Facts Part 2. (2009). Retrieved from https://www.cdt.org/files/healthprivacy/20090109mythsfacts2.pdf

HIPAA Background. (2010). Retrieved from http://hipaa.bsd.uchicago.edu/background.html

HIPAA Compliance Checklist. (n.d.). Retrieved from http://www.hipaajournal.com/hipaa-compliance-checklist/

HIPAA Privacy Rule and Its Impacts on Research. (n.d.). Retrieved from https://privacyruleandresearch.nih.gov/pr_06.asp

HITECH Act Summary. (n.d.). Retrieved from http://www.hipaasurvivalguide.com/hitech-act-summary.php

Information Technology and HIPAA. (n.d.). Retrieved from http://www.ct.gov/dph/lib/dph/ohca/hospitalstudy/it&hipaa.pdf

Leyva, C. (2013, February 3). *HIPAA Omnibus Rule Summary.* Retrieved from http://www.hipaasurvivalguide.com/hipaa-omnibus-rule.php

Privacilla.org. (2003, April). *The HIPAA Privacy Regulation — Troubled Process, Troubling Results.* Retrieved from http://www.privacilla.org/releases/HIPAA_Report.html

Rose, R. (2012, August 15). *HIPAA/HITECH Risk Assessments: Are the Standards Being Met?* Retrieved from http://www.beckershospitalreview.com/healthcare-information-technology/hipaahitech-risk-assessments-are-the-standards-being-met.html

Solove, D. J. (2003, April). HIPAA Turns 10: Analyzing the Past, Present and Future Impact. *Journal of American Health Information Management Association, 84*(4).

Summary of the HIPAA Privacy Rule. (n.d.). Retrieved from https://www.hhs.gov/hipaa/for-professionals/privacy/laws-regulations/index.html?language=es

The HIPAA Privacy Rule's Right of Access and Health Information Technology. (n.d.). Retrieved from https://www.hhs.gov/sites/default/files/ocr/privacy/hipaa/understanding/special/healthit/eaccess.pdf

The History of HIPAA & the Consequences of A HIPAA Violation. (n.d.). Retrieved from https://www.recordnations.com/articles/history-hipaa/

Wang, J. (2013, October 30). *How do I become HIPAA compliant? (A checklist).* Retrieved from https://www.truevault.com/blog/how-do-i-become-hipaa-compliant.html

Why Is the HIPAA Privacy Rule Needed? (n.d.). Retrieved from https://www.hhs.gov/hipaa/for-professionals/faq/188/why-is-the-privacy-rule-needed/index.html

Chapter 5
Navigating Through Choppy Waters of PCI DSS Compliance

Amrita Nanda
University at Buffalo, USA

Priyal Popat
University at Buffalo, USA

Deepak Vimalkumar
University at Buffalo, USA

ABSTRACT

PCI Data Security Standard is increasingly becoming one of the major compliance requirements all organizations are concerned about. This chapter taking a holistic approach, provides an overview of various components of PCI DSS. We discuss various versions of PCI DSS and the industries affected by this standard, the scope and requirements to comply and hesitation on part of most companies to imbibe it. We also look at the high-profile credit card breaches which have occurred recently and their impact on concerned industries. Additionally, we focus on the challenges faced by financial institutions to effectively meet PCI DSS requirements. Based on our analysis of different requirements of PCI DSS, challenges faced by organizations and recent security breaches of companies which were PCI DSS complaint at the time of breach, we propose recommendations to help organizations secure their cardholder data beyond the achieved compliance in place.

DOI: 10.4018/978-1-5225-2604-9.ch005

1. INTRODUCTION

Data breaches are continuously making headlines in the news today. As a result, most firms are now focusing on enforcing data protection. To make sure all entities comply with one industry accepted standard, PCI DSS was formed. This standard was introduced in 2004 to ensure security of cardholder data. PCI SSC (Payment Card Industry Security Standards Council) was established by major payment brands like Visa Inc., MasterCard Worldwide, American Express, Discover Financial Services and JCB which was responsible for development of security standards. After huge speculations and discussions, PCI SSC came up with PCI Data Security Standard (PCI DSS). All the major market players involved with storing, processing and transmitting card holder data are recommended to comply with it (PCI-SSC, 2014).

A study from (Verizon, 2013) also reported that in 2013, 11.1% of organizations were fully compliant with the standard at the time of their annual baseline assessment, up from just 7.5% in 2012. Also, according to their report organizations that are breached tend to be less compliant with PCI DSS than the average of organizations in this research. A 2011 Ponemon Institute study found 71 percent of companies do not treat PCI DSS as important and 79 percent among them have experienced data breaches (Ponemon, 2011). Codification of industry standards and complying of security standards has become top priority for all the major financial institutions since 2010. With growing political and government pressure abiding by these standards gas become very stringent.

In this paper, we conducted detailed analysis of PCI DSS scope, requirements and the industries affected by this standard. Additionally, we came across challenges faced by industries in complying with PCI DSS.

Recent news have reported many high profile breaches which have occurred in Target, Home Depot and Staples causing huge customer credit card information being lost (Tobias, 2014). The above cases instigated us to study these major breaches and analyze why the PCI DSS breach occurred even when these merchants were PCI DSS compliant at the time of breach. We analyzed the data breaches to find vulnerabilities in each case leading us to build a framework to recommending organizations on the critical aspects like Point of Sale devices, networks and software thus going beyond the PCI DSS requirements. Furthermore, we suggest that the need of advanced technologies is imminent given the fact that existing controls are being attacked immaterial of the organization being PCI DSS compliant.

2. LITERATURE REVIEW

PCI DSS compliance doesn't ensure that a company is secured against all kind of attacks. This makes the study interesting as more and more companies are investing more in becoming compliant while it doesn't guarantee results per se. Many researchers have studied about the way PCI DSS affects an organization's overall posture towards security and the following section reviews the studies conducted by them in relation to the contribution we make in this chapter. We have categorized the Literature studies into 5 areas, as shown below:

2.1. PCI DSS: A Holistic Approach on Security against Credit Card Breach

Our study's approach and adopted methodology is very similar to a recent research by (Culnan and Williams, 2009) that analyzed two high profile data breaches to provide lessons on ethics that can enhance organizational privacy. They do a great job by emphasizing on the ethical behavior and incorporating moral values along with the security standards. Similarly, in our research, we analyze recent high profile data breaches to find common factors and present recommendations to the organizations while stressing the importance of at least being PCI compliant.

(Sullivan, 2010) illustrates a holistic approach on the payment fraud issue through different sections in his study. It deals with finding the weakness of the methods used, monetary harm caused to the initiatives implemented in security standards like PCI DSS to combat these issues. It does a quantitative analysis of the data breaches from 2000 and concludes by recommendations to the policymakers.

The study by (Shaw, 2009) demonstrates the data breach problem along with the laws and regulations. It evaluates the current state and federal state data breach laws with respect to two high profile data breaches. The paper also states the importance of adhering to a standard like PCI DSS while giving equal importance to the notification law and proposes a solution for the same.

The study by (Morse and Raval, 2008) examines the roles taken by legal obligations and private ordering in payment card industry to secure the interests consumers. It evaluates the basic framework of PCI DSS and recommends it while insisting for stronger security standards.

(Gorge and Vigitrust, 2006) analyzes various data breaches that have occurred and shows us why a standard was necessary in cyber security where sensitive information were used. It answers the "Why PCI DSS?" question while describing some of the breaches happened and the cost benefit analysis of being compliant and not.

(Ataya, 2010) navigates through the process of PCI DSS audit and compliance by suggesting ways to reduce the effort in achieving it. The paper also suggests some of the actions which are to be accomplished beforehand to ease the audit process so that the audit results reflect the exact risk posture of the organization. [8]

(Coburn, 2010) in his paper deals with the importance of being PCI DSS compliant while maintaining a holistic approach to compliance and security enforced. It examines the ways to being PCI compliant starting with gap analysis, executing mock assessments and explains how it can help organizations gain a greater return on investment in IT security assets. It talks about different security methods of securing data ranging from multi-layered approach to popular measures followed in the industry.

An interesting study was done by (Sam Garfield, 2014) which deals with the popular malware called 'Backoff' responsible for millions of stolen card information. The author in this paper analyzes different data breaches caused due to the malware and further explaining how it works. At the same time, emphasis is given on the importance of ensuring PCI DSS compliance from the organization's part as well. The paper succeeds in examining why companies are reluctant in being compliant and not practicing what they should be in order to be placed one step ahead in the event of an attack.

(Owen and Dixon, 2007) discuss the PCI Data security standard, why it has been introduced and conclude it as a baseline for cardholder security. They have viewed PCI DSS as an initiative to impose best practices in information security upon the industry. This article summarizes PCI requirements, compliance dates, technologies involved and focuses on the need to secure and locate the cardholder data.

Large scale data breaches have been in the news and it is alarming with the huge numbers they come along. An article by (Peretti, 2008) provides a brief background on large scale data breaches and the criminal organizations that are responsible for exploiting the stolen data. She also examines the process by which large volumes of data are stolen, resold, and ultimately used by criminals to commit financial fraud in the underground world. Study then recommends PCI DSS compliance as the solution to organizations vulnerable to high amount of data breaches. This article backs our attempt to highlight PCI DSS's benefits to organizations in terms of enhancing security of cardholder data.

A very comprehensive illustration on Information Security Policy in the U.S. Retail Payments Industry is present in (MacCarthy, 2011) paper. Most of the breaches discussed in our chapter have failed in one of the aspects mentioned in this paper. The research here ranges from explaining PCI DSS, the information security policies that should be in place and recommendations to the payment industry on upgrading their technology. This paper also encourages retailers to share cyber threat information with each other. This would help keep track of various types of attacks being made and have a common repository of threat intelligence.

A very interesting study has been revealed in (Botha, 2011) that PCI DSS was until now considered only a baseline security measure but a correlation has been found between PCI DSS compliance and fewer data breaches. Results of this study can play a positive role in portraying PCI DSS as not an expensive compulsive audit but beneficial and secure measure of an organizations payment system. This paper enhances our claim that PCI DSS aides to an organization's security over all.

The research article by (Sussman, 2008) major components of PCI and the role of a CPA of an organization in enforcing the compliance is illustrated. The article describes the details of PCI Compliance in the light of TJX breach. Upon the wake of a breach the first question which crops up was whether the retailers were PCI Complaint or not. These standards are used as metrics by the five debit and credit card issuer organizations. Resulting to non-compliance the retailer will go through several penalties. On the other hand the CPA should develop knowledge and understanding of the standard to advise its client and employees on the scope of internal audit programs, risk assessment, anti-fraud programs, and vendor management programs and control culture. Furthermore, QSA (Quality Security Assessors) and ASV (Approved Scanning Vendors) are two types of consultants who are required to check whether PCI DSS guidelines are followed or not. But a CPA with sufficient expertise on Information security and data security can act as a QSA for a firm. Besides, CPA should suggest small merchants to have a strong relation with their financial institution that have the control on accepting credit card payment and should encourage them to make use of the PCI Compliance tools those financial institutions provide. The above hypothesis helps to determine that the companies affected with breaches should follow the guidelines laid down by PCI and have a careful scanning procedure to appoint their CPA who understands PCI guidelines well and can train others to do the same.

(Andre's, 2011) paper on relationship between PCI-DSS and security deals on why complying with PCI DSS is important for an organization. It drew a clear relation between PCI DSS and financial frauds which is the main cause of breaches these days. PCI DSS is a framework that guides small to very large organizations and is controlled by PCI-accredited auditors called QSAs (Qualified Security Assessor) with guidelines included in documentation of version 2.0 of PCI DSS. Vulnerability scans with the help of approved scanning vendor program. If the breach happens anyway, a qualified forensic investigator determines the extent of it and cause. Thus, a matchmaking is done between PCI DSS and security.

The research paper by (Jeff, 2010) focuses on a complete information security strategy beyond any particular compliance. This article deals with areas such as PCI standards and the need to use a "check-box QSA", costs of non-compliance and a data breach and lesson learnt from recent attacks. PCI DSS has definitely helped to reduce credit card breaches but there are many areas which have still not been touched including cloud computing, virtualization, smart-phone payment applications and other technologies. PCI Security Council has come up with a group called SGI (special interest group) to address this areas. Data breaches must be pre-empted. This paper has studied on such aspects as well. Few of the important points being 1. Engaging a hands-on PCI certified QSA 2. To understand where the data is located and how it can be prevented from being transmitted 3.secure the network 4. Check if the applications are PCI compliant 5.updating anti-virus program 6. Maintain a powerful password policy program 7.encryption of all hard drives 8.destroy all the data from a cell phone prior to transferring the data to a new cell phone. This paper also has made a study on the costs incurred due to a single data breach with respect to personnel costs and costs post the incidents. The study concludes that an organization should have an effective incident response plan and proper preparedness in case of a reach.

2.2. Comparison Between PCI DSS and Other Security Standards (ISO-17799, 27001, 27002), ITIL, COBIT

(Rowlingson and Winsborrow, 2006) compares two well-known security standards namely, ISO 17799 and PCI DSS. It gives and overview of both standards, explains the structure, compliance and maintenance of both standards while having a holistic view of both of them along with implementation costs.

In an article by (Mathew et al. 2011) throws light on how PCI DSS Compliance can be ensured by diverging it into a wider governance of information security comprising of not only security but also audit and control. The paper focuses on integrating the entire security governance framework for information security like Control Objective for Information and related Technology (COBIT), Information Technology Infrastructure Library (ITIL) and ISO 27002. This integrated framework will help the merchants to comply with PCI DSS more effectively with less monetary losses because a strategic alignment of PCI DSS with IS goals can ensure more security in contrast to an isolated PCI DSS standards.

Further studies on various other papers illustrate ways in which PCI DSS Compliance can be achieved with lesser resources and expenses. (Zarinka et al. 2012) came up with a mode where compliance of PCI DSS is made easy by using ISO 27001. ISO 27001 is designed to apply to a wider set of organization whereas PCI DSS is rather specific. Speaking in broader sense these standards have nothing in common. But with the help of previous studies a mapping was one between both the standards. There are many segments where both these standards overlap. There are 200 controls and 12 requirements in PCI DSS. Each control was somehow mapped to at least one of the controls specified in ISO 27001. The controls which can be mapped where mainly Communication and operations management, Access control and Information Systems acquisition, development and maintenance.

Another study by (Susanto et. al, 2011) suggests that there is no single formula that can guarantee 100% of information security. PCI DSS focuses mainly on information security relating to business transactions and smart card while ITIL and COBIT focuses on information security and its relation with the Project management and IT Governance. Other standards like ISO 27001 and BS 7799 emphasizes on information security management system as main domain and is more easily implemented and well recognized by stakeholders. This research compares attributes of all major Information Security Management System standards and concludes that only PCI DSS or only ISO 27001 does not imply complete security, hence supporting our study as well.

2.3. PCI DSS: A Merchants Point of View

For merchants to comply with PCI Compliance, a daunting task is to identify the credit card data flow, the stages of card transaction processing to be well versed with their payment infrastructure. Research paper by (Hizver and Chiueh, 2011) automates this process by developing a tool that can accurately extract the card data flow. Once compliance is achieved, it is an ongoing activity to keep updating the required logs and softwares. This paper also talks about the advantage it is to the merchants to be able to discover the process and the resulting card data flow diagram, the IT equipment's in its organization which touch the card data so as to tighten the security of these IT equipment's according to the PCI DSS compliance requirements. In support of our chapter's contribution, the tool vCardTrek developed in this research can be utilized as a recommendation to the merchants who process credit cards.

The consequences of not being PCI DSS Compliant have been addressed in detail in (Kidd, 2008) article. Kidd presents a succinct picture of the effects of non-compliance. Factors like penalties, fines, business risk, reputation, negative publicity, issuers removing the right to accept cards and costs in case a large scale breach occurs. This article aides our study as well, it gave us an understanding on how much compliance should be of importance to merchants. It is not a one-time process as well since not falling out of compliance is as well mandatory.

Another study (Adams, 2010) suggests that even though a merchant follows the guidelines and best practices and is PCI DSS compliant, it might still be a victim of the breach. What is important is what to do once attacked. There is no ideal 'one size fits all' solution as every merchant is different. A Qualified forensic investigator can lead to important answers like why it happened, who caused it and lessons learnt to not be a victim of such an attack again.

The research by (Peter et al. 's, n.d.) deals with an innovative way to examine the assessment method applicable to varying levels of merchants by using private cloud for compliance validation to PCI DSS. This paper explored the risk assessment process to observe an impact of using two different assessment methods by merchants sharing the same infrastructure. With reference to this research paper study have also been done on how the use of SAQ (self-assessment questionnaire) by level 2-4 merchants and QSA (Qualified Security Assessment) by level-1 merchants for assessment can introduce new vulnerabilities into the card holder data environment stored in the private cloud.

Research by (Harran and McKelvey, 2012) discusses merchants' objections and misunderstanding of the PCI compliance procedure. They state that merchants should themselves have a sound approach to security so that they have little difficulties with the process. Paper concludes by supporting PCI DSS's approach to security and suggests that it is highly beneficial to a business if they are compliant.

2.4. How Data Can be Protected

The core important point under all preventions of breach is data protection and its priority in an organization. This has been adequately argued in (Gorge, 2008) paper. It questions data classification and policies in place to protect them. Some decisions like how is data stored in rest, in transit and how encryption will apply to it. He states that security is more than compliance. Compliance is a necessary evil while good security practices regularly will not let you to become the next data incident headline.

An invention by (Caulkett et al., 2013) allows a method of secure payment system which can be used by payment processors for PCI DSS compliance. Generally, with changes to compliance requirements, it is daunting to review code which allows secure transmission of data again and again. This creation validates the card details and transmits them directly to payment token engine. It is nothing but cost effective solution for third parties to collect payment card details in a manner consistent with PCI DSS.

Most of the credit card breaches have occurred in the past mostly due to unawareness of the organization about the risks in the credit card breaches. A research paper by (Benj Hosack, 2004) helps to make the businesses aware of the risk in having a collection of old and legacy data lying unprotected and vulnerable. It also throws light on PA-DSS which has been brought forward by PCI SSC to protect Point of Sale (POS) systems used by the retailers. This paper discussed on how being PCI DSS complaint will costs much less than getting breached and loosing significant amount of data. Being PCI DSS Complaint and incorporating few controls will make it very difficult for the attackers to break through the company's network. There are many tools which can be used to reduce PCI risk. The tools should be accurate, would be capable of full system scanning, scanning through the archive, centralizing the management and taking a forensically sound approach. With the help of such tools significant amount of cardholder data can be protected. After selecting a particular tool an initial scan should be done to check for any risky element in the data and then subsequent scans are a must to verify for any other data leaks.

(Mark et al. 2006) came up with an apparatus that helps in payment using a credit/debit card which is secure and is able to comply with the security requirements of PCI DSS. This apparatus uses a sales transaction device which helps to determine an amount of sale and is connected to a card activated terminal (CAT) device. This secured CAT device is structured to obtain sensitive payment card information from the card, automatically requesting for a secure, encrypted manner of authorization from the sales transaction device which can be a third-party using the determined monetary amount. The sales transaction device also sends a purchase authorization approval to the CAT device. Thus the CAT device never receives any sensitive payment card information. As a result, it is compliant of certain PCI DSS requirement automatically, whereas the sales transaction device does not have to comply with any predetermined PCI requirements.

(Henry et al., 2012) came up with an idea of facilitating e-commerce via a proxy service. Their innovation mainly aims at an e-commerce solution which is capable of carrying out online ordering efficiently keeping in mind PCI DSS rules and regulations. They came up with a proxy service that can follow PCI DSS regulations and also with a Secure Socket Layer (SSL) encrypted electronic commerce web application. This proxy service can help organize data received from the e-commerce web application. This data is encrypted with a cipher according to PCI DSS regulations .The client application can make use of this data without decrypting it. Thus, usage of such kind of e-commerce systems is highly encouraged.

2.5. Is PCI DSS Enough?

The core important point under all preventions of breach is data protection and its priority in an organization. This has been adequately argued in (Gorge, 2008) paper. It questions data classification and policies in place to protect them. Some decisions like how is data stored in rest, in transit and how encryption will apply to it. He states that security is more than compliance. Compliance is a necessary evil while good security practices regularly will not let you to become the next data incident headline.

In an article by (Mathew et al. 2011) throws light on how PCI DSS Compliance can be ensured by diverging it into a wider governance of information security comprising of not only security but also audit and control. The paper focuses on integrating the entire security governance framework for information security like Control Objective for Information and related Technology (COBIT), Information Technology Infrastructure Library (ITIL) and ISO 27002. This integrated framework will help the merchants to comply with PCI DSS more effectively with less monetary losses because a strategic alignment of PCI DSS with IS goals can ensure more security in contrast to an isolated PCI DSS standards.

The research paper published by (Gunnar, 2010) deals with the improvement of security architecture getting the executive attention towards compliance activities like PCI DSS, this kind of modeling fills the gap between a system's functional requirements and checklist followed by an auditor. The study done by Gunnar aims at changing the auditor-centric approach of PCI DSS by architecture-centric approach. This approach deals with an organization's risk management, security policies and compliance decisions. Threat modeling is adopted to fill the gap between PCI DSS and the architectural approach. The challenge of a security architecture is to first tuning the functional requirement into non-functional requirements and then meeting compliance goals. This will help to establish a cost-effective architecture.

3. PAYMENT CARD INDUSTRY DATA SECURITY STANDARD

This section provides background information on Payment Card Industry Data Security Standard, how it all started and the history behind it. Initiated in the year 2004, it has been evolving over the years. We talk about the various versions of PCI DSS till date and then move on to the standardized set of requirements they have.

3.1. History

Originally started as 5 different programs by the providers, PCI-DSS took its shape in December 15 2004. Different security standard offered before PCI-DSS are showed in Table 1.

Table 1. Security standards offered before PCI-DSS

Company	Initial Security Policy
VISA	Cardholder Information Security Program
MasterCard	Site Data Protection
American Express	Data Security Operating Policy
Discover	Information Security and Compliance
JCB	Data Security Program

Each company's intentions were similar i.e. to create an additional level of protection for card issuers by ensuring that merchants meet minimum levels of security when they store, process and transmit cardholder data. Hence, Payment Card Industry Security Standards Council (PCI SSC) was formed, and on December 15, 2004, these companies aligned their individual policies and released version 1.0 of the Payment Card Industry Data Security Standard (PCI DSS) (Wikipedia, 2015).

3.1.1. Versions

Table 2 shows different PCI DSS versions released and changes incorporated in each of them.

3.1.2. Revisions

Table 3 illustrates PCI DSS versions and the detailed description on the changes done in each new version released.

3.2. Scope and Requirements

Any merchant, acquirer, issuer bank and service provider that processes, stores and transmits credit and debit card data and any connected party with them.

Major functions of PCI DSS compliance: (PCI- SSC, 2014)

1. Building and maintain a secure network
2. Protecting card holder data
3. Maintaining a vulnerability management program.
4. Regularly monitoring and testing of networks
5. Maintaining an information security policy

Table 2. PCI DSS Version history

Version No	Release Date
V 1.0	December 15 2004
V 1.1	September 2006
V 1.2	October 1 2008
V 1.2.1	August 2009
V 2.0	October 2010
V 3.0	November 2013

Table 3. PCI DSS revision history and description

Version No:	Description/Revision
V 1.0	Base version
V 1.1	To provide clarification and minor revisions to version 1.0.
V 1.2	To introduce PCI DSS v1.2 as ——PCI DSS Requirements and Security Assessment Procedures,‖ eliminating redundancy between documents, and make both general and specific changes from PCI DSS Security Audit Procedures v1.1. For complete information, see PCI Data Security Standard Summary of Changes from PCI DSS Version 1.1 to 1.2. (PCI-SSC, 2014)
V 1.2.1	Add sentence that was incorrectly deleted between PCI DSS v1.1 and v1.2. Correct "then" to "than" in testing procedures 6.3.7.a and 6.3.7.b. Remove grayed-out marking for "in place" and "not in place" columns in testing procedure 6.5.b. For Compensating Controls Worksheet – Completed Example, correct wording at top of page to say "Use this worksheet to define compensating controls for any requirement noted as 'in place' via compensating controls".(PCI-SSC, 2014)
V 2.0	Update and implement changes from v1.2.1. For details, please see "PCI DSS - Summary of Changes from PCI DSS Version 1.2.1 to 2.0." (PCI-SSC, 2014)
V 3.0	Update from v2.0. See PCI DSS – Summary of Changes from PCI DSS Version 2.0 to 3.0." (PCI-SSC, 2014)

PCI DSS is a very critical step. It's continuously getting refined and strengthen with the help of PCI SSC, credit card brands, acquirers and other third party organization. However like all other compliances, few more changes, discussions and challenges have to be overcome to make it more robust and understood by all the financial globally.

Security is necessary for all components present in a cardholder environment. The CDE as it is primarily referred to as, consist of people and technologies that store, process or transmit cardholder data. Components being servers, applications, devices etc.

Examples of system components include: (PCI-SSC, 2014)

1. Authentication servers, internal firewalls or any system which impacts the security of the CDE.
2. Virtualization components such as virtual machines, virtual switches/routers, virtual appliances and virtual applications/desktops
3. Network components like switches, routers and wireless access points

4.   Server types like web, application, database, authentication, mail, proxy, Network Time Protocol (NTP), and Domain Name System (DNS).

Significant factor in the PCI DSS requirements is the PAN i.e. primary account number and lot of dependency on the scope relevant varies with PAN usage. If PAN is not stored, processed, or transmitted, PCI DSS requirements do not apply. If cardholder name, service code, and/or expiration date are stored, processed or transmitted with the PAN, or are otherwise present in the cardholder data environment, they must be protected in accordance with all PCI DSS requirements. Having said that, these standards represent a minimum set of objectives. Further enhancement can be done through local, regional and sector laws and regulations.

PCI DSS standard specifies the below requirements to be incorporated as a part of compliance scope: (PCI-SSC, 2014)

Requirement 1: Install and maintain a firewall configuration to protect cardholder data.

Requirement 2: Do not use vendor-supplied defaults for system passwords and other security parameters.

Requirement 3: Protect stored cardholder data.

Requirement 4: Encrypt transmission of cardholder data across open, public networks.

Requirement 5: Protect all systems against malware and regularly update anti-virus software or programs.

Requirement 6: Develop and maintain secure systems and application.

Requirement 7: Restrict access to cardholder data by business need to know.

Requirement 8: Identify and authenticate access to system components.

Requirement 9: Restrict physical access to cardholder data.

Requirement 10: Track and monitor all access to network resources and cardholder data.

Requirement 11: Regularly test security systems and processes.

Requirement 12: Maintain a policy that addresses information security for all personnel.

4. INDUSTRY

These are the organizations which stores, process and transmit credit/debit card data and are supposed to comply with PCI DSS standards. In this section, we are dealing with two such industries- Merchants and Service providers.

4.1. Merchant

Merchant - Also called as the 'seller' of any item available to be bought using a card. The merchants or the seller store, process or transmit card holder data. Since the merchants accept cardholder payment card and they happen to have the card holder sensitive information, they are supposed to be PCI COMPLAINT. While the council is responsible for managing security standards, the compliance with the PCI security standards is enforced by the payment card brands. (Hosack B, 2011)

Merchant banks are responsible for making the merchants PCI compliant. A merchant compliance validation is based on following: - 1. Volume of transaction 2. Potential risk 3.exposure introduced in the payment system. (Visa Inc., 2015)

4.1.1. Merchant Levels and Compliance Validation Requirements Defined

Visa developed the PCI Compliance Acceleration Program to provide financial incentives and establish enforcement provisions for acquirers to ensure their merchants validate PCI DSS compliance.

Based on visa transaction volume all merchants fall into four merchant levels. Transaction volume is based on no. of transactions done by a merchant who is a DBA (Doing Business as- legal term for a fictional name used by a merchant under whom a business is running and presented to the world) (Visa Inc,2015).

Different levels of various merchants and their compliance requirement are discussed in Table 4.

Table 4. Different levels of merchants

Merchant Levels	Criteria	Basic Validation required
1	6 million visa transaction annually	QSA provides an Annual Report on Compliance followed by Quarterly network scan by an approved scan vendor. Finally an attested compliance form is filed
2	1 – 6 million visa transactions	In this case, the merchant has to fill an annual self-assessment questionnaire (SAQ) followed by Quarterly network scan by an approved scan vendor. Finally an attested compliance form is filed
3	20,000 – 1 million transactions mainly e-commerce	In this case, the merchant has to fill an annual self-assessment questionnaire (SAQ) followed by Quarterly network scan by an approved scan vendor. Finally an attested compliance form is filed
4	Less than 20,000	In this case, the merchant has to fill an annual self-assessment questionnaire (SAQ) followed by Quarterly network scan by an approved scan vendor. Finally an attested compliance form is filed

4.1.2. Validation Procedure and Documentation

It is the responsibility of the bank to validate the merchant at the required level and procure proper validation document from them. The merchant bank should submit the detailed report called the detailed bi-annual status reports for all the level to visa and all the compliance documents to the visa. In the same way merchant and merchant bank should verify the compliance requirements of all the other payment card brands. The other entire brand may also require proof of compliance validation.

Level-1 Merchant: The level-1 merchant are required to complete the Annual-On site PCI Data Security Assessment, according to PCI DSS V2.0 document. They should have a quality security Assessor to complete the Report on Compliance and had it over to the merchant bank. The bank in return, accepts it from the level 1 merchant's Internal Security Assessor. Level 1 merchant should also submit the PCI DSS AOC – MERCHANTS V2.0 to their merchant bank. The bank should submit all these forms and full compliance validation for to the card brand.

Level-2/level-3/level-4: The PCI DSS Self-Assessment Questionnaire (SAQ) must be completed by level 2 and 3 merchants. Level 4 merchants are required to complete the applicable PCI DSS SAQ as specified by the merchant bank. (Visa Inc., 2015)

Compliance with PCI for Merchant Includes

- Use of card readers
- Point of sale systems
- Store network and wireless access router
- Payment card data storage and transmission
- Payment card data stored in paper based records.

Penalties Under Non-Compliance Includes

- Fines and penalties
- Termination of ability to accept payment cards
- Lost confidence, so customers go to other merchants
- Lost sales
- Cost of reissuing new payment cards
- Legal costs, settlements and judgments
- Fraud losses
- Higher subsequent costs of compliance

4.2. Service Provider

Service provider are organization that processes, store and transmit Visa holder account or transaction information on behalf of visa clients, merchants or other service provider. Table 5 illustrates that there are only two level for service provider, Level 1 and level 2. Unlike Merchants, Service providers must focus on aggregate number of transaction per year to determine which level they are. (Visa Inc., 2015)

In addition, Table 6 illustrates the various levels assigned through the above table along with the Validation requirements for each level.

4.2.1. Validation Procedure

Validation is required for every 12 months for both level 1 and level 2 (Visa Inc., 2015).

Following validation requirements are required:

- **Third Party Agents**: Level 1 service providers are required to submit an Attestation of compliance (AOC), signed by both parties. Then the credit card brand has the rights to ask for Report on Compliance (ROC). This is done to verify for appropriate content. Level 2 service provider must submit a SAQ-D or an AOC with a QSA signature for re-validation.
- **Visa Clients, Visa Net Processors and Visa Vendors**: Client banks directly connected to Visa, and vendors providing services to Visa must validate compliance by submitting the full (ROC) and the AOC signed by both parties. ROCs must be sent securely via PGP encryption.

Table 5. Levels for service provider

Service provider level	Description
1	=30,000 transactions per year
2	>30,000 transactions per year

Table 6. Validation types for service providers

Level	Validation Action
1	QSA provides an Annual Report on Compliance followed by Quarterly network scan by an approved scan vendor. Finally an attested compliance form is filed
2	In this case, the merchant has to fill an annual self-assessment questionnaire (SAQ) followed by Quarterly network scan by an approved scan vendor. Finally an attested compliance form is filed

The Annual On-site PCI DATA security Assessment is done for level 1 provider. A QSA is required to complete the ROC.

The Attestation of Compliance for Onsite Assessments – must be completed by all service providers validating compliance and their assessor and submitted to the card brand.

Quarterly Network security Scan - s an automated tool that checks systems for vulnerabilities. It conducts a non-intrusive scan to remotely review networks and Web applications based in the externally-facing Internet Protocol (IP) address provided by the service provider. Level 1 and 2 service providers are responsible for ensuring that a quarterly network scan is performed on their Internet-facing perimeter systems by an Approved Scanning Vendor (Visa Inc., 2015)

4.2.2. Annual Validation

Service Providers that store, process or transmit Visa cardholder data must demonstrate PCI DSS compliance and provide the compliance validation to Visa every 12 months. The fine for non-compliance starts at 50,000 USD per service provider (assessed to the registering Visa member).

For Level 1 service providers published on the Registry, if Visa does not receive the appropriate revalidation documents:

- **Within 1:** 60 days upon expiry of the validation documents, the entity will be highlighted in Yellow on the Registry.
- **Within 61:** 90 days upon expiry of the validation documents, the entity will be highlighted Red on the Registry.
- After 90 days, the entity will be removed from the Registry.

Please note that card holder brand reserves the rights to remove any third party agent from the Registry at its discretion. (Visa Inc., 2015)

4.3. Difference Between Validation of PCI DSS in Merchant and Service Bank

One of the key differences between Merchants and Service Providers is how compliance is validated. Merchants validate their compliance by submitting evidence to their Acquirer, whereas Service Providers must submit evidence to the individual Card Brands (which are Visa, MasterCard, American Express, JCB and Discover). (Visa Inc., 2015)

Both Level 1 Merchants and Service Providers can only validate compliance with an independent assessment by a PCI QSA. Level 2 (and below) Merchants and Service Providers may be able to complete an SAQ to validate compliance. For Merchants, there are multiple SAQs, each of which represent a subset of PCI requirements and can be completed if certain criteria are met. For Service Providers who wish to self-assess (and Merchants who do not meet the criteria for any other SAQs) SAQ D must be completed. SAQ D constitutes the full set of PCI requirements.

One point to note is that, whilst Merchants assess the organization as a whole, Service Providers validate compliance for one, some or all of the services they offer. A Service Provider may be able to offer a PCI-compliant dedicated hosting solution, for example, whereas other services (e.g. their shared hosting platforms) may not be compliant.

Service Providers that are not compliant have two options open to them. They can either undergo a PCI DSS assessment to validate compliance, or have their services reviewed as part of each customer's PCI DSS assessment.

5. INDUSTRY COMPLIANCE-VERIZON REPORT

The Verizon research (Verizon, 2013) is based on quantitative data gathered by qualified security assessors (QSAs) while performing baseline assessments on PCI DSS 2.0 compliance between 2011 and 2013.

PCI DSS has achieved the below milestones in the year 2014:

- The PCI Data Security Standard (DSS) turns ten years old
- DSS 3.0 becomes effective and validation assessments start (January 1)
- DSS 2.0 expires and compliance validation against version 3.0 becomes mandatory (December 31)

The catch here is that organizations that are breached tend to be less compliant with PCI DSS than the average of organizations in this research.

Verizon report also presents few problems faced in compliance as mentioned below:

- Vast majority of organizations are still not sufficiently mature
- Struggle to provide the required compliance evidence at the time of the annual compliance validation assessment.
- Fundamental disagreements and misunderstandings around critical areas of security and compliance
- Only around one in ten organizations were fully compliant with PCI DSS 2.0 at the time of their baseline assessment (Verizon, 2014)

Figure 1 depicted below is a graphical representation of Verizon's PCI DSS compliance report (2014).

In 2013, 11.1% of organizations were fully compliant with the standard at the time of their annual baseline assessment, up from just 7.5% in 2012. This is still a very low figure, so we also looked at the percentage of organizations compliant with at least 80% of the controls and sub-controls. This showed a far greater increase: from just 32.1% (24.6% + 7.5%) in 2012, to 82.2% (71.1% + 11.1%) in 2013 showing 4 in 5 are almost there.

6. PCI DSS CHALLENGES

No company wants to be the subject of a security breach event when card information is compromised as the effects are irreparable, particularly loss of customer confidence and reputational damage. Not to forget the huge amount of fines and clear – up costs. Most companies find the PCI DSS scope challenging with respect to many themes and constantly try to get around the requirements. Some translate them into their own suitable language and some apply limited controls and attention. Some common barriers faced across organizations are. The challenges faced by the organization are mainly (Rees J, 2010)

Figure 1. Compliance Rate Source: Verizon 2014 PCI compliance report, (http:// www.verizonenterprise.com/pcireport/2014/)

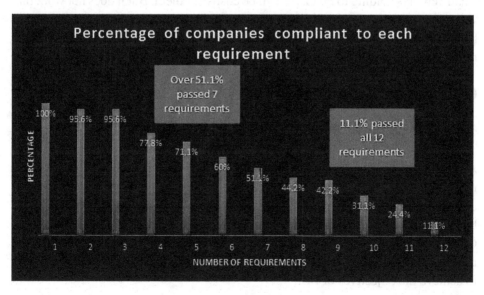

1. Costly
2. Stringent guidelines
3. Ambiguous scope
4. Casually treated

6.1. Costly

6.1.1 Expensive

Truly said, security comes with a cost. To take up the cost is an individual decision taken after considering all the implications and consequences of not complying with the same. For small firms with smaller infrastructure, it is very costly to employ all the necessary activities and attain compliance. On the flip side, fines are dead money too- really expensive. Risks come along with any new initiative organizations take or decide not to take. Companies can evaluate their need by evaluating if they can undertake business without card payments, if they can continue their operations without POS devices and decide if it seems valuable enough to put in the time and money required to comply

6.1.2. Reluctance of Small Companies to Adhere to PCI DSS Compliance

The small companies defer from complying with PCI DSS because as they are small ventures abiding to PCI DSS will be costly for them. But it does not work that way. If you take card payments you are required to adhere to PCI DSS. The small banks too are contractually obliged with the bank and the card brands through the merchant ID contractual agreement.

6.2. Stringent Guidelines

6.2.1. Too Tough

Arguments and opinions on how complex the PCI compliance model is, has become really common. It can be as complicated or as simple as you wish to make it. Lot of the items under PCI DSS can be included or excluded depending on the type of business one operates in and how they process, store and transmit card information. Qualified Security Assessors (QSA)'s who are usually from organizations authorized to assess compliance to the standard willingly help with the questions and procedure to achieve the objectives of PCI.

6.2.2. Few Aspects too Strict

PCI DSS is a very strict model. Agreed. But it does ensure that it addresses a number of security concerns concerning the wide spread use of card transactions performed. The strict nature is a blessing in disguise and it is there to protect people, financial institutions from fraud.

6.3. Ambiguous Scope

6.3.1. Guidelines too Vague

Before undertaking PCI DSS compliance project, the golden rule is to get the scope right. If an organization feels that the guidelines are not clear, then appropriate training or help needs to be taken from authorized professionals like QSA's or ISA's trained by the PCI council themselves. Since it is the first step in achieving the whole process, it is highly important to get it right.

6.3.2. Partial Agreement to PCI DSS

This is one of the major challenges that PCI DSS is going through. The organization tends to believe that they are supposed to abide by only those parts of PCI DSS which with their companies are concerned. But PCI DSS requires the organization to comply with the entire standards. PCI DSS cannot be passed unless all the components applicable to the organization being in place.

6.4. Casually Treated

6.4.1. Not a Legal Mandate

Most organizations tend to take the compliance lightly as it has not been mandated in the US yet. PCI council has been founded and promoted by major card brands as they want all card users to maintain specific level of security laid out in the compliance model. To smoothly continue your business with banks and card brands, it is essential to follow the standard. Most of the major banking institutions have been supportive of the PCI scope and are themselves trying to achieve compliance in their systems, networks, software's and banking services.

6.4.1. *Organization is Fearless of PCI DSS*

The organization does not realize the amount of penalty they would get in case of non-adherence of PCI DSS. The acquiring bank reserve to the right to fine, increase the cost per transaction or as an ultimate sanction; refuse entirely to allow a merchant to take card payments. Companies prefer not to disclose if they are fined or penalized to avoid damage. The companies do not want to be in news because of data breaches issues.

7. LARGE DATA BREACHES INVOLVING CCN

Data breach is an incident wherein sensitive, confidential or protected information are stolen or misused by compromising the security systems. We analyze recent high profile credit card breaches happened recently to validate the effectiveness status of PCI DSS compliance. Here, we discuss the extent of breach and how it happened. Some of the breaches happened are:

7.1. Breaches

In this section we analyze various data breaches happened in the recent past involving credit cards.

7.1.1 Home Depot

Home Depot can be considered lucky because even though hackers were in their network for close to five months, they stole far fewer card details than they might have otherwise. 56 million credit card details of Home Depot customers had been compromised during this attack. The Target breach lasted only three weeks and exposed 40 million of CCN data. Moreover, the same malware BlackPOS installed on Target POS had been used on Home Depot POS. Investigation Reports have come up with a report indicating that the self-checkout lanes of shopping had been the thieves choice of attack. The retailer announced the breach publicly on September 2nd 2014. 2,266 stores payment systems had been compromised during this 5 month attack period (Krebs B, 2014). With respect to the number of CCN records affected, Home Depot's 56 million come right after TJX'x co.'s breach of 90 million records. In November, the Home Depot has also announced that hackers also made off with 53 million email addresses of customers. They are also facing 44 civil lawsuits in the U.S and Canada as a result of the data breach. The retailer had been PCI Compliant but fell out of compliance during the year by not conducting periodic network scans, vulnerability assessment and having stricter security policies. It is astonishing that someone could reside in their systems for as long as 5 months unnoticed. Stolen credit cards have been up for sale and each card is indexed by the city, state and ZIP of the retail store from which each card was stolen. Hackers then make counterfeit copies of these credit and debit cards to buy high priced merchandise. The ZIP code data does not alert the bank when they perform any transaction as it can be used in the same geographic location and not stand out suspicious. Currently, Home Depot is working to deploy EuroPay MasterCard Visa (EMV) chip-and-pin security at all its stores. (Privacy Rights Clearing House, 2014)

7.1.2. Michaels

Arts and crafts chain Michaels Stores Inc. declared on April 17th 2014 that their stores have been exposed to two separate 8 month long security breaches leaking 3 million customer debit and credit cards. The company reveals that a limited portion of the point of sale systems has only been infected from May8th, 2013 to January, 2014. Aaron Brothers, Michael stores subsidiary also confirmed that 54 of their stores had some evidence of an attack between June 26, 2013 and February 27, 2014 (Krebs B, 2014). This store has wrestled with a compromise of their payment card systems for two times in three years. Being PCI Compliant, they failed to have up to date security policy and procedures in place. However most analysts argue that one cannot expect retailers to have a forensics team always on alert to trace malware. Moreover, the blame game will continue while not resulting in any solution. PCI DSS should be judiciously followed and maintained as a baseline security measure (Schwartz M, J, 2014).Having said that, a secure payment solution like P2P encryption, tokenization should be implemented nationwide by banks of all sizes, credit unions, acquirers, retailers, point-of-sale device manufacturers and industry trade group. In addition, Breach detection system products should be used to identify malware, patterns of network traffic, malicious domains and model the behavior/impact of files that are downloaded. (Kassner M, 2014)

7.1.3. Global Payment

Debit and credit card processor Global Payments suffered a massive data breach from Dec 2011 to March 2012. Publicly Global payments have only confirmed that close to 1.5 million accounts were taken during the breach, however, reports by The Wall Street Journal put that figure to 7 million (Krebs B,2012). Global Payment had been a part of PCI DSS Compliant list of service providers but was later removed from that due to unsecure processing system. In 2013, it was again added and now provides PCI DSS compliant safe and secure payment transactions. Industry standards require more than compliance, it needs to understand in depth how sensitive data can be secure. Firstly, sensitive data classification and appropriate controls have to be in place when data is across the network or at rest. Additionally, protecting the network from threats is crucial as well. (Digital Guardian, 2014)

7.1.4. Target

TARGET was ironically 'targeted' by a huge number of compromised credit and debit card information being stolen of their customers between Nov and Dec 2013. Below is the data by numbers:

- **40 Million:** The number of credit and debit cards thieves stole from Target between Nov. 27 and Dec. 15, 2013.
- **70 Million:** The number of records stolen that included the name, address, email address and phone number of Target shoppers.
- **46:** The percentage drop in profits at Target in the fourth quarter of 2013, compared with the year before.
- **200 Million:** Estimated dollar cost to credit unions and community banks for reissuing 21.8 million cards — about half of the total stolen in the Target breach.
- **100 Million:** the number of dollars Target says it will spend upgrading their payment terminals to support Chip-and-PIN enabled cards.
- **0:** The number of customer cards that Chip-and-PIN-enabled terminals would have been able to stop the bad guys from stealing had Target put the technology in place prior to the breach (without end-to-end encryption of card data, the card numbers and expiration dates can still be stolen and used in online transactions).
- **0:** The number of people in Chief Information Security Officer (CISO) or Chief Security Officer (CSO) jobs at Target (according to the AP).
- **18.00 – 35.70:** The median price range (in dollars) per card stolen from Target and resold on the black market (range covers median card price on Feb. 19, 2014 vs. Dec. 19, 2013, respectively).
- **1 Million:** 3 million – The estimated number of cards stolen from Target that were successfully sold on the black market and used for fraud before issuing banks got around to canceling the rest (based on interviews with three different banks, which found that between 3-7 percent of all cards they were told by Visa/MasterCard were compromised actually ended up experiencing fraud).
- **53.7 Million:** The income that hackers likely generated from the sale of 2 million cards stolen from Target and sold at the mid-range price of $26.85 (the median price between $18.00 and $35.70). (Krebs B, 2014)

There are no indications at this time that the breach affected customers who shopped at Target's online stores. The type of data stolen — also known as "track data" — allows crooks to create counterfeit cards by encoding the information onto any card with a magnetic stripe. If the thieves also were able to intercept PIN data for debit transactions, they would theoretically be able to reproduce stolen debit cards and use them to withdraw cash from ATMs. An examination of the malware used in the Target breach suggests that the attackers may have had help from a poorly secured feature built into a widely-used IT management software product that was running on the retailer's internal network. The attackers were able to infect Target's point-of-sale registers with a malware strain that stole credit and debit card data. The intruders also set up a control server within Target's internal network that served as a central repository for data hovered up from all of the infected registers.

Cards stolen in a recent data breach at retail giant Target have been flooding underground black markets in recent weeks, selling in batches of one million cards and going for anywhere from $20 to more than $100 per card, KrebsOnSecurity has learned.

7.1.5. Goodwill

Goodwill industries International has confirmed about credit card data breach on 18th of July 2014. They have confirmed that the breach has occurred after the third-party vendor C&K systems got compromised leading to a loss of 868,000 credit and debit card loss in nearly 330 stores (Bluemner, 2014). Goodwill also confirmed that the breach was stemmed from a malware called RAW: PoS which were used by the attacker to compromise the third party vendor. The method employed in good will is called Ram scrapping. Ram scrapers examine the list of processes on the system and inspect the memory for the data that matches credit card data such as account number, expiration date and other information in the magnetic stripe. The scrapers usually encrypt and store the stolen data in the victim's network until it is remotely retrieved (Krebs B, 2014). This was first identified by idRAR (an identity theft protection firm) which had a copy of the details of the breach sent to it by good will industries. C&K systems came up with an analysis that a magnetic stripe in a credit or debit card contains two areas called tracks. Track 1 includes cardholder's name, account number and other data. Track 2 contains cardholder's account; encrypted PIN and other information excluding card holder's name. The underground stores which sell the stolen credit and debit card tend to sell the track 2 data. After this whole incident, goodwill industries have learnt that it is dangerous to neglect third-party service provider due diligence (Krebs B, 2014). The PCI compliance highlights on gaining transparency in service provider's operations by implementing some malware prevention and it also provides proper controls so as to protect the card-holder data.

7.1.6. Staples

Multiple reported they have identified a pattern of credit and debit card fraud in December 2014 suggesting that a data breach might have occurred in several Staples Inc. office supply locations in the Northeastern United States. Staples was quoted saying it is investigating "a potential issue" and has contacted law enforcement. As per the sources at banks operating on the East Coast, it seems that fraudsters have succeeded in stealing customer card data from 119 of Staples stores, including seven Staples stores in Pennsylvania, at least three in New York City, and another in New Jersey over a period of August 10, 2014 through September 16, 2014 compromising the systems to steal about 1.19 million credit card data (Krebs B, 2014). Reporters have traced a pattern of fraudulent transactions on a group of cards which were used in a small number of Staples locations in the Northeast. The fraudulent charges happened at other (non-Staples) businesses, such as supermarkets and other big-box retailers. This suggests that the Point-Of-Sale devices in Staples locations may have fallen victim to card-stealing malware that lets thieves create counterfeit copies of cards that customer's swipe at compromised payment terminals. (Privacy Rights Clearinghouse, 2015)

7.1.7. Adobe Systems

The hackers got hold of the user passwords in Adobe and the systems were hacked using these accounts. Customer IDs, encrypted passwords, names, encrypted credit or debit card numbers, expiration dates, and other information related to customer orders were exposed. Around 3 million encrypted credit card data and encrypted passwords of almost 38 million users were exposed over a period of 2 weeks. Adobe IDs were also compromised and were later reset by Adobe. In addition to these, the hackers also stole source code data of their products like ColdFusion and Acrobat and Reader. Though the company was PCI DSS compliant, the hackers were able to break-in easily to Adobe network and did the damage. After the breach, hackers kept the source code on a hidden but unencrypted server. (Privacy Rights Clearinghouse, 2015)

7.2. Breach Analysis

This section analyzes various breaches against different parameters of study while PCI DSS compliant status being the focus as illustrated in Table 7.

It is interesting to note that, all of them were PCI DSS compliant while the breach happened. So, is PCI DSS enough? Where is the return in investment if your organization is breached even after being compliant?

Table 7. Study of various breaches against different parameters of study while being PCI DSS compliant

S.No	BREACH DETAILS				SUMMARY – DATA ANALYSIS			
	Breach Description/ Title	CCN Records	PCI Compliant Status (Y/N)	PCI requirement (s) violated	Breach method	Flaws detected	Monetary Damage	Recommendations
1	Staples Inc.	1.16 Million	Y	Requirement 3 Requirement 4 Requirement 5	Staples locations may have fallen victim to card-stealing malware that lets thieves create counterfeit copies of cards that customer swipe at compromised payment terminals. Investigation revealed that the hackers used malware that provided access to information for transactions at 115 of its stores.	1. Lack of security assessments to find potential threats. 2. Breach occurred from July 2014 to September 2014 showing the systems were compromised and the malware was undetected up to 3 months. 3. Absence of encryption mechanism made it easier for hackers to read the card data. 4. Security assessments in POS (Point Of Sale) devices were minimum. 5. Antivirus software were not up-to-date to detect the malware in POS services. 6. Vulnerability assessment were minimal.	No Data Available	1. Perform vulnerability assessment and security tests regularly. 2. Update antivirus and firewall systems. 3. Opt for EMV with tokenization Instead of Magstripe Cards. 4. Perform thorough network and device scans to detect malwares. 5. Encrypt all sensitive network communications, data in rest and motion.
2	Home Depot	56 million	Y	Requirement 5 Requirement 10	Malware on POS device named BlackPOS.	1. Outdated Symantec antivirus software from 2007. 2. Not continuously monitoring the network for suspicious behavior. 3. Performing vulnerability scans irregularly and at only a small number of stores.	$43 million	1. Do not fall out of compliance once it is achieved. 2. Regularly upgrade software for patches. 3. Avoid conventional naming of backend servers which can be easily identified by hackers. 4. Risk assessment is an ongoing activity and should be performed periodically.

continued on following page

Table 7. Continued

	BREACH DETAILS			SUMMARY – DATA ANALYSIS		
3	Good will	868,000 (330 stores)	Yes (since its third party vendor C&K systems does)	Requirement 2 Requirement 5 Requirement 10	Malware detected on a particular third party vendor system called C&K systems.	1. Forensic investigation determined that 330 goodwill stores in 20 states were compromised. But no internal good will systems were attacked. The retail point-of-sale (PoS) systems service provider C&K systems was attacked by a malware named RAW. 2. There is a possibility that the attackers are using remote access. They are using phishing or social engineering techniques to get the credentials of the databases. 3. The owners of C&K systems on the other hand claimed the credit card information cannot be stolen unless there are vulnerabilities present in the network of the store.	$111 million (only Q2 data)	1. Since, there are many incidents which are occurring at the vendor's site, it is recommended for them to use a totally different server environment with enhanced security measures while dealing with credit card and other confidential information details. 2. To prevent remote access, usage of stronger password is recommended rather than using a default admin password which can easily be hacked.
4	Michaels and Aaron Brothers Stores	3 million	Y	Requirement 5	Sophisticated malware on POS device	1. Not continuously monitoring the network for suspicious behavior 2. Performing vulnerability scans irregularly and at only a small number of stores. 3. Unsecure third party vendors	Not available	1. Partner with third party vendors which are PCI Compliant Service Providers and use authorized PCI POS devices 2. Do not fall out of compliance once it is achieved 3. Regularly upgrade software for patches

continued on following page

Table 7. Continued

	BREACH DETAILS					SUMMARY – DATA ANALYSIS		
5	Target	40 million	Yes (as per forensic investigation)	Requirement 2 Requirement 5 Requirement 10	Malware on POS device "BLACKPOS"	Multiple and conflicting reasons sighted. 1. There are allegations and cross-allegations among different party. 2. Target was blamed of storing the credit card information in an unprotected way, since CVV numbers were stolen. So, they were accused of not being PCI complaint. 3. But later digital forensics proved that the attack happened only when the card was swiped but before it got encrypted and stored. So, that signifies the credit card information was never stored. Thus, the blame game continued getting the card issuer like Master –card etc. into picture for not using EMV chips in the cards. Even, PCI was blamed for unclear guidelines.	$148 million	1. Usage of EMV chips security for credit cards rather than regular magnetic strips. 2. According to the card-issuer companies the retailers were not really complaint if they got breached which means they have not provided proper information to their assessor if they have got breached. So, the retailer should make sure they are providing all the relevant information while auditing.
6	Adobe Systems.	3 Million	Y	Requirement 2 Requirement 3 Requirement 5	Outside hack was made possible by weak password requirements. Adobe was under attack for over 2 weeks. Encrypted payment card information, codes of upcoming software and personal account information were stolen over the period.	1. Breach might have started from September 2013 and it was identified weeks later. This shows the importance of a holistic vulnerability assessment regularly. 2. Weak password requirements made it easy for the hackers. This shows the organization's inability to convey the importance of security to its employees/users. 3. Security assessment and testing carried out were minimal.	No Data Available	1. Perform vulnerability assessment and relevant tests regularly to detect suspicious activity. 2. Enforce password security requirements. Make users aware of the consequences of using easy passwords. 3. Make employees/3rd party users aware of the best practices in security and enforce it.

continued on following page

Table 7. Continued

	BREACH DETAILS				SUMMARY – DATA ANALYSIS		
7	Global Payments A third-party processor of transactions for Visa and MasterCard	1.5 million	Y	Requirement 2 Requirement 8 Requirement 10	Servers hacked	1. Administrative account not protected sufficiently. 2. Network not tracked for a long period of time giving access to hackers to be on the system unnoticed.	$94 million	1. Network scans should be performed every quarter by a qualified scan vendor (QSV). 2. Firewall should be monitored and intrusion detection services should be incorporated as a measure to check the network activity. 3. Regularly provide compliance documentation demonstrating full compliance to Visa and Mastercard and be included in the list of Compliant Service Providers. 4. Use EMV technology coupled with tokenization to ensure a more secure encryption of credit card data.

Figure 2 shows the breached organization and number of CCN records misused in their system.

Figure 3 represents the affected organization along with the number of months they were exposed by the intrusion.

Figure 2. Organization with no. of CCN records breached

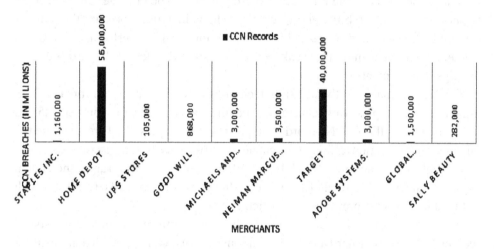

Figure 3. Organizations with the duration of breach occurred

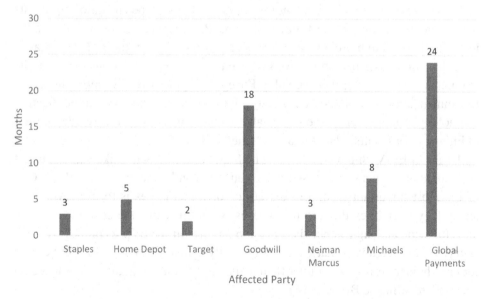

8. OUR CONTRIBUTION

The above analysis is incomplete without being able to draw meaningful value out of it. As a part of our post breach analysis, we have created a framework as shown in Figure 4. The figure consists of major credit card breaches who are PCI DSS compliant numbered from 1 to 7. Following which, the middle set of content refers to weaknesses responsible for each of these breaches. The breaches are connected to one or more vulnerability and vice versa. The vulnerability box has the number of each breach which is connected to it. In addition, we have performed arithmetic calculations to determine the weakness most responsible for credit card breaches amongst the set mentioned here.

For eg: Outdated authentication technology is the reason for breach in 3 organizations- Staples, Target and global Payment as shown by the numbers 1,5 and 7. Out of 1.16 million CCN records compromised at Staples, 0.19 are attributed to outdated authentication technology weakness (1.16 divided by total no. of weaknesses responsible for Staples breach → 1.16/5= 0.19). Similarly, adding Target and Global payment values gives a total of 1.69. This value gives a comparative result of which vulnerability is most prevalent and which is least.

The framework also connects to the third column which consists of recommendations to improve an organizations security. Our approach demonstrates two types of solutions- Existing PCI DSS recommendations and non PCI DSS recommendations segregated by the shape and color of the box. This box color and shape represent PCI DSS recommendation and box shape and color represents our recommendations to the framework (non PCI DSS requirement). The faults in the middle column are connected to recommendations on the right. Similar to the calculation described above, we give values to recommendations based on the number of vulnerabilities they can solve. For eg: - 'Upgrade to EMV chip technology' recommendation is a solution for only one weakness 'Outdated authentication technology' and it receives the same value 1.69 calculated previously. Please refer to Figure 4, for results related to all breaches and

Usage of EMV chip technology - The high profile breaches like staples, target and global payments were caused due to outdated authentication technology. One of the most important recommendation to solve this issues is to use EMV chip technology to fight credit card fraud cases. With this cards the customers do not have to swipe and sign rather than just tap and go. In the chip technology data is encrypted in such a way that it cannot be easily stolen. EMV uses PIN to be used for card-holder verification rather than using card-holder signature (Firstdata.com Smart Card Alliance Brief, 2014).

Figure 4. Framework consisting of breaches, related vulnerabilities and recommendations to overcome weaknesses

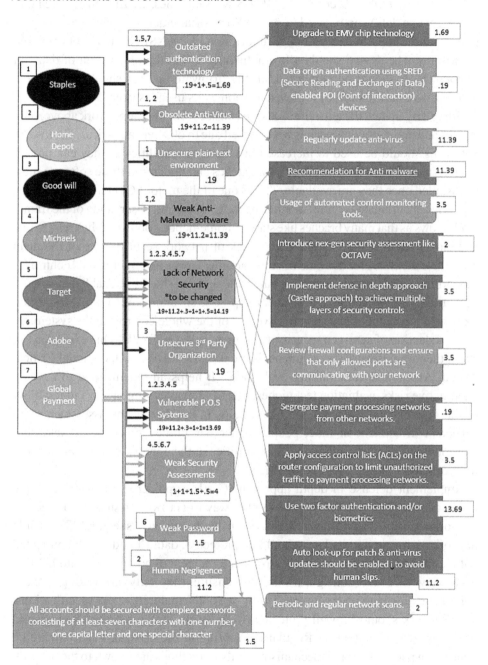

Data origin authentication using SRED (Secure Reading and Exchange of Data) enabled POI – According to PCI SSC guidelines, SRED (Secure reading and exchange data) can be used to secure Point-of interaction devices. Some of its points are the mainly encryption of algorithms like ANSI X9 and ISO approved algorithms. The device should allow authentication at the origination of data, all remote access should be monitored, all the firmware updates should be updated, and sensitive data should be removed as soon as its usage is over.

Regularly update the anti-virus - As we can see from the frame-work above, both staples and home-depot breaches were caused due to obsolete anti-virus. Up-to-date anti-virus should be used to increase the security capabilities as they can protect your systems from a possible infection. Patches and updates in these software must be installed once they are available. This is one of the major PCI DSS requirements.

Usage of automated control monitoring tools - A careful observation of the frame-work shows us that many braches like staples, home-depot, goodwill, Michaels, Target and global payments are caused due to lack of network security. One of the main preventive measures for this kind of vulnerabilities can be using automated control for monitoring tools. Auto look ups for patch and updates should be enabled in system. This ensures the protection against human slips. Use of Automated Control Monitoring tools monitoring the status and effectiveness of the whole controls in the system.

Introduction of next-gen security assessment Like OCTAVE - One of the ways to strengthen weak security assessments is the use of OCTAVE (Operational Critical Threat, Assets and vulnerability evaluation). It helps an organization to develop quantitative risks evaluation techniques, identify the assets and major vulnerability of the organization. Besides, OCTAVE helps in optimizing the assessment with sufficient investment in time, people, and other limited resources. It take into consideration people, technology, and facilities in the context of their relationship to information. (Caralli R.A et al, 2015)

Implement defense in depth approach (Castle approach) to achieve multiple layers of security controls –This is another way to get rid of issues due to lack of network-security. A multi-layered, defense in depth approach is required. The whole network perimeter and its layer should be protected, data should also be protected with proper data access control and strong enforcement of policy. (Hipolito J, 2015)

Review firewall configurations and ensure that only allowed ports are communicating with your network: This is one of the major PCI DSS specifications. The Network should be well-protected by fire-wall configurations which should be reviewed time and again. Regular monitoring of the network traffic should be done using packet-filtering mechanisms. Only ports that's are known to the network should be allowed to enter and other ports should be restricted. Next-gen fire-walls by Palo Alto are one of the most advanced methods to protect organizations from network vulnerabilities.

Segregate payment processing networks from other networks - Un-secure third-party organization was one of the major cause of the breach that happened to Goodwill. So, as a precaution for the future the third party organizations should take necessary steps. They should entirely segregate the payment processing networks from other networks. They should use a totally different server environment with enhanced security measures while dealing with credit card and other confidential information details. The third-party organizations should be insisted to reveal any security related incident even if it may not have led to an actual compromise of data. If the vendor needs remote access, make it segmented in such a way that it does not coincide with rest of the data in the network. Only essential information should be allowed for access.

Apply access control lists (ACLs) on the router configuration to limit unauthorized traffic to payment processing networks - This is one of the way to reduce loss of credit card data through lack of network security. Strict ACLs should be created to segment both front-end and back-end databases. Data leakage prevention and detection tools can be used to help in reducing credit-card breaches through weak network securities. (US-CERT, 2015)

Use two factor authentication and/or biometrics - From the framework, we can examine that five out of the seven breaches were caused due to vulnerable P.O.S systems. Every POS vendor should be requested to incorporate and support it. If they don't use bio-metric finger-printing they can use USB connected scanners. This method also helps the vendor in complying with PCI DSS standards by using of unique passwords by the owners and monitoring of the network regularly. Besides, two-factor authentication is also. Two-factor authentication is another way to protect retail stores from hackers trying to hack their P.O.S systems. Two-factor authentication enables second layer of protection against hackers and cyber-thieves. Hackers can easily decipher passwords but they have to hack the second layer of authentication require to gain accesses.

Periodic and regular network scans: Weak security assessments lead to irregularity in performing network scans. 4 breaches out of the 7 studied in this chapter attribute to weak assessments of security. This is a PCI DSS requirement and recommends regular assessment of an organizations security infrastructure which would lead to periodic scanning being performed judiciously.

All accounts should be secured with complex passwords consisting of at least seven characters with one number, one capital letter and one special character: One of the two reasons Adobe suffered an attack is due to weak password on their systems. This is a PCI DSS recommendation and suggests never to use default system generated passwords and also secure systems with complex seven character password consisting of one number, one capital letter and one special character.

9. CONCLUSION

It is the right time for every organization to realize that the same technology used to compromise their security systems can be used to strengthen it if you know your vulnerabilities. Many a times, it is the negligence from organization's part to ensure proper security which lands them in trouble. We described various aspects of different data breaches and analyzed it from the PCI DSS compliance standpoint. We saw organizations getting breached even after being PCI compliant. With the analysis, we have found that PCI DSS compliance per. se. is not enough for ensuring protection against bad guys. Maintaining compliance, as well as ensuring that specific defense mechanisms are in place as outlined in our framework should be a mandate for an organization.

Attackers are evolving every day and the number of attacks on organizations are also on the rise. Without a holistic and unbaiting approach to security, an organization is invariably susceptible to these vicious attempts. While PCI DSS compliance entails the security measures to be adopted for basic protection of card-holder data, it is the responsibility of each organization to go beyond the call of duty and ensure maximum protection.

REFERENCES

Adams, R. (2010). Prevent, protect, pursue–a paradigm for preventing fraud. *Computer Fraud & Security, 2010*(7), 5-11. Retrieved online on 23rd January 2015 from http://www.sciencedirect.com.gate.lib.buffalo.edu/science/article/pii/S1361372310700804#

André Marïen. (2011). PCI DSS appears to reduce breaches. *Computer Fraud & Security, 5*. Retrieved online on 23rd January 2015 from http://www.sciencedirect.com.gate.lib.buffalo.edu/science/article/pii/S1361372311700471

Ataya, G. (2010). PCI DSS audit and compliance. *Information Security Technical Report, 15*(4), 138-144. Retrieved Online on January 22, 2015 from http://www.sciencedirect.com/science/article/pii/S136341271100015X

Bluemner, A. (2014) *The $5.4M Question: Can POS Systems Prevent Credit Card Fraud?* Retrieved online on 10th October January 2015 from http://findaccountingsoftware.com/expert-advice/the-54m-question-can-pos-systems-prevent-credit-card-fraud/

Caralli, R. A., Stevens, J. F., Young, L. R., & Wilson, W. R. (2007). *Introducing octave allegro: Improving the information security risk assessment process* (No. CMU/SEI-2007-TR-012). Carnegie-Mellon Univ. Retrieved on 23rd January 2015 from http://resources.sei.cmu.edu/asset_files/TechnicalReport/2007_005_001_14885.pdf

Caulkett, A., Rakshit, S., Lloyd, C., & Baxendale, C. (2012). *U.S. Patent Application 13/645,805*. Retrieved online on 23rd January 2015 from http://www.google.com/patents/US20130091061

Coburn, A. (2010). Fitting PCI DSS within a wider governance framework. *Computer Fraud & Security, 2010*(9), 11-13. Retrieved Online on January 22, 2015 from http://www.sciencedirect.com/science/article/pii/S1361372310701214

Culnan, M. J., & Williams, C. C. (2009). How ethics can enhance organizational privacy: Lessons from the choicepoint and TJX data breaches. *Management Information Systems Quarterly*, 673–687.

Digital Guardian. (2014). *An Expert Guide to Securing Sensitive Data: 34 Experts Reveal the Biggest Mistakes Companies Make with Data Security.* Retrieved on 10th November 2014 from https://digitalguardian.com/blog/expert-guide-securing-sensitive-data-34-experts-reveal-biggest-mistakes-companies-make-data

Firstdata.com. (2014). *Smart Card Alliance Brief.* Retrieved from http://www.firstdata.com/smarticles/fi/home/preventing-data-breaches.html

Garfield, S. (n.d.). *Point-of-Sale Malware: Why Today's Top Retailers Are Vulnerable to Attacks.* Retrieved Online on January 22, 2015 from http://tuftsdev.github.io/DefenseOfTheDarkArts/students_works/final_project/fall2014/sgarfield.pdf

Gorge, M. (2006). The PCI standard and its implications for the security industry. *Computer Fraud & Security, 2006*(2), 6-9. Retrieved Online on January 22, 2015 from http://www.sciencedirect.com/science/article/pii/S1361372306703074

Gorge, M. (2008). Data protection: why are organisations still missing the point? *Computer Fraud & Security, 2008*(6), 5-8. Retrieved online on 23rd January 2015 from http://www.sciencedirect.com.gate.lib.buffalo.edu/science/article/pii/S1361372308700952

Harran, M., & McKelvey, N. (2012). PCI Compliance–No excuses, please. *Proceedings from International Journal of Information and Network Security (IJINS), 2*(2), 118-123. Retrieved online on 23rd January 2015 from http://iaesjournal.com/online/index.php/IJINS/article/view/1940

Hizver, J., & Chiueh, T. (2011). Automated Discovery of Credit Card Data Flow for PCI DSS Compliance. *Proceedings of 30th IEEE International Symposium on Reliable Distributed Systems.* Retrieved online on 23rd January 2015 from http://www.inf.ufpr.br/aldri/disc/TSD/2012/2012_TSD_Apre_Artigos/Gustavo_02_SRDS11_Automated.pdf

Hosack, B. (2011). Businesses still unaware of risks of account data compromise. *Computer Fraud & Security, 2011*(1), 17-19. Retrieved online on 23rd January 2015 from http://www.sciencedirect.com/science/article/pii/S1361372311700070

Kallas, C. S., Pravasi, N. I., Sievel, M. E., & Tokarski, J. P. (2009). *U.S. Patent Application 12/648,525.* Retrieved online on 23rd January 2015 from https://www.google.com/patents/US20110161231

Kassner, M. (2014). *Breach Detection Systems take aim at targeted persistent attacks.* Retrieved on 10th November 2014 from http://www.techrepublic.com/blog/it-security/breach-detection-systems-take-aim-at-targeted-persistent-attacks/

Kidd, R. (2008). Counting the cost of non-compliance with PCI DSS. *Computer Fraud & Security, 2008*(11), 13-14. Retrieved online on 23rd January 2015 from http://www.sciencedirect.com.gate.lib.buffalo.edu/science/article/pii/S1361372308701635

Krebs, B. (2012). *Global Payments Breach Window Expands.* Retrieved on 10th November 2014 from http://krebsonsecurity.com/tag/global-payments-breach/

Krebs, B. (2014a). *Home Depot Hit By Same Malware as Target.* Retrieved on 10th November 2014 from http://krebsonsecurity.com/tag/home-depot-breach/

Krebs, B. (2014b). *3 Million Customer Credit, Debit Cards Stolen in Michaels, Aaron Brothers Breaches.* Retrieved on 10th November 2014 from http://krebsonsecurity.com/2014/04/3-million-customer-credit-debit-cards-stolen-in-michaels-aaron-brothers-breaches/

Krebs, B. (2014c). *Breach at Goodwill Vendor Lasted 18 Months.* Retrieved online 10th October January from http://krebsonsecurity.com/2014/09/breach-at-goodwill-vendor-lasted-18-months/

Krebs on Security. (2014). *The Target Breach, By the Numbers.* Retrieved online on 10th November from http://krebsonsecurity.com/2014/05/the-target-breach-by-the-numbers/#more-25847

Krebsonsecurity.com. (2014). *Staples: 6-Month Breach, 1.16 Million Cards*. Retrieved online on 22nd January from http://krebsonsecurity.com/2014/12/staples-6-month-breach-1-16-million-cards-

Lovrić, Z. (2012). *Model of Simplified Implementation of PCI DSS by Using ISO 27001 Standard*. Retrieved online on 23rd January 2015 from http://www.ceciis.foi.hr/app/public/conferences/1/papers2012/iss8.pdf

MacCarthy, M. (2011). Information security policy in the US retail payments industry. *Stan. Tech. L. Rev., 2011*, 3-12. Retrieved online on 23rd January 2015 from http://www18.georgetown.edu/data/people/maccartm/publication-66522.pdf

Miller, H. S., Fleet, M. R., Celenza, B. J., & Shust, D. (2012). *U.S. Patent Application 13/417,883*. Retrieved online on 23rd January 2015 from http://www.google.com/patents/US20110161231

Morse, E. A., & Raval, V. (2008). PCI DSS: Payment card industry data security standards in context. *Computer Law & Security Review, 24*(6), 540-554. Retrieved Online on January 22, 2015 from http://www.sciencedirect.com/science/article/pii/S0267364908000976

Nicho, M., Fakhry, H., & Haiber, C. (2011). An Integrated Security Governance Framework for Effective PCI DSS Implementation. *International Journal of Information Security and Privacy (IJISP), 5*(3), 50-67. Retrieved online on 23rd January 2015 from http://www.igi-global.com/article/integrated-security-governance-framework-effective/58982

Nicho, M., & MBA, M. (2011). *Effectiveness of the PCI DSS 2.0 on Preventing Security Breaches: A Holistic perspective*. Retrieved online on 23rd January from http://www.sc2labs.com/public/uploaded/Effectiveness-of-PCI-DSS.pdf

Olajide, P., Zavarsky, P., Ruhl, R., & Lindskog, D. (n.d.). *PCI DSS Compliance Validation of Different Levels of Merchants in a Multi-tenant Private Cloud*. Retrieved online on 23rd January 2015 from http://infosec.concordia.ab.ca/files/2013/02/OlajideP.pdf

Owen, M., & Dixon, C. (2007). A new baseline for cardholder security. *Network Security, 6*. Retrieved online on 23rd January 2015 from http://www.sciencedirect.com.gate.lib.buffalo.edu/science/article/pii/S1353485807700545

PCI DSS Compliance Blog. (2013). *SRED Requirements for Point-of-Interaction Devices*. Retrieved Online on January 23rd 2015 fromhttp://blog.elementps.com/element_payment_solutions/2013/01/sred-requirements-for-point-of-interaction-devices.html

PCI Security Standards Council, LLC. (n.d.a). Retrieved on 10th November 2014 from https://www.pcisecuritystandards.org/documents/PCI_DSS_v3.pdf

PCI Security Standards Council, LLC. (n.d.b). Retrieved on 10th November 2014 from https://www.pcisecuritystandards.org/documents/pci_dss_v2_summary_of_changes.pdf

PCI-SSC. (2014). *Security Standards Council, LLC*. Retrieved on 10th October 2014 from https://www.pcisecuritystandards.org/organization_info/index.php

Peretti, K. K. (2008). Data breaches: what the underground world of carding reveals. *Santa Clara Computer & High Tech. LJ, 25*, 375. Retrieved online on 23rd January 2015 from http://digitalcommons.law.scu.edu/cgi/viewcontent.cgi?article=1472&context=chtlj&sei-redir=1&referer=http%3A%2F%2Fscholar.google.com%2Fscholar%3Fq%3Dpoint%2Bof%2Bsale%2Bdata%2Bbreach%2Bpci%2Bdss%26btnG%3D%26hl%3Den%26as_sdt%3D0%252C33%26authuser%3D1#search=%22point%20sale%20data%20breach%20pci%20dss%22

Peterson, G. (2010). From auditor-centric to architecture-centric: SDLC for PCI DSS. *Information Security Technical Report, 15*(4), 150-153. Retrieved online on 23rd January 2015 from http://www.sciencedirect.com/science/article/pii/S1363412711000148

Ponemon. (2011). *2011 PCI DSS Compliance Trends Study, Survey of IT & IT security practitioners in the U.S.* Retrieved on 10th October 2014 from http://www.imperva.com/docs/AP_Ponemon_2011_PCI_DSS_Compliance_Trends_Study.pdf

Privacy Rights Clearing House. (2014). *Chronology of Data Breaches*. Retrieved on 10th November 2014 from https://www.privacyrights.org/data-breach/new

Privacy Rights Clearinghouse. (n.d.). Retrieved on January 22, 2015 from https://www.privacyrights.org/

Rees, J. (2010). The challenges of PCI DSS compliance. *Computer Fraud & Security, 2010*(12), 14-16. Retrieved online on 23rd January 2015 from http://www.sciencedirect.com/science/article/pii/S1361372310701561

Rowlingson, R., & Winsborrow, R. (2006). A comparison of the Payment Card Industry data security standard with ISO17799. *Computer Fraud & Security, 2006*(3), 16-19. Retrieved online January 22, 2015 from http://www.sciencedirect.com/science/article/pii/S1361372306703232

Schwartz, M. J. (2014). *Michaels Data Breach Response: 7 Facts.* Retrieved on 10th November 2014 from http://www.darkreading.com/attacks-breaches/michaels-data-breach-response-7-facts/d/d-id/1204630

Shaw, A. (2009). Data breach: from notification to prevention using PCI DSS. *Column. JL & Soc. Probs., 43,* 517. Retrieved Online on January 22, 2015 from http://www.columbia.edu/cu/jlsp/pdf/Summer%202010/Shaw.JLSP.43.4.pdf

Sullivan, R. (2010, May). The Changing Nature of US Card Payment Fraud: Issues for Industry and Public Policy. In *WEIS.* Retrieved Online on January 22, 2015 from http://weis2010.econinfosec.org/papers/panel/weis2010_sullivan.pdf

Susanto, H., Almunawar, M. N., & Tuan, Y. C. (2011). *Information security management system standards: A comparative study of the big five.* Academic Press.

Sussman, B. (2008). Mastering the Payment Card Industry Standard: Private Framework Seeks to Shield Credit and Debit Card Account Information. *Journal of Accountancy, 205*(1), 50. Retrieved online on 23rd January 2015 from https://www.questia.com/read/1G1-173922998/mastering-the-payment-card-industry-standard-private

Tobias, S. (2014). *2014: The Year in Cyberattacks.* Retrieved on 10th January 2015 from http://www.newsweek.com/2014-year-cyber-attacks-295876

Trendmicro.com. (n.d.). *Anatomy of a Data Breach by Hipolito. J.* Retrieved on February 15th 2015 from http://www.trendmicro.com/vinfo/us/threat-encyclopedia/web-attack/110/anatomy-of-a-data-breach

Tutton, J. (2010). Incident response and compliance: A case study of the recent attacks. *Information Security Technical Report, 15*(4), 145-149. Retrieved online on 23rd January 2015 from http://www.sciencedirect.com/science/article/pii/S1363412711000124

United States Computer Emergency Readiness Team Alert (TA14-212A), Backoff Point-of-Sale Malware. (2014). Retrieved on February 15th 2015 from https://www.us-cert.gov/ncas/alerts/TA14-212A

Verizon. (2013). *Verizon Data Breach Investigations Report.* Retrieved on 10th October 2014 from http://www.verizonenterprise.com/resources/reports/rp_data-breach-investigations-report-2013_en_xg.pdf

Verizon Communication. (2014). Retrieved on November 4, 2014 from http://www.verizonenterprise.com/pcireport/2014/

VISA Inc. (n.d.a). Retrieved online 10th January 2015 from http://usa.visa.com/merchants/protect-your-business/cisp/service-providers.jsp

VISA Inc. (n.d.b). Retrieved on 10th January 2015 from http://usa.visa.com/merchants/protect-your-business/cisp/merchant-pci-dss-compliance.jsp

Wikipedia: The Free Encyclopedia. (2014, December 19). Retrieved on November 4, 2014, from http://www.wikipedia.org

Section 3
Human and Social Risks

Chapter 6

Fortifying Corporate Human Wall:
A Literature Review of Security Awareness and Training

Anandharaman Pattabiraman
University at Buffalo, USA

Kaushik Swaminathan
University at Buffalo, USA

Sridhar Srinivasan
University at Buffalo, USA

Manish Gupta
University at Buffalo, USA

ABSTRACT

It has been very evident from data breaches from last few years that attackers are increasingly targeting the path of least resistance to compromise the security of organizations. Cyber security threats that exploit human behavior are becoming sophisticated and difficult to prevent against. At the same time humans are the countermeasures that can adapt swiftly to changing risk landscape than technological and procedural countermeasures. Organizations are implementing and enhancing their security awareness and training programs in an attempt to ensure that risks from human elements, which pose the greatest risks, are mitigated. The chapter conducts a thorough literature review in the area of security awareness and training and presents a classification scheme and a conceptual research model to provide insights into the existing body of knowledge in the area. Trends and analyses are also presented from the reviewed papers, which can be of importance to organizations in improving their security awareness programs. The insights from the study can be leveraged to build a strong human wall against both internal and external threats that are fast evolving and causing tremendous amount of loss.

DOI: 10.4018/978-1-5225-2604-9.ch006

1. INTRODUCTION

Information is the fundamental asset of an organization and hence it is vital to protect the information. Though we have spent heavily on tools such as antivirus software, firewalls, intrusion detection and prevention systems to protect the information security, the threats aren't completely eradicated due to the gaps in the implementation of security tools and due to the reason that not all threats to security are known to the user community. We try to address the same through efficient security training which creates another level of defence for an organization in overcoming the security threats. Most of the times, employees follow organizational policies to ensure compliance however certain gaps are found which compromises the information. Few examples include ignoring the antivirus alerts, leaking out sensitive information through phone, writing passwords in desk, downloading a malicious file, etc. As the deliberate threats to information are prevalent, we deal with necessity of enforcing a strong security program which will help users in understanding the security policies of an organization and to empower the users to protect themselves and the organization from any security issues.

This paper documents the essential business case for investing in a cost-effective security awareness training program. Through proper trainings to user group, we seek to establish a proper culture which complies with the information security policies and goes a long way in helping reduce risks and cut costs for an organization. The training methods could include publishing awareness through emails, newsfeeds, blogs and also through refresher courses and by conducting regular auditing. To analyse the existing security awareness programs in the market, we performed intensive research of several related papers, the details of which have been specified below. These papers help to provide details of the current security training programs in place, the identified security gaps and how theories are framed to ensure that the information security needs of an organization are met.

The contributions of the chapter are many-fold. First it provides a comprehensive view of literature in the area of security awareness and training from last few years. Second, the filtering and classification process provides insight into the trends and emphasis of recent research which has been in response to growing needs for a robust and effective information security awareness program. Given the increasing trend of human link being the weakest and most exploited links, organizations are increasingly adapting their programs to the shifting risk landscape. The chapter shows the pattern of research to indicate the areas in security awareness that have gained importance in recent years. The chapter is organized in 5 sections. Second section provides an overview of security awareness and training, third section provides details in the research methodology used in the chapter, fourth chapter presents the results and findings of the research study and the last section concludes the chapter with suggestions for future work.

2. BACKGROUND

It has been consistently shown through numerous surveys and studies that most of the data breaches happen due to insiders' oversight or mistakes. It is usually the non-malicious and uninformed employees that lead to the breaches. The number of layers of technological defense can be as strong as possible but the people working and supporting these technologies are always vulnerable. Users with little security awareness are the biggest risks to the organization. Breaches after breaches has shown us that only a minor slip up is enough to put the whole security program for any company at huge exposure. Technology alone cannot provide protection against information security and privacy risks and people are the most important line of defense who are responsible for ensuring that risks are managed in accordance with specific risk appetite and tolerance for the company (Tipton and Krause, 2007; IT Governance Institute, 2008). Focusing only on technical countermeasures is not enough for mitigating information security risks (Mitnick and Simon, 2003). Employees of the company need to be trained and educated on security best practices, policies, compliance requirements, implemented controls, expectations for risk mitigation as part of a security awareness program (Ashenden, 2008; Williams, 2008).

A robust awareness program is essential in ensuring that people understand their security responsibilities, organizational policies, and how to detect and respond to potential security incidents. The goal of an effective security awareness program should be to help the users move from ''become aware'' to ''stay aware'' of potential security threats (Schlienger and Teufel, 2003). It is intuitive as well as shown in a recent study that any security awareness program needs to be relevant, timely, and consistent of security information because information risk profiles keep shifting and evolving (Kruger and Kearney, 2006). There has been an extensive body of literature in the field of security awareness and training in last few years, emphasizing the important part that an effective security awareness program plays in overall security of any organization. The studies have focused on different aspects of the security awareness including delivery methods, evaluating effectiveness, compliance, behavior change, gamification and others. These studies have also dealt with many challenges that companies face when trying to realize the true efficacy of security awareness program. One of the challenges is finding appropriate delivery methods for an organization because one-size-fits-all approach doesn't effectively work due to specific organizational factors (Valentine, 2006). There are many levels to be achieved when outcomes of security awareness programs are to be assessed. The chapter shows how researchers have focused on one specific area of security awareness and training. For example, Shaw et al (2009) show that one of the critical success factors for a security awareness programme is the delivery methods. Cybersecurity threats that exploit soft factors in an organization such humans and social networks are constantly evolving. However, unlike technologies humans can quickly adapt to changes in environment and provide much needed detection and response capabilities. As we will see in the coverage of the chapter, appropriate security awareness program can become a strong control to provide adequate protection needed in today's fast evolving threat landscape (Kumaraguru et al., 2007; Eminagaoglu et al., 2010; Wijnand et al., 2006)).

3. RESEARCH METHODOLOGY

Literature review is a proven research method to survey and synthesize prior literature to conceptualize the area of study (Webster and Watson, 2002). University of Wisconsin writing centre defines literature review as *"critical analysis of a segment of a published body of knowledge through summary, classification, and comparison of prior research studies, reviews of literature, and theoretical articles"* (Wisconsin writing centre, 2016). While, it directly adds to the extant literature and it has been found to hamper the progress when it is lacking (Webster and Watson, 2002). Scholars have adopted one of the four techniques for conducting literature review research - *Narrative Review, Descriptive Review, Vote Counting, and Meta-Analysis*. All of these four have different emphasis on qualitative versus quantitative methods (King and He, 2005). We follow the traditional way of conducting literature review for our study – *Descriptive review*.

Descriptive review entails qualitative analysis of extant literature to reveal an underlying pattern and trend in the studies (Guzzo et al., 1987). *Descriptive review* also is sometimes based on quantification such as frequency analysis, publication times, outcomes etc (Guzzo et al., 1987). We have used quantitative analysis also in our study at a very high level to using frequency analysis as well as publication times, as will present in section 4. Using basic principles of *Descriptive review*, we followed a systematic procedure to search, filter and classify the extant literature on security awareness and training for last 7-8 years. We conducted a comprehensive literature to collect as many relevant papers as possible in the area of security awareness and training. We used *scholar.google.com* and also a university's online academic source. We then read, analysed and coded each study one data record. Using relevant and reputable online database for searching quality academic literature has become one of the most widely used, if not the only one, process for literature survey (Petter and McLean, 2009; Sabherwal et al., 2006). Therefore, for a literature review on cloud computing, it is appropriate and practical to focus on online databases rather than library collections. The university's database that we used has subscription to most of the academic databases such as IEEE, ACM, AIS, ABI/INFORM, etc. After we completed the coding of all papers, we identified trends and patterns among the papers (King and He, 2005). The outcome is representative literature review study of the current state of security awareness and training. We also categorized the studies in specific categories based on commonality in the end objectives of the research papers. We used "Google Scholar" to search on the topic "Security Awareness Training" for time period 2012-2016 and selected 115 related papers that are found at university's online database. We then followed a staged filtered process to exclude the articles that did not directly pertain to our area of focus of security awareness and training or did not have enough adequate academic references and insights. This done through reading both the abstract and full text. At the end after 2 rounds of scanning and exclusion, we scoped a final list of 60 papers, that had a clear focus on security awareness and training, to review and analyse further.

4. RESULTS AND DISCUSSION

We follow an established method of literature review on security awareness and training to portray a landscape of current literature and provide a snapshot to aid future development. University of Wisconsin writing centre defines literature review as *"critical analysis of a segment of a published body of knowledge through summary, classification, and comparison of prior research studies, reviews of literature, and theoretical articles"* (Wisconsin writing centre, 2016). Our segment of published body of knowledge is security awareness and training. We then developed a literature classification scheme to systematically reveal and examine academic insights on security awareness and training., a literature classification scheme was developed. This classification was based on categorising the research focus of the 60 articles which we scoped-in for further review after the filtering processes.

We deployed the traditional and widely used 'bottom-up' approach as informed by grounded theory (Glaser and Strauss, 1967) to identify the categories used for this literature review. Such an approach has also been widely supported as a rigorous method for reviewing literature (Wolfswinkel et al., 2011). Specific categories and subcategories were assigned to each paper and then consolidated into top categories as described below. The first step was an initial reading of the 60 papers. In the initial coding stages, we assigned keywords for each paper that represent the theme, approach and objectives of each paper (Strauss and Corbin, 1997). This was around after careful reading of full text of the papers. There were around 40-50 unique keywords identified. In the next step, we organized 60 papers in 8 sub-categories which were further consolidated into 2 top-level categories. We also iteratively reviewed and revised these categorizations to make sure that the classification scheme is not only parsimonious but also represented the diversity of the initial analysis.

The categories in the classification scheme were also validated by the keywords that we assigned to each paper during initial coding (Barki et al., 1993). Consequently, a classification framework, as shown in Figure 1, was created. Table 1 also shows count of papers in each sub-category. For example, "gamification" that shows as one sub-category in Figure 1 under the high level category of "User Training" has 6 papers that were assigned to that category. At the end, the scoped 60 papers were full-text reviewed and eventually classified into 2 high-level categories – Behavioral

Figure 1. Classification scheme

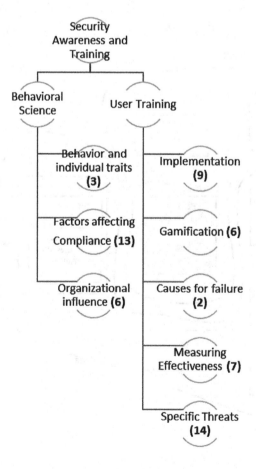

Science and User Training; and eight subcategories - Behavior and individual traits, Factors affecting, Compliance, Organizational influence, Implementation, Gamification, Causes for failure, Measuring Effectiveness and Specific Threats.

We assigned each paper to only one subcategory, to present a conceptual and structured classification of the major categories and subcategories within current cloud computing research and conceptualise the relationships between these categories. Appendix A lists all these categories and the associated references for each of them. All 60 papers are mapped to each of the category. Figure 2 shows the conceptual model of our research and analysis. It shows the dependencies and connections between different categories and how they interact for overall security awareness and training program for any company. Figure 2 summarizes the interaction between different categories and concepts related to security awareness and training.Figure 3 shows year-wise distribution of 60 papers that were reviewed and analysed as part of this study. We also did some basic content analysis by looking at the titles of the papers to \understand the trend and thematic direction for this research. Historically

Figure 2. Conceptual research model

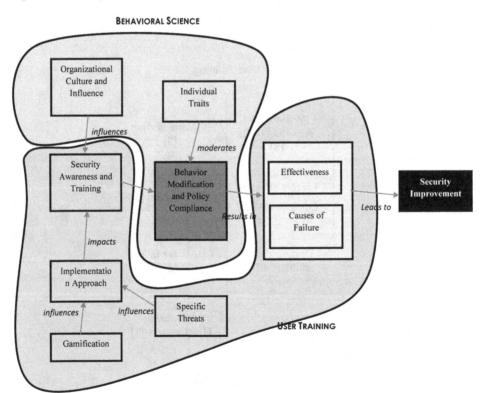

Figure 3. Year-wise distribution of papers

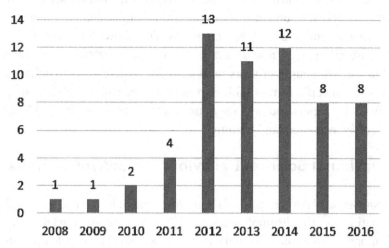

also researchers have regarded content analysis as a flexible method for analyzing text data (Cavanagh, 1997). The specific type of content analysis approach is usually based on the problem being studied.

We have shown the conceptual model in Figure 2 and provide additional insights by including titles of the papers in the frequency analysis. This is consistent with prior research and study to align the approach based on the problem being studied (Weber, 1990). Figure 4 represents keyword frequency analysis of terms that were part of the title of the papers. It reflects the emphasis of these research papers with

Figure 4. Frequency analysis

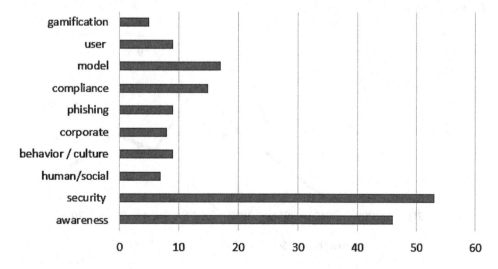

more specific areas in security awareness such as gamification showing a lower count as they also form into a sub-category in the overall classification scheme. Figure 5 shows the yearly trend of 2 top level categories. This shows how "behavior science, which consistently gained researchers' attention from 2010-2013 seems to have settled down in last couple of years with more innovative ways to deliver training and addressing specific threats taking front seat. The following sections presents insights from the papers and how they contribute to the body of knowledge in the area of securtiy awareness and training.

4.1. Behavioural Science: Behaviour and individual Traits

Information Security Awareness deals with the extent of how employees understand the information security, its implications and how they are expected to adhere to the policy. Human behavior has vital influence on individuals' attitude towards policy adherence. Individual traits such as conscientiousness, emotional stability, risk-taking propensity (McCormac et al., 2016), awareness of social engineering attacks, Attitude towards compliance, maturity and age (Wipawayangkool et al. 2015) etc., have a tremendous impact on how individuals perceive information security and their willingness to comply with organizational policies pertaining to information security. Nearly half of the information security violations are perpetuated by the insiders who belong to the organization (Crossler, et al., 2013). Therefore, it is essential to understand the difference between deviant behaviour and misbehaviour, motivation and behaviour of an attacker, cross-cultural influence and fear as a motivator of compliance in order to formulate the right information security awareness strategy.

Figure 5. Yearly trend of research

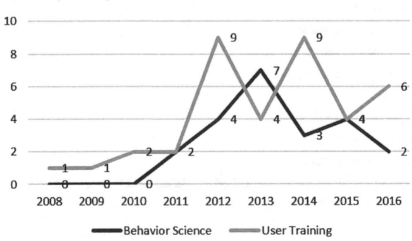

McMormac et al. (2016) try to study how individuals' Information Security Awareness (ISA) and individual difference parameters, such as age, gender, personality and risk-taking propensity are related. KAB (Knowledge, Attitude, Behavior) model is validated and Human Aspects of Information Security Questionnaire (HAIS-Q) is used for assessing the ISA. The ISA deals with the extent of how employees understand the information security, its implications and how they are expected to adhere to the policy. The HAIS-Q consists of seven focus areas namely Internet use, Email use, Social media use, Password management, Incident reporting, Information handling, Mobile computing. Each focus area has its own statements of Knowledge, Behavior and Attitude. Based on the results, it was found that conscientiousness, agreeableness, emotional stability and risk-taking propensity significantly explained variance in individuals' ISA. The findings have important implications for organizations as they can assist in the identification of InfoSec strengths and weaknesses, and can facilitate the development of tailored InfoSec training for employees. Nearly half of security violations happen due to organizational insiders. Crossler et al. (2013) focus on behavioral InfoSec research that focuses on behaviors of individuals in protecting information assets and deals with themes for future research on this topic. The results show that that fear is a powerful motivator for ensuring compliance and that collectivism better than individualism when it comes to conducting research.

Wipawayangkool, et al. (2015) conducted a survey based research, focusing on the millennials. This study explores millennials' malware awareness and intention to comply with information security policy. The main findings of the study showed that millennials' are more likely to comply with security policies as they get older and have positive attitude towards information security and that while knowledge of relatively technical types of malware such as viruses, worms, and Trojans does not lead to the millennials' intention to comply, the awareness of social engineering attacks such as phishing and spamming does.

4.2. Behavioral Science: Factors affecting Compliance

Ensuring compliance is a challenging task for any organization as humans are known for their propensity to not to adhere with regulations and are perceived as the weakest link in an organization's information security architecture. For an awareness strategy to be successful, it is important that the individuals adhere to and comply with the security policies and procedures. Behavioral science provides a fascinating insight on various factors that can influence adherence and, therefore, can help organizations employ better tactics to encourage compliance. Various behavior theories such as Protection Motivation Theory and Theory of Planned Behavior (Safa, et al., 2015), Theory of Reasoned Action (Gundu and Flowerday, 2013) etc., can be used to postulate on how various attributes such as self-efficacy, attitude, knowledge of threats etc., impact compliance. In addition, effective socialization, fear of negative impact, and motivation using rewards can help better in understanding the knowing-doing gap. (Cox, J, 2012) (Ifinedo, P, 2014) (Son, J.Y, 2011)

Williams and Akanmu (2013) demonstrate that there are positive relationships between threats and awareness training, vulnerabilities within system, perceived threat severity and compliance. This study (Williams and Akanmu, 2013) establishes that: community training, vulnerability to threats, perceived threat severity, and compliance to security policies is positively related to *information security threat.*

Safa et al. (2015) employed Structural Equation Modeling to demonstrate the influence held on users' behavior by the following factors: awareness, organization policy, experience and involvement, attitude, subjective norms, self-efficacy and threat appraisal. They have based their research on Protection Motivation Theory and Theory of Planned Behavior. The authors (Gundu and Flowerday, 2013) present an information security awareness process that seeks to cultivate positive security behavior using a behavioral intention model based on the Theory of Reasoned Action, the Protection Motivation Theory and the Behaviorism Theory. The authors show that implementation of an information security policy does not necessarily mean that employees understand their roles and comply to the policy and protect the information assets. The results showed that an increase in knowledge made a positive change in attitude and behavior.

The paper by Parsons et al. (2014) states that many vulnerabilities could be attributed to the behavior of users and explains the concept of HAIS-Q (Human Aspect Information Security Questionnaire) to quantify the human based information security vulnerabilities. The study proves that better knowledge of policy and procedures is associated with better attitude towards policy and procedures and that self-reported behaviour is more risk averse.

Cox (2012) explains the purpose of examining the information assurance understanding and security awareness by developing a structured framework of knowing-doing gap (IS users not following the corporate security policies even though they are aware of them). The structured model is built on the theory of planned behavior which states that "an individual who intends to commit a behavior, tend to commit it". The study shows that the following show more positive attitude towards observing security precautions: 1) users who perceive a higher vulnerability or higher severity to the threat to their information systems 2) users with a more positive attitude towards following security precautions and 3) users who perceive having greater perceived behavioral control, amongst others.

Ifinedo (2014) investigates socio-organisational factors that affect individuals' attitudes towards ISSP compliance and subjective norms, which in turn affect ISSP compliance behavioural intentions. The study shows that Attachment, Commitment,

Involvement and Personal norms will have a positive effect on attitude towards ISSP compliance.

Another paper (Son, 2011) explains two motivation models of human behavior - Extrinsic (fear: owing to punishments/rewards) and Intrinsic (desire: innate desire to follow the rules). The study confirms that 1) deterrent certainty is positively associated with employees' compliance with ISSP (IS security policy), 2) deterrent severity is positively associated with employees 'compliance with ISSP, 3) perceived legitimacy is positively associated with employees' compliance with ISSP and 4) perceived value congruence is positively associated with employees' compliance with ISSP

Cheng et al (2013) develop a model based on both social bond and deterrence theories to understand the factors that determine why an employee violates or deviates from an organization's Information Systems Security Policy (ISSP). Hypotheses for the study try to prove how formal (regularized rules and corresponding sanctions established by the organization) and informal (social morality and behavior) controls impact the intention to violate the IS security policy. The study (Cheng et al. (2013)) proves that both formal and informal controls have a significant effect on the ISSP violation intentions. The results of the study emphasize on the importance of deterrence, social bond and social pressure factors to prevent ISSP violation behaviors.

In a research paper by Safa et al. (2016), the authors study how knowledge sharing, collaboration, intervention, experience, attachment, commitment and personal norms affect the employee's attitude towards compliance with organizational security policies. In the course, the authors employ elements from social Bond theory and involvement theory. Vance and Siponen (2012) try to address the gap found in the research of employee violations of security policies in an organization. Rational Choice Theory, which incorporates "individuals' decisions to break rules as being utilitarian calculations based on perceived benefits, moral beliefs, formal and informal sanctions", is applied for addressing the same. The paper shows that formal sanctions (Explicit penalties), informal sanctions - Unstated social penalties (non-legal costs) and moral beliefs - Eliminates formal sanctions if they are strong negatively affect intention to violate IS security policy while perceived benefits positively affect intention to violate IS security policy.

Ifinedo (2012) conducts a research conducted to understand how two theories- Protection Motivation Theory (PMT) and Theory of Planned Behavior(TBP)- affect Information Security policy compliance. The research concluded that however strong the security measures are in an organization; it would be effective only if there is an active compliance of the security policy. The findings proved that the Information security policy compliance is positively influenced by factors such as self-efficacy, response efficacy, attitude toward compliance, perceived vulnerability, and subjective norms. Vance et al. (2012) examine the influence of habit [a routinized form of past behavior] on the employee intent to comply with security policies. The authors coupled habit with Protection Motivation Theory [PMT] to design an empirical test that demonstrated that habitual IS security compliance strongly reinforced the cognitive processes theorized by PMT as well as employee intention for future compliance. Then they conclude that addressing employees past and automatic behavior will significantly improve their compliance with security policies.

Chen et al (2012) draw from compliance theory and general deterrence theory to propose a research model in which the relations among coercive control, remuneration control and certainty of control are studied. Then a web based field experiment was used to empirically test the model. This paper addresses the effect of the following on employee compliance - punitive measures, reward mechanisms and certainty of control.

4.3. Behavioral Science: Organizational Influence

Organizations have many tactics and strategies at their disposal to ensure security policy compliance. For instance, the intent of the management in enforcing compliance (Hu. et al., 2012), framing the right deterrence policies and communication focussed on mitigating the effect of neutralization (Barlow et al., 2013), shaping the right perception on the inherent vulnerability and severity of threats (Siponen et al., 2014), Building a positive and inclusive security culture (Da Veiga, and Martin, 2015) (Flores and Ekstedt, 2016), etc., will have an immediate and serious impact on individual's intent to comply with organizational policies. These macroscopic measures, coupled with complacent individual behavior, may ensure the optimal level of compliance in an organization. A recent study (Barlow et al, 2013) investigates if security policy focussed on mitigating neutralization can reduce intentions to violation of security policy, is more effective than a security policy focused on deterrent sanctions. The research concludes that there is a need for proper design of security training and awareness programs. While both deterrence and neutralization affect employees' intentions to violate IT security policies, these intentions can be reduced by proper training that gives focus to addressing neutralization techniques rather than the traditional view of only focusing on deterrence and awareness.

Information security is at threat when the employees do not comply with the information security policies. Siponen (2014) develop a multi-theory mode that combines Protection Motivation Theory, the Theory of Reasoned Action, and the Cognitive Evaluation Theory 1 and explains employees' adherence to the security policies. The results showed that an employee's perceived severity, vulnerability, self-efficacy, normative beliefs, and attitude had a positive and significant impact on the employee's intention to comply with information security policies and procedures. The employee's intention to comply with security policies also had a significant impact on his or her actual compliance with these policies. An employee's response efficacy and rewards provided for complying with security policies, on the other hand, did not have a significant impact on his or her complying with these policies.

Awareness and training programs form a critical facet in influencing the information security culture. Da Veiga and Martins (2015) did a case study on a financial institution with global operations. In this institution, ISCA was conducted at 4 intervals over a period of eight years and the results showed that the information security culture improved from one assessment to another. The results also show that a focused awareness and training programs have a significant influence in instilling a stronger information security culture. In a recent research, authors Mejias and Balthazard (2014) explain about, how the evolvement of emerging technologies, causes organization vulnerable to cyber-attacks. Also explains how the technical knowledge, organizational impact and attacker assessment contribute to an understanding of IT attacks and their association with ISA and ISS risk assessment.

A very recent study (Flores and Ekstedt, 2016) tries to find how organizational factors and individual perception about social engineering threats affect an individual's intention to resist social engineering. The study used exploratory and confirmatory stages to research and develop hypotheses. The following constructs were derived to form hypotheses- 1) Organizational structure- Transformational Leadership (TL) and Information Security Culture (ISC), 2) Information security awareness and 3) Intrinsic beliefs- Self-Efficacy (SE), Attitude (A) and Normative Beliefs (NB). The study (Flores and Ekstedt, 2016) concluded that attitude towards resisting social engineering has the strongest direct influence on intention to resist social engineering, whereas self-efficacy and normative behavior had minimal effect on intention to resist social engineering. Similarly, Transformational leadership had a strong relationship with perceived information security culture and information security awareness.

Hu et al (2012) demonstrate that the intention of employees to comply with policies can be influenced by the following 3 factors: The intent of the top management, individual cognition of the employees and organizational culture. The study (Hu et al. 2012) showed that:

- Stronger positive attitude, subjective norm and perceived control towards information security policy compliance leads to stronger behavioral intention to comply with the policies.
- Stronger perceived goal/rule oriented cultural value leads to stronger positive attitude, subjective norm and perceived behavioral control towards compliance with information security policies
- Stronger perceived goal/rule orientated cultural value leads to stronger intention to comply with information security policies

- Stronger perceived top management participation in information security initiatives leads to stronger positive attitude, subjective norm and perceived behavioral control towards compliance with information security policies

4.4. User Training: Causes for Failure

User awareness trainings require more than just informing people and it is essential to assess the reasons for failure of such security measures to understand the gap. This could be attributed to the personal, social or environmental factors (Bada and Sasse, 2014). Also, it is essential to understand the audience's constraints and supporting beliefs for understanding why the behavior is occurring more than knowing what behaviors currently exist (Stewart and Lacey, 2012). These factors would help to understand the causes of failure of user awareness trainings and thereby, would provide means to improve the training campaigns.

The primary purpose of security awareness is to influence the adoption of secure behaviors. Bada and Sasse (2014) identify what behaviors help to deliver information security, to what extent they are adopted, and existing approaches to change information security behaviors through awareness campaigns - what works, and what not, and why. This paper reviews current information security awareness campaigns and their effectiveness, existing knowledge about behavior and behavior change, the importance of cultural differences in influencing behavioral change; and rewards and punishments method.

Stewart and Lacey (2012) put forth the following question - why mainstream information security awareness techniques have failed to evolve at the same rate as automated technical security controls? They, then, demonstrate that how advanced concepts from safety science can be used to improve information security risk communications in an organization by examining the concepts of bounded rationality, mental models and the extended parallel processing model in an information security context.

4.5. User Training: Gamification

Gamified approaches are considered emerging technologies in providing sufficient user awareness trainings in protecting the organizations assets. By engaging users in "game thinking" styles, cyber security skills of the users could be enhanced (Endicott-Popovsky et al., 2013) (Adams and Makramalla, 2015). Game design framework helps to improve the user's avoidance behavior and focuses on conceptual knowledge of URLs and emails thereby providing users with the ability to mitigate the phishing risks (Arachchilage and Love, 2013). Also, the gamified approaches are found to have better benefits to the users on providing training about the IT compliance (Baxter et al., 2015). Gamification also includes mechanisms such as progress measurement to track compliance and reward system for encouraging compliance in non-game situations. In addition, the relation between the motivation to comply to the security policy and human behavioural outcomes for success and rewards for complying with the policy is studied. (Kapp, 2012).

Endicott-Popovsky et al. (2013), in a study, prepare people for security awareness by proposing a learning environment that would raise visitor awareness of cybersecurity issues related to the digital world. This is performed by engaging in-world participants. It focuses on building trust in virtual world and provides facility to see how the people work towards achieving it. NIST special publication 800-50 recognizes people as the weakest link of security and recommends that users of IS be aware of their roles. A 2013 paper (Arachchilage and Love, 2013) aimed to design a game based framework for security awareness and training against phishing attacks in an interactive and user-friendly manner. The use of personal computers and internet has increased exponentially and the attacks related to computers have also grown and so the need for security is much more important today. The study concluded that the game design framework should enhance users' avoidance behavior through motivation and effectively reduce phishing attacks. The analysis of the results of the questionnaire and study identified the measures that need to be included in the game design framework, which were perceived threat, safeguard effectiveness, safeguard cost, self-efficacy, perceived severity, and perceived susceptibility elements.

Adams and Makramalla (2015) discuss a methodology for improving cyber security skills and leadership among employees in an organization. The authors, Adam and Makramalla (2015) studied the characteristics of an attacker and entrepreneurial perspectives and using these characteristics, created avatars for a gamified approach that develops a story and implements security training through this story. This approach allows the trainees to experience an attack through the eyes of a cyber-attacker and therefore from entrepreneurial perspectives.

In another recent paper (Labuschagne and Eloff, 2014), the authors discuss the features of various security awareness frameworks such as ENISA 2010, SANS security awareness roadmap and the NIST awareness framework. They, then proceed to list various studies that have demonstrated the effectiveness of the security awareness programs. They then proceeded to pursue the effectiveness of games within security awareness programs and to show how the gamification process was successful as a training method.

Baxter et al. (2015) use the results of lab tests and field study about IT security training conducted on employees of a bank to show that employees are more satisfied with respect to security training and gain more knowledge when gamification techniques are used for training instead of traditional non-gamification techniques. The paper's findings show that individuals find gamified training more enjoyable than other training types, individuals receiving gamified training will exhibit greater knowledge acquisition than individuals receiving non-gamified training or no training. However, does not outperform non-gamified learning approaches. Arachchilage et al. (2012) developed a mobile game to increase awareness of phishing attacks and avoidance behavior through motivation. The previous game designs focused on procedural knowledge but authors' game design focuses on conceptual knowledge about parts of the URL and email which was shown to help users detect attacks better. The study concludes that this type of interactive and user-friendly method of gamifying the awareness training of phishing attacks is effective for the current level of ever increasing number of phishing attacks.

4.6. User Training: Implementation

User awareness trainings could be implemented by different ways. The training program could be developed by studying cognitive and cultural bias' that affects the behavior of the user (Tsohou et al., 2015). Data analytics could be used to obtain data from various sources and studying the pattern to implement the training program accordingly (Korpela, 2015). Models such as Drip-Feed and IBTL could be used as well. The former focuses on passing information to the employees in phased manner whereas the latter focuses on correlating the defender's tolerance to threats with respect to the attacker's ability to attack (Caldwell, 2016; Dutt, 2011). Another model proposes achieving user training through knowledge sharing among employees (Safa and Von Solms, 2016). In few countries, ISP's directly provide trainings to the online retailers that help the retailers in detecting the threats at root level itself (Kureva et al., 2014). Furthermore, the trainings could be implemented in different methods – gaming, conventional delivery, instructor led delivery, simulation based with each method carrying certain advantages over the others (Abawajy, 2010). Tsohou et al. (2015) develop a conceptual framework for information security awareness which emphasizes the role of cognitive and cultural biases, individual perceptions, beliefs and how they affect the internalization of communicated security objectives and employees' compliance to the information security policy. The paper (Tsohou, 2015) identifies and analyses the cognitive and cultural biases that influence the user and its effects on the compliance to a security policy. It also provides recommendations on how to develop security policies taking into consideration these biases so as to be effective.

Another study (Korpela, 2015) deals with the use of data analytics to improve cyber security awareness using the existing data sources. The paper demonstrates the ability of data analytics to correlate data from a wide range of data sources across significant time periods resulting in a better understanding of end users' online and learning behaviors. The paper also shows that using analytics, organizations can develop an educating matrix personalized to the users, which have the risk level of the user, their means of security education and the respective delivery method. Caldwell (2016) suggest that training methods such as 'sheep dig training', where the employees are trained only during the induction, and annual training should be avoided as threat vectors keep changing frequently. The study suggests a drip-feed method, where little information about security are passed to the employees on a weekly basis and should involve all levels of management in the process. Additionally, the training should be made effective by adopting different methods such as involving people in a penetration testing, sending alerts through email or SMS, bug bounty program and hackathons so that the users are more involved and the training is not just a routine task. E- learning can make learning simpler and it needs to be done in such a way that all levels of users can understand and covers all topics. Effective assessment of the training program is by testing the users on their security awareness and response levels and should change the behavior and attitude of the employee towards information security. Moreover, all levels of employees of the organization must be tested for their security awareness.

Dutt et al. (2011) illustrate an Instance Based Learning Theory (IBTL) technique to explain how a defender's behavior along with the nature of adversarial behavior helps in detecting cyber-attacks. Results from an IBL model predict that defender's cognitive abilities, namely, experience and tolerance, and the attacker's strategy about timing of threats together impact a defender's cyber security awareness. The authors (Safa and Von Solms, 2016) address how knowledge sharing within an organization contributes in creating information security awareness. Behavioral attributes such as earning a reputation, and gaining promotion as an extrinsic motivation, and curiosity satisfaction as an intrinsic motivation have a positive effects on employees' attitude towards ISKS. The authors have based their study on The Theory of Planned Behavior, The Motivation Theory, and Triandis' Model.

A recent study (Bharathi and Suguna, 2014) deals with information security awareness and how it influences an organization, and develop a model to understand it. The study reviews the existing models, ranks the findings based on the importance and develop a new model. Based on the rankings the new model consists of 3 levels namely high-level, mid-level and low-level. The high-level consists of policy and knowledge management, the mid-level deals with education and methods and the low-level consists of training, campaigns, responsibility and brand. The effectiveness of the model needs to be tested by implementing it and then evaluating the security awareness of the users after the implementation. Abawajy and Kim (2010) explain the effects of various information security awareness delivery methods used in improving end-users' information security awareness and behaviour and concludes that combined methods are better than individual methods. Abawajy (2014) discusses in detail about various methods that can be employed to impart information security awareness trainings to the employees. The methods that were discussed are Conventional delivery methods, Instructor led delivery methods, online based methods, Game based methods, Video based methods and Simulation based methods. Based on tests conducted on a sample of users, the author concludes that the test results suggest that video based training approach is the most preferred one.

A paper by Kuvera et al. (2014) proposes to develop a framework (ISP-ISA) that lets the Internet Service Provider (ISP) to provide information security awareness to the online shoppers. The previous researches on information security awareness were in an organizational context and focused only on security threats and risks, omitting the importance of information security awareness. The study (Kuvera et al., 2014) concluded that a framework has been developed as to how Information Security awareness for online shoppers may be conducted with active involvement of the ISPs

4.7. User Training: Measuring Effectiveness

In most of the organizations, there is a gap between the information security policy developed and how effectively they are implemented. This gap can lead to the employees not being able to identify the threats in time, to gauge the risks and impacts of the threats. To make sure the information security awareness and training programs are effectively implemented, we need a model or a process to measure the effective of the program. Better password security awareness, increased participation in awareness programs, increased compliance to the security are some of the results of an effective security training program.

Below are some of the processes to measure the effectiveness of the program-Using the metrics such as Risky behavior scale [RBS], Conservative behavior scale [CBS], Exposure to offense scale [EOS] and Risk perception scale [RPS], behavior traits can be used to assess the security awareness level of the employees (Ogutcu et al., 2016). Measuring the user satisfaction with information security policies can help in understanding the effectiveness of the information security training program. The effort or the benefit of the user training program is directly proportional to the user satisfaction with the information security policy i.e. the training program is more effective when the users are satisfied with the information security policy (Montesdioca and Macada, 2015). Regular auditing can be used to evaluate the employee security awareness program. Auditing can identify organization's compliance with industry standards, employees' awareness of the risks and their impacts and assess if appropriate security controls are in place (Semer, 2012). Awareness can be objectively measured using Neuro-IS tools such as eye tracking that analyses the movement of the eyes, and the results obtained from these tools can be used for evaluating the awareness of the employee and provide appropriate recommendations to improve the security awareness training program (Jaeger, and Eckhardt, 2016). Self-assessment, providing feedback to experts and observing the employees can also be used to measure the effectiveness of the program (Hansch, and Benenson,, 2014).

In a recent paper (Ogutcu et al. (2016), the authors investigate the users' risky behavior that may threaten the IS security. In addition, the threats the users may be exposed to, to what extent users perceive risks, the preventive actions they employ etc, were examined. The authors then, for the assessment of security related behaviors and security awareness levels of IS users, developed the following 4 metrics: Risky behavior scale [RBS], Conservative behavior scale [CBS], Exposure to offense scale [EOS] and Risk perception scale [RPS] based on the results of data collected through a survey._

The following are the findings of the study (Ogutcu et al. (2016):

- The more the respondents perceive threats, their behavior becomes more protective.
- As the respondents' use of risky technologies increases, their ratio of being exposed to crime or having a negative experience increases as well.
- As the use of technology increases, individuals are exposed to crime more and besides their threat perceptions increase, too.
- Security related trainings improve the users' awareness.

Eminağaoğlu et al. (2009 emphasizes the importance of providing proper security awareness training to users on regular basis and how it helps the employee in contributing to the organization's security rules and implementations. As an initial step, current situation and previous reported security incidents were analysed. This was followed by conducting a technical audit of password weakness. Based on these results, KPIs was defined. Through proper trainings (visual materials used rather than articles), the following were confirmed by the research:

- Weak password usage was decreased significantly and continuously among most of the users
- Employees began to develop a continual improvement of awareness and they had a inclined tendency to choose and use their passwords more safely
- Users began to participate in information security controls and mechanisms that were included in the awareness campaign
- Most employees started to have (albeit reluctant) tendency to comply with the company's information security policies

Hänsch and Benenson (2014) provide a standardized definition for the term "security awareness". They followed three pronged approach for a complete coverage - as perception (focuses on the fact that users must be aware that security issues do exist), as protection (focuses on the fact that users must know which dangers exist and which measures are needed to protect them from dangers) and as behavior (focuses on the fact that users must know what tools to use, and by how, to protect against security incidents). Shaw et al. (2009) report on a laboratory experiment that investigates the impacts of hypermedia, multimedia and hypertext to increase information security awareness among the three awareness levels in an online training environment. The results indicate that: learners who have the better understanding at the perception and comprehension levels can improve understanding at the projection level; learners with text material perform better at the perception level; and learners with multimedia material perform better at the comprehension level and projection level.

Montesdioca and Maçada develop a measurement of user satisfaction with information security practices aids in understanding user behavior with regards to security and provides metrics to evaluate the investment that goes into planning and designing information security awareness programs. The researchers (Montesdioca and Maçada, 2015) have based their model on three behavioral theories that are expectation disconfirmation theory, needs theory and equity theory. An employee security awareness program focuses on how people can mitigate physical and information security risks, as well as keep the organization compliant with regulations and industry standards that require stronger IT security controls. A recent paper (Semer, 2012) deals with how auditing a security program can help assess whether it is executed properly. Semer (2012) suggests that auditors need to focus on the following six areas while evaluating a security awareness program- data, regulations and standards, network access, user conduct and Mobile devices and Wi-Fi, social media and social engineering. Jaeger and Eckhardt (2016) attempt to answer if employees with high levels of perceived ISA also more likely to look for indicators of security and fraud when using web browsers and emails at work and the extent to which employees give higher visual attention to these indicators after being subject to organizational awareness-raising activities. The study (Jaeger and Eckhardt, 2016) provide meaningful implications for practitioners on how to sharpen their employees' eyes for IS security threats.

4.8. User Training: Specific Threats

The number of ways the security of an organization can be compromised is increasing rapidly. The presence of technical controls alone is not sufficient to ensure an organization is secure, as the human aspect of security is equally important. Organizations are implementing BYOD policy to enable employees to work from any place using their own device. With increase in productivity through BYOD policy, there is also an increase in security risks such as lack of knowledge of security of the devices, complacency in security of smartphones, theft of devices, social engineering, malware and data tampering. To ensure the sensitive data of both the company and the individual are not compromised through mobile devices, security controls such as user authentication, antivirus applications, regular updates and encryption along with an effective security awareness program on the risks and impacts of using these devices need to be in place and properly implemented. The security applications such as antivirus need to be designed such that they are easy to use and understand. Information about various threats and how they can be overcome should be clearly conveyed to the users. Importance of privacy and security settings of an application should be reviewed before using them. Users need to be motivated to follow the security policy to make sure they understand the benefits of being secure. Phishing is a type of social engineering attack in which a victim receives an email/SMS asking the victim to give personal information such as credit card details, login credentials. The phishing mail/SMS poses itself as useful information familiar to the user, have genuine references and trust signals.

Social networking sites are used nowadays to carry out phishing attacks as there is a lack of controls for online security threats, security trainings for using social networking sites. User education and awareness programs play a vital role in curbing phishing attacks. The phishing awareness education provided is usually ignored as it provides complex information that the user cannot easily understand. Therefore, context specific and easy to understand education material along with training and public campaigns can be implemented so that the user is better prepared for phishing attacks. Another method for increasing awareness of phishing is through simulating the phishing attack and providing subsequent training. SERUM (Social Engineering Resistant User Model) (Jansson and Von Solms, 2013) can be used in which the objectives of the phishing training are defined, phishing is simulated for users and the results of the exercise are used to analyze the levels of phishing awareness. The simulation tests include database crash, lottery win and false virus scanner. Training centred on individual user's cognitive abilities (inhibition and working memory) and personality factors (Trust, Impulsivity, Computer Experience) (Mayhorn and Nyeste, 2012) can be developed along with usual training to make the training more personalized and effective. Awareness program around anti phishing techniques alone can be used instead of a general awareness program so that phishing attacks are the main objective of the program.

Furnell and Clarke (2012) seek to explain that most of the security features are concentrated on the technical aspects and the human factors are not considered much, and highlight that IT security is more than a technical problem and there is strong need to consider human aspects of security. They used examples of antivirus and authentication procedures to explain the shortcomings with technology and human aspects would better safeguard against threats. Jain and Shanbhag (2012 detail different risks associated with mobile applications and how best they can be avoided, showing that social engineering and vulnerable applications are the most common threats. Due to growth of mobile phone users, the information available through them also increases and so a need for information security awareness including the vulnerabilities and threats has to be present. Parker et al (2015) conducted a survey in the form of a questionnaire for a group of 510 of different ages, language and ethnicity, to analyze the results of the awareness of the users. The sample showed a good level of security awareness and many people used security controls such as PIN for the SIM and Screen lock with password. The findings concluded that there is more security awareness amongst younger smartphone users but the rate of knowledge about the threats and implementation of the respective controls is a concern. The study (Parker et al, 2015) also suggested that the design of a security within in a smartphone needs to be simple and non-technical to cater to the diverse user base.

Imgraben et al (2014) conducted a survey on 250 smart mobile phone users of the security awareness they have, which helps in finding where they lag to provide appropriate training. The Survey (Imgraben, 2014) was based on

- **General Security Loss (Loss/Theft of Device):** Default settings not changed, not locking sim card, not using alphanumeric password
- **Malware**: To steal owner's credentials and other personal information. "Remember Me" feature and "jailbreak" aids malware, no anti-virus installed
- **Unauthorized Access**: Storing sensitive data in devices with no locking mechanism
- **Wi-Fi/Bluetooth Security**: Leaving "on" all the time, connecting to an unknown hotspot,
- **Phishing**: Small screen size aids phishing, trusting emails based on their logos

Focusing on the behavioral aspect of information security compliance, Ophoff and Robinson (2014) assess the level of security awareness that exists with mobile phone users and to determine whether complacency about mobile phone security exists among the users. The questionnaire given to the sample of respondents included points such as if smartphone users trust applications from official app repositories, if users considered security before downloading applications and if security controls were enabled in the smartphone. The research concluded that there is high level of complacency in security of smartphones and related security controls and that users rarely consider privacy and security settings when installing an application. The research also indicated that the users have a high level of trust towards smartphone app repositories. Moreover, user's language does not impact his/her security awareness and a relationship between IT expertise and adoption of smartphone security controls by the user.

In BYOD deployment, the devices are used by the employees to access both private and corporate data, putting the security of both at risk. Security for mobile devices is often overlooked and the importance of end users' security is crucial in the overall security of the organization. Organizations spend a lot of funds in securing their network, they do not concentrate that much on the human side of vulnerabilities, which the hackers target nowadays. Chen et al. (2013) addresses the security risks associated with BYOD and how education, training and awareness address this risk. Authors (Chen et al., 2013) propose that workshops and instructor based training programs and computer based programs need to be combined to achieve maximum results from the training program and raise awareness of the security threats of mobile devices. McCroham et al.(2010) try to understand why users are careless in their password choices and are reluctant in setting strong passwords (atleast 8 characters) and if cyber security awareness training program can help. The study finds that if users have a greater degree of awareness about threats to information systems, they will engage in behaviors that enhance security. The study (McCrohan, 2010) also confirm that if individuals are informed of the threats facing their online activities, and are informed of their ability to mitigate security threats by setting strong passwords, and are provided with detailed information on how to create strong passwords, then the individuals will be more inclined to try and control it.

Kirlappos and Sasse (2012) explore the components of necessary user education that is required to safeguard from phishing attacks. The study confirms that the education currently provided is not effective as it focuses on indicators that user cannot understand and the user information must rather focus on awareness, education and training. Public awareness campaign and context specific indicators have been used for better education of users and protect them from victims of phishing attacks. Jansson and von Solms (2013) explain that if simulating phishing attacks are combined with embedded training, it can contribute towards cultivating users' resistance towards phishing attacks. The authors developed an exercise called as SERUM (Social Engineering Resistant User Model) to illustrate their analyses. The paper also explains that though technical tools would help in avoiding phishing attacks, the users should not be too reliant on the technical tools.

Successful phishing attacks have particularly strong implications for military populations, and have the potential to threaten national security. In an attempt to reduce the overall success rate of a phishing attack, a study (Coronges, 2012) uses social network analytics to identify the effect of social network structures on the spread of a phishing attack. This study attempted to explore the effects of social networks on the dissemination of information about a well-known, yet highly successful social engineering attack – phishing emails.

Mayhorn and Nyeste (2012) attempt to show an association between anti-phishing training techniques used in previous research and individual differences including: cognitive abilities (inhibition and working memory) and personality factors (Trust, Impulsivity, Computer Experience) which could affect phishing susceptibility. The inferential results of this study included various effects of training and individual differences. A positive effect of training was found in reducing phishing susceptibility and increasing awareness of fake emails. Spear phishing is a type of social engineering attack targeted at a particular individual or a group where the victim receives an email or SMS relevant to him/her, asking to give personal info such as credit card number, login credentials and so on. The rate of success of spear phishing attacks is much higher compared to a normal phishing attack. Caputo et al. (2014) try to validate the effectiveness of the current security training awareness programs and suggests some changes and improvements based on their study. The study concluded that the training did not have much effect on the likelihood that a participant would click a subsequent mail and that employees clicking a phishing mail were more likely to click a subsequent phishing mail and employees not clicking were more likely to not click subsequent phishing mails.

Silic and Back (2016) investigates how Social Networking Sites (SNS) are exploited and the risks involved in the sensitive data that is transmitted through these sites every day. The study adopted methods such as field experiments, interviews to get results on the status of SNS risks and how much aware the employees are. The field study findings indicated that females were more likely to become victims and respondents aged between 20 and 30 years were most vulnerable. Interview findings revealed that employees had little knowledge about company's policies regarding SNS, employees trust SNS and are not aware of the risks involved and the security training for using SNS is not effective.

Video Surveillance is an excellent tool for many applications including crime prevention and law enforcement. However, privacy concerns are often set aside when compared to public safety and security. In a study, the authors (Winkler and Rinner, 2012) question if sufficient efforts are made to protect the privacy of monitored people. The authors have presented a system architecture and in-depth description for a direct user feedback mechanism to realize the highest privacy protection level.

5. CONCLUSION

The chapter presented a comprehensive view of extant literature in the area of security awareness and training from last few years. The filtering and classification process provided insights into the trends and emphasis of recent research which has been in response to growing needs for a robust and effective information security awareness program. Given the increasing trend of human link being the weakest and most exploited links, organizations are increasingly adapting their programs to the shifting risk landscape. The chapter shows the pattern of research to indicate the areas in security awareness that have gained importance in recent years. The conceptual model showed interrelationships between the research classification categories that play a part in development of an effective awareness program. Additional insights were provided through trend and distribution of papers over last few years and also through frequency analysis of the keywords. Contributions, approach and findings of each paper was presented in the previous section that provides an excellent overview of coverage of the topics in extant literature.

REFERENCES

Abawajy, J. (2014). User preference of cyber security awareness delivery methods. *Behaviour & Information Technology, 33*(3), 237–248. doi:10.1080/014492 9X.2012.708787

Abawajy, J., & Kim, T. (2010). Performance Analysis of Cyber Security Awareness Delivery Methods. In T. Kim, W. Fang, M. K. Khan, K. P. Arnett, H. Kang, & D. Ślęzak (Eds.), *Security Technology, Disaster Recovery and Business Continuity. Communications in Computer and Information Science* (Vol. 122). Berlin: Springer. doi:10.1007/978-3-642-17610-4_16

Adams, M., & Makramalla, M. (2015). Cybersecurity Skills Training: An Attacker-Centric Gamified Approach. *Technology Innovation Management Review, 5*(1).

Arachchilage, N. A. G., & Love, S. (2013). A game design framework for avoiding phishing attacks. *Computers in Human Behavior, 29*(3), 706–714. doi:10.1016/j. chb.2012.12.018

Arachchilage, N. A. G., Love, S., & Scott, M. (2012). Designing a Mobile Game to Teach Conceptual Knowledge of Avoiding "Phishing Attacks". *International Journal for e-Learning Security, 2*(2), 127-132.

Ashenden, D. (2008). *Information security management: a human challenge?* Elsevier Information Security Technical Report 13.

Bada, M., & Sasse, A. (2014). *Cyber Security Awareness Campaigns: Why do they fail to change behaviour?*. Academic Press.

Barki, H., Rivard, S., & Talbot, J. (1993). A Keyword Classification Scheme for IS Research Literature: An Update. *Management Information Systems Quarterly, 17*(June), 209–225. doi:10.2307/249802

Barlow, J. B., Warkentin, M., Ormond, D., & Dennis, A. R. (2013). Dont make excuses! Discouraging neutralization to reduce IT policy violation. *Computers & Security, 39*, 145–159. doi:10.1016/j.cose.2013.05.006

Baxter, R. J., Holderness, D. K., & Wood, D. A. (2015). Applying Basic Gamification Techniques to IT Compliance Training: Evidence from the Lab and Field. *Journal of Information Systems*.

Bharathi, S., & Suguna, J. (2014). A Conceptual Model To Understand Information Security Awareness. *International Journal of Engineering, 3*(8).

Caldwell, T. (2016). Making security awareness training work. *Computer Fraud & Security*, (6): 8–14.

Caputo, D. D., Pfleeger, S. L., Freeman, J. D., & Johnson, M. E. (2014). Going spear phishing: Exploring embedded training and awareness. *IEEE Security and Privacy, 12*(1), 28–38. doi:10.1109/MSP.2013.106

Cavanagh, S. (1997). Content analysis: Concepts, methods and applications. *Nurse Researcher, 4*(3), 5–16. PMID:27285770

Chen, H., Li, J., Hoang, T., & Lou, X. (2013). *Security challenges of BYOD: a security education, training and awareness perspective*. Academic Press.

Chen, Y., Ramamurthy, K., & Wen, K. W. (2012). Organizations information security policy compliance: Stick or carrot approach? *Journal of Management Information Systems, 29*(3), 157–188. doi:10.2753/MIS0742-1222290305

Cheng, L., Li, Y., Li, W., Holm, E., & Zhai, Q. (2013). Understanding the violation of IS security policy in organizations: An integrated model based on social control and deterrence theory. *Computers & Security, 39*, 447–459. doi:10.1016/j.cose.2013.09.009

Coronges, K., Dodge, R., Mukina, C., Radwick, Z., Shevchik, J., & Rovira, E. (2012, January). The influences of social networks on phishing vulnerability. In *System Science (HICSS), 2012 45th Hawaii International Conference on* (pp. 2366-2373). IEEE. doi:10.1109/HICSS.2012.657

Cox, J. (2012). Information systems user security: A structured model of the knowing–doing gap. *Computers in Human Behavior, 28*(5), 1849–1858. doi:10.1016/j. chb.2012.05.003

Crossler, R. E., Johnston, A. C., Lowry, P. B., Hu, Q., Warkentin, M., & Baskerville, R. (2013). Future directions for behavioral information security research. *Computers & Security, 32*, 90-101.

Da Veiga, A., & Martins, N. (2015). Improving the information security culture through monitoring and implementation actions illustrated through a case study. *Computers & Security, 49*, 162–176. doi:10.1016/j.cose.2014.12.006

Dutt, V., Ahn, Y. S., & Gonzalez, C. (2011, July). Cyber situation awareness: Modeling the security analyst in a cyber-attack scenario through instance-based learning. In *IFIP Annual Conference on Data and Applications Security and Privacy* (pp. 280-292). Springer Berlin Heidelberg. doi:10.1007/978-3-642-22348-8_24

Eminağaoğlu, M., Uçar, E., & Eren, Ş. (2009). The positive outcomes of information security awareness training in companies–A case study. *Information Security Technical Report, 14*(4), 223-229.

Eminagaoglu, M., Ucar, E., & Eren, S. (2010). The positive outcomes of information security awareness training in companies – a case study. *Information Security Technical Report, 4*, 1–7.

Endicott-Popovsky, B., Hinrichs, R. J., & Frincke, D. (2013, July). Leveraging 2 nd life as a communications media: An effective tool for security awareness training. In *IEEE International Professional Communication 2013 Conference* (pp. 1-7). IEEE.

Flores, W. R., & Ekstedt, M. (2016). Shaping intention to resist social engineering through transformational leadership, information security culture and awareness. *Computers & Security, 59*, 26–44. doi:10.1016/j.cose.2016.01.004

Furnell, S., & Clarke, N. (2012). Power to the people? The evolving recognition of human aspects of security. *Computers & Security, 31*(8), 983-988.

Glaser, B., & Strauss, A. (1967). *The Discovery of Grounded Theory: Strategies for Qualitative Research*. Chicago, IL: Aldine Publishing Company.

Gundu, T., & Flowerday, S. V. (2013). Ignorance to awareness: Towards an information security awareness process. *SAIEE Africa Research Journal, 104*(2), 69–79.

Guzzo, R. A., Jackson, S. E., & Katzell, R. A. (1987). Meta-analysis Analysis. *Research in Organizational Behavior,* (9): 407–442.

Hänsch, N., & Benenson, Z. (2014, September). Specifying IT security awareness. In *2014 25th International Workshop on Database and Expert Systems Applications* (pp. 326-330). IEEE. doi:10.1109/DEXA.2014.71

Hu, Q., Dinev, T., Hart, P., & Cooke, D. (2012). Managing employee compliance with information security policies: The critical role of top management and organizational culture. *Decision Sciences, 43*(4), 615–660. doi:10.1111/j.1540-5915.2012.00361.x

Ifinedo, P. (2012). Understanding information systems security policy compliance: An integration of the theory of planned behavior and the protection motivation theory. *Computers & Security, 31*(1), 83–95. doi:10.1016/j.cose.2011.10.007

Ifinedo, P. (2014). Information systems security policy compliance: An empirical study of the effects of socialisation, influence, and cognition. *Information & Management, 51*(1), 69–79. doi:10.1016/j.im.2013.10.001

Imgraben, J., Engelbrecht, A., & Choo, K. K. R. (2014). Always connected, but are smart mobile users getting more security savvy? A survey of smart mobile device users. *Behaviour & Information Technology, 33*(12), 1347–1360. doi:10.1080/01 44929X.2014.934286

IT Governance Institute. (2008). Information security governance: guidance for information security managers. ITGI Publishing.

Jaeger, L., & Eckhardt, A. (2016). *A neurosecurity perspective on the formation of information security awareness–Proposing a multi-method approach*. Academic Press.

Jain, A. K., & Shanbhag, D. (2012). Addressing Security and Privacy Risks in Mobile Applications. *IT Professional, 14*(5), 28–33. doi:10.1109/MITP.2012.72

Jansson, K., & von Solms, R. (2013). Phishing for phishing awareness. *Behaviour & Information Technology, 32*(6), 584–593. doi:10.1080/0144929X.2011.632650

King, W. R., & He, J. (2005). Understanding the Role and Methods of Meta-Analysis in IS Research. *Communications of the Association for Information Systems,* (16), 665–686.

Kirlappos, I., & Sasse, M. A. (2012). Security education against phishing: A modest proposal for a major rethink. *IEEE Security and Privacy Magazine, 10*(2), 24–32. doi:10.1109/MSP.2011.179

Korpela, K. (2015). Improving cyber security awareness and training programs with data analytics. *Information Security Journal: A Global Perspective, 24*(1-3), 72-77.

Kruger, H. A., & Kearney, W. D. (2006). A prototype for assessing information security awareness. *Computers & Security, 25*(4), 289–296. doi:10.1016/j.cose.2006.02.008

Kumaraguru, P. (2007). Protecting people from phishing: the design and evaluation of an embedded training email system. In *Proceedings of the computer human interaction (CHI 2007)*. New York, NY: ACM Press. doi:10.1145/1240624.1240760

Kureva, G., Loock, M., & Kritzinger, E. (2014). *Towards addressing Information Security Awareness through Internet Service Providers*. Academic Press.

Labuschagne, W. A., & Eloff, M. (2014, July). The Effectiveness of Online Gaming as Part of a Security Awareness Program. *13th European Conference on Cyber Warfare and Security ECCWS-2014, 125.*

Mayhorn, C. B., & Nyeste, P. G. (2012). Training users to counteract phishing. *Work (Reading, Mass.), 41*(Supplement 1), 3549–3552. PMID:22317259

McCormac, A., Zwaans, T., Parsons, K., Calic, D., Butavicius, M., & Pattinson, M. (2016). Individual differences and Information Security Awareness. *Computers in Human Behavior.*

McCrohan, K. F., Engel, K., & Harvey, J. W. (2010). Influence of awareness and training on cyber security. *Journal of Internet Commerce, 9*(1), 23–41. doi:10.108 0/15332861.2010.487415

Mejias, R. J., & Balthazard, P. A. (2014). A model of information security awareness for assessing information security risk for emerging technologies. *Journal of Information Privacy and Security, 10*(4), 160–185. doi:10.1080/15536548.2014.974407

Montesdioca, G. P. Z., & Maçada, A. C. G. (2015). Measuring user satisfaction with information security practices. *Computers & Security, 48*, 267–280. doi:10.1016/j. cose.2014.10.015

Ogutcu, G., Testik, Ö. M., & Chouseinoglou, O. (2016). Analysis of personal information security behavior and awareness. *Computers & Security, 56*, 83–93. doi:10.1016/j.cose.2015.10.002

Ophoff, J., & Robinson, M. (2014, August). Exploring end-user smartphone security awareness within a South African context. In *2014 Information Security for South Africa* (pp. 1-7). IEEE.

Parker, F., Ophoff, J., Van Belle, J. P., & Karia, R. (2015, November). Security awareness and adoption of security controls by smartphone users. In *2015 Second International Conference on Information Security and Cyber Forensics (InfoSec)* (pp. 99-104). IEEE. doi:10.1109/InfoSec.2015.7435513

Parsons, K., McCormac, A., Butavicius, M., Pattinson, M., & Jerram, C. (2014). Determining employee awareness using the human aspects of information security questionnaire (HAIS-Q). *Computers & Security, 42*, 165-176.

Petter, S., & McLean, E. R. (2009). A Meta-analytic Assessment of the Delone and Mclean IS Success Model: An Examination of IS Success at the Individual Level. *Information & Management, 3*(46), 159–166. doi:10.1016/j.im.2008.12.006

Sabherwal, R., Jeyaraj, A., & Chowa, C. (2006). Information System Success: Individual and Organizational Determinants. *Management Science, 12*(52), 1849–1864. doi:10.1287/mnsc.1060.0583

Safa, N. S., Sookhak, M., Von Solms, R., Furnell, S., Ghani, N. A., & Herawan, T. (2015). Information security conscious care behaviour formation in organizations. *Computers & Security, 53*, 65–78. doi:10.1016/j.cose.2015.05.012

Safa, N. S., & Von Solms, R. (2016). An information security knowledge sharing model in organizations. *Computers in Human Behavior, 57*, 442–451. doi:10.1016/j.chb.2015.12.037

Safa, N. S., Von Solms, R., & Furnell, S. (2016). Information security policy compliance model in organizations. *Computers & Security, 56*, 70-82.

Schlienger, T., & Teufel, S. (2003). Information security culture – From analysis to change. *3rd annual information security South Africa conference, information security South Africa – Proceedings of ISSA 2003.*

Semer, L. J. (2012). Evaluating the employee security awareness program: Regular audits of IT safeguards can reveal whether staff members are doing their part to protect the organization's data and networks. *Internal Auditor, 69*(6), 53–57.

Shaw, R. S., Chen, C. C., Harris, A. L., & Huang, H. J. (2009). The impact of information richness on information security awareness training effectiveness. *Computers & Education, 52*(1), 92–100. doi:10.1016/j.compedu.2008.06.011

Silic, M., & Back, A. (2016). The dark side of social networking sites: Understanding phishing risks. *Computers in Human Behavior*, *60*, 35–43. doi:10.1016/j.chb.2016.02.050

Siponen, M., Mahmood, M. A., & Pahnila, S. (2014). Employees adherence to information security policies: An exploratory field study. *Information & Management*, *51*(2), 217–224. doi:10.1016/j.im.2013.08.006

Son, J. Y. (2011). Out of fear or desire? Toward a better understanding of employees motivation to follow IS security policies. *Information & Management*, *48*(7), 296–302. doi:10.1016/j.im.2011.07.002

Stewart, G., & Lacey, D. (2012). Death by a thousand facts: Criticising the technocratic approach to information security awareness. *Information Management & Computer Security*, *20*(1), 29–38. doi:10.1108/09685221211219182

Strauss, A., & Corbin, J. (1997). *Grounded Theory in Practice*. London: Sage Publications.

Tipton, H. F., & Krause, M. (2007). *Information security management handbook*. Auerbach Publications.

Tsohou, A., Karyda, M., & Kokolakis, S. (2015). Analyzing the role of cognitive and cultural biases in the internalization of information security policies: Recommendations for information security awareness programs. *Computers & Security*, *52*, 128–141. doi:10.1016/j.cose.2015.04.006

Valentine, J. A. (2006). Enhancing the employee security awareness model. *Computer Fraud & Security*, *2006*(6), 17–19. doi:10.1016/S1361-3723(06)70370-0

Vance, A., Siponen, M., & Pahnila, S. (2012). Motivating IS security compliance: Insights from habit and protection motivation theory. *Information & Management*, *49*(3), 190–198. doi:10.1016/j.im.2012.04.002

Vance, A., & Siponen, M. T. (2012). IS security policy violations: A rational choice perspective. *Journal of Organizational and End User Computing*, *24*(1), 21–41. doi:10.4018/joeuc.2012010102

Weber, R. P. (1990). *Basic content analysis*. Beverly Hills, CA: Sage. doi:10.4135/9781412983488

Webster, J., & Watson, R. T. (2002). Analyzing the Past to Prepare for the Future: Writing a Literature Review. *Management Information Systems Quarterly*, *2*(26), iii–xiii.

Wijnand, I., de Kort, Y., Midden, C., & van den Hoven, E. (2006). Persuasive Technology for Human Well-Being: Setting the Scene. Persuasive Technology, 1-5.

Williams, P. (2008). *In a 'trusting' environment, everyone is responsible for information security*. Elsevier Information Security Technical Report 13.

Williams & Ayobami. (2013). Relationship between Information Security Awareness and Information Security Threat. *International Journal of Research in Commerce, IT & Management, 3*(8).

Winkler, T., & Rinner, B. (2012). User-centric privacy awareness in video surveillance. *Multimedia Systems, 18*(2), 99–121. doi:10.1007/s00530-011-0241-1

Wipawayangkool & Villafranca. (2015). Exploring Millennials' Malware Awareness and Intention to Comply with Information Security Policy. *Review of Integrative Business and Economics Research, 4*(3), 153.

Wisconsin Writing Centre. (2016). *Learn how to write a review of literature*. Retrieved online on January 10 from http://writing.wisc.edu/Handbook/ReviewofLiterature.html#what

Wolfswinkel, Furtmueller, & Wilderom. (2011). Using Grounded Theory as a Method for Rigorously Reviewing Literature. *European Journal of Information Systems*. doi: 10.1057/ejis.2011.51

APPENDIX

Table 1.Classification categories and references

Topics / Categories	References
Behaviour and individual traits (Behavioural Science)	McMormac et al. (2016); Crossler et al. (2013); Wipawayangkool, et al. (2015)
Factors affecting Compliance (Behavioural Science)	Williams and Akanmu (2013); Safa et al. (2015); Gundu and Floweday (2013); Parsons et al. (2014); Cox (2012); Ifinedo (2014); Son (2011); Cheng et al. (2013); Safa et al. (2016); Vance and Siponen (2012); Ifinedo (2012); Vance et al. (2012); Chen et al. (2012)
Organizational influence (Behavioural Science)	Barlow et al. (2013); Siponen et al. (2014); Da Veiga and Martins. (2015); Mejias and Balthazard. (2014); Flores and Ekstedt. (2016); Hu et al. (2012)
Causes for failure (User Training)	Bada and Sasse. (2014); Stewart and Lacey. (2012)
Gamification (User Training)	Endicott-Popovsky at al. (2013); Arachchilage and Love (2013); Adams and Makramalla. (2015);Labuschagne and Eloff (2014);Baxter et al. (2015);Arachchilage et al. (2012)
Implementation (User Training)	Tsohou et al. (2015);Korpela (2015);Caldwell (2016);Dutt et al. (2011);Safa and Von Solms (2016);Bharathi and Suguna. (2014);Abawajy and Kim (2010);Abawajy (2014);Kureva et al. (???)
Measuring Effectiveness (User Training)	Ogutcu et al. (2016);Eminağaoğlu et al. (2009);Hänsch and Benenson. (2014);Shaw et al. (2009);Montesdioca and Maçada,. (2015);Semer (2012);Jaeger and Eckhardt. (2016)
Specific Threats (User Training)	Furnell and Clarke. (2012);Jain and Shanbhag. (2012);Parker et al. (2015);Imgraben et al. (2014);Ophoff and Robinson. (2014);Chen et al. (2013);McCrohan et al. (2010);Kirlappos and Sasse (2012);Jansson and von Solms (2013);Coronges et al. (2012);Mayhorn and Nyeste. (2012);Caputo et al. (2014);Silic and Back. (2016);Winkler and Rinner. (2012)

Chapter 7
A Tale of Policies and Breaches:
Analytical Approach to Construct Social Media Policy

Neha Singh
University at Buffalo, USA

Tanya Mittal
University at Buffalo, USA

Manish Gupta
University at Buffalo, USA

ABSTRACT

While the use of social media offers great opportunities to interact with customers and business partners, there are significant risks associated with this technology if a clear strategy has not been defined to address both the risks and the benefits that come along with it. The best approach for an organization to effectively utilize the benefits of this technology is to engage all relevant stakeholders and establish a strategy that addresses the pertinent issues. The organization needs to have in place relevant policies so as to be able to achieve it. To be able to identify the most frequent risks and their source, we captured breach data from various sources. In the chapter, we analyzed that the most important source of risk that can occur due to use of social media for a company is from its own workforce and an employee might find various ways of doing so.

DOI: 10.4018/978-1-5225-2604-9.ch007

1. INTRODUCTION

People that have shared interests, aspirations, backgrounds have historically found a way to establish communication and share information. Use of technology for similar functions in last few decades has given rise to tremendous opportunities and efficiencies. Merriam Webster dictionary (MW, 2016) defines social media as "forms of electronic communication (such as Web sites) through which people create online communities to share information, ideas, personal messages, etc." Social Media has been essentially characterized by attributes such as participation, community and connectedness (Mayfield, 2006; Marken, 2007). Social media technology consists of propagating or diffusing content through social networks over the Internet. Social media provides the power of enhanced interactivity, for example an individual might watch news on the television but cannot provide any kind of feedback over it whereas social media tools allow a person to comment, discuss and distribute information. It is one of the highly effective communication platforms that can connect n number of users virtually from any part of the world. Numerous studies have investigated different motivation behind individual's use of social media which range from relationships, connectedness, information gain, capital gain, amongst others (Bonds-Raacke and Raacke, 2010; Gangadharbatla, 2008; Nadkarni and Hofmann, 2012; Sheldon, et. al, 2011; Smith, 2011).

1.1. The Impact of Social Media & the Risks Involved

Social media is not an exception to any kind of business these days. Each and every business unit such as human resources, marketing, sales, R&D, and customer service have realized the importance of social media in order to hire employees, create & enhance brand recognition, generate revenue, drive innovation and improve customer satisfaction. A study conducted back in 2009 has found that there is high correlation between high financial performance and extensive social media engagement. However, since social media tools can be incorporated within an organization without any kind of new infrastructure, the business or marketing introduce them to the company without proper planning or risk identification/assessment, irrespective of the fact that social media introduces substantial risks to the organization. Use of social Media might lead to risks such as: information leakage, reputational damage, privacy breach, loss of intellectual property and copyright infringement. On the other hand, simply choosing not to use social media might result in opportunity cost. Therefore, every organization must be aware of all the risks & opportunities and should be able to properly manage the use of social media.

1.2. How Big is the Problem?

According to Proskauer's third annual global survey (Proskauer, 2014) about social media usage in the workplace nearly 90% of the organizations now use social media for business purposes amongst which only 60% of them have implemented social media policies. However, the misuse of social media in the organizations has increased drastically. More than 70% of the businesses had to take disciplinary action against its employees (which was initially 35% according to Proskauer's third annual global survey about social media usage).

Use of social media within an organization is not restricted to itself and therefore, risks associated with social media usage can come from both inside and out of the organization. Moreover, the organizations do not have direct control over these systems as they do not manage or own them. One of the risks that could arise is from the employee access to social media sites. According to a survey titled "Social Media & Workplace report 2012" (Hollon, 2012) 75% of the workers access social media sites from their mobile at least once a day and 60% access it multiple times a day, even though only 43% of them work in organizations that are open to the use of social media. This is a good indication of the motivation of the employees to use social media. An employee could be involved in a data breach or information leakage leading to financial and reputational damage to the company. On the other hand, any incorrect, irrelevant or inappropriate content posted on social media, whether by an employee or an external user, can steer the company into legal & compliance issues with the investors, customers or the government. Also, it would lead to financial and reputational loss for the company. Thus, to prevent the risks occurring due to the use of social media, the company requires both procedural (policies) and technical (technology) controls and these policies should not only be for the employees of the company but also for the external users (fans & followers). Also, apart from implementing policies it needs to take precautions and protect against specific risks and further assess and control the risks continuously in order to gain the benefits of social media usage.

1.3. Types of Risks due to Social Media Usage

- **Reputation Damage**

This is the greatest threat faced by an organization due to the use of social media. Anyone and everyone can post and publish on the social media. It provides a mechanism to spread a good news but also serves as a medium and acts as a host to complaints and grudges. If the reputation of a company is damaged and portrayed in a negative manner, then its customers no longer desire to conduct business with them.

The loss of reputation due to breaches affects the company in many ways including weakened competitiveness, loss of trust, sometimes loss of license (Rayner, 2003). The impact is sometime felt industry-wide (Xifra and Ordeix, 2009).

- **Data/Information Leakage**

This is the second most important threat faced by an organization. The information can be owned or relate to the organization itself or can be owned by someone external to the unit for example customer details in a banking or healthcare industry. The information leakage might happen by unauthorized personnel and sometimes even done innocently with intent of no harm to the company but once the information is out there on social media, there is hardly any way to get it back. As they say "There is no delete option on social media". Any information leakage or data loss can land the company into a huge risk including legal risks and the impact leads to huge costs involved in repairing the damage and getting the lost customers back.

- **Privacy**

Privacy is not security or confidentiality. Privacy is the ability of an individual or an organization to selectively release personal/confidential information. Privacy breach may result due to data loss. The impacts of privacy loss can be something like identity theft, cyber stalking for a personnel or might lead to a financial loss to an organization.

1.4. Social Media Breaches by Employees

Social media threats to an organization might be caused by internal (employees, insiders and consultants) and external (customers, activists). However, the threats form the internal employees of the company is much more prominent as they tend to have more power and knowledge about the organization they work for. The internal employees can pose a threat to the company in a number of ways such as: misuse of confidential information, inappropriate use of business, giving false and derogatory remarks about other employees and the business etc. When viewing and examining different reports and articles regarding the misuse of social media, reputation damage and information leakage are the top two most common risks incurred by a company. These both risks are highly interrelated in the sense that data leakage can lead to reputation damage. Although someone outside the organization can cause reputation damage as well, data leakage is more related to an internal employee. Many of these incidents (as you can see in Appendix-B) can happen due to lack social media usage and policies awareness amongst the employees or due to sheer innocence. Therefore, it is highly recommended that the company organize various training session on the appropriate use of social media to its employees.

There have been recent documented and research cases where employees have been fired because of their posts to social media sites. The press has coined a phrase "Facebook Fired" in wake of growing cases of similar disciplinary actions emanating from employees' negligent and abusive posts (Hidy and McDonald, 2013). To proactively address risks from social media use by employees, employers have escalated the employee activities monitoring at workplace (Mello 2012; Kaupins and Park, 2011; Gelms, 2012; Sánchez et. al., 2012).

2. LITERATURE REVIEW

The starting point of our risk that actually got us interested into the research work was due to the ISACA White Paper on "Social media: Business benefits and Security, governance and Assurance perspective" (ISACA, 2010). It provided us with the starting point which led to further research. The paper includes the risks of a corporate media presence and employee personal use of social media along with mitigation strategies and also assurance considerations.

Employee social media policies have been widely researched over last few years. There are studies that conducted existing social media policies for their research in the legal domain (Jacobson and Tufts 2013; Vaast and Kaganer 2013). There are other studies that have provided recommendations to formulate employee social media policies based on existing legal landscape and on anticipated changes to them (Hidy and Mcdonald 2013; Mooney 2013; Younkins 2013; Jennings, Blount, and Weatherly 2014; Kirby and Raphan 2014). This research is unique because no other study has provided insights and practical recommendations based on security breaches and existing employer policies at the some of the world's leading companies across several industries.

The Proskauer came up with the work "Social media in the workplace around the world" (Proskauer, 2014) mentioning that usage of social media was still in novelty in 2011 when they first published their survey but the recent survey depicts that 90% of the business now uses social media for business purposes. However, as the usage of social media increases, the risk of blurring the fine line between usage of social media for personal use and professional uses increases. The paper also confirms through surveys that there has been a tremendous increase in the number of companies that have implemented social media policies to address the risk arising out of misuse out of social media by the employees.

The research paper "Workplace and social networking- the implications of Employment relations" (Broughton et. al., 2009) states that in recent times the use of social media by employees have received a high level of attention by Employers mainly because of the disputes between the employers and employees that gained much e media attention in recent times. Initially the focus was primarily on "work bloggers" – individuals who maintain a website discussing about content relevant to their work. But now, it's been shifted to people who have social media account like Facebook and Twitter and reference their work on such sites.

"Critical Social media issues for Retail companies" (Beringer and Southwell, 2011) identified the various risks of using social media in multiple areas of business which includes Intellectual property and Brand protection, defamation, Employment issues, Regulatory scrutiny and Reputational. It also identifies the nature and scope of social media risk are often unrolled, informal, infinite reach, fast, interconnected and blurring of professional and personal lines.

The article "Protecting your practice from social media misadventures" (PRMS, 2012) suggests the elements to be included in creating an organizational social media policy. The suggestions consists of Purpose/Objective of creating the policy, Prohibited uses, Best/Permitted Uses, Violations and Enforcements. It also covers various breaches that were in the news that demonstrates lack of knowledge among healthcare workers as to what constitutes confidential patient information which that resulted in causing reputational damage to physician practices along with board complaints, regulatory fines and litigation.

The paper "ASNE 10 Best practices for Social media - helpful guidelines for news organization" (Hohmann et. al., 2012) identifies the social media guidelines for news organizations and gives the takeaways which includes application of traditional ethic rules online, assumption that everything online is public, breaking of news on the company's website and not on Twitter, no perception, independent authentication of anything found on social networking site, transparency and admission in case of being wrong, confidentiality of internal deliberations. The paper "Sample Social media policy" (ACFE., n.d.) includes principles apply to professional use of social media on Company's behalf as well as personal use when referencing Company.

The reason why social media usage in Financial Industry lagged behind and the risk associated with its usage was identified and mentioned in the paper "Social media usage in Financial Service Industry: Toward a Business- Driven compliance approach" (Chanda and Zaorski, 2013). It also provides information about the overview of the regulatory landscape, emergence of social media in financial service industry, effective use of social media, regulatory concerns. The many risk associated with social media usage to an enterprise is discussed in "Copyright SANS

Institute" (Shullich, 2011), along with ways to conduct a risk assessment and figure out which risks are applicable. The paper provides a detailed information regarding many topics like definition of Social Media, risk assessment, risk of social media use which is further classified as the impact, information leakage, data loss, piracy and infringement, corporate espionage, reconnaissance.

Another paper that efficiently put forwards the various law on social media workplace and breaches of these laws is "Blurred boundaries" (Sanchez, et. al, 2012). It consists of various information like the reasonable expectations of privacy analysis, employer evaluation of online speech and virtual identity of applicants, employer imposed limitations on Employee private life, the privacy expectation of employees, work/personal life separation. It also provides insights on the future of digital privacy of workplace. We also got some insights of recommendations for social media usage and maintaining privacy, confidentiality and professionalism for Nurse's association with the NSNA Paper (NSNA, n.d.). It gave us information regarding various examples of privacy and confidentiality breaches and suggestions to develop social media guidelines and common issues faced by its usage.

The risk involved for employers and steps taken to minimize the risk of usage of social media within organization. These questions were answered by 44 different jurisdictions in EMEA, Asia and America. The Mayer Brown publication on the "Use of social media in the workplace" (Abate et. al., 2011) helped us in collating the policies which should be mandatory to be present for successful Risk mitigation. Another key findings that we came across was from "Grant Thorton white paper"(Thompson, et al., 2011) which included the information on speed of the growth of social media, and also the finding that most companies have policies related to e-mail communication and technology but no policies that specifically address social media usage.

Another great source of information was "ace progress report" (Merrill et. al., 2011) that provides a clear understanding of reputational, legal and operational risk of social media participation and how can the company mitigate the social media risk they face. The "Accenture white paper" (Accenture, 2015) gives information regarding the shortfalls of managing social media, and a comprehensive and proactive response strategy that they came up with. They have also discussed about the evolution of social media, sources and types of social media risks and the essential components and enablers of social media risk management. Another presentation is "Learning to live with social networks: risk and rewards" (Zeltser, 2011) that explored the key risks associated with online social networking and discussed the policies and technologies that aided at mitigating these risks. It also evaluated the risk of sharing too much information online could bring value to the company or not.

3. RESEARCH METHODOLOGY

To come up with a list of critical policies that should be implemented by an organization, we started to look at and find companies that already have already implemented effective social media usage policies in their workplace. We first came up with a set of target companies from various domains (IT, financial, health, retail etc.) and then refined the list to those companies for which the policies were publically available online. The companies that we chose and the list of social media policies associated with them are appended towards the end of the paper as Appendix A.

After we were able to find the policies, we went ahead to search for articles and reports on various breaches caused by the use of social media by employees. The search terms were as follows:

Social Media AND Breaches OR Breaches by an employee OR Social media AND policy breach OR news AND social media policy AND breach OR information leakage OR data loss AND employee OR employee AND employer relations.

These were the reports that were reported by the employers and have been in the news. There would be many more breaches that were never reported. We tried to gather and analyze as many breaches as possible in this field to build our case and to come up with the most significant risks that a company could incur due to misuse of social media by its employees. The list of breaches that we found is appended towards the end of the paper as Appendix B. The list of social media policies that we analyzed is the most critical or "must have" by an employer are appended as Table 1.

4. DATA AND ANALYSIS

As mentioned in last section, we collected publicly available social media policies to represent a wide range of industries. A list of policies reviewed is shown in Table

Table 1. Analyzied social media policies

Best Buy
Cisco
Dell
Intel
Coke
IBM
Los Angeles Times
GAP

1. As shown in Figure 1, we analyzed existing policies available publicly and also articles on best approach and best practices to construct social media policy (see Prafull, 2012; Jet, 2016; Lauby, 2009) and derived a list of policy statements that companies should include in their social media policy to avoid data breach situations.

Table 3 depicts a sample of breaches that we came across and the underlying policies that should have been helpful in preventing the breaches. It also shows whether there were policies already in place or not. In cases where the policies did exist, we analyzed and worked on finding the policies whose existence could have prevented these breaches.

5. CONCLUSION

Social media has become one of the most widely used forms of communicating, information gathering and socializing for individuals and organizations alike. Most of the companies and organizations have a social media presence through sites such as Facebook, Twitter and Linkedin amongst others. Companies are increasingly using them to communicate with an extensive pool of current and potential customers. This has opened up new channels that can lead to data breaches, as we have seen in the chapter where several data breaches on social media were analyzed. To make the things worse from a risk standpoint, these social media platforms are constantly evolving and innovating. As far as social media is concerned, most of the breaches have had happened due to human lapses. Sometimes people share confidential

Figure 1. Research methodology and contributions

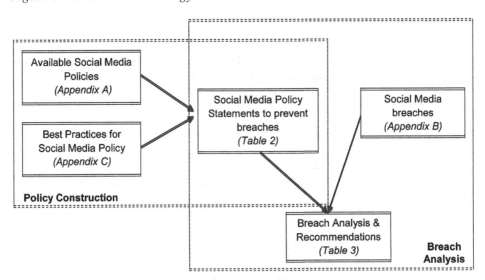

Table 2. Social Media Policy statements to prevent breaches

Social Media Policy Statements
PA1: The employee should adhere to the proper copyright and reference laws set forth by the company.
PA2: Every employee should familiarize himself/herself with the Code of Conduct.
PA3: Posting any content related to race, ethnicity, religion, gender or physical disability will not be tolerated.
PA4: Maintain transparency with the things you do. Use your real name and be clear about your role at the company.
PA5: The employees should not disparage customers, suppliers, employees, and so on, using any social media sites or blogs.
PA6: The employees are not allowed to disclose any confidential information of the company. Never post anything about the financial, operational and legal information of the company.
PA6.1: Never share personal information about our clients online or offline.
PA6.2: Never share personal information about our employees online or offline.
PA6.3: Never post anything related to the company's future strategies, sales trends or promotions
PA7: Never post anything that is false, abusive, threatening or defamatory.
PA8: The employer reserves the right to monitor employees' use of email and Internet, including access to social media sites.
PA9: The Company reserves the right to review, edit or even delete any misleading or inaccurate content found on social media or blog posts.
PA10: Be conscious when mixing your business and personal lives.
PA10.1: The employees should keep company related social media accounts separate from their personal accounts.
PA11: Employees should get permission before they refer to or post images of current or former employees, members, vendors or suppliers. Additionally, employees should get appropriate permission to use a third party's copyrights, copyrighted material, trademarks, service marks or other intellectual property.
PA12: The employee should make sure that the after-hours online activities do not violate the code of conduct.
PA13: The use of social media should not cause any interference in the employee's primary job responsibilities.
B. Social Media Policies related to Healthcare
PB1: Sending, receiving, displaying, printing, or otherwise disseminating confidential information or Personal Health Information (PHI) in violation of the Health Insurance Portability and Accountability Act (HIPAA) or the Health Information Technology, Economic and Clinical Health Act of 2009 (HITECH) is not allowed.
PB2: Abide by all applicable confidentiality laws and policies.
PB3: Never disclose any individually identifiable information regarding a member, client, or patient.
C. Social Media Policies related to IT
PC1: Employees are encouraged to participate in social media and exchange ideas but remain within limits and bound by the confidentiality obligations.
PC2: Connect and have fun but always remain transparent about your identity.
PC3: Every employee should be aware of "what not to share".

continued on following page

Table 2. Continued

Social Media Policy Statements
PC4: Your use of social media and blog posts should add value to your users, followers and fans
D. Policies related to enforcing the Social Media Policies
PD1: Anything you post that can potentially tarnish the Company's image will ultimately be your responsibility.
PD2: You are personally responsible for the content you publish.
PD3: Violations of the social media policies and code of conduct may result in disciplinary action against the employee, including but not limited to
PD3.1: Prohibiting an employee from accessing any electronic tools or equipment
PD3.2: Possible termination of employment
PD3.3: Legal action and/or criminal liability
PD4: Attending awareness training sessions and campaigns organized by the company are mandatory for each and every employee.
PD5: Every employee needs to sign and acknowledge that he/she understands and agrees to abide by the policies set forth by the organization.
PD6: The employer has the right to obtain periodic assessment and rectification of employees' understanding of existing policies.

Table 3. Breach analysis and recommendations

BREACH (Appendix - B)	WHY IT HAPPENED?	POLICY/(IES) THAT COULD HELP AVERT THE BREACH (Table 2)
St. Mary Medical Center, Long Beach *(PRMS, 2012)*	There was no policy in place.	PA6.1 PA7 PD1
Nursing Assistant Convicted, Oregon *(PRMS, 2012)*	There was no policy in place.	PB1 PB2 PB3 PD3
Derogatory Comments on Facebook *(Scutt, 2013)*	There was no policy in place.	PA3 PA10
B&O Worker dismissed for misconduct *(Scutt, 2013)*	The social media policies in place were not communicated well to the employees and/or its compliance might not be well stated.	PD4 PD6
Gosden v Lifeline (McCay Solicitors, 2015)	Although effective policies are put in place the employers need to conduct appropriate investigations and need to be alive to the potential problem of using social media.	PA8 PA5

continued on following page

Table 3. Continued

BREACH (Appendix - B)	WHY IT HAPPENED?	POLICY/(IES) THAT COULD HELP AVERT THE BREACH (Table 2)
Preece v Wetherspoons. *(McCay Solicitors, 2015)*	The employee was well aware of the company's policy regarding the usage of social media. The policies stated that employees should not write or contribute to a blog, including Facebook, where the content lowers the reputation of the company or its customers, and the company reserved the right to take disciplinary action where this occurred.	PD5 PD3
Abusive tweets by a game retailer employee *(McDonough, n.d.)*	There was no strict policy in place.	Establish new policies including how private social media accounts should be used, especially prohibiting the making of offensive remarks & reinforce the behavior they expect from their employees.
Yath v. Fairview Clinics, N.P. *(PRMS, 2012).*	The existing policy: "Fairview gives access to personal information about consumers only to employees who require it to perform their jobs. We will take every appropriate step to keep your information secure from other employees." But the clinic failed to communicate that the violations of policies would lead to serious consequences. The compliance measures were inappropriate.	PD4 PD5 PD6
Tri-City Medical Center, California *(PRMS, 2012)*	The existing policies: "Employees who choose to use social media should be careful and avoid discussing any confidential and work information" "Always obey the law and all District policies and procedures, and act in a professional, honest, and ethical manner when acting on behalf of the District" "Complete all required training in a timely manner." The policy regarding social media usage was not detailed.	PB1 PB3 PD5 PD6
Mercy Walworth Medical Center, Wisconsin *(Lake Geneva, 2009)*	There were existing policies regarding employee acceptable behavior along with consequences in case of non-compliance. Just having existing policies provide little help as controls.	PD3 PD4 PD5 PD6

information, unbeknownst to them, that they shouldn't. In response, companies are widely adopting social media policy. Most of these policies are tailored to organization-specific factors such as social media presence, propensity to risks and industry. As we saw in the chapter (Appendix A), companies take different approach on building their own social media policy. The objective of the chapter was to demonstrate how significantly different social media policies can be based on a variety of factors and how data breaches could have been prevented if only certain policy statements were in the victim company's social media policy. This chapter highlights how a well crafted and communicated social media policy can prevent data breaches and avoid companies in an adverse situation.

At the same time, companies are also turning to services that offer to monitor employees' online presence and ensure that social media policies are being enforced. This has led to serious privacy concerns and some states have enacted laws to prevent companies from checking out social media sites of their employees. Maryland and California are such states that are leading the wave and other states are considering similar legislation. Constructing a strong social media policy and increasing an awareness about the dangers of social media are one of the most effective controls that companies have. The major findings of this paper can be summarized in the below two points.

Inability of Policy Enforcement

The major finding that we came up with the paper is that most of the companies have policies related to social media usage in place but just having mere policies without any means to effectively and efficiently enforce them is an insufficient mitigation strategy. There should be policies to create awareness among employees about threats and companies' existing policies by means of training sessions and campaigns. The employees should be made aware that they themselves are the only one liable for their actions and any violations would lead to severe consequences. Regular training sessions and awareness programs can prevent breaches from occurring.

Lack of Policy

This is the age of technology where social media has become an integral part of business. The social media usage was still in it's novice stage in the year 2011 but during the recent years almost 90% of the companies use it. Although there has been tremendous increase in implementing policies addressed to social media usage. there are still some companies that have no policy in place. Absence of policies is a major threat as it does nothing in educating and guiding an employee regarding the correct usage of social media which could result in future breaches. And what that absence could lead to, has been depicted in our analysis above. Also, there are few companies that have a general policy in place but it's is equally essential to align the organizational policies to social media usage policies.

We have come up with the Master policy which states the most critical or mandatory set of policies that should exist and enforced in any organization to successfully combat the threat that technology has posed in business and hence, mitigate the risk. Many organizations are missing critical social media usage policies and their implementation strategies. At best, they are not leveraging the potential power of social media, at worst, they are exposed to social media related risks and inappropriate use by their employees.

REFERENCES

Abate, D., Hoffman, D., Robertson, N., Rogers, A., & Zeppenfeld, G. (2011, July). *The use of social media in the workplace.* Retrieved from https://www.mayerbrown.com/public_docs/ TheUseofSocialMediainTheWorkplace.pdf

Accenture. (2015). *A Comprehensive Approach to Managing Social Media Risk and Compliance.* Retrieved from https://www.accenture.com/t20150715T045906__w__/ us-en/_acnmedia/Accenture/Conversion-Assets/DotCom/Documents/Global/PDF/ Dualpub_1/accenture-comprehensive-approach-managing-social-media-risk-compliance.pdf on May 1,2016.

ACFE. (n.d.). *Sample Social media policy.* Retrieved from http://www.acfe.com/ uploadedfiles/acfe_website/content/documents/sample-documents/sample-social-media-policy.pdf

Barkan, T. (2011, January). *Social Strat – Special Report: How are the members of association using social media today?* Retrieved from https://www.uia.org/ sites/dev.uia.be/files/misc_pdfs/roundtable/Social_Media_Use_Survey_Report_ Individuals_2011.pdf on May 1, 2016.

Beringer, A., & Southwell, A. (2011, January 11). *Critical Social media issues for Retail companies.* Retrieved from http://www.gibsondunn.com/publications/ Documents/WebcastSlides-CriticalSocialMediaIssuesforRetailCompanies.pdf

Bonds-Raacke, J., & Raacke, J. (2010). MySpace and Facebook: Identifying dimensions of uses and gratifications for friend networking sites. *Individual Differences Research, 8,* 27–33.

Broughton, A., Higgins, T., Hicks, B., & Cox, A. (2009). *Workplace and social networking- the implications of Employment relations*. Retrieved from http://www.acas.org.uk/media/pdf/d/6/1111_Workplaces_and_Social_Networking.pdf

Buy, B. (2016, July 21). *Best Buy Social Media Policy*. Retrieved from http://forums.bestbuy.com/t5/Welcome-News/Best-Buy-Social-Media-Policy/td-p/20492

CDM Media. (2015, April 21). *Protecting social media assets: lessons from CDM Media*. Retrieved from http://www.law360.com/articles/643290/protecting-social-media-assets-lessons-from-cdm-media

Chanda, R., & Zaorski, S. (2013, May/June). Social media usage in Financial Service Industry: Toward a Business- Driven compliance approach. *Journal of Taxation and Regulation of Financial Institution, 26*(5), 5–20.

Cisco. (2014, April). *Cisco Social Media Policy*. Retrieved from http://www.slideshare.net/Cisco/cisco-global-social-media-policy

Coke. (2016). *Social Media Principles*. Retrieved from http://www.coca-colacompany.com/stories/online-social-media-principles/

Dell. (2011, August 15). *Dell: Global Social Media Policy*. Retrieved from http://www.dell.com/learn/us/en/uscorp1/corp-comm/social-media-policy

Duara, N. (2012, March 8). *Ore. Nurse Aide Posted Facebook Photos of Patients*. Retrieved from cnsnews.com/news/article/ore-nurse-aide-posted-facebook-photos-patients-2

Editor's Choice. (2011, March 31). *Abusive Facebook comments led to pub shift manager's dismissal*. Retrieved from http://www.xperthr.co.uk/editors-choice/abusive-facebook-comments-led-to-pub-shift-managers-dismissal/108662/

Fink, J. (June 14, 2010). *Five Nurses Fired for Facebook Postings*. Retrieved from www.scrubsmag.com/five-nurses-fired-for-facebook-postings/

Gangadharbatla, H. (2008). Facebook me: Collective self-esteem, need to belong, and Internet self-efficacy as predictors of the Igenerations attitudes toward social networking sites. *Journal of Interactive Advertising, 8*(2), 5–15. doi:10.1080/15252019.2008.10722138

Gelms, J. (2012). High-tech Harassment: Employer Liability under Title VII for Employee Social Media Misconduct. *Washington Law Review (Seattle, Wash.), 87*(1), 249–279.

Geneva, L. (2009). *Nurses fired Over Cell Photos of a patient*. Retrieved from http://www.wisn.com/Nurses-Fired-Over-Cell-Phone-Photos-Of-Patient/8076340/

Hidy, K. M., & McDonald, M. S. E. (2013). Risky business: The legal implications of social media's increasing role in employment decisions. *Journal of Legal Studies in Business*, *18*, 69–88.

Hohmann, J., & The 2010-11 ASNE Ethics and Values Committee. (2011, May). *ASNE 10 Best practices for Social media - helpful guidelines for news organization*. Retrieved from http://asne.org/Files/pdf/10_Best_Practices_for_Social_Media.pdf

Hollon, J. (2012, October 3). *Survey: 75% of Workers are accessing social media while on the job*. Retrieved from: http://www.eremedia.com/tlnt/survey-75-of-workers-are-accessing-social-media-while-on-the-job/ on April 30, 2016

IBM. (2010). *IBM Social Computing Guidelines*. Retrieved from https://www.ibm.com/blogs/zz/en/guidelines.html

Intel. (n.d.). *Intel Social Media Guidelines*. Retrieved from http://www.intel.com/content/www/us/en/legal/intel-social-media-guidelines.html

ISACA. (2010). *Social media: Business benefits and Security, governance and Assurance perspective*. Retrieved from: http://www.isaca.org/groups/professional-english/security-trend/groupdocuments/social-media-wh-paper-26-may10-research.pdf

Jacobson, W. S., & Tufts, S. H. (2013). To Post or Not to Post: Employee Rights and Social Media. *Review of Public Personnel Administration*, *33*(1), 84–107. doi:10.1177/0734371X12443265

Jennings, S. E., Blount, J. R., & Gail Weatherly, M. (2014). Social Media – A Virtual Pandoras Box: Prevalence, Possible Legal Liabilities, and Policies. *Business and Professional Communication Quarterly*, *77*(1), 96–113. doi:10.1177/2329490613517132

Jet. (2016). *5 terrific examples of Company social media policies* [Web post log]. Retrieved from http://blog.hirerabbit.com/5-terrific-examples-of-company-social-media-policies/

Jones, L. B. (2013, Mar 28). *Best practice example: GAP Social Media Policy*. Retrieved from http://oursocialtimes.com/best-practice-example-gaps-social-media-policy/

Kaupins, G., & Park, S. (2011). Legal and Ethical Implications of Corporate Social Networks. *Employee Responsibilities and Rights Journal, 23*(2), 83–99. doi:10.1007/s10672-010-9149-8

Kirby & Raphan. (2014). The NLRB's Continued Regulation of Social Media in the Workplace. *Journal of Internet Law, 18*(2), 13–17.

Lauby, S. (2009, June 02). *10 Must-Haves for your social media policy* [Web post log]. Retrieved from: http://mashable.com/2009/06/02/social-media-policy-musts/#225temiNmaqO

Marken, G. A. (2007). Social Media . . . The Hunted can Become the Hunter. *Public Relations Quarterly, 52*(4), 9–12.

Mayfield, A. (2006). *What is Social Media?*. Retrieved from http://www.spannerworks.com/fileadmin/uploads/eBooks/What_is_ Social_Media.pdf

McCay Solicitors. (2015). *Employees' use and misuse of social media*. Retrieved from http://www.mccaysolicitors.co.uk/employees-use-misuse-of-social-media/

Rayner, J. (2003). *Managing Reputational Risk: Curbing Threats, Leveraging Opportunities*. Chichester, UK: John Wiley & Sons.

Xifra, J., & Ordeix, E. (2009). Managing reputational risk in an economic downturn: The case of Banco Santander. *Public Relations Review, 35*(4), 353–360. doi:10.1016/j.pubrev.2009.08.004

McDonough, S. (n.d.). *How the use of social media can affect your employment*. Retrieved from http://www.md-solicitors.co.uk/how-the-use-of-social-media-can-affect-your-employment/

Merrill, T., Latham, K., Santalesa, D., & Navetta, D. (2011, April). *Social media: The business benefits may be enormous, but can the risks – reputational, legal, operational- be mitigated?* Retrieved from http://www.acegroup.com/us-en/news-room/wp-social-media-the-business-benefits-may-be-enormous-but-can-the-risks-reputational-legal-operational-be-mitigated.aspx?frmmob=tr

Mooney, J. A. (2013). Locked Out on LinkedIn: LinkedIn Account Belongs to Employee, Not Employer. *Intellectual Property & Technology Law Journal, 25*(6), 16–18.

MW. (2016). *Dictionary Definition of Social Media*. Retrieved from http://www.merriam-webster.com/dictionary/social%20media

Nadkarni, A., & Hofmann, S. G. (2012). Why do people use Facebook? *Personality and Individual Differences, 52*(3), 243–249. doi:10.1016/j.paid.2011.11.007 PMID:22544987

NSNA. (n.d.). *Recommendations For: Social Media Usage and Maintaining Privacy, Confidentiality and Professionalism*. Retrieved from: http://www.nsna.org/Portals/0/Skins/NSNA/pdf/NSNA_Social_Media_Recommendations.pdf

Prafull. (2012). *5 great corporate social media policy examples* [Web post log]. Retrieved from http://blog.hirerabbit.com/5-great-corporate-social-media-policy-examples/

PRMS. (2012). Protecting your practice from social media misadventures. *Rx for Risk, 20*(4).

Proskauer, D. (2014, July 5). *Employee access to social media in the workplace decreases*. Retrieved from http://www.danpontefract.com/employee-access-to-social-media-in-the-workplace-decreases/

Proskauer. (2014). *Social media in the workplace around the world*. Retrieved from http://www.proskauer.com/files/uploads/social-media-in-the-workplace-2014.pdf

Scutt, M. (2013, Sept). *Misuse of Social media by Employees*. Retrieved from http://www.infolaw.co.uk/newsletter/2013/09/misuse-of-social-media-by-employees/

Sheldon, K. M., Abad, N., & Hinsch, C. (2011). A two-process view of Facebook use and relatedness need-satisfaction: Disconnection drives use, and connection rewards it. *Journal of Personality and Social Psychology, 100*(4), 766–775. doi:10.1037/a0022407 PMID:21280967

Shullich, R. (2011, December 5). *Risk assessment of Social Media*. Retrieved from https://www.sans.org/reading-room/whitepapers/privacy/risk-assessment-social-media-33940

Smith, A. (2011, November 14). *Why Americans use social media*. Pew Research Center.

Thompson, T., Jr., Hertzberg, J., & Sullivan, M. (2011). *Social media and its associated risks*. Retrieved from https://www.grantthornton.ca/resources/insights/white_papers/ social%20media_whitepaper%20CDN%20-%20FINAL.pdf

Times. (2009). *Times updates social media guidelines*. Retrieved from http://latimesblogs.latimes.com/readers/2009/11/updated-social-media-guidelines.html

Vaast, E., & Kaganer, E. (2013). Social Media Affordances and Governance in the Workplace: An Examination of Organizational Policies. *Journal of Computer-Mediated Communication*, *19*(1), 78–101. doi:10.1111/jcc4.12032

Welles, K. (2008, Dec 4). *Online Comments lead to privacy complaint*. Retrieved from http://www.databreaches.net/online-comments-lead-to-privacy-complaint/

Yath v. Fairview Clinics, N. P. (2009). Retrieved from http://www.casebriefs.com /blog/law/health-law/health-law-keyed-to-furrow/the-professional-patient-relationship/yath-v-fairview-clinics-n-p/

Younkins, L. R. (2013). #IHateMyBoss: Rethinking the NLRB's Approach to Social Media Policies. *Brooklyn Journal of Corporate, Financial & Commercial Law*, *8*(1), 222–252.

Zeltser, L. (2011). *Learning to live with social networks: risk and rewards*. Retrieved from: https://zeltser.com/media/docs/social-networking-risks-rewards.pdf

APPENDIX A: SOCIAL MEDIA POLICIES

(Retrieved online per details in the References)

A1. BEST BUY (Best Buy, 2016)

Guidelines for functioning in an electronic world are the same as the values, ethics and confidentiality policies employees are expected to live every day, whether you're Tweeting, talking with customers or chatting over the neighbor's fence. Remember, your responsibility to Best Buy doesn't end when you are off the clock. For that reason, this policy applies to both company sponsored social media and personal use as it relates to Best Buy.

What You Should Do

- *Disclose your Affiliation: If you talk about work related matters that are within your area of job responsibility you must disclose your affiliation with Best Buy.*
- *State That It's YOUR Opinion: When commenting on the business. Unless authorized to speak on behalf of Best Buy, you must state that the views expressed are your own. Hourly employees should not speak on behalf of Best Buy when they are off the clock.*
- *Protect Yourself: Be careful about what personal information you share online.*
- *Act responsibly and ethically: When participating in online communities, do not misrepresent yourself. If you are not a vice president, don't say you are.*
- *Honor Our Differences: Live the values. Best Buy will not tolerate discrimination (including age, sex, race, color, creed, religion, ethnicity, sexual orientation, gender identity, national origin, citizenship, disability, or marital status or any other legally recognized protected basis under federal, state, or local laws, regulations or ordinances).*
- *Offers and Contests: Follow the normal legal review process. If you are in the store, offers must be approved through the retail marketing toolkit.*

What You Should Never Disclose:

- *The Numbers: Non-public financial or operational information. This includes strategies, forecasts and most anything with a dollar-figure attached to it. If it's not already public information, it's not your job to make it so.*

- **Promotions:** *Internal communication regarding drive times, promotional activities or inventory allocations. Including: advance ads, drive time playbooks, holiday strategies and Retail Insider editions.*
- **Personal Information:** *Never share personal information about our customers. See the Customer Information Policies for more information.*
- **Legal Information:** *Anything to do with a legal issue, legal case, or attorneys without first checking with legal.*
- **Anything that belongs to someone else:** *Let them post their own stuff; you stick to posting your own creations. This includes illegal music sharing, copyrighted publications, and all logos or other images that are trademarked by Best Buy.*
- **Confidential Information:** *Do not publish, post, or release information that is considered confidential or top secret.*

Basically, if you find yourself wondering if you can talk about something you learned at work -- don't. Follow Best Buy's policies and live the company's values and philosophies. They're there for a reason.

Just in case you are forgetful or ignore the guidelines above, here's what could happen. You could:

- *Get fired (and it's embarrassing to lose your job for something that's so easily avoided)*
- *Get Best Buy in legal trouble with customers or investors*
- *Cost us the ability to get and keep customers*

Remember: protect the brand, protect yourself.

Finally, here are some policies you should keep in mind whenever you are communicating about or on behalf of Best Buy:

- *Customer Information Policies*
- *Information Security Policy*
- *Code of Business Ethics*
- *Confidentiality Policy*
- *Policy Against Sexual Harassment*
- *Policy Against All Forms of Harassment*
- *Inappropriate Conduct Policy*
- *Securities Trading Policy*

If you still have questions please contact your leadership.

A2. CISCO (Cisco, 2014)

Policy

- *When you are participating on social networking sites using your personal social media accounts, be transparent that your thoughts are your own if discussing official Cisco business. Use your real identity— no aliases—and disclose your affiliation with Cisco. If you believe your posting might lead to any confusion with viewers about whether you are speaking on behalf of Cisco, you should clearly and specifically state as follows:*
  - *Twitter disclaimer: "These tweets are my own, not Cisco's."*
  - *Disclaimer for blogs sponsored by Cisco: "Some of the individuals posting to this site, including the moderators, work for Cisco. Opinions expressed here and in any corresponding comments are the personal opinions of the original authors, not those of Cisco."*
  - *Third-party blog disclaimer: "The opinions expressed in this blog are my own views and not those of Cisco."*
- *Do not commit Cisco to any action unless you have the authority to do so.*
- *Do not post any business-related confidential or internal-use–only information (marked "For Internal Use Only")that you obtain or learn about as part of your job duties with Cisco. Such information includes the following examples: information regarding the development of systems, products, processes and technology; personally identifiable information (such as telephone numbers, Social Security numbers, credit and debit card numbers or financial account numbers) of the company's employees, customers, vendors, or competitors; nonpublic financial information; marketing strategies; inventions not yet patented; or other business-related confidential or proprietary information.*
- *Respect all copyright and intellectual property laws including those protecting music, videos, text and photographs belonging to Cisco or third parties.*
- *Respect financial disclosure laws. Be very careful when making statements about Cisco's financial performance, and do not make statements that in any way could violate federal or state securities laws such as the disclosure of material, nonpublic information. For example, it is illegal to communicate or give a "tip" on inside information to others so that they may buy or sell stocks or securities. Refer any questions to a Cisco Investor Relations representative.*
- *If you are representing yourself as a Cisco employee on social networking sites like LinkedIn, you may not provide professional references for any current or former Cisco employee, contractor, vendor, or contingent worker on Cisco's behalf. However, you may provide a personal reference or recommendation r for current or former Cisco employees, contractors, vendors, and contingent*

workers provided a) the statements made and information provided in the reference are factually accurate; and b) you include the following disclaimer:

"This reference is being made by me in a personal capacity. It is not intended and should not be construed as a reference from Cisco Systems, Inc. or any of its affiliated entities."

- *Respect privacy; never ask for personal social networking passwords.*
- *Do not post anything that is maliciously false, abusive, threatening or defamatory. You should not post content that is defamatory, discriminatory, harassing, or in violation of Cisco's policies against discrimination, harassment, or hostility on account of age, race, religion, sex, ethnicity, nationality, disability, or other protected class, status, or characteristic. You should not unlawfully disparage Cisco products or services, or the products or services of our vendors or competitors. Examples of such conduct include offensive posts meant to intentionally harm someone's reputation and posts that could contribute to a hostile work environment on the basis of age, race, religion, sex, ethnicity, nationality, disability or other protected class, status or characteristic.*
- *Do not engage with the news media or industry analysts (for example, Wall Street Journal, InformationWeek, Gartner, and Forrester) to discuss official Cisco strategy and/or business on Cisco's behalf without Public Relations (PR) and Analyst Relations (AR) consultation and approval. To ensure that Cisco communicates with the media in a consistent, timely, and professional manner about matters related to the company, consult your manager and your PR representative or AR representative before responding.*
- *If you see something online that alleges potentially unlawful or unethical conduct (for example, illegal, unsafe or unethical conduct by a Cisco employee, contractor or vendor), please immediately escalate this event to the internetpostings@cisco.com alias. Representatives from Legal, PR, Social Media, and HR monitor this alias. If you are uncomfortable reaching out to the internetpostings@cisco.com alias, you can contact the Ethics Resource Center, which is confidential and anonymous and is the best resource to resolve problems such as the following:*
  - *Theft, fraud or any other dishonest conduct*
  - *Discrimination or harassment*
  - *Waste or abuse of Cisco resources*
  - *Conflicts of interest*
  - *Unsafe situations*
  - *Mismanagement*
  - *Any actions that violate the COBC*

A3. DELL (Dell, 2011)

There's a lot of talk about Social Media these days both at Dell and around the world. Dell encourages all employees to use Social Media the right way and this policy should help you on that path. This policy is the first step, not the last; so if you're interested in Social Media, whether personally or professionally, you should look into our Social Media and Communities University (SMaC U) classes. Since the term Social Media is used a number of different ways, we want to make sure you understand what we mean when we say Social Media. Social Media is any tool or service that facilitates conversations over the internet. Social Media applies not only to traditional big names, such as Facebook®, Twitter and Renren, but also applies to other platforms you may use that include user conversations, which you may not think of as Social Media. Platforms such as, YouTube™, Flickr™, blogs and wikis are all part of Social Media.

Finally, even though this policy is written so it's easy to understand and conversational in tone, it's an actual policy. If you don't follow the principles laid out below when engaging in Social Media you could face serious consequences up to termination in accordance with the laws of the country where you are employed. Nobody wants that to happen though, so read over this policy and make sure you understand it. Dell has five Social Media principles that you should know before engaging in any type of online conversation that might impact Dell. You'll know these principles if you've already taken the Social Media Principles course from SMaC U.

Protect Information

Social Media encourages you to share information and connect with people. When you use Social Media, you should try and build relationships, but you should also be aware that through your relationship with Dell, you have access to confidential information that shouldn't be made public. So, you shouldn't share our confidential company information or any of our customers' personally identifiable information. Every year, you take a course on how you should protect privacy and personal information. The same thing applies on Social Media, because you mistakenly post confidential information on a Social Media platform, it will be hard to take down that information completely.

Be Transparent and Disclose

When you talk about Dell on Social Media, you should disclose that you work for Dell. Your friends may know you work for Dell, but their network of friends and colleagues may not and you don't want to accidentally mislead someone. You should know and remember the 10 magic words: "Hello, my name is [NAME], and I work for Dell." Be sure to replace [NAME] with your name because that looks odd.

Follow the Law, Follow the Code of Conduct

Social Media lets you communicate incredibly fast and have your message go viral in seconds. This makes it difficult to fix an inaccurate message once you've shared it. The best thing to do is double check all content before you share it, both for accuracy and to make sure it fits into Dell's overall Social Media strategy, our Code of Conduct and any restrictions that may apply to your content based on local law (such as the FTC Endorsement Guidelines in the US) and the platform you are using (such as terms of service for the site upon which you are sharing). One of Dell's core values is winning with integrity, and that applies to Social Media as well. Dell employees hold ourselves to high ethical standards, as our Code of Conduct spells out, and that applies to Social Media just like everything else you do as a Dell employee.

Be Responsible

Make sure you're engaging in Social Media conversations the right way. If you aren't an authority on a subject, send someone to the expert rather than responding yourself. Don't speak on behalf of Dell if you aren't giving an official Dell response, and be sure your audience knows the difference. If you see something being shared related to Dell on a Social Media platform that shouldn't be happening, immediately inform the Social Media and Communities team, your manager, Ethics and Compliance or some other appropriate contact. And always remember that anything posted in social media can go viral, no matter what your privacy settings may be, so be sure you're only posting content you would feel comfortable showing up in your boss' inbox, your coworker's Twitter feed or the front page of a major news site.

Be Nice, Have Fun and Connect

Social Media is a place to have conversations and build connections, whether you're doing it for Dell or for yourself. The connections you'll make on Social Media will be much more rewarding if you remember to have conversations rather than push agendas. Dell has always been a leader in using technology to directly connect with our customers. Social Media is another tool you can use to build our brand, just be sure you do it the right way.

Social Media Account Ownership

This section isn't a Social Media principle, but it's still important enough to be in this policy. If you participate in Social Media activities as part of your job at Dell, that account may be considered Dell property. If that account is Dell property, you don't get to take it with you if you leave the company — meaning you will not try to change the password or the account name or create a similar sounding account or have any ownership of the contacts and connections you have gained through the account. This doesn't apply to personal accounts that you may access at work, but would certainly apply to all Dell-branded accounts created as part of your job. If you have any questions about an account you operate, please reach out to the SMaC team to discuss the account.

A4. INTEL (Intel, n.d.)

- ***Disclose:*** *Your honesty—or dishonesty—will be quickly noticed in the social media environment. Please represent Intel ethically and with integrity.*
- ***Be transparent:*** *If you make an endorsement or recommendation about Intel's products/technologies, you must disclose that you work for Intel. If you do not have an "Intel" handle, then use "#iwork4intel" in your postings. Using a disclaimer in your bio or profile is not enough per the FTC.*
- ***Be truthful:*** *If you have a vested interest in something you are discussing, be the first to point it out and be specific about what it is.*
- ***Be yourself:*** *Stick to your area of expertise; only write what you know. If you publish to a website outside Intel, please use a disclaimer like this one: "The postings on this site are my own and don't necessarily represent Intel's positions, strategies, or opinions."*
- ***Be up-to-date:*** *If you are leaving Intel, please remember to update your employment information on social media sites.*
- ***Protect:*** Make sure all that transparency doesn't violate Intel's confidentiality or legal guidelines for commercial speech—or your own privacy. Remember, if you're online, you're on the record—everything on the Internet is public and searchable. And what you write is ultimately your responsibility.
- ***Don't tell secrets:*** *Never reveal Intel classified or confidential information. If you are posting your job description on LinkedIn, be sure not to reveal confidential product information. If you're unsure, check with Intel PR or Global Communications Group. Off-limit topics include litigation, non-published financials, and unreleased product info. Also, please respect brand,*

trademark, copyright, fair use, and trade secrets. If it gives you pause—pause rather than publish.

- **Don't slam the competition (or Intel):** *Play nice. Anything you publish must be true and not misleading, and all claims must be substantiated and approved.* *

- **Don't overshare:** *Be careful out there—once you hit "share," you usually can't get it back. Plus, being judicious will help make your content more crisp and audience-relevant.*

- **Use Common Sense:** Perception is reality and in online social networks, the lines between public and private, personal and professional, are blurred. Just by identifying yourself as an Intel employee, you are creating perceptions about your expertise and about Intel. Do us all proud.

- **Add value:** *There are millions of words out there—make yours helpful and thought-provoking. Remember, it's a conversation, so keep it real. Build community by posting content that invites responses—then stay engaged. You can also broaden the dialogue by citing others who are writing about the same topic and allowing your content to be shared.*

- ***Don't make claims:** *We must use FTC mandated disclaimers **in all communications** when benchmarking or comparing processors. So stay away from saying our products are smarter/ faster/ higher-performing in your social media postings. Leave that to the experts.*

- **Did you screw up?** *If you make a mistake, admit it. Be upfront and be quick with your correction. If you're posting to a blog, you may choose to modify an earlier post—just make it clear that you have done so.*

- **Contractors and Endorsements:** *As the Intel Social Media Guidelines describe, we support transparency and are committed to clear disclosure of relationships and endorsements. If you are contracted, seeded, or in any way compensated by Intel to create social media, please be sure to read and follow the Intel Sponsored, Seeded, or Incentivized Social Media Practitioner Guidelines. As part of these guidelines, you need to disclose that you have been seeded or otherwise compensated by Intel. Your blog will be monitored for compliance with our guidelines and accurate descriptions of products and claims.*

- **Moderation:** *Moderation (reviewing and approving content) applies to any social media content written on behalf of Intel by people outside the company, whether the site is on or off Intel.com. We do not endorse or take responsibility for content posted by third parties, also known as user-generated content (UGC). This includes text input and uploaded files, including video, images, audio, executables, and documents. While we strongly encourage user* *participation, there are some guidelines we ask third parties to follow to keep it safe for everyone.*

- **Post moderation:** *Even when a site requires the user to register before posting, simple user name and email entry doesn't really validate the person. To ensure least risk/most security, we require moderation of all UGC posts. The designated moderator scans all posts to be sure they adhere to Intel's guidelines.*

- **Community moderation (reactive moderation):** *For established, healthy communities, group moderation by regular users can work well. This will sometimes be allowed to take the place of post moderation—but it must be applied for and approved.*

- **The "house rules":** *Whether content is post moderated or community moderated, we use this rule of thumb: the Good, the Bad, but not the Ugly. If the content is positive or negative and in context to the conversation, then it can be approved, regardless of whether it's favorable or unfavorable to Intel. But if the content is ugly, offensive, denigrating, and/or completely out of context, then we ask our moderators and communities to reject the content.*

- **Intel Sponsored, Seeded, or Incentivized Social Media Practitioner Guidelines:** *Intel supports transparency. We are committed to ensuring that our social media practitioners (SMPs) clearly disclose relationships and endorsements, and that statements about Intel® products are truthful and substantiated. If you are a social media practitioner who has been seeded with product, incentivized, or otherwise has an ongoing relationship with Intel, these guidelines apply to you. If you have any questions or concerns about them, get in touch with your Intel sponsor.*

Please keep in mind that Intel monitors social media related to our business, including the activities of our sponsored, seeded, or incentivized SMPs. If we find any non-disclosed relationships or statements that are false or misleading, we will contact you for correction. If, as a sponsored SMP, you are found to repetitively make inaccurate statements about Intel, Intel® products, or Intel® services, we may discontinue our relationship with you.

Rules of Engagement for Intel Sponsored, Seeded, or Incentivized SMPs

- **Be transparent:** *Please clearly and conspicuously disclose your relationship to Intel, including any incentives or sponsorships. Be sure this information is readily apparent to the public and to readers of each of your posts.*

- **Be specific:** *Do not make general claims about Intel® products, but talk specifically about what you experienced.*
- **Be yourself:** *We encourage you to write in the first person and stick to your area of expertise as it relates to Intel® technology.*
- **Be conscientious:** *Keep in mind that what you write is your responsibility, and failure to abide by these guidelines could put your Intel sponsorship or incentive at risk. Also, please always follow the terms and conditions for any third-party sites in which you participate.*

A5. COCA COLA (Coke, 2016)

There's a big difference in speaking "on behalf of the Company" and speaking "about" the Company. This set of 5 principles refers to those personal or unofficial online activities where you might refer to Coca-Cola.

- **Adhere to the Code of Business Conduct and other applicable policies.** *All Company associates, from the Chairman to every intern, are subject to the Company's Code of Business Conduct in every public setting. In addition, other policies, including the Information Protection Policy and the Insider Trading Policy, govern associates' behavior with respect to the disclosure of information; these policies are applicable to your personal activities online.*
- **You are responsible for your actions.** *Anything you post that can potentially tarnish the Company's image will ultimately be your responsibility. We do encourage you to participate in the online social media space, but urge you to do so properly, exercising sound judgment and common sense.*
- **Be a "scout" for compliments and criticism.** *Even if you are not an official online spokesperson for the Company, you are one of our most vital assets for monitoring the social media landscape. If you come across positive or negative remarks about the*
- **Let the subject matter experts respond to negative posts.** *You may come across negative or disparaging posts about the Company or its brands, or see third parties trying to spark negative conversations. Unless you are a certified online spokesperson, avoid the temptation to react yourself.*
- **Be conscious when mixing your business and personal lives.** *Online, your personal and business personas are likely to intersect. The Company respects the free speech rights of all of its associates, but you must remember that customers, colleagues and supervisors often have access to the online content you post. Keep this in mind when publishing information online that can be seen by more than friends and family, and know that information originally*

intended just for friends and family can be forwarded on. Remember NEVER to disclose non-public information of the Company (including confidential information), and be aware that taking public positions online that are counter to the Company's interests might cause conflict.

A6. IBM (IBM, 2010)

- *Know and follow IBM's* Business Conduct Guidelines.
- *IBMers are personally responsible for the content they publish on-line, whether in a blog, social computing site or any other form of user-generated media. Be mindful that what you publish will be public for a long time-protect your privacy and take care to understand a site's terms of service.*
- *Identify yourself-name and, when relevant, role at IBM-when you discuss IBM-related matters such as IBM products or services. You must make it clear that you are speaking for yourself and not on behalf of IBM.*
- *If you publish content online relevant to IBM in your personal capacity it is best to use a disclaimer such as this: "The postings on this site are my own and don't necessarily represent IBM's positions, strategies or opinions."*
- *Respect copyright, fair use and financial disclosure laws.*
- *Don't provide IBM's or a client's, partner's or suppliers' confidential or other proprietary information and never discuss IBM business performance or other sensitive matters about business results or plans publicly.*
- *Don't cite or reference clients, partners or suppliers on business-related matters without their approval. When you do make a reference, link back to the source and do not publish content that might allow inferences to be drawn which could damage a client relationship with IBM.*
- *Respect your audience. Don't use ethnic slurs, discriminatory remarks, personal insults, obscenity, or engage in any similar conduct that would not be appropriate or acceptable in IBM's workplace. You should also show proper consideration for others' privacy.*
- *Be aware of your association with IBM in online social networks. If you identify yourself as an IBMer, ensure your profile and related content is consistent with how you wish to present yourself with colleagues and clients.*
- *Spirited and passionate discussions and debates are fine, but you should be respectful of others and their opinions. Be the first to correct your own mistakes.*

- *Try to add value. Provide worthwhile information and perspective. IBM's brand is best represented by its people and what you publish may reflect on IBM's brand.*
- *Don't misuse IBM logos or trademarks and only use them if you have the authority to do so. For example, you shouldn't use IBM in your screen name or other social media ID.*

A7. LOS ANGELES TIMES (Times, 2009)

Social media networks – Facebook, MySpace, Twitter and others – provide useful reporting and promotional tools for Los Angeles Times journalists. The Times' Ethics Guidelines will largely cover issues that arise when using social media, but this brief document should provide additional guidance on specific questions.

Basic Principles

- *Integrity is our most important commodity: Avoid writing or posting anything that would embarrass The Times or compromise your ability to do your job.*
- *Assume that your professional life and your personal life will merge online regardless of your care in separating them.*
- *Even if you use privacy tools (determining who can view your page or profile, for instance), assume that everything you write, exchange or receive on a social media site is public.*
- *Just as political bumper stickers and lawn signs are to be avoided in the offline world, so too are partisan expressions online.*
- *Be aware of perceptions. If you "friend" a source or join a group on one side of a debate, do so with the other side as well. Also understand that readers may view your participation in a group as your acceptance of its views; be clear that you're looking for story ideas or simply collecting information. Consider that you may be an observer of online content without actively participating.*

Guidelines for Reporting

- *Be aware of inadvertent disclosures or the perception of disclosures. For example, consider that "friending" a professional contact may publicly identify that person as one of your sources.*
- *You should identify yourself as a Times employee online if you would do so in a similar situation offline.*

- *Authentication is essential: Verify sourcing after collecting information online. When transmitting information online – as in re-Tweeting material from other sources – apply the same standards and level of caution you would in more formal publication.*

Additional Notes

- *Using social media sites means that you (and the content you exchange) are subject to their terms of service. This can have legal implications, including the possibility that your interactions could be subject to a third-party subpoena. The social media network has access to and control over everything you have disclosed to or on that site. For instance, any information might be turned over to law enforcement without your consent or even your knowledge.*
- *These passages from the "Outside affiliations and community work" section of the Ethics Guidelines may be helpful as you navigate social media sites. For the complete guidelines, please see The Times' library's intranet site or, if you are outside the company network, see the* Readers' Representative Journal.

Editorial employees may not use their positions at the paper to promote personal agendas or causes. Nor should they allow their outside activities to undermine the impartiality of Times coverage, in fact or appearance.

Staff members may not engage in political advocacy – as members of a campaign or an organization specifically concerned with political change. Nor may they contribute money to a partisan campaign or candidate. No staff member may run for or accept appointment to any public office. Staff members should avoid public expressions or demonstrations of their political views – bumper stickers, lawn signs and the like.

Although The Times does not seek to restrict staff members' participation in civic life or journalistic organizations, they should be aware that outside affiliations and memberships may create real or apparent ethical conflicts. When those affiliations have even the slightest potential to damage the newspaper's credibility, staff members should proceed with caution and take care to advise supervisors.

Some types of civic participation may be deemed inappropriate. An environmental writer, for instance, would be prohibited from affiliating with environmental organizations, a health writer from joining medical groups, a business editor from membership in certain trade or financial associations.

A8. GAP (Jones, 2013)

These guidelines are important—because if you don't follow them a few things could happen: your posts can get deleted, we could lose customers and investors, we could get in trouble, or, worst of all, you could even lose your job … So do the right thing, stick to the guidelines.

Keep in mind…

There's really no such thing as "delete" *on the Internet, so please—think before you post.*

Some subjects can invite a flame war. *Be careful discussing things where emotions run high (e.g. politics and religion) and show respect for others' opinions.*

It's a small world and we're a global company. *Remember that what you say can be seen by customers and employees all over the world and something you say in one country might be inaccurate or offensive in another.*

Respect other people's stuff. *Just because something's online doesn't mean it's OK to copy it.*

Your job comes first. *Unless you are an authorized Social Media Manager, don't let social media affect your job performance.*

How to be the best …

Play nice. *Be respectful and considerate, no trolling, troll baiting, or flaming anybody, even our competitors.*

Be yourself. *Be the first to out that you are a Gap Inc. employee—and make it clear that you are not a company spokesperson.*

If you #!%#@# up? *Correct it immediately and be clear about what you've done to fix it. Contact the social media team if it's a real doozy.*

Add value. *Make sure your posts really add to the conversation. If it promotes Gap Inc.'s goals and values, supports our customers, improves or helps us sell products, or helps us do our jobs better, then you are adding value.*

Don't even think about it…

Talking about financial information, sales trends, strategies, forecasts, legal issues, future promotional activities.

Giving out personal information about customers or employees.

Posting confidential or non-public information.

Responding to an offensive or negative post by a customer. There's no winner in that game.

APPENDIX B: SOCIAL MEDIA BREACHES

B.1. Yath v. Fairview Clinics, N.P.

In a 2009 Minnesota case, Yath v. Fairview Clinics, (Yath v. Fairview Clinics, 2009) a patient attempted to impose liability upon the clinic and its employee through the theory of vicarious liability due to an employee's unauthorized access and dissemination of her medical record.[1] The employee, wondering why an acquaintance was at the clinic, improperly accessed and read the patient's medical file learning that she had a sexually transmitted disease and a new sex partner other than her husband. The employee shared this information with another employee, who then disclosed it to others, and eventually the information reached the patient's estranged husband. During this time, someone created a MySpace webpage posting the information on the Internet. The patient sued the clinic and the individuals allegedly involved in the disclosure. The district court granted summary judgment to the clinic on the invasion-of-privacy and vicarious liability claims and the patient appealed. The court of appeals overturned the trial court on the invasion-of-privacy argument, stating that the "number of actual viewers [of the site] was irrelevant." Rather, the determination depends on "whether the content is conveyed through a medium that delivers the information directly to the public." Since the MySpace webpage was not password protected, and it was available to the public for at least 24 hours, the publicity element of the invasion-of-privacy claim was satisfied.

In this case, the court found that the clinic could not be held liable for the employee's wrongful access and dissemination of patient information because the patient did not present any evidence that the employee's actions were foreseeable. Notably, the clinic did have a policy against such behavior by employees, which the court acknowledged in its opinion. Without such a policy in place, the court may have found that an employee's wrongful access and dissemination of private information would be foreseeable, and thereby hold the employer responsible." (PRMS, 2012).

B.2. Mercy Walworth Medical Center, Wisconsin

Two nurses were fired from Mercy Walworth Medical Center in Lake Geneva, Wisconsin, after an anonymous call from another employee led police to investigate a story that the two had taken photos of a patient and posted them on the Internet. Each was found to have taken photos of x-rays of a patient who was admitted to the emergency room with an object lodged in his body. Although investigators were unable to find anyone who had actually seen the photos posted online, discussion of the incident was posted to one of the nurse's Facebook pages. (PRMS, 2012).

"There were two nurses that independently took a picture each of an X-ray of a patient," Walworth County Undersheriff Kurt Picknell said. (Lake Geneva, 2009)

B.3. Tri-City Medical Center, California

In June 2010, five California nurses were fired from Tri-City Medical Center in Oceanside for discussing patients on Facebook.[5] Notably, no patient names, photos, or other identifying information was included in the posts. Just a short month later, Tri-City implemented a new policy, requiring employees to sign a new social media agreement concerning such sites as MySpace, Zoho, and Eventful, specifically stating, "Even if the patient is not identified by name or by the medical record number the information you disclose may identify that patient," in an effort to educate employees about what constitutes private medical information. (PRMS, 2012)

B.4. St. Mary Medical Center, Long Beach

In a particularly gruesome and cruel case, an elderly man who was stabbed more than a dozen times by a fellow nursing home resident and almost decapitated, became a source of entertainment for the nurses assigned to treat him at St. Mary Medical Center in Long Beach. At least seven staff members and two nurses snapped pictures of the dying man, instead of focusing on saving his life, and posted them on Facebook. The incident brought the hospital under intense scrutiny from the California Department of Health, who along with investigating the particular incident, also opened investigation on eight other potential breaches of patient information reported at the hospital in the same year. (PRMS, 2012)

B.5. Nursing Assistant Convicted, Oregon

A nursing assistant in Oregon was convicted by a jury for invasion of privacy for posting graphic photos of patients using bed pans.[6] Not only did she spend several days in jail for her conduct, she was forced to surrender her nursing certificate and fired by her employer, Regency Pacific Nursing and Rehab Center in the Portland suburb of Gresham. The Nursing Center was subjected to a thorough investigation by the Oregon Department of Human Services in order to determine whether the Center, along with the nursing assistant, was responsible for the invasion of privacy. According to a statement released by the Center, the employee's actions were immediately reported to the local police department, the Oregon State Department of Human Services, and the Oregon State Board of Nursing to ensure their immediate involvement in the investigation, and all appropriate notifications were made to the family members involved. (PRMS, 2012)

B.6. Derogatory Comments on Facebook

Derogatory comments on Facebook as was held in Whitham v Club 24 Ltd t/a Ventura ET/1810462/10. Mrs Whitham, a team leader employed by the Respondent, engaged in an exchange of messages with colleagues on Facebook after a difficult day: "I think I work in a nursery and I do not mean working with plants" and "Don't worry it takes a lot for the bastard to grind me down". She also sent a message saying "2 true xx" to the suggestion that she worked with a "lot of planks". Her messages were only visible to her 50 Facebook friends.

The employer took the view that these comments could damage its relationship with its main client and suspended her and issued disciplinary proceedings. (Scutt, 2013)

B.7. B&Q Worker Dismissed for Misconduct

In another example, a B&Q worker was dismissed for gross misconduct for posting on Facebook that his "place of work is beyond a ******* joke". He also posted he would do some "busting", which the employer took to be a breach of its social media policy and was threatening in tone. (Scutt, 2013)

B.8. Gosden v Lifeline

In Gosden v Lifeline, the tribunal held that the Claimant had been dismissed fairly for sending an offensive email from his personal computer to a former colleague's personal computer on the grounds that he acted in a way which could damage the employer's reputation. (McCay Solicitors, 2015)

B.9. Preece v Wetherspoons

In Preece v Wetherspoons, a pub manager posted derogatory comments about two abusive customers on Facebook whilst at work. The employee thought her privacy settings were private but her comments could in fact be viewed much more widely, including by family members of the customers in question. Wetherspoons had a clearly worded IT policy which reserves the right to take disciplinary action should the contents of any Facebook page "be found to lower the reputation of the organisation, staff or customers and/or contravene the company's equal opportunity policy". (McCay Solicitors, 2015)

Miss Preece was employed by JD Wetherspoons plc as a shift manager, working at the company's Ferry Boat Pub in Runcorn, Cheshire. She was aware of the company's policies regarding "blogging", which expressly referred to sites such as MySpace and Facebook. The policies stated that employees should not write or contribute to a blog, including Facebook, where the content lowers the reputation of the company or its customers, and the company reserved the right to take disciplinary action where this occurred. (Editor's choice, 2011)

B.10. Abusive Tweets by a Game Retailer Employee

A recent case involved offensive and abusive tweets posted by an employee of a games retailer resulting in him being summarily dismissed for gross misconduct. The employee brought an unfair dismissal claim against his employer which was originally upheld by the Employment Tribunal on the basis that the tweets were posted for 'private use'. However, this decision has since been overturned as the Employment Appeal Tribunal found the employee's failure to use privacy settings coupled with the fact that his tweets could have been seen by both staff and potential customers sufficient to justify his dismissal. (McDonough, n.d.)

Section 4
Technology Risks

Chapter 8
Information Technology Outsourcing Risk Factors and Provider Selection

Salim Lahmiri
ESCA School of Management, Morocco

ABSTRACT

Information technology outsourcing has become a major issue in business and received a large attention from both business managers and scholars. Indeed, it helps a business company to reduce it costs and to maintain its competitiveness. The purpose of this chapter is to introduce the utility of information technology outsourcing for the enterprise and to review some recent works in outsourcing risk factors identification and provider selection. Finally, drawbacks of information technology outsourcing will be presented along with future research directions.

INTRODUCTION

Since the 1980s, business outsourcing has increasingly become a common practice (Liou & Chuang, 2010; Kaya, 2011; Chen et al, 2011; Shi et al, 2011; Liou & Chuang, 2010; Cai et al, 2013) because of a combination of environmental pressure, efficiency, and competitive pressure (Hsu et al, 2013). There exist several definitions of outsourcing. For instance, it is defined as ongoing purchasing of services and parts from an outside company that is already provided by the outsourcing company (Linder, 2004). It is also defined as transfer of production functions of goods or

DOI: 10.4018/978-1-5225-2604-9.ch008

services to external providers (Araz et al., 2007). More general, outsourcing occurs when one company hands over a part of their existing internal activity to another company by contract (McCarthy & Anagroustou, 2004). Companies outsource for various reasons, including receiving efficient procurement services, having access to specialized technology and operational platforms, and reducing the staffing levels (Chen et al., 2011).

Information technology (IT) outsourcing is one of the most outsourcing practices (Chen et al, 2011; Hsu et al, 2013). For companies, the drivers of IT functions outsourcing are cost savings, access to expertise and new technologies, a decrease in IT professional recruitment, flexibility in managing IT resources and an increase in capital utilization, effectively manage time and costs, and to improve productivity, quality, and customer satisfaction (Jurison, 1995; Quinn & Hilmer, 1994; Sobol & Apte, 1995; Dhar & Balakrishnan, 2006). Other identified reasons include increasing the flexibility of the IT department, reducing technology costs, improving IT quality, increasing access to new technologies, and decreasing risk (Claver et al., 2002). Consequently, companies have increased efficiencies and abilities to focus on core competencies; and therefore, they increased both profits and customer satisfaction (Hsu et al., 2013).

However, the IT outsourcing which is a very complex process is affected by several risk factors; including the provider reliability, technical competence, financial stability, and manufacturing capability (Li & Wan, 2014). But, choosing outsourcing providers is an important key to increase the success rate of outsourcing (Hsu et al, 2013). Unfortunately, it is also a difficult task due to the fact that outsourcing providers cannot meet all selection criteria (Li & Wan, 2014). According to (Li & Wan, 2014), the IT outsourcing process may be divided into seven phases: IT demand, application status, and department performance evaluation; IT development and programming; outsourcing strategy; contract object design and outsourcing provider selection; contract negotiation; implementation and supervision; and project approval. The overall process is shown in Figure 1 as in (Li & Wan, 2014).

The purpose of this chapter is to provide an overview of IT outsourcing risk factors and provider selection methods. The chapter is organized as follows. IT outsourcing process and risk factors identification will be presented. Then, some recent advances related to IT outsourcing provider selection will be presented. Finally, we conclude by presenting some of IT outsourcing disadvantages and provide future research directions in the area of IT outsourcing risk factors identification and provider selection.

Figure 1. IT outsourcing process as in Li and Wan (2014)

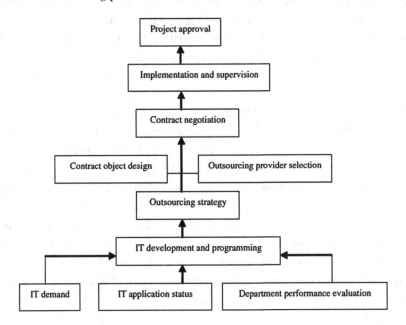

BACKGROUND

IT Outsourcing Risk Factors and Assessment

The effective risk management process is highly needed because of risk caused by application of information technology systems (Blakley, McDermott, & Geer, 2001). Therefore, an effective risk management process will result in a successful security program (Blakley, McDermott, & Geer, 2001). Indeed, the risk management process is based on three basic elements: the process of identifying risks, assessing risks, and taking steps to reduce risks to an acceptable level (Stoneburner, Goguen, & Feringa, 2002). There is an increasing interest on identification of IT outsourcing risk factors because appropriate identification is significant to capture the source of IT outsourcing risk (Fan et al, 2012). Besides, according to Peltier (2005) risk assessment is the most important process of information risk management.

In terms of IT outsourcing risk factors identification, Fan et al, (2012) conducted a comprehensive study to examine various risk factors of IT outsourcing mentioned in the literature, and interviewed 23 experts in IT industry to finally select eight risk factors. They are described in Table 1 as in Fan et al, (2012). Furthermore, Fan et al, (2012) investigated a method for identifying risk factors of IT outsourcing, in which the interrelationships among risk factors are considered. In particular,

Table 1. Risk factors as identified and described by Fan et al., (2012)

Risk Factors	Description
Technological indivisibility	Since much of information technology is not divisible, trying to divide it into parts for different vendors can be problematical
Possibility of weak management	Weak management could increase costs and lead to conflict and dissatisfaction because new type of IT outsourcing management may be more difficult
Cultural fit	Poor cultural fit may damage the outsourcing relationships between client and vendor and lead to the conflict between them
Requirements instability	Future direction and requirements of the client may change in the process of IT outsourcing operation
Coordination between client and vendor	Effective coordination between client and vendor could facilitate the favorable cooperation in the process of IT outsourcing operation
Reliability of selected vendor(s)	Unreliable vendor(s) may influence the schedule and quality of IT outsourcing operation
Uncertainty about the legal environment	Legal environment is the external condition for IT outsourcing. Uncertain legal environment could influence IT outsourcing operation
Technological complexity	Technological complexity may influence the schedule of IT outsourcing operation and the quality of task accomplishment

based on the 2-tuple fuzzy linguistic representation model (Herrera & Martínez, 2000, 2001) and the classical Decision Making Trial and Evaluation Laboratory (DEMATEL) method (Fontela & Gabus, 1976; Gabus & Fontela, 1972, 1973), they developed an extended DEMATEL method to identify the importance and classification of risk factors. The authors concluded that compared with the existing fuzzy DEMATEL methods (Wu & Lee, 2007 & Lin & Wu, 2008), their proposed method for risk factors identification in IT outsourcing is more suitable to deal with the interdependent information in the form of linguistic terms. Indeed, they concluded that their method for risk factors identification using interdependent information in linguistic environment gives decision makers one more choice for identifying risk factors of IT outsourcing.

In terms of IT outsourcing risk assessment, a large number of recent studies have analyzed various issues including risk assessment, mitigation, and devolvement of best practices in information technology outsourcing. For instance, Chou and Chou (2009) developed an information system outsourcing life cycle model based on various risks factors encountered during different contracting phases; including pre-contract, contract, and post-contract phases. Thouin et al, (2009) used transaction cost economics of information technology outsourcing examining the effect of level of low asset specificity on firm level financial performance. In particular, the transaction cost economics closely corresponded to optimal allocation of firm-resources so that firms that outsourced low asset specificity resources experienced superior financial performance. Alaghehband et al, (2011) used transaction cost theory in information technology outsourcing in terms of faithfulness and concluded that the model hardly capture all the essential elements of transaction cost theory. In a similar study, Rusu and Hudosi (2011) proposed a model of an information technology outsourcing that includes a procedure based on transaction cost theory to examine and assess the risk exposure in information technology. Al-Hamadany and Kanapathy (2012) examined the effect of perceived risks and benefits on the intention to increase level of information technology outsourcing using a questionnaire survey. The results from 83 companies in Malyasia indicated that financial risk factor is the most significant factor amongst all perceived risks, whereas technical resources and time are found as the most influencing factors for perceived benefits. Based on a comprehensive review of the literature, Abdullah and Verner (2012) developed a literature based conceptual risk framework for strategic information technology system development outsourcing from the clients perspective. They identified complexity, contract, execution, financial, legal, organizational environment and user as influencing factors on the outcome of strategic information systems.

Kim et al, (2013) proposed a model for information technology outsourcing management by considering governance effectiveness as key factor to facilitate success. Bachlechner et al, (2014) found that factors like auditing clouds, heterogeneity of services, coordination between parties, relationships between clients and vendors, and lack of data security awareness can be considered as risks if these are not adequately managed. Recently, in an interesting study, Samantra et al, (2014) proposed a hierarchical information technology outsourcing risk structure representation to develop a formal model for qualitative risk assessment. The proposed models consisted on an improved decision making method using fuzzy set theory for converting linguistic data into numeric risk ratings. Their presented hierarchical risk assessment model outlined numerous outsourcing risks; including strategic, business, technical, financial, legal, operational, environmental, information, managerial, relationship, and time management risk. The outsourcing risks and their influencing factors are shown in Table 2 adapted from Samantra et al, (2014).

Recent Advances in Provider Selection

As a strategy, outsourcing is suitable to reduce firm operating costs and consequently improve its competitiveness. Indeed, outsourcing could be used by and for a company to strengthen its position in today's competitive markets (Liou & Chuang, 2010). However, it is crucial to select appropriate outsourcing provider following a rigorous scientific methodology. There exists a large body of works where different approaches have been proposed to select optimal provider. For instance, Lee and

Table 2. Outsourcing risks and their influencing factors (adapted from Samantra et al., 2014)

Outsourcing Risk	Influencing Factors
Strategic risk	Loss of organizational competency, Proximity of core competency, Interdependence of activities, Technological invisibility, Endemic uncertainty Out-dated technology skill, Lack of information flow to support ITO (IT outsourcing) strategy, Lack of strategy focused on attaining reduction in cost, Fuzzy focus, Poorly managed Mergers and Acquisitions (M&A) and partnerships, Loosing ownership of the client
Business risk	Business uncertainty, Small number of suppliers, Asset specificity, Interdependence of activities
Technical risk	Lack of use of new technology, Complexity of new and emerging technology and interface, Loss of key technical person, Lack of technical knowledge and education, Lack of research on IT service, Task complexity, Loss of innovative capacity, Technological discontinuity
Financial risk	Lack of experience and expertise of the enterprise with the activity, Lack of planning and inaccurate budgeting, Endemic uncertainty, Ineffective infrastructure investment, Increased cost of services
Legal risk	Different rules and regulations in global trading, Dangers of eternal triangle, Lack of experience of the client with outsourcing, Uncertainty about the legal environment, Privacy, piracy and security
Operational risk	Lack of experience and expertise of client with contract management, Measurement problem, Lack of talent and innovation, Possibility of weak management, Lack of organizational learning, Lack of experience and expertise of the supplier with the activities
Environmental risk	Measurement problems, Social responsibility, Lack of experience and expertise of the organization and/or of the supplier with outsourcing contracts, Poor cultural fit, Danger of eternal triangle
Information risk	Interdependence of activities, Lack of experience and expertise of the supplier with the activities, Supplier size, Supplier financial stability, Task complexity
Managerial risk	Lack of conflict management, Lack of upper management involvement, Lack of contingency plan, Lack of understanding individual authorities and responsibilities, Unclear decision making process, Lack of expertise and experience in IT field
Relationship risk	Inadequate terms and ambiguous contract with supplier, Suppliers' service quality, Lack of buyer and supplier relationship, Suppliers' transparency in information sharing on its capabilities, Supplier hold-up, expropriation and loss of bargaining power, Misaligned incentives between supplier and buyer, Ineffective bidding mechanisms
Time management risk	No proper follow up, Not paying attention to details in the starting stages, Deadlines not met, Less manpower, Sorting delay

Kim (2005) analyzed the structural relationship among the determinants of an outsourcing partnership and identified six key factors including shared knowledge, organizational linkage, mutual dependency, benefits, commitment, and predisposition. Several techniques have been proposed in the literature to identify best providers.

For instance, Yang et al. (2007) identified factors affecting the business process outsourcing decision and constructed a decision model using the analytic hierarchy process (AHP) method. Hsu and Hsu (2008) presented an entropy-combined technique for order preference by similarity to ideal solution (TOPSIS) based decision-making method for medical information system outsourcing.

Recently, hybrid methods have been proposed to better select outsourcing provider. For instance, Liou & Chuang (2010) proposed a new hybrid multiple criteria decision-making (MCDM) model, which addresses the dependent relationships among criteria with the aid of the Decision-Making Trial and Evaluation Laboratory (DEMATEL) method to build a relations-structure among criteria. The authors used the Analytical Network Process (ANP) of Saaty (1996) to determine the relative weights of each criterion with dependence and feedback. They also adopted VIKOR method (Opricovic, 1998; Opricovic and Tzeng, 2004) to prioritize the alternatives. Using data from a Taiwanese airline and fifteen criterions (compatibility, relationship, flexibility, information sharing, quality, knowledge skills, customer satisfaction, on time rate, cost, cost saving, flexibility in billing, risk, labor unions, loss of management control, and information security) they concluded that their model can help practitioners improve their decision process, particularly when criteria are numerous and inter-related. Other successful hybrid models were also proposed in the literature to deal with the problem of outsourcing provider selection. For example, Lin et al. (2010) proposed a hybrid MADM method for outsourcing provider selection by combining interpretive structural modeling and the ANP method. Chen et al, (2011) presented the fuzzy Preference Ranking Organization Method for Enrichment Evaluation (fuzzy PROMETHEE) to evaluate four potential suppliers using seven criteria and four decision makers using data from Taiwanese bank. They concluded that rankings results provide help assisting decision-makers or organizations seeking to improve the efficiency of the information technology outsourcing decision processes. Liou et al. (2011) proposed a hybrid MADM model to address the dependent relationships among various criteria. Finally, they used fuzzy preference programming and ANP to construct a model for outsourcing provider selection. Ho et al. (2012) integrated the quality function deployment (QFD), fuzzy set, and AHP method for evaluating and selecting optimal third-party logistics service providers. Buyukozkan and Cifci (2012) proposed a hybrid MADM method for evaluating green suppliers based on fuzzy decision making Trial and evaluation laboratory (DEMATEL), fuzzy ANP and fuzzy technique for order preference by similarity to ideal solution (TOPSIS) of Hwang and Yoon (1981). Hsu et al, (2013) proposed a hybrid model that combines DEMATEL and ANP to addresses the dependent relationships between the various criteria. They also applied a modified grey relation method to select and improve the criterion-gaps to the aspiration levels instead of ranking the alternatives.

More recently, Li and Wan (2014) proposed an interesting model that combined Linear Programming Technique for Multidimensional Analysis of Preference (LINMAP) (Srinivasan & Shocker, 1973) and TOPSIS to propose a new fuzzy linear programming method for selecting IT outsourcing providers. The LINMAP was adopted because of its superiority to determine attribute weights objectively and thus overcome the drawback of TOPSIS. Besides, the relative closeness degrees of TOPSIS we used to sufficiently consider both the positive and negative ideal solutions: PIS and NIS. Indeed, according to TOPSIS method chosen alternative should have the shortest distance from the PIS and the farthest distance from the NIS. By summarizing the existing research, they considered five criteria and their factors to apply their model to a national high-tech enterprise of China. They are provided in Table 3 as in Yang & Huang (2000).

FUTURE RESEARCH DIRECTIONS

Recent works on information technology outsourcing risk factors identification and provider selection has proposed several directions for future works in order to better manage information technology risks.

In terms of future research in the area of information technology outsourcing risk factors identification, Fan et al, (2012) suggested to develop new methods to solve the problems of risk factor identification with hybrid interdependent information such as numerical values, interval numbers and linguistic terms. According to Kou and Lu (2013), individual knowledge, experience and intuitive judgment provide

Table 3. The attributes of evaluating IT outsourcing providers as in Li and Wan (2014)

Attributes	Factors
Management	Stimulate IT department to improve performance and enhance morale, Improve communication problems and selfishness between IT department and operational department, Solve the floating and scarcity of employee, Increase the ability of management and control of IT department, Keep the flexibility to adjust department, including consolidation or decentralization
Economics	Focus on core competence, Make strategic alliance with vendor to make up the shortage of resources or technology, Form a new company by concatenating core competencies of these strategic alliances to develop new product and sell, Share the risk, Time to market
Strategy	Get new technology, Learn new technology of software management and development from vendors
Technology	Reduce the developing and maintaining cost of information technology, Make the fixed costs to become to variable costs, Increase the flexibility in finance
Quality	Procure higher reliability and performance of IT, Reach higher service level

better assessment of risk than probabilistic approach. As a result, they proposed to use fuzzy set theory for risk assessment and capturing the individual intuitive assessment. As future works to improve the hierarchical information technology outsourcing risk assessment model, Samantra et al, (2014) proposed several routes: to use trapezoidal fuzzy numbers for extracting linguistic representation of risk assessment, to investigate appropriateness of different types of fuzzy numbers for risk estimation, to determine accurate number of decision makers in order to save data collection time, and to use client as well as vendor perspective to compare the risks from different perspectives.

In terms of future research in the area of information technology outsourcing provider selection, Chen et al, (2011) suggested to use fuzzy preference relations and fuzzy linguistic preference relations and to be compared for the outsourcing supplier selection problem. Hsu et al, (2013) proposed test their hybrid DEMATEL-ANP model on other industries such as manufacturing, government or telecommunication. Li and Wan (2014) proposed to investigate in future how to solve fuzzy nonlinear programming models in the context of provider selection, and to develop some effective and efficient methods for solving outsourcing provider selection problems with intuitionistic fuzzy information in which attribute ratings and truth degrees of alternatives' comparisons are expressed with intuitionistic fuzzy sets.

CONCLUSION

In recent years, information technology outsourcing has received a large attention from both business managers and scholars because of its role in reducing costs and maintaining company competitiveness. However, information technology outsourcing has several related shortcomings; including information security, loss of management control, morale problems, and labor union issues. It also may cause unexpected complexities, increase costs and friction to the value chain, and require more senior management attention and deeper management skills than initially anticipated (Howell, 1999). For these aforementioned reasons, there is an increasing interest on (1) identification of IT outsourcing risk factors because appropriate identification is significant to capture the source of IT outsourcing risk, and (2) appropriate selection of outsourcing provider.

Different models have been proposed in the literature to better identify various risk factors that may influence information technology outsourcing to help decision makers capture risk source including DEMATEL method, transaction cost theory in information technology, or a comprehensive review of the literature. Besides, various mathematical models were adopted to identify appropriate outsourcing provider. They include AHP, TOPSIS, MCDM, DEMATEL, ANP, VIKOR, MADM, fuzzy

PROMETHEE, QFD, fuzzy set, and LINMAP. To better identify risk factors and optimally select outsourcing provider, it was suggested that future works will focus on design of sophisticated hybrid models, development of advanced models, and usage of different industries to validate new proposed methods.

REFERENCES

Abdullah, L. M., & Verner, J. M. (2012). Analysis and application of an outsourcing risk framework. *Journal of Systems and Software, 85*(8), 1930–1952. doi:10.1016/j.jss.2012.02.040

Al-Hamadany, W. A., & Kanapathy, K. (2012). Information technology outsourcing decisions in an emerging economy: The influence of perceived risks and benefits. *World Applied Sciences Journal, 19*, 1078–1086.

Alaghehband, F. K., Rivard, S., Wu, S., & Goyette, S. (2011). An assessment of the use of transaction cost theory in information technology outsourcing. *The Journal of Strategic Information Systems, 20*(2), 125–138. doi:10.1016/j.jsis.2011.04.003

Araz, C., Ozfirat, P. M., & Ozkarahan, I. (2007). An integrated multicriteria decision making methodology for outsourcing management. *Computers & Operations Research, 34*(12), 3738–3756. doi:10.1016/j.cor.2006.01.014

Bachlechner, D., Thalmann, S., & Maier, R. (2014). Security and compliance challenges in complex IT outsourcing arrangements: A multi-stakeholder perspective. *Computers & Security, 40*, 38–59. doi:10.1016/j.cose.2013.11.002

Blakley, B., McDermott, E., & Geer, D. (2001). Information security is information risk management. *In Proceedings of the workshop on New security paradigms*. Cloudcroft, NM: ACM.

Buyukozkan, G., & Cifci, G. (2012). A novel hybrid MCDM approach based on fuzzy DEMATEL, fuzzy ANP and fuzzy TOPSIS to evaluate green suppliers. *Expert Systems with Applications, 39*(3), 3000–3011. doi:10.1016/j.eswa.2011.08.162

Cai, X. Q., Chen, J., Xiao, Y. B., Xu, X. L., & Yu, G. (2013). Fresh-product supply chain management with logistics outsourcing. *Omega, 41*(4), 752–765. doi:10.1016/j.omega.2012.09.004

Chen, Y.-H., Wang, T.-C., & Wu, C.-Y. (2011). Strategic decisions using the fuzzy PROMETHEE for IS outsourcing. *Expert Systems with Applications, 38*(10), 13216–13222. doi:10.1016/j.eswa.2011.04.137

Chou, D. C., & Chou, A. Y. (2009). Information systems outsourcing life cycle and risks analysis. *Computer Standards & Interfaces, 31*(5), 1036–1043. doi:10.1016/j.csi.2008.09.032

Claver, E., Gonzalez, R., Gasco, J., & Llopis, J. (2002). Information systems outsourcing: Reasons, reservations and success factors. *Logistics Information Management, 15*(4), 294–308. doi:10.1108/09576050210436138

Dhar, S., & Balakrishnan, B. (2006). Risks, benefits, and challenges in global IT outsourcing: Perspectives and practices. *Journal of Global Information Management, 14*(3), 39–69. doi:10.4018/jgim.2006070104

Fan, Z.-P., Suo, W.-L., & Feng, B. (2012). Identifying risk factors of IT outsourcing using interdependent information: An extended DEMATEL method. *Expert Systems with Applications, 39*(3), 3832–3840. doi:10.1016/j.eswa.2011.09.092

Fontela, E., & Gabus, A. (1976). *The DEMATEL observer, DEMATEL 1976 report.* Geneva, Switzerland: Battelle Geneva Research Centre.

Gabus, A., & Fontela, E. (1972). *World problems, an invitation to further thought within the framework of DEMATEL.* Geneva, Switzerland: Battelle Geneva Research Centre.

Gabus, A., & Fontela, E. (1973). *Perceptions of the world problematic: Communication procedure, communicating with those bearing collective responsibility, (DEMATEL report no. 1).* Geneva, Switzerland: Battelle Geneva Research Centre.

Herrera, F., & Martínez, L. (2000). A 2-tuple fuzzy linguistic representation model for computing with words. *IEEE Transactions on Fuzzy Systems, 8*(6), 746–752. doi:10.1109/91.890332

Herrera, F., & Martínez, L. (2001). A model based on linguistic 2-tuples for dealing with multigranular hierarchical linguistic contexts in multi-expert decision making. *IEEE Transactions on Systems, Man, and Cybernetics. Part B, Cybernetics, 31*(2), 227–234. doi:10.1109/3477.915345 PMID:18244784

Ho, W., He, T., Lee, C. K. M., & Emrouznejad, A. (2012). Strategic logistics outsourcing: An integrated QFD and fuzzy AHP approach. *Expert Systems with Applications, 39*(12), 10841–10850. doi:10.1016/j.eswa.2012.03.009

Howell, J. (1999). Research and technology outsourcing. *Technology Analysis and Strategic Management, 11*(1), 17–29. doi:10.1080/095373299107555

Hsu, C.-C., Liou, J. J. H., & Chuang, Y.-C. (2013). Integrating DANP and modified grey relation theory for the selection of an outsourcing provider. *Expert Systems with Applications*, *40*(6), 2297–2304. doi:10.1016/j.eswa.2012.10.040

Hsu, C.-I., Chiu, C., & Hsu, P.-L. (2004). Predicting information systems outsourcing success using a hierarchical design of case-based reasoning. *Expert Systems with Applications*, *26*(3), 435–441. doi:10.1016/j.eswa.2003.10.002

Hsu, P. F., & Hsu, M. G. (2008). Optimizing the information outsourcing practices of primary care medical organizations using entropy and TOPSIS. *Quality & Quantity*, *42*(2), 181–201. doi:10.1007/s11135-006-9040-8

Hwang, C. L., & Yoon, K. (1981). *Multiple attributes decision making methods and applications*. Berlin: Springer. doi:10.1007/978-3-642-48318-9

Jurison, J. (1995). The role of risk and return in information technology outsourcing decisions. *Journal of Information Technology*, *10*(4), 239–247. doi:10.1057/jit.1995.27

Kaya, O. (2011). Outsourcing vs. in-house production: A comparison of supply chain contracts with effort dependent demand. *Omega*, *39*(2), 168–178. doi:10.1016/j.omega.2010.06.002

Kim, Y. J., Lee, J. M., Koo, C., & Nam, K. (2013). The role of governance effectiveness in explaining IT outsourcing performance. *International Journal of Information Management*, *33*(5), 850–860. doi:10.1016/j.ijinfomgt.2013.07.003

Kou, Y.-C., & Lu, S.-T. (2013). Using fuzzy multiple criteria decision making approach to enhance risk assessment for metropolitan construction projects. *International Journal of Project Management*, *31*(4), 602–614. doi:10.1016/j.ijproman.2012.10.003

Lee, J. N., & Kim, Y. G. (2005). Understanding outsourcing partnership: A comparison of three theoretical perspectives. *IEEE Transactions on Engineering Management*, *52*(1), 43–57. doi:10.1109/TEM.2004.839958

Li, D.-F., & Wan, S.-P. (2014). Fuzzy heterogeneous multiattribute decision making method for outsourcing provider selection. *Expert Systems with Applications*, *41*(6), 3047–3059. doi:10.1016/j.eswa.2013.10.036

Lin, C. J., & Wu, W. W. (2008). A causal analytical method for group decision-making under fuzzy environment. *Expert Systems with Applications*, *34*(1), 205–213. doi:10.1016/j.eswa.2006.08.012

Lin, Y. T., Lin, C. L., Yu, H. C., & Tzeng, G. H. (2010). A novel hybrid MCDM approach for outsourcing vendor selection: A case study for a semiconductor company in Taiwan. *Expert Systems with Applications, 37*(7), 4796–4804. doi:10.1016/j.eswa.2009.12.036

Linder, J. G. (2004). *Outsourcing for radical change: A bold approach to enterprise transformation.* New York: AMACOM.

Liou, J. J. H., & Chuang, Y.-T. (2010). Developing a hybrid multi-criteria model for selection of outsourcing providers. *Expert Systems with Applications, 37*(5), 3755–3761. doi:10.1016/j.eswa.2009.11.048

McCarthy, I., & Anagroustou, A. (2004). The impact of outsourcing on the transaction costs and boundaries of manufacturing. *International Journal of Production Economics, 88*(1), 61–71. doi:10.1016/S0925-5273(03)00183-X

Opricovic, S. (1998). *Multicriteria optimization of civil engineering systems.* Belgrade: Faculty of Civil Engineering.

Opricovic, S., & Tzeng, G. H. (2004). Compromise solution by MCDM methods: A comparative analysis of VIKOR and TOPSIS. *European Journal of Operational Research, 156*(2), 445–455. doi:10.1016/S0377-2217(03)00020-1

Peltier, T. R. (2005). *Information security risk analysis.* Auerbach Pub. doi:10.1201/9781420031195

Quinn, J., & Hilmer, F. (1994). Strategic outsourcing. *Sloan Management Review,* (Summer), 43–55.

Rusu, L., & Hudosi, G. (2011). Assessing the risk exposure in IT outsourcing for large companies. *International Journal of Information Technology and Management, 10*(1), 24–44. doi:10.1504/IJITM.2011.037760

Saaty, T. L. (1996). *Decision making with dependence and feedback: Analytic network process.* Pittsburgh, PA: RWS Publications.

Samantra, D., Datta, S., & Mahapatra, S. S. (2014). Risk assessment in IT outsourcing using fuzzy decision-making approach: An Indian perspective. *Expert Systems with Applications, 41*(8), 4010–4022. doi:10.1016/j.eswa.2013.12.024

Shi, X. J., Tsuji, H., & Zhang, S. M. (2011). Eliciting experts perceived risk of software offshore outsourcing incorporating individual heterogeneity. *Expert Systems with Applications, 38*(3), 2283–2291. doi:10.1016/j.eswa.2010.08.016

Sobol, M., & Apte, U. (1995). Domestic and global outsourcing practices of Americas most effective IS users. *Journal of Information Technology, 10*(4), 269–280. doi:10.1057/jit.1995.30

Srinivasan, V., & Shocker, A. D. (1973). Linear programming techniques for multidimensional analysis of preference. *Psychometrica, 38*(3), 337–342. doi:10.1007/BF02291658

Stoneburner, G., Goguen, A., & Feringa, A. (2002). Risk management guide for information technology systems. National Institute of Standards and Technology. doi:10.6028/NIST.SP.800-30

Thouin, M. F., Hoffman, J. J., & Ford, E. W. (2009). IT outsourcing and firm-level performance: A transaction cost perspective. *Information & Management, 46*(8), 463–469. doi:10.1016/j.im.2009.08.006

Wu, W. W., & Lee, Y. T. (2007). Developing global managers competencies using the fuzzy DEMATEL method. *Expert Systems with Applications, 32*(2), 499–507. doi:10.1016/j.eswa.2005.12.005

Yang, C. Y., & Huang, J. B. (2000). A decision model for IS outsourcing. *International Journal of Information Management, 20*(3), 225–239. doi:10.1016/S0268-4012(00)00007-4

Yang, D. H., Kim, S., Nam, C., & Min, J. W. (2007). Developing a decision model for business process outsourcing. *Computers & Operations Research, 34*(12), 3769–3778. doi:10.1016/j.cor.2006.01.012

KEY TERMS AND DEFINITIONS

AHP: Analytic Hierarchy Process.

ANP: Analytical Network Process.

DEMATEL: Decision-Making Trial and Evaluation Laboratory.

LINMAP: Linear Programming Technique for Multidimensional Analysis of Preference.

MADM: Multi-Attribute Decision Making.

MCDM: Multiple-Criteria Decision-Making.

PROMETHEE: Preference Ranking Organization Method for Enrichment Evaluation.

QFD: Quality Function Deployment.
TOPSIS: Order preference by similarity to ideal solution.
VIKOR: Vlsekriterijumska Optimizacija I Kompromisno Resenje.

Chapter 9
Impact of Technology Innovation:
A Study on Cloud Risk Mitigation

Niranjali Suresh
University at Buffalo, USA

Manish Gupta
University at Buffalo, USA

ABSTRACT

Cloud enables computing as a utility by offering convenient, on-demand network access to a centralized pool of configurable computing resources that can be rapidly deployed with great efficiency and minimal management overhead. In order to realize the benefits of the innovative cloud computing paradigm, companies must overcome heightened risks and security threats associated with it. Security and privacy in cloud is complex owing to newer dimensions in problem scope such as multi-tenant architectures and shared infrastructure, elasticity, measured services, viability etc. In this paper, we survey existing literature on cloud security issues and risks which then guides us to provide a section on auditing based to address the identified risks. We also provide a discourse on risk assessment frameworks to highlight benefits using such structured methods for understanding risks. The main contribution of the paper is investigation of current innovations in cloud computing that are targeted towards assisting in effective management of aforementioned risks and security issues. The compilation of discussed solutions has been developed to cater to specific cloud security, compliance and privacy requirements across industries by cloud service providers, software-as-a-service (SaaS) application vendors and advisory firms.

DOI: 10.4018/978-1-5225-2604-9.ch009

1. INTRODUCTION

Cloud computing is transforming and redefining the design and procurement of IT infrastructure and software thereby providing attractive services to its users across the globe. The US National Institute of Standards and Technology (NIST) defines cloud computing as "a model for enabling ubiquitous, convenient, on - demand network access to a shared pool of configurable computing resources (e.g. networks, servers, storage, applications, and services) that can be rapidly provisioned and released with minimal management effort or service provider interaction" (Mell and Grance, 2011). The technology allows individuals and enterprises to avoid committing large capital outlays when purchasing and managing or operating software and hardware. Cloud reduces strain on developers by allowing them to focus their efforts on coding business logic rather than concerning about over or under provisioning resources for a service based on the market for a service. Large batch oriented tasks can be efficiently executed with minimal resources simply through scalable programming. In cloud, 1000 servers for one hour costs no more than using one server for 1,000 hours. This elasticity of resources, without paying a premium for large scale, is unprecedented in the history of IT. As Heiser and Nicolett (2008) of Gartner mention that cloud computing lacks transparency because it is, for most part, provided by an external entity and is a method for "storing and processing your data externally in multiple unspecified locations, often sourced from other, unnamed providers, and containing data from multiple customers." In the same vein, companies are also advised they consider all the involved risks in moving to cloud and also evaluate all the required controls around the protection of data and processes before migrating to cloud.

One of the main contributions of the chapter is reviewing recent innovations in cloud computing in security space and how they are aligned to manage risks from specific areas of cloud implementation. The discussions on extant literature on cloud, auditing focus areas and risk assessment frameworks help the chapter highlight how recent innovations are poised to manage risks. The primary tenet of the research is innovation in cloud computing. Innovation in IT is one of the widely studied topics (Baregheh et al., 2009) with many acceptable definitions. We use Rogers' (1998) definition as ''introduction of a new product or a 'qualitative change' in a product, a process…". Not all innovations have the same impact and vary based on type of innovation (Grover et al., 1997; Adomavicius et al., 2007; Christensen et al., 2007; Carlo et al., 2011). Innovation has been linked to higher productivity, growth, and development. (Fagerberg, 2005; Kaplinsky et al., 2009). In recent years, with increasing adoption of IT, the impact of innovations is on rise as well and has been of high interest to researchers (Avgerou, 2008; Xiao et al., 2013).

This chapter is organized in six sections that delve deep into cloud security and innovations. Having introduced cloud computing as a technology platform in the first section, we move on to discuss key risks in cloud, their impact on environmental security and customer's business processes. The third section elaborates on significant aspects of cloud that require additional attention through continuous auditing. Audit challenges and suggested approaches have been delineated in line with industry best practices. This is followed by a description of some of the most prominent cloud computing frameworks and working groups that are widely used accepted across industries and geographies as enablers and benchmarks while setting up cloud systems. The following section briefly examines additional challenges specific to particular cloud computing domains such as banking, medical, and government sectors. The final section discusses recent innovations in cloud computing and its impact on transforming enterprise cloud implementations and managing cloud computing risks. Figure 1 shows how different sections and approach for the study.

2. EXTANT RESEARCH: CLOUD COMPUTING RISKS

Cloud computing is fraught with security risks, according to analyst firm Gartner. Smart customers would consider a third party security assessment before committing

Figure 1. Components and approach of the study

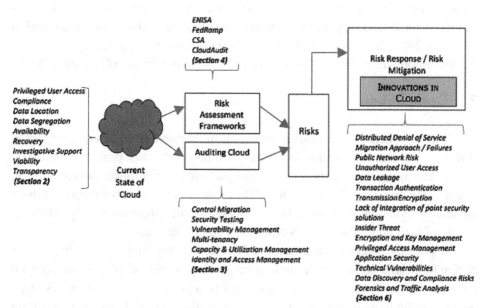

their business to a cloud vendor. Gartner says in a June report titled "Assessing the Security Risks of Cloud Computing" that cloud computing has "unique attributes that require risk assessment in areas such as data integrity, recovery, and privacy, and an evaluation of legal issues in areas such as e-discovery, regulatory compliance, and auditing". Some of the above mentioned areas have been discussed below.

2.1. Privileged User Access

Cloud users, who are also content providers, publish data on cloud and require fine grained access controls. In healthcare, access to patient records stored in cloud would have to be regulated by policies admitted by HIPAA (Yu et al.,2010). In spite of emerging standards, the process of managing identities in cloud environments still presents a level of architectural complexity. Agreement on the implementation of role based and attribute based access controls become difficult to achieve when extended across several agencies and domains. We therefore see the emergence of Identity as a Service (IDaaS) as a potential opportunity to address complexity in IAM in cloud environments. The use of such a service in itself can facilitate the management of identity throughout its lifecycle including the provisioning/ de-provisioning and the capture of relevant event information that is required for monitoring and audit purposes as well as the provision of self-service mechanisms for use by end users (Dorey, 2011).

In Cloud, an externally sourced IT service can bypasses the physical, logical and personnel controls that IT normally provides for in-house applications. The cloud service vendors must be requested to state clearly hiring policies and access privileges for data administrators who are allowed to handle the client's' information (Brodkin, 2008). Users, on the other hand, must also consider appointing trustworthy administrators who can be allowed to handle the stored information (Teneyuca, 2011).

2.2. Compliance

Compliance with the regulations is important for businesses. Businesses subject to compliance obligations are audited on a regular basis; and must provide compliance evidence. Any proof of compliance violation or absence of compliance evidence can lead auditors to impose financial fines. These fines may lead to bankruptcy if there are serious violations. Moreover, businesses such as the financial sector publish the results of their compliance audits to increase their client base.

The inability to monitor the cloud directly makes it a very difficult rather impossible choice for businesses to deploy applications as they would not be able meet certain compliance requirements. One specific class of legislations and regulations place restrictions on trans-border data flows and thus places restrictions on the location of data. Many countries in the world ask for the same requirement, the data and applications servers should be located in the country. Compliance also requires meaningful traceability of the various administration actions. These actions should be auditable so that a fine-grained evaluation of the actions can be carried out. The most auditable way of answering this requirement is to produce logs of these actions in a reliable manner. This implies that confidentiality and integrity of these logs should be ensured together with trusted time stamping. Cloud customers should be able to access the logs of every action pertaining to his application on various virtual machines (Massonet, et al., 2011).

Most corporations start using the cloud to launch critical applications without realizing the full impact of putting data in cloud. Cloud providers must therefore ensure environments are secure and intrusion proof in order to maintain users trust. Access guarantee must be provided for client data hosted on cloud. A company hosting sensitive data on cloud might require information on the location of data or may also require the data to be stored only in a particular region. It is advised that a contractual agreement be signed between the provider and user of cloud services to ensure that all consumer data resides on a known server (Kalpana, et al., 2012).

2.3. Data Location

Unique properties of cloud computing such as openness and multi-tenancy have led to the increasing emphasis on data security and privacy protection on cloud environments. In a typical SaaS model customer does not know where the data is stored, hence to avoid the leakage of potentially sensitive information, data privacy laws in many countries including some EU countries forbid certain types of sensitive data to leave the country. In Canada, both the Freedom of Information and Protection of Privacy Act (FOIPPA) in British Columbia and the Personal Information International Disclosure Protection Act in Nova Scotia prohibit the access to, disclosure of, and storage of data outside Canada without consent. This makes locality of data be an extremely important consideration in many enterprise architectures (Kadam, 2011). Organizations that rely on multiple cloud service providers may have little or no control over the movement of their data through different data centers around the world. Similarly, it is not always clear whether the data custodian or the third-party service provider is accountable to protect the data, or which sets of data protection laws apply. To comply with global privacy regulations, organizations need to ensure that their cloud providers implement technical and administrative controls to protect their data. These measures should include adequate technical controls, such as end-to-end encryption or tokenization. Security and privacy SLA's and Data loss prevention tools can also help enforce policies for data movement. For these legal agreements to have practical effect, organizations must also actively manage them. In other words, organizations should require regular reports on the adequacy of their providers' privacy and security measures and database activities, as well as disclosure of any incidents or issues that may put data at risk (Deloitte, 2016).

2.4. Data Segregation

While multi-tenancy maximizes cost benefits to businesses it also allows multiple users to collocate their data using SaaS applications which can lead to intrusion of data of one user by another becomes possible. Hacking a user's application or injecting malicious code in a SaaS system may be called an intrusion. SaaS model should therefore ensure a clear boundary that segregates each user's data at both physical and application layers (Subashini, et al., 2011). The GovCloud service offered by AWS offers an isolated AWS region for hosting highly regulated and sensitive workloads to support compliance requirements such as International Traffic in Arms Regulations (ITAR) and Federal Risk and Authorization Management Program (FedRAMP).

Full data segregation is not possible on cloud, users must come to terms with the fact that their data and VM's share space with other users. Cloud service providers and clients must therefore ensure that encryption is available at all stages, and that these encryption schemes were designed and tested by experienced professionals. Asking for evidence that the encryption implementation was designed and tested by experienced specialists, finding out who performed the protocol analysis and code reviews would be essential. This is important because encryption accidents might lead to lack of availability of critical and sensitive data or might even make the data unusable. Knowing who has access to decryption keys is key while establishing authorised access to data (Brodkin, 2008).

2.5. Availability

A major concern for users with respect to migration to public cloud has been its lack of availability and reliability. There have been several incidences where well-known cloud providers have experienced temporary lack of availability lasting at least several hours and striking loss of personal customer data. For example, Amazon's Elastic Compute Cloud (EC2) service in North America was temporarily unavailable at significant times due to 'lightning storm that caused damage to a single power distribution unit (PDU) in a single availability zone'.

There are three reasons why cloud users must be concerned with the availability of their valued assets in the cloud. First, most cloud providers rent computing and data-center infrastructures from other cloud providers. This means that when one cloud infrastructure is affected (unavailable), most probably, other providers will suffer similar losses, hindering the availability of resources to a wider audience. Second, the possibility that a cloud provider can file for bankruptcy, where the provider goes out of business with consequential financial liability to offset makes the availability of cloud resources a serious issue to consider. Finally, cross-vulnerability in the cloud due to the multi-tenancy implementation of cloud infrastructures and services makes the availability of resources in the cloud an important issue to consider. Users must engage with service providers to understand disaster recovery processes for their cloud based applications. Best practices may include providing backup copies of data on a monthly basis as part of the agreement. Further, users must be aware of their provider's business continuity plans, for instance, whether the provider has hot-standby sites and whether resilience is built as an abstraction to all layers of its services (Onwubiko, 2010).

2.6. Recovery

Disaster recovery and continuity of operations on cloud are among top customer concerns. Cloud providers are expected to replicate user data and application infrastructure across multiple sites to prevent any possibility of total failure. Even if a service provider refuses to divulge the exact location of customer data, it should be able to provide the customer with information on what would happen to their data if cloud data center(s) succumb to a disaster (Brodkin, 2008).

Cloud providers must employ risk models to estimate the number of servers in a data center and determine the distribution of customers across data centers in a manner that minimizes risk. In the event of stress on any single data center due to correlated failures, dynamic migration of a group of customers to another site can be employed. To achieve all of these tasks seamlessly, the cloud provider should be able to treat all of its data centers as a single pool of resources available to its DR customers. To prevent correlated of DR sites (due to factors like electrical grid failure or natural disaster in a geographical location) from stressing any one data center, the cloud provider should attempt to distribute its DR customers across multiple data centers in a way that minimizes potential conflicts—e.g. multiple customers from the same geographic region should be backed up to different cloud data centers (Wood, 2010).

2.7. Investigative Support

In cloud computing, lack of physical access to infrastructure, remote nature of evidence and transparency issues complicate forensics. Gathering forensics data is further restricted by service providers who intentionally avoid providing interfaces for the same. For instance, IaaS providers may not provide images of disks or virtual machines which are of high value during a forensics investigation. Since CSP's are generally dependent on partner CSP's and SaaS providers, investigation must be performed for each link in this dependency chain. It is important for all parties in the chain must be trustworthy, corruption free and willing to support an investigation.

Log records play a significant role in digital forensic analysis of systems. Regulations such as HIPAA, Payment Card Industry Data Security Standard, or Sarbanes-Oxley often require forensically sound preservation of information. Detailed logs may disclose private and sensitive information, hence it must be adequately protected with access controls.

Zonal planning can help determine safe and unsafe zones within a network which could reduce complexities and vulnerabilities of network data transfer in a cloud network. A service provider's own network may be marked as 'safe' while their suppliers or other external networks could be part 'unsafe' (Ko, et al., 2011). CSPs need to adopt and implement efficient mechanisms for the retrieval of data, for backups and to implement a data retention policy. Specific training activities focused in forensic analysis of cloud incidents should be promoted within a cloud service provider organization. CSP should also identify and indicate a "point of contact" to assist a customer with forensic investigation activities. As per the SLA or contract, the CSP should ensure quick and dependable access to the information/ data needed at any time during the investigation through specific and documented procedures (ENISA, 2014).

2.8. Viability

The risk of the CSP suddenly going out of business, either through a "soft" cessation (i.e., filing for bankruptcy), or in a more abrupt way (simply ceasing operations and removing assets) concerns the uncertainty about the stability of the CSP. While relying on major CSPs, large enterprises with an insignificant risk of abruptly shutting down, mitigates the problem, the type and cost of service offered by these CSPs might not be suited for the needs of the would-be customer. Small, start-up cloud providers are more subject to market fluctuations, and might at some time decide to stop providing hosting services to their customers, or to move to another business model. In these cases the customer might be left stranded and unable to use the infrastructure anymore without any forewarning (Bartolini, et al., 2015).

Due diligence should be conducted to determine the viability of the vendor/ service provider. Consider such factors as vendor reputation, transparency, references, financial (means and resources), and independent third-party assessments of vendor safeguards and processes (Bisong, et al., 2011). To ensure long term viability, issues such as disaster recovery, data portability and exit strategy must be addressed in the service level agreement by both the provider and user. An insurance of the CSP in favor of the customer can reduce the risks by covering the losses suffered by the customer. Software escrow techniques must be revisited for cloud-based services (Bartolini, et al., 2015).

2.9. Transparency

In order to become trusted partners to enterprises, CSP's need to be more transparent about their security practices. Cloud providers have their own firewalls, monitoring and controls to ensure that attacks, APTs, malware and otherwise unauthorized activity, but much of that information is not made available to customers for use in their security and monitoring capabilities. This is a problem that potentially impacts a cloud customers' ability to ensure complete visibility and protection for their own assets by being unable to incorporate all security intelligence and log information from beginning to end of a potential threat vector. While large cloud security providers (CSPs), like Amazon, Rackspace, Verizon's Terremark and Google have well-documented and publicized security practices, several organizations do businesses with smaller service providers in one vertical for purposes like billing or marketing. These vertical-specific CSP's reveal limited security information on their websites and during interactions making it difficult for customers to gain complete insight into their security policies and control implementations (Leinwand, 2016).

One interesting early example of service provider transparency is trust.salesforce. com, a site that salesforce.com, this website provides public information on its performance statistics. The site also guides users on general best practices that can be employed while using salesforce application to avoid attack vectors and comply to legal standards. This website takes the first step towards improved transparency between service provider and customer which is acknowledging that compromise of customer system is indeed possible. The less information that is hidden, the easier it is to trust a provider (Ryoo et al., 2014).

3. AUDITING CLOUD COMPUTING

Decisions to use cloud are generally not part of business road map but are results of economic desire. Lack of adherence to regulatory environment or business not understanding changes in IT introduce significant risk. True cost of cloud implementations, hence need to take into account audit, compliance and risk management. IT audit helps organizations identify and manage compliance and security risk to cloud infrastructure. This in turn reduces cost, improves security and helps make cloud ventures successful. Most cloud providers use core functions, security services and monitoring functions similar to their clients. This enables the use of control frameworks such as COBIT or NIST for auditing systems hosted on cloud. However, it is essential that an auditor recognises the risks to systems as IT moves to cloud and changes that it might bring about to the scope of the audit. Below are some specific areas that an auditor must pay close attention to while auditing cloud.

3.1. Migration of Controls

Migration of an application to cloud involves consideration of certain key factors such as existing IT infrastructure, security architecture and complexity. Security controls would have to adapt and evolve to meet cloud requirements. Existing mechanisms to secure data during rest and transmission, encryption and key management and identity and access management have to be migrated, tested and updated to secure cloud environments. For instance, some corporate systems and data may not be encrypted owing to their reliance on tightly secured internal networks and LAN security. When these systems are moved to cloud they pass over the internet and could be compromised due to lack of secure authentication and data integrity checks (Halpert, Ben 17). Simpler applications such as E Mail can be directly ported to cloud based SaaS applications like Office 365, Google Apps or Lotus live. However, migration of complex applications or legacy systems to cloud might require code changes, elaborate planning and extensive testing (Rashmi, et al., 2012). Migration of a virtual host may also change the legality of actions occurring on that host. In such cases, restrictions and liability of the cloud service provider and user must be clearly stated in contractual agreements.

Ensuring migration of controls must be followed by ensuring application availability and business continuity. Devices that enable network connectivity and data access such as firewalls, traffic-filtering routers and web gateways have to be configured correctly for the application to function as expected. Migration of security policies can be a complex and tedious effort for several organizations despite automation (Reichenberg, 2013).

3.2. Security Testing

Custom applications developed in-house may not be extensively tested for common vulnerabilities of the internet. In a public setting it might be vulnerable to a variety of security incidents like data breaches, malware, bot-nets, worms etc. (Halpert, 2011).

With respect to cloud applications, focus needs to be laid on security testing due to the business implications that come along with security flaws in the application. In a cloud computing environment security testing should be applied on three layers, namely the service, the infrastructure and the platform layer. Testing must be a combined effort by both, the SaaS provider and PaaS or IaaS consumer of cloud services. Application specific code may also introduce risks which have to be resolved by developers or a dedicated security testing team (Zech, et al., 2011). Internal cloud testing to check the quality of infrastructure and cloud capabilities can be done only by the service provider due to their elevated access into cloud systems. Similarly cloud based application system providers must test their services over private, public and hybrid clouds. Engineers must deal with the integration of various SaaS applications through the API's and connectivity protocols provided. Factors such as QoS requirements for applications, testing environment requirements, test models, test adequacy, test techniques and tools for security testing must be addressed and agreed upon by the cloud vendor and client (Gao, J et al., 2011). Auditors must ensure that web applications are carefully tested to ensure adequacy in access, authentication and monitoring (Halpert, 2011).

3.3. Vulnerability Management

Patching is so important that CSIS 20 Critical Security Controls includes as number 4: Continuous Vulnerability Assessment and Remediation (CSIS, 2013). Cloud SaaS applications do not provide much control to a customer where application patching is concerned. A service provider's improper patch management process could have serious ramifications on a user's business. WordPress experienced a serious outage due to a bad patch in the year 2010.

Cloud Security Alliance (CSA) recommends that a service provider and user establish policies, procedures and mechanisms for vulnerability and patch management. A user must employ a risk based approach to prioritize and deploy vendor supplied patches. In PaaS environments, users would have better control over patching, however the biggest challenge lies in environment management. Infrastructure engineers must coordinate with application development, testing teams and cloud service providers while applying patches. In IaaS environments, providers generally install patch management agents which report to a central data center. Apart from these scenarios, cloud service providers are also responsible for fixing vulnerabilities in their API's which are used by customers to access cloud services (Shackleford, 2016)

3.4. Multitenancy

Cloud computing allows greater economy in scale by hosting several virtual machines on a single server, this is known as multi-tenancy. Over provisioning of resources in a multi-tenant environment may cause applications to contend for resources and lead to lack of availability and create a denial of service condition. This could be caused as a result of adverse behaviour of other tenants in a physical server whose application consumes large amount of memory or CPU. Lack of physical controls lead to an excessive dependency on logical controls to prevent tenants from inadvertently interfering with each other's security. Weak logical controls might enable a malicious tenant to compromise the security posture of other tenants. Share services may also be considered a single point of failure when misconfigurations or uncontrolled changes are implemented. Co-mingled tenant data may make data destruction difficult especially if data is stored in shared media (OWASP, 2016).

Auditors must verify that multi-tenant architectures take into account the local segregation of environment, applications, data encryption, key management and storage. Segregation of shared or public cloud can also be achieved through virtual private cloud that allows quarantining virtual infrastructure and linking it back to internal resources via encrypted networks. An auditor should make sure that VPC's are appropriately implemented by the client while configuring cloud setup. They must also advise the client to negotiate isolation of critical and highly sensitive application with the cloud service provider although this may lead to an increase in cost (Ren et al., 2012).

3.5. Capacity and Utilization Management

Cloud service providers charge users according to the resources that they consume. Users are often unable to connect their resource consumption to the amount charged by providers. It is in a multitenant virtualized environment that providers incorrectly apply charges to a user's billing when a software or a bug running on another user's account could be utilizing more than expected resources. A unified mechanism must be in place to fairly measure resource consumption and subsequent charges levied. This mechanism must be able to guarantee the user of the amount of cloud resources that they are likely to consume based on which cloud strategy can be decided (K. Ren et al., 2012).

End-to-End mapping and aggregation of all metered components can be done for specific scenarios like performing a complex business transaction of ordering a product. Many cloud hosting environments do not expose metering information other than the standard billing details accessible to the account owner. Although this allows users to gauge the usage of cloud features within their account, it does not allow users to identify individual application or instance usage. Auditors must ensure that cloud service providers share a granular report of service usage metering and billing. Ensuring accountability for usage and chargeback results in improved services and better alignment between business and IT costs.

3.6. Identity and Access Management

Identity and access management function on cloud must be able to track and provide information on who has access to what information and if this access is monitored or logged by the system. Log of activities, including all authentication and access attempts (success and failed) must be preserved. These metrics must be used by auditors to enforce segregation of duties, identify and prevent access violations and quantify risk exposure (CSA, 2012).

The dynamic nature of cloud requires access management to be flexible enough to support updation of policies dynamically as users enter and leave the system. It is important to keep all roles and data access structures related information confidential and secured. Auditors must monitor and audit compliance with information security policies and best practices to mitigate lack of transparency, if any, among cloud service providers, users and data owners (Habiba, et al., 2013). While some cloud providers may provide a high degree of granularity in access management, auditors must also ensure that these are tested and applied properly to IT systems on cloud. Single, centrally controlled access models such as active directory can become more complicated to implement on cloud (Halpert, 2011)

4. CLOUD CONTROL FRAMEWORKS

Established risk assessment frameworks have been widely used to conduct a through and risk-based auditing of IT and related processes. In recent years, with the emergence of cloud and IOT technologies, these frameworks have also been updated to include auditing criteria and practices for Cloud computing and IOT. Use of a recognized and accepted framework also helps provide assurance that it is objective and independent of biases in evaluation. Below are a few control frameworks that might prove useful for an auditor considering cloud audits.

4.1. ENISA

ENISA is the European Network and Information security agency, papers published by ENSI provide detailed risk assessment models for cloud and specifically advice organizations that do business in the European Union. Since its inception in 2004, ENISA has been contributing greatly to the development and increasing awareness of network and information security within the European Union. Some solutions delivered by the agency include pan-European Cyber Security Exercises, the development of National Cyber Security Strategies, CSIRTs cooperation and capacity building.

ENISA classifies Cloud Computing (CC) risks into three categories: Organizational, Technical and Legal. Organizational risk pertains to risks to the structure or business of an organization in case of instances such as co-tenant activities or termination of business by cloud service provider. Technical risks arise due to common problems on cloud such as malicious attacks or resource sharing issues which lead to failure of cloud services. Legal risks due to non-adherence of laws or regulations such as privacy law violation due to change in jurisdiction for data in motion (Dahbur, et al.,2011). ENISA (2014b) also studies the cyber threat landscape in cloud and is involved in various issues related to cloud adoption such as privacy, data protection, trust services, emerging technologies etc. The organization also enables optimization of information security by advising on setting up and monitoring service contracts with cloud vendors. In December 2011 ENISA has published a survey and analysis of security parameters in cloud SLAs across the European public sector. Experts across industries work with ENISA to publish papers on cloud computing through a group called ENISA Cloud Security and Resilience Expert Group. The organization also works with public sector, in EU member states, for cloud adoption by understanding current barriers and assisting with solutions and best practices (ENISA, 2014a).

4.2. FedRAMP

FedRAMP is the US government program to apply the Federal Information Security Management Act (FISMA) to cloud computing. The success of FedRAMP has led to its use across East Asia, Northern Europe, and the Americas for cloud security implementations. FedRAMP provides a comprehensive set of cloud security requirements and an independent assessment program backed by the chief information officers (CIOs) of the Department of Defense (DoD), the Department of Homeland Security (DHS), and the GSA. Cloud service providers (CSPs) that implement the required security controls and meet independent assessment requirements can be authorized for use by the federal government. FedRAMP standardized the process of FISMA authorization such that they can be performed once and reused by multiple agencies. This saves both government and private sector CSPs a lot of time and money and enables fast adoption of new systems and services.

FedRAMP also ensures consistency across all government agencies and instills a sense of trust between agencies. An authorized CSP can be leveraged by any agency without having to repeat the process. Continuous monitoring is a critical part of FedRAMP, CSP's must ensure the alignment of business processes like patch management and configuration management across their cloud systems. Authorized CSPs must perform monthly scans and send the scan results to their government authorization point of contact. High vulnerabilities are expected to be mitigated within 30 days and moderate vulnerabilities within 90 days. Failure to mitigate vulnerabilities according to these requirements could lead to a CSP having its authorization suspended or revoked (Taylor, L.,2014). Auditors are allowed to rely on the scope of this certification to forgo independent audits of these systems. The framework stresses the importance of the vendor being a committed partner to meeting standards, monetary security and controls of client's systems (Halpert, Ben, 2011).

4.3. The Cloud Security Alliance (CSA)

The Cloud Security Alliance (CSA) is a nonprofit organization led by industry practitioners, corporations, and other important stakeholders. CSA defines best practices for a secure cloud environment. It aims at enabling customers make an informed decision while transitioning their IT infrastructure to the cloud. In 2010, CSA published the the CSA Governance, Risk Management, and Compliance (GRC) Stack to help customers assess cloud service providers practices against industry standards and their compliance with regulations. In 2013, the CSA and the British Standards Institution launched the Security, Trust & Assurance Registry (STAR), a free, publicly accessible registry in which to publish CSA-related assessments for the reference of cloud users. CSA STAR introduced a control framework covering fundamental security for customers to evaluate overall risk of CSP's, this was called the Cloud Controls Matrix (CCM). CSA STAR self-assessment is open and free for all CSP's while higher levels of assurance through third-party assessments are based on continuous improvement certifications (Microsoft, 2016).

The CSA Top Threats Working Group released the list of top 12 threats in cloud for 2016 called 'The Treacherous 12', specifically related to shared on-demand nature of cloud computing. Risk of data breaches and weak identity management top this list closely followed by insecure API's, system vulnerabilities and account hijacking (Cloud Security Alliance, 2016).

4.4. Cloud Audit

Launched in January 2010 as a CSA working group, CloudAudit is a volunteer cross-industry effort from the best minds and talent in Cloud, networking, security, audit, assurance and architecture backgrounds. There are over 250 participants/interested parties supporting CloudAudit/A6. The "core team" are those that have committed to participate on a regular basis and establish leadership roles within the group. Anyone and everyone is welcome to contribute and participate. CloudAudit provides a common interface for enterprises to streamline their audit process in cloud environments. It also enables providers automate the Audit, Assertion, Assessment, and Assurance of their infrastructure (IaaS), platform (PaaS), and application (SaaS) environments and also allow authorized consumers of their services to do the same through an open, extensible and secure interface and methodology. The group provides light and easy to implement definitions and language structures using HTTP(s) and allow for their extension by providers. CloudAudit assists service providers by automating typically one-off labor-intensive, repetitive and costly auditing, assurance and compliance functions. Consumers, on the other hand, benefit by receiving a consistent and standardized interface to the information produced by the service provider (Cloud Security Alliance, 2010).

While this effort may not alleviate all of the audit concerns, it would begin to provide customers access to data that would differentiate cloud providers based on the information they provide. This will allow customers to partner with providers with whom they can achieve standard compliance. When audit information becomes a differentiating factor for competing service providers, it is possible that companies will continue to improve their work in this area (Rasheed, 2011).

5. DOMAINS

Cloud computing services vary based on industry needs, legal and regulatory requirements. This section provides brief summary of how cloud computing impacts specific industries highlighting main concerns.

5.1. Healthcare Domain

This domain must facilitate sharing of information that is confidential and sensitive. For this purpose medical institutions have started using cloud for sharing. Breach could result in loss to both patients and the institution. Some legal regulations that the medical industry must comply with include Health Insurance Portability and Accountability Act (HIPAA), the Health Information Technology for Economic and Clinical Health (HITECH) Act, the Food and Drug Administration Amendments Act (FDAAA), and the American Recovery and Reinvestment Act (ARRA) of 2009. This gives rise to the need for specifically tailored audit approaches to audit medical cloud systems. Organisations need to cooperate among themselves to tackle cloud security and audits.

5.2. Banking Domain

Owing to high inflow of confidential data, banks would have to update and secure their information incessantly while also making it accessible to customers. Banks can reduce cost by sharing customer information through cloud systems. This could potentially enable reducing interest rates. However, a big security concern faced by banks on cloud is to prevent client information from being misused or stolen. For this, data stored on cloud must be encrypted and access must be restricted by banks. Breach of data of one bank could potentially put other banks data also at risk.

5.3. Government Domain

With government agencies entering cloud domain, auditing cloud service providers is even more important due to sensitive nature of data. Today the Federal Risk and Authorization Management Program (FedRAMP) assesses cloud providers based on visibility, change control process and incident response. CSPs are expected to submit automated data feeds on system performance and reports. CSP's also have to report controls that they have in place to monitor and prevent data breach due to new risks or vulnerabilities (Ryoo et al., 2013).

6. RECENT INNOVATIONS IN CLOUD COMPUTING

While the use of Internet and web-based utilities that companies are embracing for cost savings, productivity and technology agility (Marston et al., 2011) has given them the competitive advantage there is no doubt that they are increasingly becoming more attractive target for hackers (ENISA, 2009). Both the adopting companies and the ones providing cloud services are making strides in implementing processes and technologies based on innovation. However, the providers have the economies of scale and scope on their side to innovate with their services and their security practices. As Kaufman (2009) also explains, larger "providers like Amazon and Microsoft, for example, have the capabilities to deflect and survive cyber-attacks that not all providers have". At the same time, the distributed nature of the cloud with data stored in multiple data centers limits impact from certain kinds of cyber threats (Biswas, 2011). At the same time, potential adopters of cloud services should ensure before signing up for a service that the security that the provider offers meets their risk appetite. There are advancements in underlying technologies that providers have leveraged to offer more robust security solutions around their products. There have been several studies that have explored how companies respond to new innovations in technology and how their adoption of emerging technology is impacted by various factors including evolution of their own offerings, resistance to change and compatibility issues (Nelson and Winter, 1982; Levinthal and March, 1993; Tushman and Anderson, 1986).

Companies also make changes in their management structures and investment decisions to facilitate their ability to innovate in situations that improve their ability to provide more secure offerings (Hargadon, 2003; Sanidas, 2004). Studies have shown failure in the transition to new core technologies to support their own products and services have hampered their own growth (Gilbert, 2005; Taylor and Helfat, 2009). Also, there have been studies to distinguish between types of technological innovation based on divergent requirements and business mandates (Gibson and Birkinshaw, 2004; Gilbert, 2005; Raisch and Birkinshaw, 2008). Innovation in security aspects of cloud offerings also propose differentiated benefits and coverage against known and emerging risks. This section of the chapter investigates how recent technological innovations in managing risks in cloud services have helped both adopters and providers mitigate risks from cloud. Articles were collected from recent media announcements for last one year. These media announcements highlight that providers are keen on spreading the word about their innovation to provide assurance to the world that security is one of their top priorities. We also show how these innovations are mapped to cloud risks that we have identified in section 2 and how specifically they map to audit focus areas from section 3. Table 1 provides a summary of the articles with information on provider company, their services and what cloud risks are being addressed by that service.

Table 1 also shows the references on the media announcements and specific subsection where the announcement is discussed. Table 2 shows how specific cloud risk addressed are mapped to cloud risks that were identified in the section on extant literature on existing cloud computing risks. Table 3 shows mapping of cloud risks and how specific audit focus area can be used to test the control effectiveness and strength of each risk addressed. This will help the auditors and managers understand how the innovation is ranked in terms of providing security that the innovation aims to. At the same time auditors can also see how these specific risks can be incorporated in their overall audit plan when they collectively evaluate the control category to ensure that redundancies are reduced and defence in depth or layered control approach is maintained. The second column in Tables 2 and 3 represent the specific sub-section in Sections 2 and 3, respectively that deals with the specific risk. The first column in these tables is aggregation of similar types of addressed risks. Table 4 shows the cloud risks and specific media announcements that attempt to address them. In the next subsections, each of the announcements are discussed where the section title is also the title(s) of the media announcements that announced the specific innovation.

Table 1. Summary of recent innovations and addressed cloud risks

Cloud Risk Addressed	Provider / Domain	Service(s) / Process(es)	Reference(s)	Chapter Section
Distributed Denial of Service	Amazon Inc	AWS Shield	(Greene and Stevens, 2016; AWS Shield, 2016)	6.1
Migration Approach	Healthcare	Staged Migration	(McKendrick, 2016)	6.2
Public Network Risk	Console Inc.	Console	(Pesek, G, 2016; Hardesty, 2016; Console, 2016)	6.3
Unauthorized User Access & Data Leakage	Various	CASB	(Skyhigh, 2016)	6.4
Transaction Security	IBM	Blockchain network	(Prisco, 2016; Olavsrud, 2016; Castillo, 2016)	6.5
Insider Threat	Various	UEBA, Behavior Analysis	(Sarukkai, 2015)	6.6
Migration Failures	Amazon	AWS Elastic Block Store	(Frank, 2016)	6.7
Encryption and Key Management	Valutive and Gemalto	Safenet	(Vaultive, 2016)	6.8
Privileged Access / Insider Threat	Lieberman	Enterprise Random Password Manager	(Lieberman, 2016a; Lieberman, 2016b)	6.9
Web Application Firewall	Barracuda	Web Application Security	(Barracuda, 2016)	6.10
Public Network Risk	Zscaler	ZScaler Private Access	(Zscaler, 2016)	6.11
Application Security	Amazon	AWS X-Ray	(Amazon, 2016a; (Amazon, 2016c)	6.12
Technical Vulnerabilities	Menlo Security	Isolation Platform	Menlo, 2016)	6.13
Migration Failures	CloudVelox	CloudVelox	(Kepes, 2016)	6.14
Technical Vulnerabilities	Amazon	Amazon Inspector	(Amazon, 2016b)	6.15
Data Discovery and Compliance Risks	Dataguise	DgSecure (Analytics, Governance)	(Amazon, 2016d)	6.16
Insider Threat	Dataguise	DgSecure (RBAC, UEBA)	(Amazon, 2016d)	6.16
Data Encryption	IBM	Z13s servers	(Morgan, 2016; (Bhartiya, 2016; Taft, 2016)	6.17
Forensics and Traffic Analysis	ProtectWise	ProtectWise	(Protectwise, 2016)	6.18
Encryption and Key Management	Google	CSEK	(Vijayan, J, 2016)	6.19

Table 2. Mapping of cloud risk addressed and current risks focus area

Cloud Risks Addressed	Sub-Sections in 2 (Current Risks)
Distributed Denial of Service	2.3, 2.5, 2.6, 2.7
Migration Approach / Failures	2.2, 2.9
Public Network Risk	2.3, 2.5, 2.9
Unauthorized User Access	2.1, 2.2, 2.4
Transaction Security	2.2, 2.4, 2.7
Data Leakage	2.2, 2.3, 2.4, 2.7
Encryption and Key Management	2.2, 2.3, 2.5, 2.8, 2.9
Privileged Access Management	2.1, 2.2
Web Application Firewall	2.2, 2.7
Application Security	2.2, 2.3, 2.5, 2.6
Technical Vulnerabilities	2.2, 2.3, 2.5, 2.6
Data Discovery and Compliance Risks	2.2, 2.3, 2.4, 2.7, 2.8
Insider Threat	2.1, 2.2, 2.4, 2.6, 2.7
Forensics and Traffic Analysis	2.2, 2.3 2.7, 2.9

Table 3. Mapping of cloud risk addressed and audit focus area

Cloud Risks Addressed	Audit Focus Areas
Distributed Denial of Service	3.5
Migration Approach / Failures	3.1
Public Network Risk	3.4, 3.2
Unauthorized User Access	3.6
Transaction Security	3.6, 3.2
Data Leakage	3.2, 3.6
Encryption and Key Management	3.1, 3.6
Privileged Access Management	3.6
Web Application Firewall	3.3
Application Security	3.3
Technical Vulnerabilities	3.2, 3.3
Data Discovery and Compliance Risks	3.2, 3.4
Insider Threat	3.2, 3.6
Forensics and Traffic Analysis	3.2, 3.5

Table 4. Mapping of cloud risk addressed through innovations

Cloud Risks Addressed	Recent Innovations (Sub-Sections in 6)
Distributed Denial of Service	6.1
Migration Approach / Failures	6.2, 6.7, 6.14
Public Network Risk	6.3, 6.11
Unauthorized User Access	6.4
Transaction Security	6.5
Data Leakage	6.4
Encryption and Key Management	6.8, 6.12, 6.17, 6.19
Privileged Access Management	6.09
Web Application Firewall	6.10
Application Security	6.12
Technical Vulnerabilities	6.13, 6.15
Data Discovery and Compliance Risks	6.16
Insider Threat	6.09, 6.16
Forensics and Traffic Analysis	6.18

6.1. Amazon Cloud Computing Division Unveils New Cyber Security Service (Greene and Stevens, 2016) / AWS Shield (AWS Shield, 2016)

In wake of the recent Distributed denial of services attack launched against market giants like twitter, PayPal and Netflix, Amazon launches AWS Shield to protect its customers from such attacks that can make websites unreachable for a period of time. AWS shield has been introduced with two tiers – Standard and Advanced. Standard version is free of cost and automatically enabled for all customers of AWS. It protects web applications from commonly known attacks occurring at the network and transport layers. This is done by analysing incoming traffic to detecting anomalies, malicious code inserts or malware signatures. Inline and automatic mitigation techniques are also available to protect application from impact of attacks. AWS Shield advanced is a paid service and can protect applications from larger and more sophisticated attacks and is integrated with AWS Web Application Firewall (AWS WAF). Enhanced resource specific monitoring, the ability to set proactive firewall rules with AWS WAF and advanced automatic mitigation techniques are some key features. AWS Shield advanced provides access to 24*7 DDoS Response team who can be engaged before, during or after attack for specialised services. It also comes with 'DDoS cost protection' which identify spikes on Elastic load balancer that could be caused by a potential DDoS attack and provides service credits for any charges levied because of this spike.

6.2. For Healthcare, Cloud Computing Comes in Measured Doses (McKendrick, 2016)

Health care providers taking to cloud has significantly grown over the past two years despite concerns regarding data protection and HIPPA laws. Most healthcare organizations prefer staged migration to cloud starting with testing cloud platforms with back office applications and then managing analytics and storage on cloud before rolling out patient facing web applications. Companies are opting for a combination of private cloud, for storing sensitive information like patient records, and public cloud for disaster recovery and setting up POC environments.

6.3. Bringing Cloud Security Innovations to the Enterprise (Pesek, G, 2016) / IIX Reinvents Itself as Console (Hardesty, L, 2016) / Console Inc. (Console, 2016)

Console Inc. enables programmable interconnection between two enterprises or an enterprise and a cloud network like Microsoft Azure, Google Cloud platform or AWS via a software platform. With public internet one does not have control over the path taken by data packets, network performance and exposure to threats. A data packet travelling across public internet is, on an average, exposed to four different networks each having several vulnerable points such as routers, switches, gateways etc. Console has a built a global network with 160 points of presence connected by a fibre for direct private connection that can bypass the public internet. Console is the first company to fully automate switching and routing for seamless interconnection, avoiding the risks of sending traffic over the public Internet and providing a more secure, reliable and consistent environment. Console provides other features like social networking among enterprises, SaaS solution providers and business partners. They also provide advanced monitoring that enables an enterprise to repurpose capacity across network ports.

6.4. What is a Cloud Access Security Broker (CASB) (Skyhigh, 2016)

CASB is an on premise or cloud hosted software that act as policy enforcement points and are placed between cloud service providers and consumers. CASB can combine security policies including Authentication, single sign-on, authorization, credential mapping, device profiling, encryption, tokenization, logging, alerting, malware detection/prevention.

Gartner names cloud access security broker the #1 security technology of 2016 and believes that by 2020, 85% of large enterprises will use CASB for their cloud services.

CASB's can help organizations identify threats and misuse of cloud services by identifying usage of shadow IT cloud services and risks they pose to organizational data. Shadow IT can also pose a threat to the IP of a company when employees put corporate information on cloud during unauthorized deployments. A CASB can monitor data traffic sent between organizational endpoints and cloud applications which will enable IT to uncover rogue deployments and cloud services used by employees.

6.5. IBM Launches Blockchain Cloud Services on High Security Server, LinuxONE (Prisco, 2016) / IBM Building Blockchain Ecosystem (Olavsrud, 2016) / IBM Unveils New Cloud Blockchain Security Service (Castillo, 2016)

IBM has launched a new functionality as part of its cloud services for businesses to test and run blockchain networks. This service will ensure security for private data and is ideal for industries that require strong compliance. Blockchain is a distributed database that can record digital events or transactions. Records cannot be altered and can only be amended. Each block of item in a chain is timestamped and also contains a hash value of the previous block thus creating a link between the two. Each new transaction has to be authenticated by all participants in the distributed network forming the block chain thus providing transparency and creating awareness among stakeholders. IBM looks to improve security of private blockchains running in cloud by securing end points and fighting insider threats. The IBM Blockchain runs on LinuxOne emperor system that can scale up to 8000 VMs and is designed to protect against backdoor attacks. IBM's secure services container technology provides firmware protection and prevents system administrators and root users from accessing the blockchain on cloud. All software built on IBM Blockchain will be encrypted and attested to prevent installation of malware on client systems. It is currently being used to securely track high value goods such as diamonds and artwork. Microsoft has also rolled out BaaS for Microsoft azure.

6.6. How Data Science and Machine Learning is Enabling Cloud Threat Protection (Sarukkai, 2015)

User and Entity behavioral analytics (UEBA) creates behavior based models for cloud services wherein these models adapt depending on user behavior. Anomalies in user behavior can be easily identified and reported. Machine learning algorithms in UEBA performs data exploration thus enabling prioritization of security incidents. For example, while traditional detection systems might flag every transaction above a certain threshold, UEBA would spot unusual user activities by sifting through large datasets. Given that an average company sees over 2 billion cloud based transactions each day, UEBA can be used against factors such as service action, service action category, number of bytes uploaded/downloaded and rate/time of access of services across a service action or even an entire cloud service provider to identify behavioral anomalies.

Behavior analysis takes security beyond rule writing by looking at activities and behaviors so that even if someone is able to compromise a user's identity, they still have to be able to act like the user, which is when the alarms start to go off. Gartner predicts the UEBA market revenue to rise to approximately US$200 million by the end of 2017.

6.7. Amazon Quietly Launches Tools for Migrating on Premise Apps to Cloud (Frank, 2016)

Migration of legacy and on premise applications to cloud is risky especially if those applications require low downtime. Amazons Server Migration service helps IT replicate on premise VMs to Amazon Cloud by supporting incremental replication. IT administrators install a connector that will analyze their virtualized server environment and collect information about the instances they are using. The AWS Management console provides a view of all operating connectors and virtualized servers in an environment. From there, administrators can create and manage replication jobs to take the contents of a VM and reproduce it as an Amazon Machine Image stored in the AWS Elastic Block Store (EBS) service.

Each incremental replication will sync only what's been changed to minimize network bandwidth use. Allows servers to be tested incrementally. From there, it's possible to spin up a new instance that should be a duplicate of what's running on-premises, either for testing the replicated VM or for getting it running in production. This feature ensures that migration to cloud is simplified. It also allows orchestration of multi-server migrations, incremental testing of migrated servers, supports widely used operating systems and minimizes downtime due to migration.

6.8. Vaultive and Gemalto Team Up to Deliver Increased Cloud Data Security Control for SaaS Applications (Vaultive, 2016)

Vaultive and Gemalto have teamed up to provide an encryption and key management solution by which companies can encrypt data before moving it to cloud and also maintain ownership of encryption keys across SaaS applications. More control over key management allows organization to demonstrate better control of their sensitive data. This approach also allows separation of controls between cloud administrators and security professionals who are responsible for protecting data and keys. Gemalto's SafeNet, which is their multi factor authentication service, can be integrated with this platform for identity and access management.

Some key features of this solution:

1. Rule based policy engine enables rapid integration with SaaS applications and encryption best practices ensures securing data at organizational boundaries;
2. Cost effective method to secure multiple cloud applications. Ease of deployment across physical, public and virtual cloud environments;
3. Uses Key Management Interoperability protocol standard and SafeNet can centrally manage and preserve integrity of encryption keys.

6.9. Lieberman Software to Present Cloud Security Session at Gartner Identity and Access Management Summit (Lieberman, 2016a; Lieberman, 2016b)

Some concerns of companies migrating to cloud revolve around the growing number of unmanaged administrator accounts and cryptographic keys. Lieberman Software's cyber security technology automatically discovers privileged accounts in cloud and hybrid environments at scale, and audits access to those accounts. The Enterprise Random Password Manager (ERPM) is a cyber-defense platform that can protect organizations from insider threats, advanced persist threats and cyber-attacks across on-premise and cloud environments. ERPM tracks privileged accounts and provides them with unique and frequently changing credentials. These identities are available only to authorized users on a temporary basis thus preventing unauthorized or anonymous access to critical systems. The software also allows users to configure rules for password complexity, diversity, change frequency and synchronize changes for across dependencies. ERPM can be used to secure identity of super user accounts, service accounts, application credentials, encryption keys and cloud identities on Azure, AWS, Softlayer etc. It also helps organizations meet compliance requirements by providing a comprehensive view of risks across privileged accounts and enforcing credential policies.

6.10. Barracuda Simplifies Web Application Security for AWS Customers (Barracuda, 2016)

Barracuda has released a new metered billing option for its Web Application Firewall that enables customers to deploy an unlimited number of firewalls but pay only for what is consumed. This is in contrast to practices followed by AWS marketplace applications where customer usage is aggregated and charged as part of AWS bill. This offering provides AWS customers greater flexibility and control over operational costs while securing their cloud environments. Meter firewalls allow cost to economically scale with increasing application workloads.

6.11. Zscaler Private Access - Remote Access Without the Security Risks of VPNs (Zscaler, 2016)

VPNs have always been the standard method of providing users remote access to corporate applications on an internal network. However, cost of installation, deployment, maintenance and upgrade is high for VPN. Additional requirements in terms of increased number of datacenters, load balancers, Site-to-Site VPN tunnels and licenses may be required for providing high availability of VPN. The most important risk with VPN is security, since remote access is actually network access. Once in a network malware can propagate and users may be able to gain access to adjacent applications from which they should be restricted.

To address this issue, Zscaler Private Access uses the global Zscaler cloud infrastructure to enable application access independent of network access. Zscaler Private Access decouples applications from the physical network and delivers granular, per-user access to apps and services running in the internal corporate network, in a data center, or in a public cloud like Amazon or Azure. The service is based on Zscaler's global cloud (with over 100 data centers globally), Zscalar App and Zscalar's software connectors, so there is no requirement for additional hardware or upgrades of existing hardware. If there are more than two instances of the same application deployed in two different locations the software will choose the path that provides best performance.

6.12. Amazon Unveils AWS X-Ray and Personal Health Dashboard to Help Monitor Application Health in the Cloud (Amazon, 2016a) / AWS X-Rays (Amazon, 2016c)

With the emergence of distributed systems, ensuring functioning of modules at scale has gained importance. There has been no easy way for developers to "follow-the-thread" as execution traverses EC2 instances, ECS containers, micro-services, AWS database and messaging services. AWS X-Ray is a service that allows developers to debug their distributed applications. X-Ray captures trace data from code running on EC2 instances, AWS Elastic beanstalk AWS Gateway API and more. The data collected at each point is called a segment, and is stored as a chunk of JSON data. A segment represents a unit of work, and includes request and response timing, along with optional sub-segments that represent smaller work units down to lines of code. It allows developers to follow thread execution by adding HTTP headers to requests. The X-Ray UI is built around the concept of filter expressions. The UI is powered by free-form filters that allows to filter results based on response time, duration, service, dates, trace ID, HTTP methods etc.

6.13. Half of the Web is Vulnerable to Malware (Menlo, 2016)

According to Menlo Software's 'State of the web 2016' report, 46% of internet's top 1 million sites are risky. Menlo considers a site 'risky' if the homepage or associated background sites: is running vulnerable software, is known-bad, or has had a security incident in the last 12 months. Traditional methods like firewalls, anti-virus, network sandboxing or intrusion prevention systems attempt to prevent attacks by distinguishing between "good" and "bad" elements, and then implement policies intended to allow "good" content and block the "bad." However, this strategy has not been effective in eliminating malware and phishing attacks has also generated several false reports.

Menlo Security's cloud based Isolation Platform is aimed at solving the malware problem completely by executing all of the content from the internet in an isolated environment. The application can perform isolation at scale in a distributed cloud environment and render malware free content to the end user without requiring any end point software. The platform is inserted between user and the web and configured via proxy chaining with web gateway or firewall. A user's web request is sent to the platform that browses the web on the users behalf and fetches and executed web content within the platform on the user's behalf. Only 100% safe rendering information is sent to the users device to the native web browser. All of the good or bad content from the web remains in the isolation platform. Platform also helps secure E Mails protecting organization from data theft or fraud.

6.14. CloudVelox Offers Automated Cloud Network Customizations (Kepes, 2016)

CloudVelox software automates migration of on premise applications to public cloud including AWS and Azure with reduced time, complexity and hassle. The software has already automated storage and compute migration and has not added automation for network migration customizations too. Enterprises can "map" their existing networking topologies within a data center and recreate that within a cloud network paradigm. This automation can ease the migration to cloud for large data centers with complex network configurations and enterprise workloads running on specific VLANs and subnets. During migration, Data security and access is managed by SSH, HTTPS, Volume encryption and IPSeC VPN. System security is handled by launching the application in a separate AWS VPC and configuring security groups and virtual access control lists. Application security is ensured by utilizing CloudVelox's ability to authenticate users from LDAP servers running in customer data center, customers can assert control over appropriate resource access in the cloud.

6.15. Amazon Web Services Makes Amazon Inspector Available to All Customers (Amazon, 2016b)

Amazon Inspector identifies potential security issues, vulnerabilities and deviations from security norms to help customers improve security compliance for applications running on AWS cloud servers. This reduces effort required to assess security risks and provides a simplified mechanism for developers to integrate security assessments within the application development cycle. This integration can be done by using API's provided by inspector on specific EC2 instances and associated applications that customers would like to assess. Security tests and duration can be selected and adjusted as required. Once tests are selected, the inspector analyses the application activities and looks for a wide variety of potential vulnerabilities in the system. Information such as application communication flow and channels are gathered and compared against AWS rule packages that comprise of several thousand security vulnerabilities. Once an assessment is completed customers are provided with detailed recommendations for application remediation. This service along with CloudTrail allows auditors to view details and logs of security tests performed thereby simplifying the process of demonstrating compliance for AWS customers.

6.16. Dataguise Shows Security and Compliance Innovations for Cloud-Based Data Infrastructure at AWS Summit in New York (Amazon, 2016d)

Dataguise DgSecure on AWS is a data centric security platform. It scans Amazon S3 (storage) and identifies the location and status of sensitive information that is also accessed via Amazon Elastic MapReduce (Amazon EMR) for data analytics, compliance, and information governance purposes. The solution features transparent, role-based sensitive asset provisioning on the Amazon EMR platform so that users have access to sensitive data hosted on Amazon S3 through DgSecure role-based access policies. The technology also provides detection, monitoring, auditing of sensitive information across cloud based repositories. DgSecure can help businesses understand data breach, privacy and compliance risk, make risk based decisions and provide additional layers of security for data driven initiatives. DgSecure also supports all major distributions including Hortonworks, Cloudera, and MapR as well as major relational databases including Oracle, SQLServer, MySQL, and PostgreSQL. Dataguise also uses machine learning and behavioral analytics to alert administrators when system, device, or human behavior deviates from the norm. It makes sure that any move to the cloud remains compliant with privacy and regulatory requirements by allowing companies to keep track of all the data across the enterprise and ensuring it doesn't fall into the wrong hands.

6.17. IBM's New Cyberframe is the World's Most Secure Server for Datacenters, Cloud and Mobile (Morgan, 2016) / IBM Encrypts the Cloud with Z13s Mainframes (Bhartiya, 2016) / IBM Takes the Power of Mainframe to Cloud (Taft, 2016)

IBM announced the Z13s (s for security) mainframe servers with speedy encryption, cyber analytics and other security innovations. IBM has spent 5 years and $1 bn on Z13s development efforts. It can process 2.5 bn transactions a day with advanced cryptographic features to encrypt and decrypt data two times faster than previous generation servers with loss in performance. Clients can encrypt data right from the point where order is made on mobile to the financial transactions done in the data center or on cloud. IBM is also offering new analytics service to Z systems that is based on UEBA to identify malicious activity. The Z13 costs half that of public cloud for comparable configuration and equivalent workloads.

The new offerings include IBM Bluemix integration with z Systems. IBM's bluemix environment combined with enhancements to connector technology within bluemix and Z systems now allows enterprises to leverage their own single-tenant version of Bluemix to build applications around their most sensitive data and existing services. IBM also introduced z Systems Hybrid Cloud Connect Test Drive, which enables enterprises to connect their on-premises enterprise systems to a public cloud. IBM z Systems will offer IBM Cloud Manager with OpenStack for the z13 to simplify the management of virtualized environments.

6.18. ProtectWise Achieves Advanced Partner Status in the Amazon Web Services Partner Network (Protectwise, 2016)

ProtectWise offers a cloud detection visibility and response platform that uses software sensors deployed on networks for packet capture of all network traffic. The data is then streamed back to the cloud platform for threat detection and analysis and stored for up to a year, you will know with absolute confidence whether or not events have impacted your environment. The ProtectWise Grid captures high fidelity network traffic, creates a lasting memory for the network and delivers analysis and alerting through a visualizer. The Grid helps users not only understand what is happening in real time, but also to go back in time and show progression in attacks. Users know when and how an attack happens, and are able to pinpoint the attack for rapid remediation. This provides security teams the strategic advantage to hunt and investigate threats through every stage of an attack. The ProtectWise Visualizer is an overview of your network security which allows exploration for collaboration and forensic analysis by cutting through the noise to quickly identify the high-priority threats.

6.19. Google Initiates Customer-Supplied Cloud Data Encryption Keys (Vijayan, J, 2016)

Although many cloud vendors encrypt customer data at rest these days, the fact that they also hold the decryption keys has proved to be an issue for many organizations. Google this week announced general availability of an option that lets customers of its cloud services use their own keys for encrypting sensitive data stored online. Currently, Google's cloud platform encrypts all customer data stored on its servers by default but with this new service Google enables enterprises to bring their own Customer-Supplied Encryption Keys (CSEK) to protect data. The company will only require and hold customer keys temporarily to fulfill requests such as starting a virtual machine or attaching a disk. Google will use CSEK to protect the Google-generated keys used to encrypt and decrypt the data. Any key the customer provides must be 256-bit string encoded in the RFC 4648 standard. Since CSEK's are not stored anywhere by Google, if keys are lost there will be no way for Google to retrieve data encrypted with those keys. Amazon and Box provide similar facilities to its customers for data security.

7. CONCLUSION

It has been evident last few years that cloud computing's offers a lot of promises for small and large enterprises alike. Security risks have been largely seen as main concerns and voiced by companies. Cloud service providers have been on an upward trajectory to improve their offerings' flexibility and scalability and improving security and availability levels. This chapter elaborates on 1) the most important risks inherent to the cloud as are evidenced by extant literature as well as 2) audit focus areas that can provide assurance on control strength of controls that mitigate risks. Companies have taken a hybrid approach with direct and compensating controls for lack of appropriate technology to support their security objectives. This chapter presents how companies (cloud service providers) have responded with innovations in security and how they are in response to risks that have already been highlighted by extant research. This chapter can be useful for managers, auditors and security professionals on how recent innovations are shaping cloud industry and they are providing the much needed respite from the pressure of cloud computing risks. At the same time, it also provides insights into the trend of innovation in security solutions in cloud. As future work on this chapter, we plan on collecting additional data from previous years (older than 2016) and interpret the results to show how the evolution has been for cloud computing. Also, specific risks could be investigated as part of future work to unravel any underlying themes and categories in countermeasures that provide most benefit from the risks that arise due to adoption of cloud computing services.

REFERENCES

Adomavicius, G., Bockstedt, J., Gupta, A., & Kauffman, R. J. (2007). Technology roles and paths of influence in an ecosystem model of technology evolution. *Information Technology Management*, 8(2), 185–202. doi:10.1007/s10799-007-0012-z

Amazon. (2016a). *Amazon unveils AWS X-Ray and Personal Health Dashboard to help monitor application health in the cloud*. Retrieved online on December 15, 2016 from http://www.geekwire.com/2016/amazon-unveils-aws-x-ray-personal-health-dashboard-help-monitor-application-health-cloud/

Amazon. (2016b). *Amazon Web Services Makes Amazon Inspector Available to All Customers*. Retrieved online on December 15, 2016 from http://www.businesswire.com/news/home/20160419006466/en/Amazon-Web-Services-Amazon-Inspector-Customers

Amazon. (2016c). *AWS XRAY. Amazon Website.* Retrieved online on December 15, 2016 from https://aws.amazon.com/blogs/aws/aws-x-ray-see-inside-of-your-distributed-application/

Amazon. (2016d). *Dataguise Shows Security and Compliance Innovations for Cloud-Based Data Infrastructure at AWS Summit in New York.* Retrieved online on December 15, 2016 from http://www.businesswire.com/news/home/20161205005340/en/Global-Cybersecurity-Confidence-Falls-70-Percent-%E2%80%9CC-%E2%80%9D

Avgerou, C. (2008). Information systems in developing countries: a critical research review. *J. Inform. Technol., 23*(3), 133–146.

AWS Shield. (2016). *AWS Shield: managed DDOS Protection.* Retrieved online on December 15, 2016 from https://aws.amazon.com/shield/

Baregheh, A., Rowley, J., & Sambrook, S. (2009). Towards a multidisciplinary definition of innovation. *Management Decision, 47*(8), 1323–1339.

Barracuda. (2016). *Barracuda Simplifies Web Application Security for AWS Customers.* Retrieved online on December 15, 2016 from http://www.broadwayworld.com/bwwgeeks/article/Barracuda-Simplifies-Web-Application-Security-for-AWS-Customers-20161130

Bartolini, C., El Kateb, D., Le Traon, Y., & Hagen, D. (2015). *Cloud Providers Viability: How to Address it from an IT and Legal Perspective? Economics of Grids.* Clouds, Systems, and Services.

Bhartiya, S. (2016). *IBM encrypts the cloud with Z13s mainframe.* Retrieved online on December 15, 2016 from http://www.cio.com/article/3033967/linux/ibm-encrypts-the-cloud-with-z13s-mainframe.html

Bisong, A., & Rahman, M. (2011). *An overview of the security concerns in enterprise cloud computing.* arXiv preprint arXiv:1101.5613

Biswas, S. (2011, January 20). *Is cloud computing secure? Yes, another perspective* [Web log post]. Retrieved online on January 6, 2017 from http://www.cloudtweaks.com/2011/01/the-question-should-be-is-anything-truly-secure

Brodkin, J. (2008). Gartner: Seven cloud-computing security risks. *InfoWorld, 2008,* 1–3.

Businesswire. (2016). *World First: Outscale Introduces Per-Second Billing to Boost Cloud Adoption.* Retrieved online on December 15, 2016 from http://www.businesswire.com/news/home/20160915005885/en/World-Outscale-Introduces-Per-Second-Billing-Boost-Cloud

Carlo, J. L., Lyytinen, K., & Rose, G. M. (2011). Internet computing as a disruptive information technology innovation: The role of strong order effects. *Information Systems Journal, 21*(1), 91–122. doi:10.1111/j.1365-2575.2009.00345.x

Castillo, M. (2016). *IBM Unveils New Cloud Blockchain Security Service.* Retrieved from http://www.coindesk.com

Chang, V., Kuo, Y. H., & Ramachandran, M. (2016). Cloud computing adoption framework: A security framework for business clouds. *Future Generation Computer Systems, 57,* 24–41. doi:10.1016/j.future.2015.09.031

Christensen, C. M., Baumann, H., Ruggles, R., & Sadtler, T. M. (2007). Disruptive Innovation for Social Change. In *Harvard Business Review* (pp. 136–136). Harvard Business School Publication Corp.

Cloud Security Alliance. (2010). *Cloud Audit Working Group.* Retrieved online on December 15, 2016 from https://cloudsecurityalliance.org/group/cloudaudit/

Cloud Security Alliance. (2016). *The Treacherous 12.* Retrieved online on December 15, 2016 from https://downloads.cloudsecurityalliance.org/assets/research/top-threats/Treacherous-12_Cloud-Computing_Top-Threats.pdf

Console. (2016). Console Inc. Retrieved online on December 15, 2016 from https://www.console.to/

Cooper, C. (2016). *Fixing the weakest link in cloud security.* Retrieved online on December 15, 2016 from http://mspmentor.net/cloud-services/fixing-weakest-link-cloud-security

Dahbur, K., Mohammad, B., & Tarakji, A. B. (2011, April). A survey of risks, threats and vulnerabilities in cloud computing. In *Proceedings of the 2011 International conference on intelligent semantic Web-services and applications* (p. 12). ACM. doi:10.1145/1980822.1980834

Deloitte. (2016). *Data privacy in the cloud Navigating the new privacy regime in a cloud environment.* Retrieved online on December 15, 2016 from http://www.wsj.com/articles/amazon-cloud-computing-division-unveils-new-cyber-security-service-1480620359

Dorey, P. G., & Leite, A. (2011). Commentary: Cloud computing–A security problem or solution?. *Information Security Technical Report, 16*(3), 89-96.

ENISA. (2009). *Cloud Computing: Benefits, Risks and Recommendations for Information Security.* Retrieved online on January 6, 2017 from: http://www.enisa.europa.eu/act/rm/files/deliverables/cloud-computing-risk-assessment

ENISA. (2014a). *Making the cloud more transparent - a boost for secure, trustworthy services*. ENISA.

ENISA. (2014b). *Exploring Cloud Incidents*. Retrieved online on December 15, 2016 from https://www.enisa.europa.eu/publications/exploring-cloud-incidents

Fagerberg, J. (2005). Innovation: a guide to the literature. In J. Fagerberg, D. C. Mowery, & R. R. Nelson (Eds.), *The Oxford Handbook of Innovation* (pp. 1–26). New York: Oxford University Press.

Frank, B. (2016). *Amazon Quietly Launches tools for migrating on premise apps to cloud*. Retrieved online on December 15, 2016 from http://www.pcworld.com/article/3135060/cloud-computing/aws-quietly-launches-tool-for-migrating-on-premesis-apps-to-the-cloud.html

Gao, J., Bai, X., & Tsai, W. T. (2011). Cloud testing-issues, challenges, needs and practice. *Software Engineering: An International Journal, 1*(1), 9–23.

Gilbert, C. (2005). Unbundling the structure of inertia: Resource versus routine rigidity. *Academy of Management Journal, 48*(5), 741–763. doi:10.5465/AMJ.2005.18803920

Greene, J., & Stevens, L. (2016). Amazon Cloud Computing Division Unveils New Cyber Security Service. *Wall Street Journal*. Retrieved online on December 15, 2016 from http://www.wsj.com/articles/amazon-cloud-computing-division-unveils-new-cyber-security-service-1480620359

Greene, T. (2015). *SANS: 20 critical security controls you need to add*. Retrieved online on December 15, 2016 from http://www.networkworld.com/article/2992503/security/sans-20-critical-security-controls-you-need-to-add.html

Grover, V., Fiedler, K., & Teng, J. (1997). Empirical evidence on Swansons tri-core model of information systems innovation. *Information Systems Research, 8*(3), 273–287. doi:10.1287/isre.8.3.273

Habiba, M., Islam, M. R., & Ali, A. S. (2013, July). Access control management for cloud. In *2013 12th IEEE International Conference on Trust, Security and Privacy in Computing and Communications* (pp. 485-492). doi:10.1109/TrustCom.2013.61

Halpert, B. (2011). *Auditing cloud computing: A security and privacy guide* (Vol. 21). John Wiley & Sons. doi:10.1002/9781118269091

Hardesty, L. (2016). *IIX Reinvents Itself as Console*. Retrieved online on December 15, 2016 from https://www.sdxcentral.com/articles/news/iix-reinvents-itself-console/2016/05/

Hargadon, A. (2003). *How breakthroughs happen: The surprising truth about how companies innovate*. Boston, MA: Harvard Business School Press.

Heiser, J., & Nicolett, M. (2008). *Assessing the security risks of cloud computing*. Stamford, CT: Gartner Research. Retrieved online on January 6, 2017 from http://www.globalcloudbusiness.com/SharedFiles/Download.aspx?pageid=138&mid=220&fileid=12

Kadam, Y. (2011). Security Issues in Cloud Computing A Transparent View. *International Journal of Computer Science Emerging Technology, 2*(5), 316–322.

Kaplinsky, R., Chataway, J., Clark, N., Hanlin, R., Kale, D., Muraguri, L, Papaioannou, T., Robbins, P. and Wamae, W. (2009). Below the radar: what does innovation in emerging economies have to offer other low-income economies? *International Journal Technology Management Sustenance Development, 8*(3), 177–197.

Kaufman, L. M. (2009). Data security in the world of cloud computing. *IEEE Security and Privacy, 7*(4), 61–64. doi:10.1109/MSP.2009.87

Kepes, B. (2016). *CloudVelox offers automated cloud network customizations*. Retrieved online on December 15, 2016 from http://www.networkworld.com/article/3142742/cloud-computing/cloudvelox-offers-automated-cloud-network-customizations.html

Ko, R. K., Jagadpramana, P., Mowbray, M., Pearson, S., Kirchberg, M., Liang, Q., & Lee, B. S. (2011, July). TrustCloud: A framework for accountability and trust in cloud computing. In *2011 IEEE World Congress on Services* (pp. 584-588). doi:10.1109/SERVICES.2011.91

Kroes, N. (2014). *Making the cloud more transparent - a boost for secure, trustworthy services*. Retrieved online on December 15, 2016 from http://ec.europa.eu.gate.lib.buffalo.edu/commission_2010-2014/kroes/en/content/making-cloud-more-transparent-boost-secure-trustworthy-services

Kwang, T. W. (2016). *Cloud technology for public sector innovation*. Retrieved online on December 15, 2016 from http://www.enterpriseinnovation.net/article/cloud-technology-public-sector-innovation-2130602017

Leinwand, A. (2016). *Transparency in the cloud or the lack of thereof*. Retrieved online on December 15, 2016 from http://cloudtweaks.com/2016/11/transparency-cloud/

Levinthal, D. A., & March, J. G. (1993). The myopia of learning. *Strategic Management Journal, 14*(S2), 95–112. doi:10.1002/smj.4250141009

Lieberman. (2016a). *Lieberman Software to Present Cloud Security Session at Gartner Identity and Access*. Retrieved online on December 15, 2016 from http://www.marketwired.com/press-release/lieberman-software-present-cloud-security-session-gartner-identity-access-management-2178865.htm

Lieberman. (2016b). *Enterprise Random Password Manager*. Retrieved online on December 15, 2016 from https://liebsoft.com/products/Enterprise_Random_Password_Manager/

Marston, S., Li, Z., Bandyopadhyay, S., Zhang, J., & Ghalsasi, A. (2011). Cloud computing – the business perspective. *Decision Support Systems*, *51*(1), 176–189. doi:10.1016/j.dss.2010.12.006

Massonet, P., Naqvi, S., Ponsard, C., Latanicki, J., Rochwerger, B., & Villari, M. (2011, May). A monitoring and audit logging architecture for data location compliance in federated cloud infrastructures. In *Parallel and Distributed Processing Workshops and Phd Forum (IPDPSW), 2011 IEEE International Symposium on* (pp. 1510-1517). IEEE. doi:10.1109/IPDPS.2011.304

McKendrick, J. (2016). For healthcare: cloud computing comes in measured doses. *Forbes*. Retrieved online on December 15, 2016 from http://www.forbes.com/sites/joemckendrick/2016/11/27/for-healthcare-cloud-computing-comes-in-measured-doses/#62b6087d6894

Mell, P., & Grance, T. (2011). *The NIST definition of cloud computing: Recommendations of the 33666 Institute of Standards and Technology*. Retrieved online on January 6 from http://csrc.nist.gov/publications/nistpubs/800-145/SP800-145.pdf

Menlo. (2016). *Half of the Web is Vulnerable to Malware*. Retrieved online on December 15, 2016 from http://www.prnewswire.com/news-releases/half-of-the-web-is-vulnerable-to-malware-300376971.html

Microsoft. (2016). *Cloud Security Alliance*. Retrieved online on December 15, 2016 from https://www.microsoft.com/en-us/trustcenter/Compliance/CSA

Morgan, S. (2016). IBM's new cyberframe is the world's most secure server for datacenters, cloud and mobile. *Forbes*. Retrieved online on December 15, 2016 from http://www.forbes.com/sites/stevemorgan/2016/02/16/ibms-new-cyberframe-is-the-worlds-most-secure-server/#e0781e868fa6

Nelson, R. R., & Winter, S. G. (1982). *An evolutionary theory of economic change*. Cambridge, MA: Belknap Press/Harvard University Press.

Olavsrud, T. (2016). *IBM Buiding blockchain ecosystem.* Retrieved online on December 15, 2016. http://www.cio.com/article/3147358/it-industry/ibm-building-blockchain-ecosystem.html

Onwubiko, C. (2010). Security issues to cloud computing. In *Cloud Computing* (pp. 271–288). Springer London. doi:10.1007/978-1-84996-241-4_16

OWASP. (2010). *Cloud-10 Multi Tenancy and Physical Security.* Retrieved online on December 15, 2016 from https://www.owasp.org/index.php/Cloud-10_Multi_Tenancy_and_Physical_Security

Pesek, G. (2016). *Bringing cloud security innovations to the enterprise.* Retrieved online on December 15, 2016 from http://siliconangle.com/blog/2016/12/02/bringing-cloud-security-innovations-enterprise-reinvent/

Prisco, G. (2016). *IBM Launches Blockchain Cloud Services on High Security Server.* Retrieved online on December 15, 2016 from https://bitcoinmagazine.com/articles/ibm-launches-blockchain-cloud-services-on-high-security-server-linuxone-1469043762

ProtectWise. (2016). *ProtectWise Achieves Advanced Partner Status in the Amazon Web Services Partner Network.* Retrieved online on December 15, 2016 from http://www.businesswire.com/news/home/20161201005006/en/ProtectWise-Achieves-Advanced-Partner-Status-Amazon-Web

Raisch, S., & Birkinshaw, J. (2008). Organizational ambidexterity: Antecedents, outcomes, and moderators. *Journal of Management, 34*(3), 375–409. doi:10.1177/0149206308316058

Rasheed, H. (2011). *Auditing for standards compliance in the cloud: Challenges and directions.* Academic Press.

Rashmi, M. S., & Sahoo, G. (2012). A five-phased approach for the cloud migration. *Int J Emerg Technol Adv Eng, 2*(4), 286–291.

Ren, K., Wang, C., & Wang, Q. (2012, January-February). Security Challenges for the Public Cloud. *IEEE Internet Computing, 16*(1), 69–73. doi:10.1109/MIC.2012.14

Rogers, M. (1998). *The Definition and Measurement of Innovation* (Working paper no. 9/ 98). Melbourne Institute of Applied Economic and Social Research. Retrieved online on January 6, 2017 from http://melbourneinstitute.com/downloads/working_paper_series/ wp1998n09.pdf

Ryoo, J., Rizvi, S., Aiken, W., & Kissell, J. (2013). Cloud Security Auditing: Challenges and Emerging Approaches. *IEEE Security & Privacy, 12*(6), 68-74. doi: 10.1109/MSP.2013.132

Sanidas, E. (2004). Technology, technical and organizational innovations, economic and societal growth. *Technology in Society, 26*(1), 67–84. doi:10.1016/j.techsoc.2003.10.006

Sarukkai, S. (2015). *How Data Science And Machine Learning Is Enabling Cloud Threat Protection.* Retrieved online on December 15, 2016 from http://cloudtweaks.com/2015/12/data-science-machine-learning/

Shackleford, D. (n.d.). *How to overcome unique cloud-based patch management challenges* Retrieved online on December 15, 2016 from http://searchcloudsecurity.techtarget.com/tip/How-to-overcome-unique-cloud-based-patch-management-challenges

SkyHigh. (2016). *What is a cloud access security broker.* Academic Press.

Subashini, S., & Kavitha, V. (2011). A survey on security issues in service delivery models of cloud computing. *Journal of Network and Computer Applications, 34*(1), 1–11. doi:10.1016/j.jnca.2010.07.006

Taft, D. (2016a). *IBM takes the power of mainframe to cloud.* Retrieved online on December 15, 2016 from http://www.eweek.com/cloud/ibm-takes-the-power-of-the-mainframe-to-the-cloud.html

Taft, D. (2016b). *IBM Delivers Secure Blockchain Services in the Cloud.* Retrieved online on December 15, 2016 from http://www.eweek.com/cloud/ibm-delivers-secure-blockchain-services-in-the-cloud.html

Taylor, A., & Helfat, C. E. (2009). Organizational Linkages for Surviving Technological Change: Complementary Assets, Middle Management, and Ambidexterity. *Organization Science, 20*(4), 718–739. doi:10.1287/orsc.1090.0429

Taylor, L. (2014). FedRAMP: History and Future Direction. *IEEE Cloud Computing, 1*(3), 10–14. doi:10.1109/MCC.2014.54

Teneyuca, D. (2011). Internet cloud security: The illusion of inclusion. *Information Security Technical Report, 16*(3).

Tushman, M. L., & Anderson, P. C. (1986). Technological discontinuities and organizational environments. *Administrative Science Quarterly, 31*(3), 439–465. doi:10.2307/2392832

Vaultive. (2016). *Vaultive and Gemalto Team Up to Deliver Increased Cloud Data Security Control for SaaS Applications*. Retrieved online on December 15, 2016 from http://www.prnewswire.com/news-releases/vaultive-and-gemalto-team-up-to-deliver-increased-cloud-data-security-control-for-saas-applications-300342211.html

Vijayan, J. (2016). *Google Initiates Customer-Supplied Cloud Data Encryption Keys*. Retrieved online on December 15, 2016 from http://www.eweek.com/cloud/google-initiates-customer-supplied-cloud-data-encryption-keys.html

Wood, T., Cecchet, E., Ramakrishnan, K. K., Shenoy, P. J., van der Merwe, J. E., & Venkataramani, A. (2010). Disaster Recovery as a Cloud Service: Economic Benefits & Deployment Challenges. *HotCloud, 10*, 8–15.

Xiao, X., Califf, C.B., Sarker, S., & Sarker, S. (2013). ICT innovation in emerging economies: a review of the existing literature and a framework for future research. *Journal Information Technology, 28*(4), 264–278.

Yu, S., Wang, C., Ren, K., & Lou, W. (2010). Achieving Secure, Scalable, and Fine-grained Data Access Control in Cloud Computing. *Proceedings IEEE INFOCOM*. doi:10.1109/INFCOM.2010.5462174

Zech, P. (2011, March). Risk-based security testing in cloud computing environments. In *2011 Fourth IEEE International Conference on Software Testing, Verification and Validation* (pp. 411-414). doi:10.1109/ICST.2011.23

Zscaler. (2016). *Zscaler Private Access—Remote Access without the Security Risks of VPNs*. Retrieved online on December 15, 2016 from https://www.zscaler.com/press/zscaler-private-access/remote-access-without-security-risks-vpns

Chapter 10
Swimming Upstream in Turbulent Waters:
Auditing Agile Development

Priyadarsini Kannan Krishnamachariar
State University of New York, Buffalo, USA

Manish Gupta
State University of New York, Buffalo, USA

ABSTRACT

Agile approach is a pragmatic fashion of software development, wherein the requirements are flexible to the changing needs of the customers, fast paced markets and the iterations of software are implemented and delivered based on business priorities. A risky or experimental project where the project requirements are not clear/not defined well in advance, are the most suitable candidates for adopting agile approach, as agile enables us to work with calculated risks during development, aiming to reduce the risks. The value of any implementation is realized only if it delivers benefits to organization and users, which could be assured by effective auditing of the implementation by understanding the implications of agile approach and figuring out right audit techniques and processes. Many organizations already have well established audit functions and matured IT Audit procedures for auditing traditional SDLC waterfall processes. Yet the methods for auditing software development based on agile approach requires a different attitude and audit techniques that goes well with the proactive nature of agile approach. This paper aims to present risk based audit approach on the agile implementation of software development, how risk identification and assessment can be merged along with the phases of software development and the ways by which agile techniques can be effectively utilized as tools for audit.

DOI: 10.4018/978-1-5225-2604-9.ch010

1. INTRODUCTION

In today's dynamic business environment, where there is need to be on par with changing business requirements and the needs of users to survive in the market, it is advisable to adopt a flexible and effective software development approach. An Agile approach as opposed to other development methods, enables organizations to respond fast to changes, gaining competitive advantages on the market and ensures user satisfaction too. 'A system development methodology refers to the framework that is used to structure, plan, and control the process of developing an information system (CMS & HHS, 2008). Several software development methodologies have emerged over years each having its own benefits and weaknesses and each of which works well for certain kinds of software development projects, teams and contexts. A methodology can help a project reach its goals by help track the productivity, project status and by providing the ability to manage the project, also it specifies the deliverables of each phases or the development process itself (CMS & HHS, 2008). Software development methodologies helps in achieving quality not only in final deliverable but also enables the successful delivery of artifacts like software design in a development process, if the methodology is customized and practiced to suit the project culture and requirements. The effectiveness of the development process practiced by a project team/organization directly affects the software design quality (Suryanarayana et al, 2015).

The traditional waterfall methodology works in a linear fashion, which requires to have the requirement clear before design/development starts and each phase is completed in specified period after that it moves to next phase and which is not open to new changes in the current development life cycle. Whereas, Agile projects deliver working software in frequent iterations(sprints), this helps to reap the benefits soon and the software is available to get feedback from the users achieving active user participation. In traditional waterfall, more importance given on planning, timelines, staffing and budgets in initial phases only and the entire system is delivered at the end of the project (CMS & HHS, 2008). Moreover, practicing agile methodology also reduces the development time frame for new processes and increasing flexibility for existing processes, when extra requirements are to be modified. This in turn allows us for solving client demands in less time, gaining more clients, lowering adaptation costs and finally increased revenue (Stoica et al, 2013).

Agile organizations can respond to the needs and changes quickly and encourages to be flexible. But to be successful, an agile organization must also know how to balance structure and flexibility. If everything changes all the time, then the planned forward motion becomes problematic. It is important for agile organizations or project to understand that balancing on the edge between order and chaos determines success. This clearly depicts that an agile process can be disadvantageous if the agility factor is not regulated properly, and so the level of agility needs constant monitoring in a project implementation scenario (Highsmith, 2002). A recent survey (Techbeacon, 2016) it was found that agile approach has been adopted worldwide by many organizations and a recent survey of development and IT professionals supports that. In a 2014 survey (Techbeacon, 2016), HP interviewed 601 development and IT professionals using an online survey. Most organizations surveyed reported that they primarily use agile methods. In fact, two-thirds described their company as either "pure agile" or "leaning towards agile," A hybrid approach is used by 24 percent of respondents, which shows that they are practicing at least some agile principles in their implementation and management of their software development projects. Only nine percent responded that they are using "pure waterfall" or "leaning towards waterfall".

Being known the nature of agile approach, the importance of agility and its contribution to the growth and success of an organization, this creates an inevitable need to ensure if the agile processes are really serving the organization's objectives and to evaluate the agile software development's ability to respond to changes and delivering business value. The auditing methods of agile software development now is instrumental in providing assurance on the effectiveness of the agile implementation. Auditing of agile development cannot be laid out as one single standard process containing several procedures that can be adopted for auditing an agile based project, it requires the understanding of project, organizational context and the evaluation of risks to define a clear audit scope and procedures. This creates challenges for IT Auditor in terms of ensuring that his/her objectivity, independence is not affected but at the same time interact with the team to understand the maturity of agile processes and plan the audit process accordingly.

This paper proposes a risk driven audit model for auditing agile software development & processes, highlighting the roles of IS auditors in the auditing process across the phases of development. This paper also identifies different ways of using the agile processes followed in project and gear them as an aid for audit, without changing any existing processes. The motivation for this paper is to help auditors acquire an agile attitude and adapt their audit approach to be able to audit an agile project. Our model is designed from an agile perspective, considering the pace of project implementation.

The rest of the paper is structured as follows. In the next (second) section, we present an overview of research on agile approach in software development and the importance of IT Auditing. In the third section, we discuss about the publications and citations related to agile development and the challenges and risks in auditing agile software development process to set forth the researches in this field. Subsequently, we summarize prior research on agile and the audit techniques/issues auditing agile development, followed by a brief account of the contributions made by the papers in this special issue. In the fourth section, we talk about the proposed model for risk driven audit process of agile software development and the role of IT auditors. This also includes the effective use of agile techniques in continuous auditing. Also, the auditing process check points are defined, which aids an auditor to perform verification in the process front. In the fifth section, ERP risks are discussed and the sixth section describes the auditing of agile implementation considering the ERP development. Finally, the conclusions, key findings and directions for future research are discussed.

2. BACKGROUND AND PRELIMINARIES

"Agile is a software development approach that help teams respond to unpredictability through incremental, iterative work cadences and empirical feedback" (Agile, 2016). The concept of agile started emerging in the early 1990s, as PC computing began to grow rapidly in the enterprise and which led to a problem called "the application development crisis," or "application delivery lag." This estimation showed that it took about 3 years to develop and deploy a qualified application, even after knowing the exact business need that need to be fulfilled. This was considered as a problem as businesses moved faster than that, and the requirements, systems, and even entire businesses were likely to change within that development time span. This has led to canceling many projects partway and projects that didn't meet the current business requirements. This issue that revolves around traditional software development methodology was the reason behind the birth of agile principles and methods (Varhol, 2016). As agile started getting attention amongst the organizations, many people viewed it as a challenger to other practices such as waterfall, which are followed for long accepting their weaknesses. Like other traditional software development methodologies like Waterfall, Agile also requires requirements gathering and requirement analysis in the initial stages of the project, and based on that, the project release plans are laid. However, how agile projects use this information to manage/run the project through the development process is somewhat different (Charleston, 2016).

2.1. Study of a Proven Development Practice: Agile

In an Agile software development, a work is confined to a regular, repeatable work cycle, known as a sprint or iteration. Agile(Scrum) sprints used to be one-week or two-week sprints or sometimes a month. Every sprint produces a usable tested software product, in the order of business priorities set. Testing occurs at the end of each sprint, and issues are fixed accordingly, rather than fixing the bugs at the end of the development cycle, which reduces the cost of defect fixing and prevents the transport of defects along the phases. The agile development is within a fixed time box, with short term goals defined which prevents project overruns. The Product owner is the one who prioritizes the features to be delivered for a release from the backlog of user stories and this helps team in delivering a tangible output for each sprint/release to the customer. The process is iterative and incremental. A release may require multiple sprints, each iteration of work is built on the previous iterations or sprints, adding to or modifying some of the previous work to produce the next iteration. And agile teams are self-organizing, traditional project manager for coordination activities are not required, and collaborating with each other and getting things done is the norm.

In agile practices, A Scrum Master is a servant leader helping the team be accountable to themselves for the commitments they make (Hartman, 2009). This means that the agile team works together and builds the ability to manage themselves, their work and the scrum master helps the team in getting this attitude. He helps in removing the hurdles or issues that is affecting the progress of sprint deliveries and team performance. These are basic entities for an effective agile implementation. Agile software development entered the scene decades ago, as a reaction to traditional approaches to software development projects and has an increasing number of organizations adopting that approach till today. The success of agile approach has many reasons (Miller, 2001), few of the characteristics that attracted the organizations and the benefits that brought are given below:

- **Delivering the Tested Working Software Iterations in Regular Intervals:** Ability to correct the things that went wrong.
- **Fixed Time-Bound for Each Iteration:** Implementing only the necessary features in the initial sprints.
- **Adapting the Process and Project Activities in Case of New Risks:** Ensures goals are met.
- **Favors People Over Process and Technology:** Increased utilization of talent.
- **Collaborative Environment:** Effective project delivery integrating the sprint deliverable.

2.2. Why IT Auditing?

Organizations spend lot of money on IT to gain the benefits that IT can bring to their business operations and services. But IT can also introduce risks to the organizations by means of weaknesses and vulnerabilities in the IT systems, business processes and so on. So, it takes a professional, such as an IT auditor, to identify and assess the inherent risk associated with IT. Those risk factors include systems-related issues, such as systems development, change management and vulnerabilities, and other technology specific-factors (Singleton,2014).

IT audit function is required for an organization to get an assurance that the IT systems are properly managed to meet their intended requirements and are maintained and used with appropriate controls in place. IT auditing is an indispensable part of the corporate audit function because it underpins the auditor's judgment on the quality of the information processed by IT systems. There are many types of audit needs within IT auditing, such as organizational IT audits (management control over IT), technical IT audits (infrastructure, data centers), application IT audit (business/financial/operational), implementation IT audits, and compliance IT audits involving national or international standards (Senft et al., 2012).

The IT auditor's role has evolved to provide reasonable assurance that adequate and appropriate controls are in place. The primary role of an audit function, except in areas of advisory services, is to provide a reasonable assurance as to whether competent and reliable internal controls are set up and are working as expected in an efficient and effective manner (Senft et al., 2012). So, the IT audit functions is important for effective IT and project functioning, and when auditing an agile environment, still more diligence is needed from an auditor as the agile audit procedures and tests should check if the agile implementation is in accordance with compliance and organizational goals as well. An IT auditor when auditing agile implementation needs to possess open mindset to understand the nature of process followed and at the same time require deliberation in verifying the controls, processes and metrics as the improper implementation of agile, due to lack of in-depth understanding of process by the management or team, can cause serious problems impacting the success of the project.

3. LITERATURE REVIEW

The literature review consisted of reviewing agile software development approach, project management publications and the challenges and ways of auditing agile software development and processes. The articles reviewed met the criteria for analysis by containing some information regarding project management, agile development, risks, barriers and challenges of agile development and the auditing benefits and capabilities for auditing agile implementation. In today's business setup, organizations are facing more pressure than ever, to respond to market's dynamic demands with speed and precision by delivering new business value as quickly as possible to gain competitive edge. Adding to the unpredictable nature of business needs- the multifaceted nature of organizations and the interest for project initiatives that execute new business ideas, also the need for implementation that take advantage of the recent technical innovations seeks attention ("Oracle Primavera",2011).

Software development is a complex activity characterized by tasks and requirements that exhibit a high degree of variability (Boehm & Turner, 2004; Highsmith, 2003). The author mentioned that there are several differences in software development approaches, with respect to how they are implemented, managed and how they respond to the expectations of the customer and other stakeholders. Planning, control, and communication are crucial to success, but the way they are incorporated or achieved is different in agile and plan-driven methods (Boehm & Turner, 2004). For a traditional development project, squeezing project schedule, defects and changes in requirements changes can drive endless redesign, which causes project overruns and increased budget. J. Highsmith says that the success of the waterfall development life cycle is dependent upon a stable business environment (i.e. stable requirements) and breaks down in a high change environment (Highsmith,2002). The paper by Rico D.F. tells that the software producers are expected to be nimble enough to mirror the fast-paced changes in their customer's needs and environment changes, which paves way for agile methodology. The author after studying the major factors of agile methods that improves the success of agile, he concluded that the benefits of using agile methods range from 10% to 100% for increased cost-effectiveness, productivity, quality, cycle-time reduction, and customer satisfaction. (Rico, 2008)

It is discussed in the paper by Cockburn, A. and Highsmith, J that extensive upfront planning is the basis for predicting, measuring, and controlling problems and variations during the development life cycle. And the traditional software development approach is process-centric, on the basis that the changes can be identified and may be eliminated by continually measuring and refining processes (Cockburn & Highsmith, 2001). For a matured development based organization, the primary focus is on realizing highly optimized and repeatable processes. Thus, planning and control accomplished by a command and control style of management provide the support and motivation for developing a software product (Highsmith, 2003). Boehm says that the agile methods derive much of their agility by relying on the tacit knowledge embodied in the team, rather than writing the knowledge down in plans (Boehm, 2002). The agile project management principles are explained in the paper by Highsmith & Cutter where an important note is mentioned on selection of agile methodologies for project- Agile methodologies are ideal for projects that exhibit high variability in tasks (because of changing requirements), in the capabilities of people, and in the technology, being used (Highsmith, 2003).

In setting up an agile implementation and following agile methods not just requires the project to be ideal candidate for agile, but also requires the transitioning from individual work to self-managing teams requires a reorientation not only by developers but also by management. This transition takes time and resources, but should not be neglected (Moe et al., 2010). In the paper on 'Balancing Agility and Discipline', the authors mentioned that, Agile encourages a dedicated collocated customer, and compares the agile and plan driven processes specifying that, the main agile stress point is the interface between the customer representative and the users, the main plan driven stress point is the interface between the developer and the customer. This shows that the success of agile is mostly based on the synch of agile customer representatives with the system users they represent and the development team (Boehm & Turner, 2004). Krueger talks about the need to handle the barriers in implementing agile methods. Software products yield benefits only if they are used, the benefits associated with agile software development methods are realized only if these methods are used successfully in production environment. In adopting a new process technology like Agile, it should be relatively easy to perform since it is not feasible or affordable for the organizations to slow or stop the production to reorganize or to find out other ways of doing their business (Krueger, 2002)

Highsmith, in his research paper on Agile development ecosystems defines that all the agile methods can be characterized as placing emphasis on the following aspects: 1) delivering something useful; 2) reliance on people; 3) encouraging collaboration; 4) promoting technical excellence; 5) doing the simplest thing possible; 6) being continuously adaptable (Highsmith, 2002).

And a software will succeed when the people involved notice errors and they take responsibility in their work to move out of their job description to see if it the issues are fixed." (Manzo, 2003).

The paper by Holler (2010) explains the basic need of organizations to adopt agile implementations. As the most of the software organizations are working under stringent time constraints and the development environment is highly volatile, which introduces frequent changes and unpredictability in the system requirements, so there is need for transformation of the development approach from traditional heavyweight processes to lightweight incremental and iterative methods like Agile. Hence, many organizations are adopting agile methodology for software development, which helps them to accelerate delivery schedules, adapt to the changing business needs, align business and technology goals and generate competitive advantage (Holler, 2010).

Robert Holler, in his paper unveils and explains about the myths about agile approach, which are (1) Agile development is undisciplined, (2) Agile teams do not plan, (3) Agile development is not predictable, (4) Agile development does not scale, (5) Agile development is just another fad.

He explains that that Agile teams do perform planning and the planning is spread across the whole development phases, the continuous planning approach is followed in agile driven projects which allows the team with the necessary process-based ammunition to much more easily and efficiently adapt to the changes. He explains how large projects work by scaling up and how risks are managed. For large projects, agile method works by taking large projects and breaking them down into a coordinated series of smaller projects staffed by smaller, cross-functional teams. The agile projects also manage risk inherently by integrating the output of various teams at least every iteration in order to reduce risk and ensure functional and technical compatibility (Holler, 2010).

In the paper by Jaana Nyfjord and Mira Kajko-Mattsson (2008), the main emphasis is on the challenges of using agile processes in certain development organizations, and tells us that the capability levels of agile process implementation need to be extended to fulfill the process needs of the organizations. Places importance on discussion one of the missing capabilities, concerning risk management. On observing the practices of agile pre-implementation phases in small and medium sized organizations, they have found that the traditional development activities like planning are also included in the pre-implementation phases, specifically planning activities are performed in initial phases for large processes in medium sized organizations. This paper tells that planning is required even for the success of further agile development activities (Nyfjord and Kajko-Mattsson, 2008).

There has been is a growing trend in software development through agile approach and so, the study of risks in such environments becomes imperative (Shrivastava & Rathod, 2015). This paper talks about the Evaluating the Industrial Practice of Integrating Risk Management with Software Development and the following criteria are considered: Organizational levels, Integration aspects, Integration problems, Importance of process integration, Applicability of risk management in agile context.

An investigation is performed on how the companies studied have integrated their risk management with software development. All the companies studied agree that the integration of risk management with software development is important. They claim that a properly integrated process is of great help in managing risks effectively. They have also said that risk management is needed in any development model, like traditional, agile or any other models. Agile models include risk management by nature but they provide very general guidance for managing risks (Nyfjord and Kajko-Mattsson, 2008). Risk management models, on the other hand, provide detailed guidance. In accordance with majority of the organizations, we believe that agile models should be more active in integrating more risk management aspects.

The findings made in this study indicate that the standard models have not sufficiently reflected the practice and needs of the organizations studied. They also show that the industry studied has not implemented all the activities as prescribed by these models and that the integration of risk management with development is still in its infancy (Nyfjord & Kajko-Mattsson, 2007). Risk management has been described as the "activity of identifying and controlling undesired project outcomes proactively" (Smith & Merritt, 2002). One of the main reasons highlighted for the increasing failure in software projects is that "managers are not taking prudent measures to assess and manage the risks involved" in their projects (Keil et al, 1998). Many books that talk about Agile do not have any information on how a project team identifies, prioritizes and manages the risk to nullify their impact in the development life cycle. (Smith & Pichler, 2005). Essentially, agile methods must "tailor conventional risk management approaches meant for years-long projects into a risk driven agile iteration lasting only seven to thirty days" (Smith et al.,2005). How agile projects go about doing this remains unknown. In addition, the research participants involved in this study showed a clear appreciation for the importance of managing risk on projects outlining how the stakeholder collaboration has a huge impact on risk management as it promotes the formal management of business risks, improves overall awareness of risk management among the project team, increases the number of risks identified throughout the project and ensures logical ownership of risks (Coyle & Conboy, 2009).

In the ISACA Ireland conference on Audit and Control of Agile Projects, there was discussion on how the auditing of agile projects is different from traditional auditing. It was discussed that there are agile methods that can respond to emerging threats, also added that an auditor auditing agile development projects should not try to stop the agile tide and auditors need to approach agile controls in agile way. The auditors should be asking open questions to the project team when auditing an agile project to get an understanding and should draw useful information from the answers and the discussion with auditees that help in auditing. The auditors must base their work on the Agile manifesto, and the Agile Manifesto can guide them to ask useful questions, but it can't provide them with answers (Wright, 2014).

4. PROCESS FOR AUDITING AGILE

An auditor auditing agile development must be receptive to information and the best way to learn the subject before auditing an agile project is by listening, observing and understanding the project context and the maturity of agile method implementation in the project. The auditor should also be aware and consider the specific risks associated with Agile. There are some challenges for auditors and project teams in ensuring an efficient audit, as it requires them to work together. For a successful audit, it requires the project team and auditor to share the same objective of developing a product with low risk, effective and efficient controls. Auditing agile development is a team effort combining both the auditor and the auditee and which requires trust and understanding, right from the early stages of the audit. The following are important notes that will help an auditor get started on their Agile Audit (Wright, 2014)

1.   Auditors must be open to accept and understand the nature of agile approach and the benefits of using Agile, considering the project needs.
2.   Rather than sticking to traditional auditing methods, auditors must adapt to the context of an Agile project and consider the challenges and risks introduced by practicing this approach.
3.   In Agile projects, the auditor cannot expect stringent controls to be implemented and should allow for required flexibility and agility in processes.
4.   The auditor must be open to discussions with project team and auditors must give importance to the quality of outputs as, it is not a matter of choosing either working software *or* documentation, but valuing the former over the latter.

To be successful auditing Agile projects, the auditor must have knowledge of the Agile Framework as well as knowledge of project management methodologies. Auditors also will find that they must expand their technological knowledge and skills, devise more effective audit approaches by taking advantage of technology, and design different types of audit tests to respond to new business processes. Technology experts can also be part of audit engagement teams, to make it more effective.

Role of IS Auditor in an Implementation Based on Agile Approach

The IS audit function can help to identify, review, and provide suggestions for the key controls associated with the project and can provide assurance that the system will support effective business processes and enforce business controls on an ongoing basis.

- The internal auditor's participation is required and spread across all the critical phases of a project implementation and which helps for successful implementation and deployment.
- In an implementation project, an internal auditor plays a key role in identifying the project risks, can be involved in project initiation and progress meetings and the risks can be addressed earlier and effectively, also an auditor can help identify business and project management risks.

Figure 1 shows the process of auditing agile based implementation where the roles of IS Auditor is explained when it goes through the phases.

Figure 1. Process of auditing implementation based on Agile approach

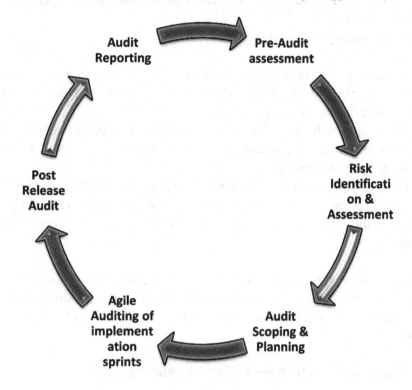

4.1. Gather Background Information and Pre-Audit Assessment

Thorough analysis of business processes and the project knowledge is required before auditing the development and understanding of the development methodology employed in the project is important. A successful audit depends on the prior preparation by both the Audit team and the Auditee, before the onsite audit. Acquiring understanding of agile methods by an auditor can be assisted by 'Agile champions' to help auditors who are less familiar with the agile methods. Auditing agile is dependent on the project context and implementation, not a standard procedure that applies to any agile project, for a flexible agile implementation, the following techniques can be used by an auditor to help kick start an audit: Pre-Audit survey is a tool for audit team to learn more about the auditee's organization, includes a set of questionnaires to gather necessary information prior to performing an onsite audit, this survey covers assets, organization structure, some important aspects of the auditee's systems/project to be audited. The lack of a pre-audit phase seriously reduces the effect of an audit, leads to delays and/or time wasting on site and in the worst case prevents an audit from being completed. Information checklists specifies the list of documents required for an effective audit, which aids project team to be well prepared for audit.

Pre-Audit survey execution steps:

- The auditors will also try to contact the senior manager/s, technical people and executives like CIO and CEO, to get idea about the items that will be reviewed during the audit.
- The auditors will be involved in requesting the documentation and business processes documents, system design and business requirement documents and the previous audit papers.
- The organization normally nominates one or more individuals from the team to assist auditors to move freely in the organization and help find the people, information etc. necessary to perform audit, they act as management liaison points.

The primary output of this phase is audit engagement letter, also the contact lists and other preliminary documents are also obtained. The documentation given by the auditee and the information gathered in pre-audit, greatly helps in drafting the audit plan.

4.2. Risk Identification and Risk Assessment

An Agile-like implementation methodology will greatly reduce the risk of an enterprise software implementation project not being running overtime or beyond the defined and beyond the defined budget. When performing system development in an agile approach requires more emphasis on risk analysis and be cognizant of the risks involved in the current environment. Figure 2 shows the risk management framework to be adopted for an effective agile based implementation.

4.2.1. Identifying Risks: Developing Risk Profile

Compiling a comprehensive list of internal operational challenges and risks is vital to developing a risk profile. Risk profile is an organization wide risk registry that must be updated throughout the project as risks are identified, including the unanticipated risks caused by new investments. Proactive, consultative engagement is required for risk profile to be effective. Identify and prioritize all related risks and perform root cause analysis to understand the effect of those risks, if left unattended, may cause higher levels of risks. Mike Cottmeyer has discussed in his paper that, implementing agile helps us manage risk effectively as the risk management techniques are ingrained into the agile processes followed and the way the project is run (Cottmeyer, 2014).

Figure 2. Exemplary risk management framework

In Agile environments, the development project team shares the responsibility for identifying risks that might impact a sprint, project or the course of development. The following agile processes aid in identifying risks in an agile development project:

- **Daily Scrum:** Strong forum for identifying risks when performing daily tasks.
- **Requirements workshop:** The team and the project manager discusses new ideas, this allows to adjust or correct the requirements so that it minimizes risk.
- **Sprint Planning:** Planning poker used to estimate the relative size of user story, gives opportunity to reduce the risk associated or break down the stories.
- **Retrospective Meeting:** Identify the problems that were hurdles/risks for the implementation.
- **Sprint Review:** Gives opportunity to identify, access and respond to risk ("Agile Risk", 2009).

4.2.2. Classify and Quantify Risks

Risk assessment requires adopting a suitable framework that enables the prioritization of risks and the ability to classify risks as real risks or opportunities. The risk appetite of an organization decides the risk assessment methods and the risk treatment that can be performed on the identified risks. It requires to have a prior plan on what data or metrics needs to be collected and managed, to enable an effective risk management as well as for agile process implementation, periodically measuring the risks. Generally traditional development methodologies do not encompass management of risks within the phases of their process life cycle, whereas the agile models are efficient enough to deliver planned development artifacts, and also the fixes that resolves the risks or problems faced in one and the same iteration, and other primary and supporting processes. (Nyfjord and Kajko-Mattsson, 2007). The following risk analysis and management process can be adopted for the agile development scenario:

1. Think about, what are the risks that could happen to the assets of the organizations (IT systems etc.)?
2. The risks, if occurs, what impact it can bring to the organization? The risk mitigation costs and the cost of accepting the risks are to be analyzed and quantified.
3. How often the recorded risks may occur? Need to qualify the likelihood of risk with relevant justification.
4. What prevention steps or mitigation steps can be taken to minimize the occurrence of these risks and to reduce the impact of these risks?
5. What are the costs in setting up countermeasures and are these justifiable in terms of monetary returns, feasibility and relevancy? (Saltmarsh & Browne, 1983; Siponen, et al, 2005).

The risk factors identified/to be identified by the auditor can be classified into four categories: Operational, Financial, Technological and Miscellaneous. Considering the implementation of system, the following areas or risk factors may be considered: Product risk, Customer Relationships, Production- Network & Hardware availability, Human Resources- Personnel issues and Quality Assurance- Maintenance issues. The suggestion of the risk assessment procedures for an agile based implementation is to use a mix of qualitative and quantitative risk approaches. Quantitative risk analysis to be employed for situations where the risk can be anticipated numerically based on a data set and quantitative risk analysis to be used to weigh and rank the risks based on relative comparison to the risk appetite and exposure of the organization.

The basic flow in assessing the risks identified:

- Assemble the identified risks across the sprints.
- Identify the occurrence and impact of the risks identified in the project implementation and its processes.
- Categorize the risks by using the categories defined across the organization or by the project, depending on the purpose of the project.
- Prioritize the risk event and update the findings in risk register along with risk-event matrix.

4.2.3. Risk Treatment

Risk treatment is the crucial step in risk management, where we decide about what action to be taken on the risks that are identified, ranked and assessed. The general options available are Avoidance, Mitigation, Transference, Acceptance. This decision to be taken based on the occurrence of the risk and its impact on the business and its processes. Risks in the agile implementation are to be managed by associating user stories to themes and ensuring that risks are identified in the project sprints. The target of each sprint should include 'minimizing risk in the project'. A risk adjusted backlog is efficient in controlling and managing risks in an agile environment. A risk adjusted backlog takes into consideration the amount of risk a feature or a story places on the project. The need to have a risk adjusted backlog is to make sure the agile implementation delivers artifacts that are of business value and the risk reduction items, which inherently maximizes the value. Risk adjustment enables us to identify and mitigate critical risks in the initial sprints development (Canty, 2015).

4.2.4. Review and Retrospection

This phase is about Tracking, Monitoring and Auditing the identified risks. The retrospective meetings enable the review of risks faced during project and helps in continuous risk assessments throughout the implementation. The risk register is reviewed to see if the high severity risks are treated and the root cause analysis report updated if any. The retrospective methods are employed to analyses the weaknesses or deficiencies and to prevent their recurrence. Possible Risk areas to be reviewed continuously when auditing an agile based development project include cost (Hardware, Software, licenses, updates, maintenance), extensive training for faculty and staff; and productivity across sprint deliveries.

4.3. Audit Scoping and Planning

In this phase, the auditors determine the main areas of focus & any areas that are explicitly to be tagged as out of scope. This decision drives the audit process and the audit planning also involves the important tasks such as interviewing the product owner and Scrum Master to determine their "success criteria" for this agile project audit. This will help auditors to check if the success criteria reflect the needs and how it is measured. When defining the Audit Scope for an implementation on agile approach, the following are to be considered:

- Understanding the organizational setup, culture, policies and security implications.
- Understanding the project context and technical complications.
- Getting access to the release plan and the sprint plan, including the planned components that are to be delivered.
- Looking if there are plans for automated integration of the developed components with any existing systems.
- Analyze and identify the existing IT controls, process controls, general controls and other security controls.

Audit requirements need to be identified and finalized in audit planning phase, the following will be included:

- Organizational requirements pertaining to system implementation.
- Customer's expectations.
- Regulatory requirements.
- Security requirements.

4.4. Agile Auditing of Implementation Sprints

The main purpose of implementation audit is to ensure if the sprint is working towards delivering the incremental and iterative development of business objectives planned. Also, focuses on the verifying the design and Implementation of controls for new systems, considering project risk and capability assessment. Figure 3 shows the areas that are predominantly covered for Implementation audit of the sprints. We next discuss each of these areas.

4.4.1. Project Execution Evaluation

For status of activities or tasks of current sprint, Sprint dashboard can be reviewed. Also, as part of evaluation, ensuring if the user stories that are of higher priority based on the risk assessment procedures and ensured if they meet the completion criteria for project schedule can be done. Release backlog can be verified to evaluate if the implementation goes as per business priorities. Also, evaluating the way, the

Figure 3. Areas for implementation audit of Sprints

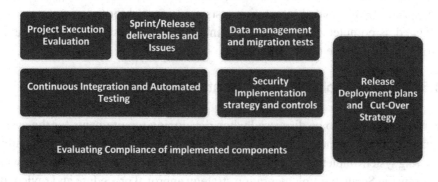

project tasks were divided across sprints -Work breakdown structures would be useful. Lastly, another way is through reviewing of user stories about estimation procedure which drives the project schedule.

4.4.2. Sprint/Release Deliverables and Issues

Some of deliverables and issues could be known through the following:

- Reviewing User stories and Requirement engineering processes of system.
- Reviewing plans for user training and project team training plans on the implementation.
- Evaluating how the issues raised in scrum meetings are handled.
- Accountability for the completed user stories by the user story owner.
- Verify if user stories are closed only based on completion of agreed "done" criteria.

4.4.3. Data Management and Migration Tests

As we are working on auditing a new implementation, the business data and other transactions performed prior may have to be migrated to the new environment. Audit procedures must include procedures to validate the data conversion and must review the data migration strategies and appropriate approval cycles involved.

4.4.4. Continuous Integration and Testing

Continuous integration is an ongoing activity in the agile development process adopted for our implementation. For successful integration of components implemented in sprints, it is suggested that an auditor must ensure if the following are performed:

1) Configuration management tool is updated with the modules implemented in every sprint, 2) Automated integration tests are triggered for the components that are tagged as completed as part of a sprint and 3) Test results are reviewed and appropriate actions are taken by the team.

4.4.5. Security Implementation Strategy and Controls

Security issues need to be discussed when developing requirements for the system because it should be intertwined along with the system to be effective. An auditor evaluating system implementation on agile methodology should perform the following: 1) Review the Security Implementation strategy approval procedure and review if it aligns with organization's security policies, 2) Review the data classification scheme and the guidelines for access controls based on that, 3) Review the release plan to verify for sprints involving security controls deployment and testing and 4) Verify if the implemented existing access controls, process controls are working as designed.

4.4.6. Evaluating Compliance of Implemented Components

- Reviewing implemented components using appropriate sampling techniques to confirm that the it is performing as planned, or was appropriately adjusted.
- Compliance tests are performed to ensure if the implemented controls are performing as per control objectives. The general and Technical Controls are evaluated for its compliance and verified if the controls are implemented based on the results of cost benefit analysis.
- Substantive tests are to be performed by an auditor on suspected and critical transactions among modules, which need further analysis to ensure its correctness and integrity.
- The audit function can help to identify, review, and provide suggestions for key controls associated with the project and can provide assurance that the system will support business processes.

4.4.7. Release Deployment Plans and Cut-Over Strategy

The auditor needs to take care of the following when verifying the release management:

- Release deployment plans mentioning the timelines and the sprints included in the release need to be laid down and approved by management.
- Verify if the cut-over strategy is chosen considering the factors, less on-going risk, Cost-Effective, enhance business process, should include roll back strategy as well.

- Verify if the cutover plan document is owned by a manager or key stakeholder, and managed very tightly.

4.5. Post Release Audit

Post Release audit is an important audit function, which verifies if the user requirements and the purpose of the project is met, this is most crucial for an agile development project, as it can be performed for every release. In an agile based implementation, retrospection meeting is a post-implementation activity, which will be happening after every release or for every sprint, by the project team, where auditors might be passively involved to understand how the project release went through. The retrospective is a collaborative process among the project team, the product owner, and the Scrum Master and other members involved in the project. An auditor might be observing these meetings to understand how a sprint/release worked. The following are the key elements of retrospective meetings: 1) This gives way for process improvements at the end of every sprint. This ensures that the project team is always improving the way it works, 2) All team members identify what went well and what could be improved and 3) the team members give suggestions for process improvement.

This is done to ensure that the project meets the promised objectives and it happens mostly in a collaborative way involving the team involved in the agile implementation. The Product Owner is responsible for organizing the review and accountable for the results. The post-implementation strategy should be in place to execute, as soon as acceptance tests are run, but mostly executed after few months of deployment. The auditor needs to ensure if the if 'DONE' definitions set for sprints or release based on the completion of user stories, component delivery is completed. This is a measure of agile implementation's success. Benefit realization will be performed by the auditor by verifying the user stories for its completion and the verification of completed stories in release backlog to see if they are prioritized based on the business needs. The following questions may be asked to assess benefits realization 1) Did the implementation meet the business need? 2) Did it achieve the estimated ROI? And 3) Did it capture the market needs; did it meet the client needs?

4.6. Audit Reporting

After completing testing auditor summarizes the audit result, draw conclusions on the findings and control weaknesses identified. For the agile implementation of any system, Auditor's report should include results specific to the processes audited, and the system and its interactions tested, inconsistencies in the agile development processes followed in project, impact of the identified weaknesses on the completeness, validity and functioning of system. And the audit evidence must be based on the right sample set chosen from the population, to perform the audit procedure and weaknesses should be associated with appropriate action plans to be implemented. engagements are to be established between the auditor and the auditee, and have to mutually accept on the findings and the follow up plans are discussed.

4.7. Compliance Monitoring and Enforcement

For an implementation project, which runs for years, Monitoring and auditing are essential to verify that a business activity is performing as intended and continues the same in a long run. It is required to include monitoring controls in the processes which assists the auditors to perform an independent, objective audit. In our agile implementation as the work is based on the prioritization of the tasks by the team based on the business value, and coming up with the stories for each release. The sprints are timebound, usually 2 weeks and run within fixed budget and the project scope can be altered by the team to finish a sprint and deliver it on time. This shows that the main controls to be established is on the project team and activities, which are not easy to measure and can go wrong and affect the project's progress. Thus, continuous monitoring is most important in our agile development scenario. The monitoring controls adopted by the auditor can be,

- Checking Sprint release Minutes of meetings.
- Reviewing Sprint planning document.
- Monitoring Agile dashboard showing the schedule, progress of activities.
- Reviewing technical controls like logs.
- Reviewing the user story estimation and prioritization procedures.
- Attending project initiation meetings.
- Passively listening the scrum calls/meetings.

An auditor can choose a self-monitoring or continuous monitoring to be employed in the implementation project. It will be at the discretion of auditor deciding on the process or system to be monitored.

4.7.1. Auditing Process Checkpoints

The auditor must ensure that the following agile processes have been performed through proper approval, within timelines at different phases of the project, the Table 1 shows the documents and checkpoints to be verified by an auditor.

Table 1. Auditing process checkpoints

Project Phases	Agile Practices/Processes
Requirements engineering	User stories log & prioritization, product backlog and sprint backlog maintenance
Project Planning	Sprint Planning document, Release planning document
Project Management and Monitoring	Agile/SCRUM stand-up meetings, Burn down charts, Sprint review meetings, minutes of meetings
Software Quality Assurance	Automated user acceptance tests, Automated unit tests, System tests results
Risk Identification and Monitoring	Retrospective meetings, Root cause analysis of risks

5. ERP RISK ANALYSIS AND AUDITING PROCESS

5.1. ERP and Business Capability and Risks

An Enterprise Resource Planning can be described as, "An enterprise-wide set of management tools that balances demand and supply, linking the customers and suppliers into a complete supply chain, providing high degrees of cross-functional integration among departments like sales, marketing, manufacturing, operations, logistics, purchasing, finance, new product development, and human resources, employing proven business processes for decision-making, and helps people in running business with high levels of customer service and productivity, and simultaneously lower costs and inventories; and providing the foundation for effective e-commerce (Aldammas and Al-mudimigh, 2011). In today's business environment, the capacity and agility to respond to the changing customer needs, business competitions, and being cognizant of the potential threats are considered a critical business capability (Prahalad, 2009).

This need of the business can be fulfilled by the agility nature of our implementation and by identifying and managing the risks in the system to be implemented. The major step towards attaining business capability can be done by investigating the system and its environment for the existing risks and finding out the chances of emerging risks which can be a threat to the system/organization. Implementing ERP system could integrate the internal and external flow of information within an organization. Such innovations would also improve SCM performance, enhance decision-making based on accurate information and improve the relationship, collaboration, and exchange of information. (Wieder et al., 2006; Kremzar & Wallace, 2001). Information systems auditors' assessments of the following risks categories will be significantly higher in an ERP setting than a non-ERP setting: a. business interruption risk; b. network security risk; c. database security risk; d. application security risk; e. process interdependency risk; and f. overall internal control risk (Hunton et al., 2001). The following are the major benefits an ERP system can provide to an organization that implements ERP system:

• Improved integration of processes among departments, shared pool of data, achieve data integrity.
• Reduces the operational and maintenance costs of IT operations and organization's IS.
• Serves as excellent decision support tool (Mabert et al., 2001).

When implementing an ERP system, our value will be based on the benefits that the system delivers and it is good to understand the reality of difficulty and challenges that are to be overcome to reap those benefits, which makes an implementation success.

5.2. ERP Implementation Risks

The changes to the ERP and other systems being integrated will not work in isolation and may impact each other during integration. The result may not be as expected and the integrity of the data might be lost if the formal change management procedures are not followed. Any organization that implements ERP and deploys in real time, must reengineer their key business processes in fundamental ways, changing the current way of doing business, restructure the organization, job roles and functions. Also, ERP systems must be able to be customized to address global issues in terms when deploying them for business in different countries, as different countries do business in different ways and have country-specific business regulations and practices for accounting, tax requirements etc. This shows that when integrating the information systems that works across various countries, there can be challenges in doing that, the major types of misfits (relating to data, process, and output) can occur due to incompatibilities between software functionality and organizational requirements as well as differences in cultural and regulatory environments (Lau, 2003). This shows that implementation of an ERP system creates a major drift in the way the business is performed and so the changes incorporated should be verified, tested and the integrations must go through formal acceptance procedures.

5.2.1. Lack of Clear Business Value

ERP systems are inherently complex! Implementing an ERP system by any organization is a difficult, long-term project, and requires huge budget for its implementation. As multiple modules, must operate and work together, this requires commitment and support from different divisions, and a clear business purpose to be defined that helps the company do business in a better way, as adopting ERP changes the way a company does business. It can take so many years to complete an ERP development project and if not directed towards the business needs, generally leads to failure of project and there is no guarantee of the expected outcome (Mabert et al., 2001). So, an approved business case is most important before commencing the implementation of ERP system.

5.2.2. Lack of Project Scope

Define your project scope from a perspective of the project, the purpose and describe what the project is intended to perform. The scope of an ERP project has several components. The business processes that are required implementation must be decided well before and it should not be changed frequently which will impact the project schedules and timeline. The scope should be built to prevent "never ending project". To resolve this issue, it is recommended that the business requirements are understood and plan how they are going to be transformed as project requirements. Also, it is recommended to breakdown the scope into individual units of work and document the items that are not in scope.

5.2.3. Lack of Top Management Commitment

The research conducted on IT management practices on several companies around the globe has concluded that active top management support and commitment are essential to the success of any system implementation. It is recommended to have form executive councils and steering groups consisting of top managers to plan and manage the IT initiatives. Such operating top management involvement tends to increase the optimization of IT business values (Ross & Weill, 2002).

5.2.4. Lack of User Involvement

User involvement is important in meeting expectations. The users need to be convinced of system usage and the purpose; so that they can help the users in further training sessions. User commitment and a "project champion" (who has the vision to get the project going and pushes for the project to be accepted where there are competing priorities) are useful in the early stages of the project and during the implementation phase.

5.2.5. Lack of Integration Approach

It is an important risk to be dealt when designing ERP systems as lack of integration impacts the purpose of ERP system as an ERP system must integrate seamlessly with existing business information systems in the organizations to deliver the expected benefits. Also, when working on an agile based ERP implementation, the integration is crucial as we are working on producing pieces of software deliverables in iterations and which must be integrated to form the required end product. So, this demands the need of proper evaluation of enterprise wide architecture to fit our system in and there has to be an integration framework designed at organization-level also to work well with existing architectures (Kähkönen et al., 2016). Also, there should be appropriate integration strategy defined when integrating the modules of ERP system as there are interactions involved between components.

5.3. ERP and IT Auditing

In order to maximize the probability of success, the risks associated with a task must be minimized (Barki, 1993; Jiang & Klein, 1999). And, audit firms minimize the risk of audit failure through the identification of inherent, control and detection risks and provides reasonable assurance that material risks are within the limit and an acceptable audit risk level (Arens & Loebbecke,1997). Also, for the implementation of an ERP system, to maximize the probability of success, need to identify the risks and respond to them by placing appropriate controls to minimize those risks. To ensure the success of ERP system implementations in project-based environment, sound risk management is the key; also, it is stated that, based on the severity of impact, low top management support and involvement and inadequate financial management are regarded as top risk factors, and there are management, technical and non-technical factors involved (Zeng, 2010). It is important for internal auditors to be aware of the unique risks associated with ERP systems to plan and execute an audit and assurance activities. It is important to identify how the internal audit function should measure the risks and perform a customized audit process to maintain the quality of ERP implementation and at the same time managing the agility in the process.

6. AUDITING OF AGILE BASED ERP IMPLEMENTATION

As illustrated in the previous section, the auditing process of agile based ERP can be performed by following the audit procedures and tools discussed and there are specific procedures or audit tests that need to be performed especially for an ERP implementation, some of which will be discussed in this section. The risks that prevail pertaining to the area of ERP implementation and the role of auditors in handling them are also discussed.

Step 1

To start with auditing process, the first step is to identify the required business processes to be implemented and analyzing them as business processes form the basis for the success of ERP system. This step includes 1) analyzing business processes, 2) Evaluating if the current processes maps to the organization's strategy, 3) analyzing the importance, purpose and quality of each process.

Step 2

There are high chances that ERP systems introduce numerous business risks, as there are automated interdependencies among business processes and the data are managed on databases and shared among processes. And several of these risks may lead to control risks like lack of segregation of duties and/or have a direct, material financial statement impact (e.g., invalid transactions, duplicate payments to vendors, and potential issues relating to business interruptions) (Hunton et al., 2001). Internal auditor need to have ability to identify and manage operational, financial, technological, compliance and other risks when auditing an ERP implementation in business context.

Step 3

The audit requirements which are evolved from audit scope, that are specific for an ERP system implementation should include the following on a high level – 1) Effective data extraction from ERP systems, 2) Increase the data access across departments, 3) Improve workflow and efficiency, 4) Improve process and technical controls, 5) Ease of Use among business users, 6) Streamline the business processes and transactions, 7) Provide an organizational level common repository and 8) Role based access controls provided to users at different levels.

Step 4

The main purpose of implementation audit is to ensure if the sprint is working towards delivering the intended artifacts in incremental and iterative fashion based on the business priorities set. The key success factors of an agile ERP implementation are as follows and these are the areas that may lead to failure of project if the risks related to those areas are not managed or controlled.

1.   Top management support;
2.   Project team structure and expertise;
3.   Communications structure and training plan;
4.   Change management and configuration management;
5.   Project Scoping;
6.   Project Risk Evaluation;
7.   Budget estimation and planning delivery of modules.

These are taken as factors and measured or verified as part of auditing across the sprints. Implementation risks occurs predominantly in the following eight areas. These areas included: 1. contract & project management; 2. integration testing; 3. data conversion; 4. reporting; 5. cut-over & stabilization; 6. retiring of legacy systems; 7. security; and 8. Training (OCA-City of San Diego, 2011). The audit process of ERP implementation across sprints begins with the field work- Interviews and Analysis, followed by observing the activities performed by the project team and lastly, reviewing release implementation plan and sprint status. Auditor will be involved in performing mock data conversion and migration tests onto the implemented ERP system. The key verification point for an ERP system is reviewing the access control guidelines and role to access mapping defined for the ERP system implementation.

Step 5

Audit results are to be reported and the discussion of findings with the auditees need to be performed once the review of implementation sprints is done. As part of this process results specific to the ERP modules audited, the workflows tested, and findings pertaining to the reviewed business processes needs to be reported. For an ERP system, Post Implementation audit is very crucial, as the success of an ERP system can be decided only after it is deployed and used in production for at least 1-2 years by the customers/organizations. Many post-go-live activities need to be planned well in advance and executed after the launch. In this step, the basic activities that an auditor expects are 1) A post-go-live plan should be in place addressing the People, Processes, and Technology of the operational ERP environment and verification that if the ERP modules planned for the release, to see if they have met the business objectives.

Step 6

When implementing processes in our ERP implementation, it is essential to include both monitoring and auditing during the process design to ensure that the internal controls are intact. The auditor need to ensure if the ERP access control functions and its operations require keen continuous monitoring controls and the data flow between modules of ERP are to be monitored to ensure accountability of actions and for further analysis in future if needed.

7. PRACTICAL IMPLICATIONS AND CONCLUSION

Organizations are moving towards collaborative agile development approaches for running their software development projects, in order to respond to this positive change in organization's culture, the role of IT auditors in embracing the growing development methodology is essential. There is need for customizing the current audit practices that are designed mostly based on the traditional development methods. The research methodology suggested in this paper provides strategies for an IT auditor to help get out of their traditional approach of auditing and being able to understand the changes and adaptations required in their approaches to audit the agile development methodology implementation. Enterprises are facing problems in managing risks in agile delivery and many fails to understand the inherent risk management in agile processes. We have discussed about how the agile processes and techniques facilitates the identification of risks and in controlling the risks during development. The audit model proposed gives ideas for the auditors in incorporating embedded audit/monitoring out of existing agile approach methods without much extra effort.

The paper has proposed primarily a conceptual framework for auditing an agile implementation, considering the implications and nature of agile and discussed the role of IT auditor across the phases. The paper also depicts the risk management steps and methods to ensure successful implementation of agile. Also, how the agile methods like daily stand-up and retrospective meetings, can inherently enable risk management is explained across the different phases of development. The emphasis here is placed on the necessity of understanding of the agile methodology and its nuances by an IT auditor to conduct an effective audit. The need for adopting different audit procedures for auditing agile implementation, is justified and discussed on how the traditional audit procedures can be customized or employ new audit methods to suit the context of an agile implementation.

REFERENCES

Agile Methodology: The Agile Movement. (2008, October 23). Retrieved from http://agilemethodology.org/

Agile Risk Management – Identifying Risks (1 of 4). (2009, July 29). Retrieved from https://agile101.wordpress.com/2009/07/27/agile-risk-management-identifying-risks-step-1-of-4/

Aldammas, A., & Al-Mudimigh, A. (2011). Critical success and failure factors of ERP implementations: Two cases from Kingdom of Saudi Arabia. *Journal of Theoretical and Applied Information Technology*.

Arens, A., & Loebbecke, J. (1997). *Overview of Integrated Auditing. Auditing: An Integrated Approach*. Academic Press.

Audit of the Enterprise Resource Planning System implementation: management identified and addressed most system implementation risks but improvements are needed related to security, payment controls and training. (2011). San Diego, CA: Office of the City Auditor, City of San Diego.

Barki, H., Rivard, S., & Talbot, J. (1993). Toward an Assessment of Software Development Risk. *Journal of Management Information Systems, 10*(2), 203–225. doi:10.1080/07421222.1993.11518006

Boehm, B. (2002). Get ready for agile methods, with care. *Computer, 35*(1), 64–69. doi:10.1109/2.976920

Boehm, B., & Turner, R. (2004). *Balancing Agility and Discipline: A Guide for the Perplexed*. Software Engineering Research and Applications Lecture Notes in Computer Science.

Canty, D. (2015). *Agile for project managers*. Academic Press.

Cavaleri, S., & Obloj, K. (1993). Management Systems: A Global Perspective. *Agile Project Management: Principles and Tools*.

Charleston, R. (2016, May 9). *ERP Implementation Approaches: Waterfall vs. Agile*. Retrieved from https://www.handshake.com/blog/erp-implementation/

CMS & HHS. (2008). *Selecting a development approach*. Centers for Medicare and Medicaid Services Research Publication. Retrieved from https://www.cms.gov/research-statistics-data-and-systems/cms-information-technology/xlc/downloads/selectingdevelopmentapproach.pdf

Cockburn, A. (2002). Agile software development. *Computer, 34*(9).

Cockburn, A., & Highsmith, J. (2001). Agile software development, the people factor. *Computer, 131-133.* doi:10.1109/2.963450

Cottmeyer, M. (2014, July 24). *Agile is Risk Management.* Retrieved from https://www.leadingagile.com/2008/05/agile-is-risk-management/

Coyle, S., & Conboy, K. (2009). A case study of risk management in agile systems development. *17th European Conference on Information Systems,* 2567-2578.

Goldman, S. L., Nagel, R. N., & Preiss, K. (1995). *Agile competitors and virtual organizations: strategies for enriching the customer.* New York: Van Nostrand Reinhold.

Grabski, S. V., Leach, S. A., & Lu, B. (2001). Risks and Controls in the Implementation of ERP Systems. *The International Journal of Digital Accounting Research.* doi:10.4192/1577-8517-v1_3

Hartman, B. (2009). *New to Agile? What Does the ScrumMaster Do Anyway?.* Retrieved from http://agileforall.com/new-to-agile-what-does-the-scrummaster-do-anyway/

Highsmith, J. (2003). *Agile Project Management: Principles and Tools.* Academic Press.

Highsmith, J., & Cockburn, A. (2001). Agile software development: The business of innovation. *Computer, 34*(9), 120–127. doi:10.1109/2.947100

Highsmith, J. A. (2002). *Agile software development ecosystems.* Boston: Addison-Wesley.

Holler, R. (n.d.). *Five Myths of Agile Development.* Retrieved from http://www.versionone.com/pdf/AgileMyths_BetterSoftware.pdf

Hunton, A., & Wright, S. (2001). *Business and audit risks associated with ERP systems: knowledge differences between information systems audit specialists and financial auditors.* Academic Press.

Jiang, J. J., & Klein, G. (1999). Risks to different aspects of system success. *Information & Management, 36*(5), 263–272. doi:10.1016/S0378-7206(99)00024-5

Kähkönen, T., Smolander, K., & Maglyas, A. (2016). Lack of integration governance in ERP development: a case study on causes and effects. *Enterprise Information Systems,* 1-34. doi:10.1080/17517575.2016.1179347

Keil, M., Cule, P. E., Lyytinen, K., & Schmidt, R. C. (1998). A framework for identifying software project risks. *Communications of the ACM, 41*(11), 76–83. doi:10.1145/287831.287843

Kremzar, M. H., & Wallace, T. F. (2001). *ERP: Making It Happen: The Implementers' Guide to Success with Enterprise Resource Planning*. New York: John Wiley & Sons, Inc.

Krueger, C. (2002). Eliminating the adoption barrier. *IEEE Software, 19*(4), 29–31. doi:10.1109/MS.2002.1020284

Lau, L. (2003). Developing a successful implementation plan for ERP: Issues and challenges. *Proceedings of the International Association for Computer Information Systems*, 223-229.

Mabert, V. A., Soni, A., & Venkataramanan, M. (2001). Enterprise resource planning: Common myths versus evolving reality. *Business Horizons, 44*(3), 69–76. doi:10.1016/S0007-6813(01)80037-9

Manzo, J. (2003). Agile Development Methods, the Myths, and the Reality: A user perspective. *Proceedings, USC-CSE Agile Methods Workshop*. Retrieved from http://sunset.usc.edu/events/past

Miller, G. (2001). *The Characteristics of Agile Software Processes*. IEEE Computer Society.

Moe, N. B., Dingsøyr, T., & Dybå, T. (2010). A teamwork model for understanding an agile team: A case study of a Scrum project. *Information and Software Technology, 52*(5), 480–491. doi:10.1016/j.infsof.2009.11.004

Nyfjord, J., & Kajko-Mattsson, M. (2007). Commonalities in Risk Management and Agile Process Models. *International Conference on Software Engineering Advances (ICSEA 2007)*. doi:10.1109/ICSEA.2007.22

Nyfjord, J., & Mattsson, M. (2008). *Degree of Agility in Pre-Implementation Process Phases*. Academic Press.

Oracle Primavera. (2011). *The Yin and Yang of Enterprise Project Portfolio Management and Agile Software Development: Combining Creativity and Governance*. Academic Press.

Prahalad, C. K. (2009). In volatile times, agility rules. *Business Week, 80*(September), 21.

Rico, D. F. (2008). What is the Return on Investment (ROI) of agile methods? *Methods (San Diego, Calif.)*, 1–7.

Ross, J. W., & Weill, P. (2002). Six IT decisions your IT people shouldn't make. *Harvard Business Review*, *80*(11), 84–95.

Saltmarsh, T. J., & Browne, P. S. (1983). Data Processing – Risk Assessment. In M. M. Wofsey (Ed.), *Advances in Computer Security Management* (Vol. 2, pp. 93–116). John Wiley and Sons Ltd.

Senft, S., Gallegos, F., & Davis, A. (2012). *Information technology control and audit*. Auerbach Publications.

Shrivastava, S., & Rathod, U. (2015). Categorization of risk factors for distributed agile projects. *Information and Software Technology*, *58*(February), 373–387. doi:10.1016/j.infsof.2014.07.007

Singleton, T. (2014). The Core of IT Auditing. *ISACA Journal, 6*. Retrieved from https://www.isaca.org/Journal/archives/2014/Volume-6/Pages/The-Core-of-IT-Auditing.aspx

Siponen, M., Baskerville, R., & Kuivalainen, T. (2005, January). Integrating security into agile development methods. In *Proceedings of the 38th Annual Hawaii International Conference on System Sciences, HICSS'05* (pp. 185a-185a). IEEE.

Smith, P., & Pichler, R. (2005). *Agile Risks/Agile Rewards*. Software Development.

Smith, P. G., & Merritt, G. M. (2002). *Proactive risk management*. New York: Productivity Press.

Stapleton, J. (1997). DSDM: Dynamic Systems Development Method. *Proceedings Technology of Object-Oriented Languages and Systems. TOOLS* 29 (Cat. No.PR00275).

State of Software Risk Management Practice. (2008). *Software Engineering*.

Stoica, M., Mircea, M., & Ghilic-Micu, B. (2013). Software Development: Agile vs. Traditional. *Informatica Economica, 17*(4), 64-76. doi:10.12948/issn14531305/17.4.2013.06

Suryanarayana, G., Sharma, T., & Samarthyam, G. (2015). Software Process versus Design Quality: Tug of War? *IEEE Software*, *32*(4), 7–11. doi:10.1109/MS.2015.87

TeachBeacon. (2016). *Survey: Is agile the new norm?* Retrieved from https://techbeacon.com/survey-agile-new-norm

Varhol, P. (2016, November 21). *The complete history of agile software development.* Retrieved from https://techbeacon.com/agility-beyond-history%E2%80%94-legacy%E2%80%94-agile-development

Wieder, B., Booth, P., Matolcsy, Z. P., & Ossimitz, M. (2006). The impact of ERP systems on firm and business process performance. *Journal of Enterprise Information Management, 19*(1), 13–29. doi:10.1108/17410390610636850

Wright, C. (2014). Agile Project need Agile Controls and Audit. *ISACA Ireland Conference GRC 2.0 - Breaking Down The Silos Conference.*

Wright, C. (2014). *Agile governance and audit: an overview for auditors and agile teams.* Cambridge, UK: IT Governance.

Zeng, Y. (2010). *Risk management for enterprise resource planning system implementations in project-based firms* (Doctoral dissertation).

Chapter 11

Do Privacy Concerns Affect Information Seeking via Smartphones?

Mohamed Abdelhamid
University at Buffalo, USA

Joana Gaia
University at Buffalo, USA

Srikanth Venkatesan
University at Buffalo, USA

Raj Sharman
University at Buffalo, USA

ABSTRACT

The innovation and evolution of technologies in smartphone industry has enabled users to efficiently achieve many tasks including utilizing search engines for instant information retrieval anytime and anywhere. Nonetheless, some users choose not to use these smartphone features including search engines to seek information. This study explores the factors that impact the likelihood of information seeking via smartphones. Privacy concern was found to be one of the main factors influencing the likelihood of seeking information. Android users were more likely to seek information compared to iPhone users, possibly due to the differences in the features of the operating systems of these phones. Motivation to seek information captured by technology ownership increases the likelihood of information seeking. The diversity of social network connections also plays a significant in information seeking behavior of the users.

DOI: 10.4018/978-1-5225-2604-9.ch011

INTRODUCTION

The past decade has witnessed a meteoric rise in the innovation of smartphones. The two main players in smartphones operating systems are IOS and Android, the latter being used in several hardware sets while IOS is only used in Apple products. Recent innovations have resulted in remarkable changes in industries and fields outside the cell phone industry. Among these changes, search engines have taken on a new challenge since smartphone users may want to acquire and seek information using their smartphones rather than a desktop computer or a laptops. The traditional way of using public desktops or personal computers may not be practical nowadays as people are on the go all the time. Given these circumstances, search engine players such as Google, Bing, and Yahoo have made functional changes to make this experience (seeking information using smartphones) more practical and efficient. Search engines are now smartphone compatible and have been integrated into smartphones operating systems. Users can seek information without even going to a smartphone web browser. Smartphone applications for search engines can be downloaded which makes search functionality available quicker than ever.

As of 2014, 34% of cell internet users don't use their laptops or desktops to go online but mostly use their cell phones. About 30% of cell owners think they cannot live without their phones (Pew Research Center, 2014). Indeed smartphones have become a primary tool in people's everyday personal, academic, and professional lives. However, some owners of smartphones don't use their device to seek information. This brings up a very important question: in the era of smartphone technology innovation, what would deter users from using some of the functionalities that make these innovations smart? Why do some people seek information through smartphones while others do not? What factors contribute to more information seeking through smartphone search engines?

THEORY AND MODEL DEVELOPMENT

This study investigates the factors that impact users to utilize the search engines in their smartphone to seek information. The model has been theoretically developed based on the information foraging theory (IFT) (Pirolli & Card, 1999). The behavioral patterns described in IFT were derived from Optimal Foraging Theory (OFT) (Stephens & Krebs, 1986) and the Adaptive Control of Thought-Rational Theory (ACT-R) (Anderson et al., 2004). We adapt the theory to investigate users' information seeking behavior using the search engines of their smartphones. The theory explores users' online search behavior and the factors that impact their decisions to seek or search for information on the web (Pirolli, 2007). The structure of the interface between the information seeker and information repositories determines the time costs, resource costs, and opportunity costs of different information foraging and sense-making strategies. Based on the trade-off between the value of information gained and the cost of foraging using a particular strategy drives the individuals towards adopting a particular foraging behavior. The theory is based on two important concepts namely "information patch" and "information scent". An information patch is an area of the search environment with similar information (McCart et al., 2013; Pirolli, 2007). It may be defined based on the task in hand. Information scent is the driving force behind why a person makes a navigational selection amongst a group of competing/ alternative options (McCart et al., 2013). The interplay between information foraging costs (including search effort) or information scent and the perceived value derived from pursuing an information patch determines the preference to search strategies. With recent advancement in the information technology industry, people have the ability to access and seek information anytime, anywhere, and with minimal efforts (Pettigrew et al., 2002). Smartphones have many of the features that laptops or desktops have. It is, therefore, interesting to investigate why some users would choose not to utilize the features in their smartphones to seek information. We argue that users' decisions to use search engines in their smartphones for seeking information depends on Information Technology (IT) barriers and IT enablers, which essentially is an interplay between foraging costs and value derived.

The IT barrier is captured by the users' perceived privacy concerns. Smartphones are associated with a single user who uses a specific account to download applications and use the smartphone. Information about the user may be collected in real-time, which includes locations and online activities. Thus, privacy may be a bigger issue for smartphones compared to laptops or desktops.

IT enablers are captured through the users' engagement and diversity in social networking sites such as Facebook, Twitter, YouTube, Google Plus, etc. The factor is captured through the diversity instrument of social networking sites, which consists of the total number of social networking accounts users have, and how often they use these accounts.

People who are more engaged in these social networking sites are usually keener on using digital technology. Frequency of use can be used as proxy for diversity (Gray et al. 2011). Diversity in social networking sites means that those people are more enabled by IT. Other studies have also found that diversity of information sources such as from social networking sites were found to improve the information seeking effectiveness (Chi & Pirolli, 2006; Pirolli, 2009). Moreover, people who are more involved on virtual social networks have less interactions with people offline (Kraut et al., 1998) and therefore may tend to use their smartphones to seek information when a need for information arises. Since users are IT enabled and less interactive with people in non-virtual settings, they tend to seek information online via smartphones. Therefore, based on the theoretical foundation of Information Foraging Theory, we arrive at hypothesis 1:

H1: The diversity of social networking sites is associated with increasing the likelihood of online information seeking via the search engines in smartphones.

Moreover, self-determination theory suggests that peoples' decisions to engage in a particular behavior depends on their ability to interact proficiently in the environment and their autonomous motivation (Grant, 2007; Grant, 2008). Motivation and ability have shown positive impact on seeking information (Reinholt et al., 2011). We argue that in the context of online information seeking, the ability to interact with the environment is captured through SNS diversity, which captures user memberships and their frequency of use. Thus, users who are very active and are members of multiple SNS are able to interact proficiently in an online environment.

Furthermore, people who have the ability to interact in the online environment are expected to be more likely to seek information via smartphone search engines. That relationship is expected to have an interaction effect with the motivation to seek

Figure 1. Conceptual model

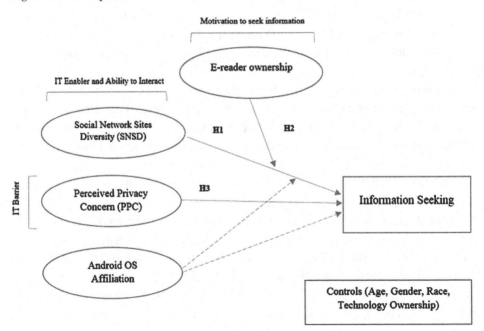

information. For the purpose of this study, e-reader ownership has been utilized to capture users' motivation to seek information:

H2: E-reader ownership and SNS diversity have a significant interaction effect on seeking information.

To test hypothesis 2 we capture the motivation of users to seek information through their ownership of e-readers such as kindle. People who own such devices are motivated to seek information and knowledge.

Based on the theoretical foundation of information foraging theory, privacy concern has been used as a factor to capture IT barrier that is expected to predict user behavior in information seeking. Chi and Pirolli (2006) argue that trust has been found to be an important barrier for information seeking while privacy concern is an important trust factor that can be a significant barrier. While information technology innovations solve some practical problems they bring other problems and issues in their wake. In this context, privacy is perhaps the most important issue when it comes to using some of the functionalities of smartphones. There are several issues that come with these functionalities. For example, a probable risk is that information seeking using a personal smartphone can always be associated and matched with the smartphone user. People use their personal emails and electronic IDs to register and use Android and IOS applications on their phones. People may avoid such engagement because they are concerned that their privacy may be violated. Users might not mind downloading a smartphone application to play a game for example, but seeking information may relate to sensitive personal information that the user would wish to keep private. Lindenbaum et al. (1988) describe privacy as a flexible concept, suggesting that it has little shared meaning amongst individuals. Even privacy scholars acknowledge that the construct has not taken on a common meaning as it applies to research (Margulis, 1977).

Researchers have debated the conceptualization of privacy as a social and/or psychological construct (Margulis, 1977). Recent research explores concerns about information privacy as reflecting the extent to which individuals are disturbed by the information collection practices of others and their anxiety over how the acquired information will be subsequently used. A stream of research in the context of privacy aims to investigate how people manage their privacy. Moreover, many researchers have investigated how different contextual factors play different roles that impact the decision-making process when privacy is a concern (Bansal et al., 2010). Many studies try to explain the privacy paradox and clarify why the actual behavior of consumers do not always follow their revealed privacy preferences (Anderson & Agarwal, 2011). Dinev and Hart (2006) indicate the aggregated effects of both personal Internet interest and trust can dampen the negative effects of privacy concerns in conducting e-commerce transactions. In the context of online chat rooms, they show that the gratification that individuals derive from participating in interpersonal interactions offsets the restraining effects of their privacy concerns and leads to self-disclosure. Lab experiments have shown that consumers are more likely to purchase from retailers who have better privacy protection policies in place (Tsai et al., 2011). Based on the theoretical foundation of Information Foraging Theory and the prior literature on privacy, we arrive at hypothesis 3:

H3: Privacy Concern is negatively associated with the likelihood of online information seeking via smartphone search engines.

METHODOLOGY

Data

The dataset used in this study has been obtained from Pew Research Center's Internet and American Life Project collected in 2012. The survey asked questions about search engine usage and interactions on social networking sites. Survey responses have been conditioned to include observations from participants that use the internet, who have smartphone devices, and are members of social networking sites. The final number of participants after the conditioning was 953 participants for which 585 (61.4%) reported a use of smartphone search engines to seek information while 368 (38.6%) reported that they did not use smartphone search engines to seek information.

Measurements

Exploratory Factor Analysis (EFA) using Principal Component Analysis (PCA) and Principal Factor Analysis (PFA) have been used to construct the instruments. The PCA suggested two factors with eigenvalue higher than 1 to be extracted. Table 1 shows factor loading which indicate sufficient convergent and discriminant validity.

Table 1. Factor loadings

Construct	Item	SNSD	PPC
Perceived Privacy Concern (PPC)	PrPrivacy1	-0.27297	**0.61815**
	PrPrivacy2	0.11431	**0.84753**
SNS Diversity (SNSD)	Frequency of Use	**0.81781**	-0.09939
	Total Accounts	**0.78440**	-0.02952

The amount of explained variance by each of the factors is relatively the same. The total explained variance is around 62%. Since correlations between factors are very low, the orthogonal rotation is more appropriate than oblique. The orthogonal rotation has been performed to obtain a clear pattern of loading. The method is used to maximize the correlation between variables that load high on factors and thereby this minimizes correlations between variables that load low on factors.

Table 2 shows the correlation matrix and the level of significance among the main variables in the model. The numbers in the diagonal indicate the variable correlation with itself. The dependent variable seeking information is coded as a binary variable: 1 for seeking information through smartphones search engines, and 0 for not using smartphones search engines to seek information. Tablet ownership and e-reader ownership are both coded 1 and 0 indicating the ownership of such a device and not owning a device respectively. Facebook is also a binary variable indicating whether a user is a member of Facebook or not. The Android variable refers to whether the users have smartphone with an Android system or an IOS. Gender is coded Male=1 for males and Male=0 for females. Age is used as an integer to indicate the user's age.

Common Method Variance

Data collected through a common method can suffer from common method variance (CMV) in which the relationship between the construct is affected by the use of a

Table 2. Correlation matrix

	Info. Seeking	SNSD	PPC	Tablet Ownership	E-reader Ownership	Age	Male	Facebook
Info. Seeking	1.00							
SNSD	0.31***	1.00						
PPC	-0.15***	-0.10***	1.00					
Tablet Ownership	0.17***	0.07**	-0.06*	1.00				
E-reader Ownership	0.08**	0.05	-0.06*	0.15***	1.00			
Age	-0.30***	-0.26***	0.19***	0.02	0.04	1.00		
Male	0.10***	0.00	-0.06*	0.02	-0.06*	-0.11***	1.00	
Facebook	0.12***	0.41***	-0.03	-0.01	0.09**	-0.17***	-0.07**	1.00
Android	0.37***	0.17***	-0.04	-0.01	0.05	-0.20***	0.04	0.11***

*** = $p < .01$; ** = $p < .05$; * = $p < .10$

single method (Podsakoff et al., 2003). Common method variance has been assessed through the marker variable technique (Lindell & Whitney, 2001).

The marker variable can be identified after data has been collected. The smallest positive correlation can be used to identify the MV. E-reader ownership has been used as marker variable since its correlation with SNS diversity is 0.05.

Formulas introduced by Lindell & Whitney (2001) have been used to calculate the correlation of the constructs. After controlling for the MV, the level of significance between SNS diversity and every other variable does not change. Thus, there is no evidence for common method variance.

RESULTS AND ANALYSIS

SAS 9.4 base has been used to clean the data and run statistical analysis. Logistic regression is used to estimate the likelihood of seeking information via smartphone search engines using the reported dichotomous variable for seeking information via smartphone search engines; the variable is used as a response variable.

Results

Logistic regression has been used to test the hypotheses. As reported in Table 3, four models are estimated. Model 1 is the most basic model without interaction effects. The c statistics for the models are between 0.822 and 0.823, which are above the 0.80 cutoff indicating that the model is a good model to distinguish between the people who seek information through smartphone search engines and those who don't. A c statistic higher than 0.8 indicates that the model is strong in discriminating the subjects (Hosmer et al., 2000). The c statistics increases incrementally from model 2 and model 4 indicating improvements of the models. Likewise, Pseudo R2 shows an improvement of the model especially in models 2 and 4. Model 4 shows the best fit statistics among all four models.

Social networking site diversity is found to have a significant effect on increasing the odds for seeking information through smartphone. The factor is found to be significant under all four models where the estimates hardly change. This result supports hypothesis 1. Therefore, SNS diversity does have a big impact on enabling users to take advantage of features available in their smartphones. This is a relatively positive impact of social networking sites on people's behavior which promotes knowledge and information seeking behavior.

Likewise, the estimates of perceived privacy concern don't change at all under all four models. Perceived privacy concerns are found to have a significant negative impact on the likelihood of information seeking. This finding supports hypothesis

3 indicating that the higher the privacy concern, the less likely it is that the users will seek information via their smartphones search engines. This finding perhaps suggests that as the smartphone industry continues to evolve and innovate, more and more information is collected from the users, invading their privacy and making their lives more traceable. These innovations could have a negative impact on the use of some of the smart features. The users might sacrifice using some of those advanced features such as the information seeking through smartphones because these features may involve putting their privacy at risk.

Although not hypothesized, the impact of operating systems on seeking information has also been investigated. The following questions need to be investigated: are Android users different from iPhone users in their information seeking behavior? If yes, then why? Are there features, advantages, or disadvantages that make certain users more likely to seek information through their smartphones than others? The findings show that Android users are more likely to seek information using their smartphones compared to iPhone users. Thus, the smartphone operating system has a significant impact on information seeking. This finding is quite interesting and calls for an explanation. There are two probable reasons that could have caused such behavior. The first possible reason comes from the fact that the iPhone screen size is much smaller compared to most Android phones screen sizes. This results in inefficiency when trying to use very small screen sizes to look for information and then read using those small screens. On the other hand, Android phones are very efficient and practical in this regard, offering relatively large screens that are easy to use and read from. Also, notice that the survey was collected in 2012 and iPhone screen size was very small at that time. Only recently has the iPhone started adjusting its screen size to compete with other players and has started gaining market share over them. The second explanation is an advantage of iPhones over other competitors especially at that time period (2012). iPhone introduced Siri in 2011 which is a feature that enabled users to search for information online using their voices and without the need to go to a search engine. The feature also supported earlier 3rd generation versions.

Since the survey specifically asked participants whether they used search engines or not to seek information, the users who use Siri do not need to use search engines and thus have answered no to the question. Android phones did not have a competing feature back then and have only recently started competing in this domain. It will be interesting to investigate the impact of the bigger screen sizes of the new iPhones generation on the likelihood of using search engines to search for information. Table 3 shows the logistic regression results of all four models.

To test hypothesis 2 we introduced the interaction term between e-reader ownership and SNS diversity. However, the interaction effect in a nonlinear model is more complex than in a linear model (Norton et al. 2004). The true level of significance

Table 3. Results of logistic regression (DV: Seeking information via Smartphones)

Variables	Model 1		Model 2		Model 3		Model 4	
	Coef.	Std. Err.	Coef.	Std. Err.	Coef.	Std. Err.	Coef.	Std. Err.
Constant	1.57***	0.52	-0.002	0.78	1.58***	0.52	1.61***	0.52
SNS Diversity	0.64***	0.10	0.67***	0.11	0.66***	0.11	0.73***	0.12
Privacy Concern	-0.20**	0.09	-0.20**	0.09	-0.20***	0.09	-0.21***	0.09
Android	2.16***	0.24	2.15***	0.24	2.13***	0.24	2.13***	0.24
E-reader ownership	0.41**	0.20	-0.76	0.69	0.41**	0.21	0.37**	0.20
Tablet ownership	1.07***	0.21	1.13***	0.21	1.07***	0.21	1.07***	0.21
Age	-0.03***	0.01	0.04	0.03	-0.03***	0.01	-0.03***	0.01
Male	0.39**	0.16	0.44***	0.17	0.40**	0.16	0.41**	0.16
Facebook	-0.32	0.27	-0.30	0.30	-0.33	0.27	-0.37	0.28
White	-0.45	0.41	-0.50	0.41	-0.45	0.41	-0.45	0.41
Black	0.15	0.47	0.12	0.47	0.15	0.47	0.15	0.47
Asian	-0.66	0.57	-0.65	0.57	-0.67	0.57	-0.66	0.57
Mixed race	-0.21	0.70	-0.23	0.71	-0.23	0.70	-0.18	0.70
Native	-0.18	0.74	-0.21	0.74	-0.17	0.74	-0.15	0.75
Diversity X E-reader ownership			0.167***	0.62			-0.33	0.22
Diversity X Android OS					-0.16	0.27	-0.16	0.27
c	0.822		0.823		0.822		0.823	
Pseudo R2	0.2486		0.2504		0.2489		0.2506	
Log likelihood	-477.6		-476.5		-477.4		-476.3	

***= p < .01; ** = p < .05; * = p < .10

cannot be derived from the basic logistic regression results and thus results may be biased. The interaction effect is not significant based on results from the logistic regression in model 2. However, these do not reflect true significance and standard errors of the interaction effect in a nonlinear model such as logistic regression. The method introduced by Norton (2004) has been used in this study. The method can be used for two continuous variables, a continuous and a dummy variable, or two dummy variables.

The interaction effect in a nonlinear model might not always be negative or positive, significant or insignificant. The predicted probability depends on other variables in the model. Thus, as seen in Figures 2 and 3 the effect is positive for some

*Figure 2. Interaction effect diversity * e-reader ownership*

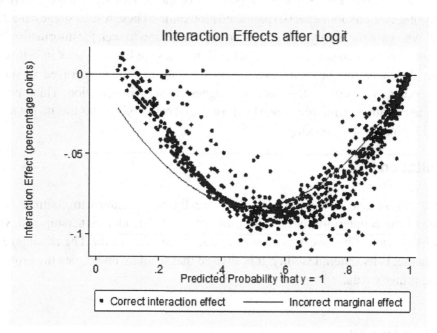

Figure 3. Z-statistics of interaction effects Diversity X E-reader ownership

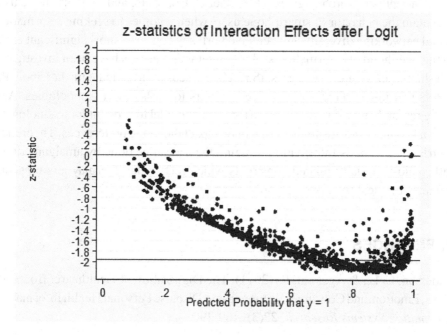

observation around the 0.2 predicted probability and is significant and negative for many observations above the 0.6 predicted probability. These results suggest that the users who have the ability to interact and the motivation to seek for information but are not extremely engaged in social networking sites are likely to seek information using their smartphones. However, users who are extremely involved in social networking sites perhaps lose their willingness to seek information. This may be associated with the time consumed by those social networking sites that do not leave room for information seeking.

Limitation

Since this is a secondary dataset, there are limited variables to control. Also, some of the counterintuitive results (interaction of E-reader ownership and SNS Diversity) cannot be investigated further due to data limitation. The advantage of the dataset is its generalizability. It is advised that scholars investigate the problem using primary data.

CONCLUSION

A theoretical approach has been adopted to explain why users seek information through their smartphone search engines. IT enablers, IT barriers, and motivation are used to explain the behavior of smartphone users when it comes to seeking information. Social networking diversity and perceived privacy concerns show significant effect on the likelihood of information seeking. Interaction effects have been investigated and show counterintuitive results. IS research needs to investigate further about the factors that impact IT use preferences of users towards newer technologies. As a future research, we aim to expand the theoretical model to account for technological design variables and affordances that may impact the usage preferences. Theoretical contribution towards Information foraging theory can be done by amalgamating it with socio-materialty related constructs which reflect the interplay among social and technological factors.

REFERENCES

Anderson, C. L., & Agarwal, R. (2011). The Digitization of Healthcare: Boundary Risks, Emotion, and Consumer Willingness to Disclose Personal Health Information. *Information Systems Research*, 22(3), 469-490.

Anderson, J. R., Bothell, D., Byrne, M. D., Douglass, S., Lebiere, C., & Qin, Y. (2004). An Integrated Theory of the Mind. *Psychological Review*, *111*(4), 1036.

Bansal, G., Zahedi, F., & Gefen, D. (2010). The Impact of Personal Dispositions on Information Sensitivity, Privacy Concern and Trust in Disclosing Health Information Online. *Decision Support Systems*, *49*(2), 138-150.

Chi, E. H., & Pirolli, P. (2006). *Social Information Foraging and Collaborative Search*. Human Computer Interaction Consortium.

Dinev, T., & Hart, P. (2006). An Extended Privacy Calculus Model for E-Commerce Transactions. *Information Systems Research*, *17*(1), 61-80.

Grant, A. M. (2007). Relational Job Design and the Motivation to Make a Prosocial Difference. *Academy of Management Review*, *32*(2), 393-417.

Grant, A. M. (2008). Does Intrinsic Motivation Fuel the Prosocial Fire? Motivational Synergy in Predicting Persistence, Performance, and Productivity. *Journal of Applied Psychology*, *93*(1), 48.

Gray, P. H., Parise, S., & Iyer, B. (2011). Innovation Impacts of Using Social Bookmarking Systems. *MIS Quarterly*, *35*(3), 629-643.

Hosmer, D. W., Lemeshow, S., & Cook, E. (2000). *Applied Logistic Regression* (2nd ed.). John Wiley & Sons. doi:10.1002/0471722146

Kraut, R., Patterson, M., Lundmark, V., Kiesler, S., Mukophadhyay, T., & Scherlis, W. (1998). Internet Paradox: A Social Technology That Reduces Social Involvement and Psychological Well-Being?. *American Psychologist*, *53*(9), 1017.

Lindell, M. K., & Whitney, D. J. (2001). Accounting for Common Method Variance in Cross-Sectional Research Designs. *Journal of Applied Psychology*, *86*(1), 114.

Lindenbaum, J., Healton, E. B., Savage, D. G., Brust, J. C., Garrett, T. J., Podell, E. R., … Allen, R. H. (1988). Neuropsychiatric Disorders Caused by Cobalamin Deficiency in the Absence of Anemia or Macrocytosis. *New England Journal of Medicine*, *318*(26), 1720-1728.

Margulis, S. T. (1977). Conceptions of Privacy: Current Status and Next Steps. *Journal of Social Issues*, *33*(3), 5-21.

McCart, J. A., Padmanabhan, B., & Berndt, D. J. (2013). Goal Attainment on Long Tail Web Sites: An Information Foraging Approach. *Decision Support Systems*, *55*(1), 235-246.

Norton, E. C., Wang, H., & Ai, C. (2004). Computing Interaction Effects and Standard Errors in Logit and Probit Models. *The Stata Journal*, (4): 154–167.

Pettigrew, K. E., Durrance, J. C., & Unruh, K. T. (2002). Facilitating Community Information Seeking Using the Internet: Findings from Three Public Library–Community Network Systems. *Journal of the American Society for Information Science and Technology*, *53*(11), 894-903.

Pew Research Center. (2014). *Mobile Technology Fact Sheet*. Retrieved October, 2014, from http://www.pewinternet.org/fact-sheets/mobile-technology-fact-sheet/

Pirolli, P. (2007). *Information Foraging Theory: Adaptive Interaction with Information*. Oxford University Press. doi:10.1093/acprof:oso/9780195173321.001.0001

Pirolli, P. (2009). An Elementary Social Information Foraging Model. *Proceedings of the SIGCHI Conference on Human Factors in Computing Systems*, 605-614.

Pirolli, P., & Card, S. (1999). Information Foraging. *Psychological Review*, *106*(4), 643.

Podsakoff, P. M., MacKenzie, S. B., Lee, J.-Y., & Podsakoff, N. P. (2003). Common Method Biases in Behavioral Research: A Critical Review of the Literature and Recommended Remedies. *Journal of Applied Psychology*, *88*(5), 879.

Reinholt, M., Pedersen, T., & Foss, N. J. (2011). Why a Central Network Position Isn't Enough: The Role of Motivation and Ability for Knowledge Sharing in Employee Networks. *Academy of Management Journal*, *54*(6), 1277-1297.

Stephens, D. W., & Krebs, J. R. (1986). *Foraging Theory*. Princeton University Press.

Tsai, J. Y., Egelman, S., Cranor, L., & Acquisti, A. (2011). The Effect of Online Privacy Information on Purchasing Behavior: An Experimental Study. *Information Systems Research*, *22*(2), 254-268.

Compilation of References

Abate, D., Hoffman, D., Robertson, N., Rogers, A., & Zeppenfeld, G. (2011, July). *The use of social media in the workplace*. Retrieved from https://www.mayerbrown.com/public_docs/ TheUseofSocialMediainTheWorkplace.pdf

Abawajy, J. (2014). User preference of cyber security awareness delivery methods. *Behaviour & Information Technology, 33*(3), 237–248. doi:10.1080/0144929X.2012.708787

Abawajy, J., & Kim, T. (2010). Performance Analysis of Cyber Security Awareness Delivery Methods. In T. Kim, W. Fang, M. K. Khan, K. P. Arnett, H. Kang, & D. Ślęzak (Eds.), *Security Technology, Disaster Recovery and Business Continuity. Communications in Computer and Information Science* (Vol. 122). Berlin: Springer. doi:10.1007/978-3-642-17610-4_16

Abdullah, L. M., & Verner, J. M. (2012). Analysis and application of an outsourcing risk framework. *Journal of Systems and Software, 85*(8), 1930–1952. doi:10.1016/j.jss.2012.02.040

Abu-Musa, A. (2008). Exploring the importance and implementation of COBIT processes in Saudi organizations: An empirical study. *Information Management & Computer Security, 17*(2), 73–95. doi:10.1108/09685220910963974

Accenture. (2015). *A Comprehensive Approach to Managing Social Media Risk and Compliance*. Retrieved from https://www.accenture.com/t20150715T045906__w__/us-en/_acnmedia/ Accenture/Conversion-Assets/DotCom/Documents/Global/PDF/Dualpub_1/accenture-comprehensive-approach-managing-social-media-risk-compliance.pdf on May 1,2016.

ACFE. (n.d.). *Sample Social media policy*. Retrieved from http://www.acfe.com/uploadedfiles/ acfe_website/content/documents/sample-documents/sample-social-media-policy.pdf

Adams, M., & Makramalla, M. (2015). Cybersecurity Skills Training: An Attacker-Centric Gamified Approach. *Technology Innovation Management Review, 5*(1).

Adams, R. (2010). Prevent, protect, pursue–a paradigm for preventing fraud. *Computer Fraud & Security, 2010*(7), 5-11. Retrieved online on 23rd January 2015 from http://www.sciencedirect.com.gate.lib.buffalo.edu/science/article/pii/S1361372310700804#

Adomavicius, G., Bockstedt, J., Gupta, A., & Kauffman, R. J. (2007). Technology roles and paths of influence in an ecosystem model of technology evolution. *Information Technology Management*, 8(2), 185–202. doi:10.1007/s10799-007-0012-z

Afzali, P., Azmayandeh, E., Nassiri, R., & Shabgahi, G. L. (2010). Effective Governance through Simultaneous Use of COBIT and Val IT. *2010 International Conference on Education and Management Technology*. doi:10.1109/ICEMT.2010.5657549

Agile Methodology: The Agile Movement. (2008, October 23). Retrieved from http://agilemethodology.org/

Agile Risk Management – Identifying Risks (1 of 4). (2009, July 29). Retrieved from https://agile101.wordpress.com/2009/07/27/agile-risk-management-identifying-risks-step-1-of-4/

Agrawal, V. (2015). A Comparative Study on Information Security Risk Analysis Methods. *International Journal of Computers*. DOI: 10.17706/jcp.12.1.57-67

Ahmed, N., & Matulevicius, R. (2013). Securing business processes using security risk-oriented patterns. *International Journal of Computer Standards & Interfaces*, 36(4), 723–733. doi:10.1016/j.csi.2013.12.007

Alaghehband, F. K., Rivard, S., Wu, S., & Goyette, S. (2011). An assessment of the use of transaction cost theory in information technology outsourcing. *The Journal of Strategic Information Systems*, 20(2), 125–138. doi:10.1016/j.jsis.2011.04.003

Alberts, C. (2005). *OCTAVE-S Implementation Guide, Version 1*. Software Engineering Institute, Carnegie Mellon University. Retrieved August 12, 2015, from http://repository.cmu.edu/cgi/viewcontent.cgi?article=1478&context=sei

Alberts, C., & Dorofee, A. (2001). *OCTAVE Criteria, Version 2.0*. Software Engineering Institute, Carnegie Mellon University. Retrieved August 12, 2015, from http://repository.cmu.edu/cgi/viewcontent.cgi?article=1217&context=sei

Aldammas, A., & Al-Mudimigh, A. (2011). Critical success and failure factors of ERP implementations: Two cases from Kingdom of Saudi Arabia. *Journal of Theoretical and Applied Information Technology*.

Alese, B. K. (2014). Evaluation of Information Security Risks Using Hybrid Assessment Model. *Proceedings of the 9th International Conference for Internet Technology and Secured Transactions (ICITST-2014)*, 387 - 395. doi:10.1109/ICITST.2014.7038843

Al-Hamadany, W. A., & Kanapathy, K. (2012). Information technology outsourcing decisions in an emerging economy: The influence of perceived risks and benefits. *World Applied Sciences Journal*, 19, 1078–1086.

Aliquo, J. F., Jr., & Fu, Z. (2014). DuPont Drives Continuous Improvement with COBIT 5 Process Assessment Model. *COBIT Focus Journal*.

Alizadeh, M., & Zannone, N. (2016). Risk-based Analysis of Business Process Executions. *Proceedings of the 6th ACM Conference on Data and Application Security and Privacy (CODASPY'16)*, 130-132. doi:10.1145/2857705.2857742

Amazon. (2016a). *Amazon unveils AWS X-Ray and Personal Health Dashboard to help monitor application health in the cloud.* Retrieved online on December 15, 2016 from http://www.geekwire.com/2016/amazon-unveils-aws-x-ray-personal-health-dashboard-help-monitor-application-health-cloud/

Amazon. (2016b). *Amazon Web Services Makes Amazon Inspector Available to All Customers.* Retrieved online on December 15, 2016 from http://www.businesswire.com/news/home/20160419006466/en/Amazon-Web-Services-Amazon-Inspector-Customers

Amazon. (2016c). *AWS XRAY. Amazon Website.* Retrieved online on December 15, 2016 from https://aws.amazon.com/blogs/aws/aws-x-ray-see-inside-of-your-distributed-application/

Amazon. (2016d). *Dataguise Shows Security and Compliance Innovations for Cloud-Based Data Infrastructure at AWS Summit in New York.* Retrieved online on December 15, 2016 from http://www.businesswire.com/news/home/20161205005340/en/Global-Cybersecurity-Confidence-Falls-70-Percent-%E2%80%9CC-%E2%80%9D

Amid, A., & Moradi, S. (2013). A Hybrid Evaluation Framework of CMM and COBIT for Improving the Software Development Quality. *Journal of Software Engineering and Applications*, 6(05), 280–288. doi:10.4236/jsea.2013.65035

Anderson, C. L., & Agarwal, R. (2011). The Digitization of Healthcare: Boundary Risks, Emotion, and Consumer Willingness to Disclose Personal Health Information. *Information Systems Research*, 22(3), 469-490.

Anderson, J. R., Bothell, D., Byrne, M. D., Douglass, S., Lebiere, C., & Qin, Y. (2004). An Integrated Theory of the Mind. *Psychological Review*, 111(4), 1036.

André Marïen. (2011). PCI DSS appears to reduce breaches. *Computer Fraud & Security, 5*. Retrieved online on 23rd January 2015 from http://www.sciencedirect.com.gate.lib.buffalo.edu/science/article/pii/S1361372311700471

Arachchilage, N. A. G., Love, S., & Scott, M. (2012). Designing a Mobile Game to Teach Conceptual Knowledge of Avoiding "Phishing Attacks". *International Journal for e-Learning Security, 2*(2), 127-132.

Arachchilage, N. A. G., & Love, S. (2013). A game design framework for avoiding phishing attacks. *Computers in Human Behavior*, 29(3), 706–714. doi:10.1016/j.chb.2012.12.018

Araz, C., Ozfirat, P. M., & Ozkarahan, I. (2007). An integrated multicriteria decision making methodology for outsourcing management. *Computers & Operations Research*, 34(12), 3738–3756. doi:10.1016/j.cor.2006.01.014

Arens, A., & Loebbecke, J. (1997). *Overview of Integrated Auditing. Auditing: An Integrated Approach*. Academic Press.

Ashenden, D. (2008). *Information security management: a human challenge?* Elsevier Information Security Technical Report 13.

Ataya, G. (2010). PCI DSS audit and compliance. *Information Security Technical Report, 15*(4), 138-144. Retrieved Online on January 22, 2015 from http://www.sciencedirect.com/science/article/pii/S136341271100015X

Atchinson, B., & Fox, D. (n.d.). *The Politics Of The Health Insurance Portability And Accountability Act*. Academic Press.

Audit of the Enterprise Resource Planning System implementation: management identified and addressed most system implementation risks but improvements are needed related to security, payment controls and training. (2011). San Diego, CA: Office of the City Auditor, City of San Diego.

Avgerou, C. (2008). Information systems in developing countries: a critical research review. *J. Inform. Technol., 23*(3), 133–146.

AWS Shield. (2016). *AWS Shield: managed DDOS Protection*. Retrieved online on December 15, 2016 from https://aws.amazon.com/shield/

Bachlechner, D., Thalmann, S., & Maier, R. (2014). Security and compliance challenges in complex IT outsourcing arrangements: A multi-stakeholder perspective. *Computers & Security, 40*, 38–59. doi:10.1016/j.cose.2013.11.002

Bada, M., & Sasse, A. (2014). *Cyber Security Awareness Campaigns: Why do they fail to change behaviour?*. Academic Press.

Bakshi, S. (2012). Risk IT framework for IT risk management: A case study of National Stock Exchange of India Limited. *COBIT Focus, 1*, 5–10.

Bansal, G., Zahedi, F., & Gefen, D. (2010). The Impact of Personal Dispositions on Information Sensitivity, Privacy Concern and Trust in Disclosing Health Information Online. *Decision Support Systems, 49*(2), 138-150.

Baregheh, A., Rowley, J., & Sambrook, S. (2009). Towards a multidisciplinary definition of innovation. *Management Decision, 47*(8), 1323–1339.

Barkan, T. (2011, January). *Social Strat – Special Report: How are the members of association using social media today?* Retrieved from https://www.uia.org/sites/dev.uia.be/files/misc_pdfs/roundtable/Social_Media_Use_Survey_Report_Individuals_2011.pdf on May 1, 2016.

Barki, H., Rivard, S., & Talbot, J. (1993). A Keyword Classification Scheme for IS Research Literature: An Update. *Management Information Systems Quarterly, 17*(June), 209–225. doi:10.2307/249802

Barki, H., Rivard, S., & Talbot, J. (1993). Toward an Assessment of Software Development Risk. *Journal of Management Information Systems, 10*(2), 203–225. doi:10.1080/07421222.1993.11518006

Barlow, J. B., Warkentin, M., Ormond, D., & Dennis, A. R. (2013). Dont make excuses! Discouraging neutralization to reduce IT policy violation. *Computers & Security, 39*, 145–159. doi:10.1016/j.cose.2013.05.006

Barracuda. (2016). *Barracuda Simplifies Web Application Security for AWS Customers*. Retrieved online on December 15, 2016 from http://www.broadwayworld.com/bwwgeeks/article/Barracuda-Simplifies-Web-Application-Security-for-AWS-Customers-20161130

Bartens, Y., de Haes, S., Eggert, L., Heilig, L., Maes, K., Frederik, S., & Voß, S. (2014). A Visualization Approach for Reducing the Perceived Complexity of COBIT 5. *9th International Conference, DESRIST 2014*. doi:10.1007/978-3-319-06701-8_34

Bartens, Y., Schulte, F., & Voß, S. (2014). E-Business IT Governance Revisited: An Attempt towards Outlining a Novel Bi-directional Business/IT Alignment in COBIT5. *47th Hawaii International Conference on System Science*. doi:10.1109/HICSS.2014.538

Bartolini, C., El Kateb, D., Le Traon, Y., & Hagen, D. (2015). *Cloud Providers Viability: How to Address it from an IT and Legal Perspective? Economics of Grids*. Clouds, Systems, and Services.

Baxter, R. J., Holderness, D. K., & Wood, D. A. (2015). Applying Basic Gamification Techniques to IT Compliance Training: Evidence from the Lab and Field. *Journal of Information Systems*.

Behnia, A., Rashid, R. A., & Chaudhry, J. A. (2012). A Survey of Information Security Risk Analysis Methods. *Journal of Smart Computing Review, 2*(1), 79–94. doi:10.6029/smartcr.2012.01.007

Belcourt, M. (2006, June). Outsourcing — The benefits and the risks. *Human Resource Management Review, 16*(2), 269–279. doi:10.1016/j.hrmr.2006.03.011

Berg, H.-P. (2010). Risk management: Procedures, methods and experiences. *Journal of International Group on Reliability: Theory and &Applications, 2*(17), 79–88.

Beringer, A., & Southwell, A. (2011, January 11). *Critical Social media issues for Retail companies*. Retrieved from http://www.gibsondunn.com/publications/Documents/WebcastSlides-CriticalSocialMediaIssuesforRetailCompanies.pdf

Bernroider, E. W. N., & Ivanov, M. (2010). IT Project management control and the control objectives for IT and related Technology (COBIT) framework. *International Journal of Project Management*.

Betz, C. T. (2011). *ITIL, COBIT and CMMI: Ongoing confusion of process and function*. BP Trends.

Bharathi, S., & Suguna, J. (2014). A Conceptual Model To Understand Information Security Awareness. *International Journal of Engineering, 3*(8).

Bhartiya, S. (2016). *IBM encrypts the cloud with Z13s mainframe*. Retrieved online on December 15, 2016 from http://www.cio.com/article/3033967/linux/ibm-encrypts-the-cloud-with-z13s-mainframe.html

Bhattacharjee, J., Sengupta, A., & Mazumdar, C. (2013). A Formal Methodology for Enterprise Information Security Risk Assessment. *Proceedings of the CRiSIS'13, 8th International Conference on Risks and Security of Internet and Systems*, 1-9. doi:10.1109/CRiSIS.2013.6766354

Bhattacharjee, J., Sengupta, A., & Mazumdar, C. (2016). A Quantitative Methodology for Security Risk Assessment of Enterprise Business Processes. *Proceedings of the 2nd International Conference on Information Systems Security and Privacy (ICISSP 2016)*, 388-399. doi:10.5220/0005739703880399

Bin-Abbas, H., & Haj Bakry, S. (2014). Assessment of IT Governance in organizations: A simple integrated approach. *Computer in Human Behavior Journal*.

Bisong, A., & Rahman, M. (2011). *An overview of the security concerns in enterprise cloud computing*. arXiv preprint arXiv:1101.5613

Biswas, S. (2011, January 20). *Is cloud computing secure? Yes, another perspective* [Web log post]. Retrieved online on January 6, 2017 from http://www.cloudtweaks.com/2011/01/the-question-should-be-is-anything-truly-secure

Blackburn, M. (n.d.). *HIPAA, Heal Thyself*. Retrieved from http://pages.jh.edu/jhumag/1104web/hipaa.html

Blakley, B., McDermott, E., & Geer, D. (2001). Information security is information risk management. *In Proceedings of the workshop on New security paradigms*. Cloudcroft, NM: ACM.

Bluemner, A. (2014) *The $5.4M Question: Can POS Systems Prevent Credit Card Fraud?* Retrieved online on 10th October January 2015 from http://findaccountingsoftware.com/expert-advice/the-54m-question-can-pos-systems-prevent-credit-card-fraud/

Boehm, B. (2002). Get ready for agile methods, with care. *Computer, 35*(1), 64–69. doi:10.1109/2.976920

Boehm, B., & Turner, R. (2004). *Balancing Agility and Discipline: A Guide for the Perplexed*. Software Engineering Research and Applications Lecture Notes in Computer Science.

Bonds-Raacke, J., & Raacke, J. (2010). MySpace and Facebook: Identifying dimensions of uses and gratifications for friend networking sites. *Individual Differences Research, 8*, 27–33.

Braendeland, G., Refsdal, A., & Stolen, K. (2010). Modular Analysis and Modeling of Risk Scenarios with Dependencies. *International Journal of Systems and Software, 83*(10), 1995–2013. doi:10.1016/j.jss.2010.05.069

Brandas, C., Stirbu, D., & Didraga, O. (2013). *Integrated approach model of risk, control and auditing of accounting information systems* (Vol. 17). Informatica Economica.

Brodkin, J. (2008). Gartner: Seven cloud-computing security risks. *InfoWorld, 2008*, 1–3.

Broughton, A., Higgins, T., Hicks, B., & Cox, A. (2009). *Workplace and social networking-the implications of Employment relations.* Retrieved from http://www.acas.org.uk/media/pdf/d/6/1111_Workplaces_and_Social_Networking.pdf

Businesswire. (2016). *World First: Outscale Introduces Per-Second Billing to Boost Cloud Adoption.* Retrieved online on December 15, 2016 from http://www.businesswire.com/news/home/20160915005885/en/World-Outscale-Introduces-Per-Second-Billing-Boost-Cloud

Buy, B. (2016, July 21). *Best Buy Social Media Policy.* Retrieved from http://forums.bestbuy.com/t5/Welcome-News/Best-Buy-Social-Media-Policy/td-p/20492

Buyukozkan, G., & Cifci, G. (2012). A novel hybrid MCDM approach based on fuzzy DEMATEL, fuzzy ANP and fuzzy TOPSIS to evaluate green suppliers. *Expert Systems with Applications, 39*(3), 3000–3011. doi:10.1016/j.eswa.2011.08.162

Cai, X. Q., Chen, J., Xiao, Y. B., Xu, X. L., & Yu, G. (2013). Fresh-product supply chain management with logistics outsourcing. *Omega, 41*(4), 752–765. doi:10.1016/j.omega.2012.09.004

Caldwell, T. (2016). Making security awareness training work. *Computer Fraud & Security,* (6): 8–14.

Califf, R., & Muhlbaier, L. (n.d.). *Health Insurance Portability and Accountability Act (HIPAA).* Academic Press.

Campbell, P. L. (2005). *A COBIT Primer.* Sandia Report.

Canty, D. (2015). *Agile for project managers.* Academic Press.

Caputo, D. D., Pfleeger, S. L., Freeman, J. D., & Johnson, M. E. (2014). Going spear phishing: Exploring embedded training and awareness. *IEEE Security and Privacy, 12*(1), 28–38. doi:10.1109/MSP.2013.106

Caralli, R. A., Stevens, J. F., Young, L. R., & Wilson, W. R. (2007). *Introducing octave allegro: Improving the information security risk assessment process* (No. CMU/SEI-2007-TR-012). Carnegie-Mellon Univ. Retrieved on 23rd January 2015 from http://resources.sei.cmu.edu/asset_files/TechnicalReport/2007_005_001_14885.pdf

Carcary, M. (2013). IT risk management: A capability maturity model perspective. *Electronic Journal Information Systems Evaluation, 16,* 3–13.

Carlo, J. L., Lyytinen, K., & Rose, G. M. (2011). Internet computing as a disruptive information technology innovation: The role of strong order effects. *Information Systems Journal, 21*(1), 91–122. doi:10.1111/j.1365-2575.2009.00345.x

Castillo, M. (2016). *IBM Unveils New Cloud Blockchain Security Service.* Retrieved from http://www.coindesk.com

Caulkett, A., Rakshit, S., Lloyd, C., & Baxendale, C. (2012). *U.S. Patent Application 13/645,805.* Retrieved online on 23rd January 2015 from http://www.google.com/patents/US20130091061

Cavaleri, S., & Obloj, K. (1993). Management Systems: A Global Perspective. *Agile Project Management: Principles and Tools.*

Cavanagh, S. (1997). Content analysis: Concepts, methods and applications. *Nurse Researcher*, *4*(3), 5–16. PMID:27285770

CDM Media. (2015, April 21). *Protecting social media assets: lessons from CDM Media.* Retrieved from http://www.law360.com/articles/643290/protecting-social-media-assets-lessons-from-cdm-media

Chanda, R., & Zaorski, S. (2013, May/June). Social media usage in Financial Service Industry: Toward a Business-Driven compliance approach. *Journal of Taxation and Regulation of Financial Institution*, *26*(5), 5–20.

Chang, V., Kuo, Y. H., & Ramachandran, M. (2016). Cloud computing adoption framework: A security framework for business clouds. *Future Generation Computer Systems*, *57*, 24–41. doi:10.1016/j.future.2015.09.031

Charleston, R. (2016, May 9). *ERP Implementation Approaches: Waterfall vs. Agile.* Retrieved from https://www.handshake.com/blog/erp-implementation/

Chen, H., Li, J., Hoang, T., & Lou, X. (2013). *Security challenges of BYOD: a security education, training and awareness perspective.* Academic Press.

Cheng, L., Li, Y., Li, W., Holm, E., & Zhai, Q. (2013). Understanding the violation of IS security policy in organizations: An integrated model based on social control and deterrence theory. *Computers & Security*, *39*, 447–459. doi:10.1016/j.cose.2013.09.009

Chen, Y.-H., Wang, T.-C., & Wu, C.-Y. (2011). Strategic decisions using the fuzzy PROMETHEE for IS outsourcing. *Expert Systems with Applications*, *38*(10), 13216–13222. doi:10.1016/j.eswa.2011.04.137

Chen, Y., Ramamurthy, K., & Wen, K. W. (2012). Organizations information security policy compliance: Stick or carrot approach? *Journal of Management Information Systems*, *29*(3), 157–188. doi:10.2753/MIS0742-1222290305

Chi, E. H., & Pirolli, P. (2006). *Social Information Foraging and Collaborative Search.* Human Computer Interaction Consortium.

Chou, D. C., & Chou, A. Y. (2009). Information systems outsourcing life cycle and risks analysis. *Computer Standards & Interfaces*, *31*(5), 1036–1043. doi:10.1016/j.csi.2008.09.032

Christensen, C. M., Baumann, H., Ruggles, R., & Sadtler, T. M. (2007). Disruptive Innovation for Social Change. In *Harvard Business Review* (pp. 136–136). Harvard Business School Publication Corp.

Chujiao, W. & Guoyuan, L. (2006). The Model of Network Security Risk Assess Based on Fuzzy Algorithm and Hierarchy. *Journal of Wuhan University (Natural Science Edition)*, *5*, 24.

Cisco. (2014, April). *Cisco Social Media Policy*. Retrieved from http://www.slideshare.net/Cisco/cisco-global-social-media-policy

Clark, K. (n.d.). *How HIPAA Final Rules Affect Health Information Technology Vendors*. Retrieved from http://www.duanemorris.com/articles/static/clark_bilimoria_jmpm_0713.pdf

Claver, E., Gonzalez, R., Gasco, J., & Llopis, J. (2002). Information systems outsourcing: Reasons, reservations and success factors. *Logistics Information Management, 15*(4), 294–308. doi:10.1108/09576050210436138

Cloud Security Alliance. (2010). *Cloud Audit Working Group*. Retrieved online on December 15, 2016 from https://cloudsecurityalliance.org/group/cloudaudit/

Cloud Security Alliance. (2016). *The Treacherous 12*. Retrieved online on December 15, 2016 from https://downloads.cloudsecurityalliance.org/assets/research/top-threats/Treacherous-12_Cloud-Computing_Top-Threats.pdf

CMS & HHS. (2008). *Selecting a development approach*. Centers for Medicare and Medicaid Services Research Publication. Retrieved from https://www.cms.gov/research-statistics-data-and-systems/cms-information-technology/xlc/downloads/selectingdevelopmentapproach.pdf

COBRA. (2003). *Introduction to Security Risk Analysis*. Retrieved August 12, 2015, from http://www.security-risk-analysis.com/

Coburn, A. (2010). Fitting PCI DSS within a wider governance framework. *Computer Fraud & Security, 2010*(9), 11-13. Retrieved Online on January 22, 2015 from http://www.sciencedirect.com/science/article/pii/S1361372310701214

Cockburn, A. (2002). Agile software development. *Computer, 34*(9).

Cockburn, A., & Highsmith, J. (2001). Agile software development, the people factor. *Computer, 131-133*. doi:10.1109/2.963450

Coke. (2016). *Social Media Principles*. Retrieved from http://www.coca-colacompany.com/stories/online-social-media-principles/

Committee for Oversight and Assessment of U.S. Department of Energy Project Management, Board on Infrastructure and the Constructed Environment, Division on Engineering and Physical Sciences. (2005). Risk identification and analysis: The owner's role in project risk management. The National Academies Press.

Console. (2016). Console Inc. Retrieved online on December 15, 2016 from https://www.console.to/

Cooper, C. (2016). *Fixing the weakest link in cloud security*. Retrieved online on December 15, 2016 from http://mspmentor.net/cloud-services/fixing-weakest-link-cloud-security

Cooper. (2007). *Risk Management, Reporting and Governance*. Broadleaf Capital International.

Coronges, K., Dodge, R., Mukina, C., Radwick, Z., Shevchik, J., & Rovira, E. (2012, January). The influences of social networks on phishing vulnerability. In *System Science (HICSS), 2012 45th Hawaii International Conference on* (pp. 2366-2373). IEEE. doi:10.1109/HICSS.2012.657

Cottmeyer, M. (2014, July 24). *Agile is Risk Management*. Retrieved from https://www.leadingagile. com/2008/05/agile-is-risk-management/

Cox, J. (2012). Information systems user security: A structured model of the knowing–doing gap. *Computers in Human Behavior, 28*(5), 1849–1858. doi:10.1016/j.chb.2012.05.003

Coyle, S., & Conboy, K. (2009). A case study of risk management in agile systems development. *17th European Conference on Information Systems*, 2567-2578.

Crossler, R. E., Johnston, A. C., Lowry, P. B., Hu, Q., Warkentin, M., & Baskerville, R. (2013). Future directions for behavioral information security research. *Computers & Security, 32*, 90-101.

Culnan, M. J., & Williams, C. C. (2009). How ethics can enhance organizational privacy: Lessons from the choicepoint and TJX data breaches. *Management Information Systems Quarterly*, 673–687.

Da Veiga, A., & Martins, N. (2015). Improving the information security culture through monitoring and implementation actions illustrated through a case study. *Computers & Security, 49*, 162–176. doi:10.1016/j.cose.2014.12.006

Dahbur, K., Mohammad, B., & Tarakji, A. B. (2011, April). A survey of risks, threats and vulnerabilities in cloud computing. In *Proceedings of the 2011 International conference on intelligent semantic Web-services and applications* (p. 12). ACM. doi:10.1145/1980822.1980834

Dai, F., Hu, Y., Zheng, K., & Wu, B. (2015). Exploring risk flow attack graph for security risk assessment. *International Journal of IET Information Security, 9*(6), 344–353. doi:10.1049/iet-ifs.2014.0272

De Haes, S., Van Grembergen, W., & Debreceny, R. S. (2013). COBIT 5 and Enterprise Governance of Information Technology: Building Blocks and Research Opportunities. *Journal of Information Systems, 27*.

Debreceny, R. (2013). Research on IT governance, risk, and value: Challenges and Opportunities. *Journal of Information Systems, 27*(1), 129–135. doi:10.2308/isys-10339

Dell. (2011, August 15). *Dell: Global Social Media Policy*. Retrieved from http://www.dell.com/learn/us/en/uscorp1/corp-comm/social-media-policy

Deloitte. (2016). *2016 EMEA Financial Services IT Risk Management Survey*. Retrieved online on January 30, 2017, from https://www2.deloitte.com/content/dam/Deloitte/ch/Documents/risk/ch-en-it-risk-management-survey-16.pdf

Deloitte. (2016). *Data privacy in the cloud Navigating the new privacy regime in a cloud environment*. Retrieved online on December 15, 2016 from http://www.wsj.com/articles/amazon-cloud-computing-division-unveils-new-cyber-security-service-1480620359

Dhar, S., & Balakrishnan, B. (2006). Risks, benefits, and challenges in global IT outsourcing: Perspectives and practices. *Journal of Global Information Management, 14*(3), 39–69. doi:10.4018/jgim.2006070104

Digital Guardian. (2014). *An Expert Guide to Securing Sensitive Data: 34 Experts Reveal the Biggest Mistakes Companies Make with Data Security.* Retrieved on 10th November 2014 from https://digitalguardian.com/blog/expert-guide-securing-sensitive-data-34-experts-reveal-biggest-mistakes-companies-make-data

Dinev, T., & Hart, P. (2006). An Extended Privacy Calculus Model for E-Commerce Transactions. *Information Systems Research, 17*(1), 61-80.

Dorey, P. G., & Leite, A. (2011). Commentary: Cloud computing–A security problem or solution?. *Information Security Technical Report, 16*(3), 89-96.

Duara, N. (2012, March 8). *Ore. Nurse Aide Posted Facebook Photos of Patients.* Retrieved from cnsnews.com/news/article/ore-nurse-aide-posted-facebook-photos-patients-2

Dutt, V., Ahn, Y. S., & Gonzalez, C. (2011, July). Cyber situation awareness: Modeling the security analyst in a cyber-attack scenario through instance-based learning. In *IFIP Annual Conference on Data and Applications Security and Privacy* (pp. 280-292). Springer Berlin Heidelberg. doi:10.1007/978-3-642-22348-8_24

Dwyer, S. (n.d.). *Health Insurance Portability and Accountability Act.* Academic Press.

Editor's Choice. (2011, March 31). *Abusive Facebook comments led to pub shift manager's dismissal.* Retrieved from http://www.xperthr.co.uk/editors-choice/abusive-facebook-comments-led-to-pub-shift-managers-dismissal/108662/

Elhasnaoui, S., Medromi, H., Faris, S., Iguer, H., & Sayouti, A. (2014). Designing a Multi Agent System Architecture for IT Governance Platform. *International Journal of Advanced Computer Science and Applications.*

Elky, S. (2006). An Introduction to Information System Risk Management. SANS Institute.

Eminağaoğlu, M., Uçar, E., & Eren, Ş. (2009). The positive outcomes of information security awareness training in companies–A case study. *Information Security Technical Report, 14*(4), 223-229.

Eminagaoglu, M., Ucar, E., & Eren, S. (2010). The positive outcomes of information security awareness training in companies – a case study. *Information Security Technical Report, 4*, 1–7.

Endicott-Popovsky, B., Hinrichs, R. J., & Frincke, D. (2013, July). Leveraging 2 nd life as a communications media: An effective tool for security awareness training. In *IEEE International Professional Communication 2013 Conference* (pp. 1-7). IEEE.

ENISA. (2009). *Cloud Computing: Benefits, Risks and Recommendations for Information Security.* Retrieved online on January 6, 2017 from: http://www.enisa.europa.eu/act/rm/files/deliverables/cloud-computing-risk-assessment

ENISA. (2014a). *Making the cloud more transparent - a boost for secure, trustworthy services.* ENISA.

ENISA. (2014b). *Exploring Cloud Incidents.* Retrieved online on December 15, 2016 from https://www.enisa.europa.eu/publications/exploring-cloud-incidents

Exploration System Mission Directorate. (2007). *Exploration Systems, Risk Management Plan.* ESMD-RMP-04.06 Rev 2 (3-12). NASA.

Fagerberg, J. (2005). Innovation: a guide to the literature. In J. Fagerberg, D. C. Mowery, & R. R. Nelson (Eds.), *The Oxford Handbook of Innovation* (pp. 1–26). New York: Oxford University Press.

Fan, Z.-P., Suo, W.-L., & Feng, B. (2012). Identifying risk factors of IT outsourcing using interdependent information: An extended DEMATEL method. *Expert Systems with Applications*, *39*(3), 3832–3840. doi:10.1016/j.eswa.2011.09.092

Farah, B. (2011). A maturity model for the management of information technology risk. International Journal of Technology. *Knowledge in Society*, *7*(1), 13–25.

Feltus, C., Petit, M., & Dubois, E. (2009). Strengthening Employee's Responsibility to Enhance Governance of IT – COBIT RACI Chart Case Study. *Proceedings of the first ACM workshop on Information security governance.* doi:10.1145/1655168.1655174

Feng, N., Wang, H. J., & Li, M. (2013). A security risk analysis model for information systems: Causal relationships of risk factors and vulnerability propagation analysis. *International Journal of Information Sciences.*, *256*, 57–73. doi:10.1016/j.ins.2013.02.036

Fink, J. (June 14, 2010). *Five Nurses Fired for Facebook Postings.* Retrieved from www.scrubsmag.com/five-nurses-fired-for-facebook-postings/

Firstdata.com. (2014). *Smart Card Alliance Brief.* Retrieved from http://www.firstdata.com/smarticles/fi/home/preventing-data-breaches.html

Flores, W. R., & Ekstedt, M. (2016). Shaping intention to resist social engineering through transformational leadership, information security culture and awareness. *Computers & Security*, *59*, 26–44. doi:10.1016/j.cose.2016.01.004

Fontela, E., & Gabus, A. (1976). *The DEMATEL observer, DEMATEL 1976 report.* Geneva, Switzerland: Battelle Geneva Research Centre.

Frank, B. (2016). *Amazon Quietly Launches tools for migrating on premise apps to cloud.* Retrieved online on December 15, 2016 from http://www.pcworld.com/article/3135060/cloud-computing/aws-quietly-launches-tool-for-migrating-on-premesis-apps-to-the-cloud.html

Furnell, S., & Clarke, N. (2012). Power to the people? The evolving recognition of human aspects of security. *Computers & Security, 31*(8), 983-988.

Fu, S., Liu, Z., Sun, G., Zhou, H., & Liu, W. (2015). Study on Security Risk Assessment for Information System Based on Fuzzy Set and Entropy Theory. *International Journal of Software Engineering, 9*(4), 818–827. doi:10.3923/jse.2015.818.827

Gabus, A., & Fontela, E. (1972). *World problems, an invitation to further thought within the framework of DEMATEL.* Geneva, Switzerland: Battelle Geneva Research Centre.

Gabus, A., & Fontela, E. (1973). *Perceptions of the world problematic: Communication procedure, communicating with those bearing collective responsibility, (DEMATEL report no. 1).* Geneva, Switzerland: Battelle Geneva Research Centre.

Gamble, M. (2013, August 13). *15 Things to Know About the HIPAA Omnibus Final Rule Before Sept. 23.* Retrieved from http://www.beckershospitalreview.com/legal-regulatory-issues/15-things-to-know-about-the-hipaa-omnibus-final-rule-before-sept-23.html

Gangadharbatla, H. (2008). Facebook me: Collective self-esteem, need to belong, and Internet self-efficacy as predictors of the Igenerations attitudes toward social networking sites. *Journal of Interactive Advertising, 8*(2), 5–15. doi:10.1080/15252019.2008.10722138

Gao, J., Bai, X., & Tsai, W. T. (2011). Cloud testing-issues, challenges, needs and practice. *Software Engineering: An International Journal, 1*(1), 9–23.

Garfield, S. (n.d.). *Point-of-Sale Malware: Why Today's Top Retailers Are Vulnerable to Attacks.* Retrieved Online on January 22, 2015 from http://tuftsdev.github.io/DefenseOfTheDarkArts/students_works/final_project/fall2014/sgarfield.pdf

Gelms, J. (2012). High-tech Harassment: Employer Liability under Title VII for Employee Social Media Misconduct. *Washington Law Review (Seattle, Wash.), 87*(1), 249–279.

Geneva, L. (2009). *Nurses fired Over Cell Photos of a patient.* Retrieved from http://www.wisn.com/Nurses-Fired-Over-Cell-Phone-Photos-Of-Patient/8076340/

Ghazouani, M., Faris, S., Medromi, H., & Sayouti, A. (2014). Information Security Risk Assessment - A Practical Approach with a Mathematical Formulation of Risk. International Journal of Computer Applications, 103(8).

Gilbert, C. (2005). Unbundling the structure of inertia: Resource versus routine rigidity. *Academy of Management Journal, 48*(5), 741–763. doi:10.5465/AMJ.2005.18803920

Gill, M. (2012). IT risk is business risk. *COBIT Focus, 2*, 10–11.

Glaser, B., & Strauss, A. (1967). *The Discovery of Grounded Theory: Strategies for Qualitative Research.* Chicago, IL: Aldine Publishing Company.

Goldman, S. L., Nagel, R. N., & Preiss, K. (1995). *Agile competitors and virtual organizations: strategies for enriching the customer.* New York: Van Nostrand Reinhold.

Gorge, M. (2006). The PCI standard and its implications for the security industry. *Computer Fraud & Security, 2006*(2), 6-9. Retrieved Online on January 22, 2015 from http://www.sciencedirect.com/science/article/pii/S1361372306703074

Gorge, M. (2008). Data protection: why are organisations still missing the point? *Computer Fraud & Security, 2008*(6), 5-8. Retrieved online on 23rd January 2015 from http://www.sciencedirect.com.gate.lib.buffalo.edu/science/article/pii/S1361372308700952

Grabski, S. V., Leach, S. A., & Lu, B. (2001). Risks and Controls in the Implementation of ERP Systems. *The International Journal of Digital Accounting Research*. doi:10.4192/1577-8517-v1_3

Grant, A. M. (2007). Relational Job Design and the Motivation to Make a Prosocial Difference. *Academy of Management Review, 32*(2), 393-417.

Grant, A. M. (2008). Does Intrinsic Motivation Fuel the Prosocial Fire? Motivational Synergy in Predicting Persistence, Performance, and Productivity. *Journal of Applied Psychology, 93*(1), 48.

Gray, P. H., Parise, S., & Iyer, B. (2011). Innovation Impacts of Using Social Bookmarking Systems. *MIS Quarterly, 35*(3), 629-643.

Greene, J., & Stevens, L. (2016). Amazon Cloud Computing Division Unveils New Cyber Security Service. *Wall Street Journal*. Retrieved online on December 15, 2016 from http://www.wsj.com/articles/amazon-cloud-computing-division-unveils-new-cyber-security-service-1480620359

Greene, T. (2015). *SANS: 20 critical security controls you need to add*. Retrieved online on December 15, 2016 from http://www.networkworld.com/article/2992503/security/sans-20-critical-security-controls-you-need-to-add.html

Grover, V., Fiedler, K., & Teng, J. (1997). Empirical evidence on Swansons tri-core model of information systems innovation. *Information Systems Research, 8*(3), 273–287. doi:10.1287/isre.8.3.273

Gundu, T., & Flowerday, S. V. (2013). Ignorance to awareness: Towards an information security awareness process. *SAIEE Africa Research Journal, 104*(2), 69–79.

Guzzo, R. A., Jackson, S. E., & Katzell, R. A. (1987). Meta-analysis Analysis. *Research in Organizational Behavior*, (9): 407–442.

Habiba, M., Islam, M. R., & Ali, A. S. (2013, July). Access control management for cloud. In *2013 12th IEEE International Conference on Trust, Security and Privacy in Computing and Communications* (pp. 485-492). doi:10.1109/TrustCom.2013.61

Haj Bakry, Saad, & Alfantookh. (2012). *IT-governance practices: COBIT*. Academic Press.

Halpert, B. (2011). *Auditing cloud computing: A security and privacy guide* (Vol. 21). John Wiley & Sons. doi:10.1002/9781118269091

Halpin, D. W., & Martinez, L.-H. (1999). Real-world Applications of Construction Process Simulation. *Proceedings of the 1999 Winter Simulation Conference.* Available online at http://www.informs-cs.org/wsc99papers/prog99.html

Hänsch, N., & Benenson, Z. (2014, September). Specifying IT security awareness. In *2014 25th International Workshop on Database and Expert Systems Applications* (pp. 326-330). IEEE. doi:10.1109/DEXA.2014.71

Hardesty, L. (2016). *IIX Reinvents Itself as Console.* Retrieved online on December 15, 2016 from https://www.sdxcentral.com/articles/news/iix-reinvents-itself-console/2016/05/

Hardy, G. (2006). Using IT governance and COBIT to deliver value with IT and respond to legal, regulatory and compliance challenges. *Information Security Technical Report, 11*(1), 55–61. doi:10.1016/j.istr.2005.12.004

Hargadon, A. (2003). *How breakthroughs happen: The surprising truth about how companies innovate.* Boston, MA: Harvard Business School Press.

Harran, M., & McKelvey, N. (2012). PCI Compliance–No excuses, please. *Proceedings from International Journal of Information and Network Security (IJINS), 2*(2), 118-123. Retrieved online on 23rd January 2015 from http://iaesjournal.com/online/index.php/IJINS/article/view/1940

Hartman, B. (2009). *New to Agile? What Does the ScrumMaster Do Anyway?.* Retrieved from http://agileforall.com/new-to-agile-what-does-the-scrummaster-do-anyway/

HB 436. (2004). *Handbook Risk Management Guidelines.* Standards Australia International Ltd.

Heiser, J., & Nicolett, M. (2008). *Assessing the security risks of cloud computing.* Stamford, CT: Gartner Research. Retrieved online on January 6, 2017 from http://www.globalcloudbusiness.com/SharedFiles/Download.aspx?pageid=138&mid=220&fileid=12

Heroux, S., & Fortin, A. (2013). The internal audit function in information technology governance: A holistic perspective. *Journal of Information Systems, 27*(1), 189–217. doi:10.2308/isys-50331

Herrera, F., & Martínez, L. (2000). A 2-tuple fuzzy linguistic representation model for computing with words. *IEEE Transactions on Fuzzy Systems, 8*(6), 746–752. doi:10.1109/91.890332

Herrera, F., & Martínez, L. (2001). A model based on linguistic 2-tuples for dealing with multigranular hierarchical linguistic contexts in multi-expert decision making. *IEEE Transactions on Systems, Man, and Cybernetics. Part B, Cybernetics, 31*(2), 227–234. doi:10.1109/3477.915345 PMID:18244784

Hidy, K. M., & McDonald, M. S. E. (2013). Risky business: The legal implications of social media's increasing role in employment decisions. *Journal of Legal Studies in Business, 18,* 69–88.

Highsmith, J. (2003). *Agile Project Management: Principles and Tools.* Academic Press.

Highsmith, J. A. (2002). *Agile software development ecosystems.* Boston: Addison-Wesley.

Highsmith, J., & Cockburn, A. (2001). Agile software development: The business of innovation. *Computer, 34*(9), 120–127. doi:10.1109/2.947100

HIPAA and Health Privacy: Myths and Facts Part 2. (2009). Retrieved from https://www.cdt.org/files/healthprivacy/20090109mythsfacts2.pdf

HIPAA Background. (2010). Retrieved from http://hipaa.bsd.uchicago.edu/background.html

HIPAA Compliance Checklist. (n.d.). Retrieved from http://www.hipaajournal.com/hipaa-compliance-checklist/

HIPAA Privacy Rule and Its Impacts on Research. (n.d.). Retrieved from https://privacyruleandresearch.nih.gov/pr_06.asp

HITECH Act Summary. (n.d.). Retrieved from http://www.hipaasurvivalguide.com/hitech-act-summary.php

Hizver, J., & Chiueh, T. (2011). Automated Discovery of Credit Card Data Flow for PCI DSS Compliance. *Proceedings of 30th IEEE International Symposium on Reliable Distributed Systems.* Retrieved online on 23rd January 2015 from http://www.inf.ufpr.br/aldri/disc/TSD/2012/2012_TSD_Apre_Artigos/Gustavo_02_SRDS11_Automated.pdf

Hogganvik, I., & Stølen, K. (2006). Lecture Notes in Computer Science: Vol. 4199. A Graphical Approach to Risk Identification, Motivated by Empirical Investigations. Springer. doi:10.1007/11880240_40

Hohmann, J., & The 2010-11 ASNE Ethics and Values Committee. (2011, May). *ASNE 10 Best practices for Social media - helpful guidelines for news organization.* Retrieved from http://asne.org/Files/pdf/10_Best_Practices_for_Social_Media.pdf

Holler, R. (n.d.). *Five Myths of Agile Development.* Retrieved from http://www.versionone.com/pdf/AgileMyths_BetterSoftware.pdf

Hollon, J. (2012, October 3). *Survey: 75% of Workers are accessing social media while on the job.* Retrieved from: http://www.eremedia.com/tlnt/survey-75-of-workers-are-accessing-social-media-while-on-the-job/ on April 30, 2016

Hosack, B. (2011). Businesses still unaware of risks of account data compromise. *Computer Fraud & Security, 2011*(1), 17-19. Retrieved online on 23rd January 2015 from http://www.sciencedirect.com/science/article/pii/S1361372311700070

Hosmer, D. W., Lemeshow, S., & Cook, E. (2000). *Applied Logistic Regression* (2nd ed.). John Wiley & Sons. doi:10.1002/0471722146

Ho, W., He, T., Lee, C. K. M., & Emrouznejad, A. (2012). Strategic logistics outsourcing: An integrated QFD and fuzzy AHP approach. *Expert Systems with Applications, 39*(12), 10841–10850. doi:10.1016/j.eswa.2012.03.009

Howell, J. (1999). Research and technology outsourcing. *Technology Analysis and Strategic Management, 11*(1), 17–29. doi:10.1080/095373299107555

Hsu, C.-C., Liou, J. J. H., & Chuang, Y.-C. (2013). Integrating DANP and modified grey relation theory for the selection of an outsourcing provider. *Expert Systems with Applications, 40*(6), 2297–2304. doi:10.1016/j.eswa.2012.10.040

Hsu, C.-I., Chiu, C., & Hsu, P.-L. (2004). Predicting information systems outsourcing success using a hierarchical design of case-based reasoning. *Expert Systems with Applications, 26*(3), 435–441. doi:10.1016/j.eswa.2003.10.002

Hsu, P. F., & Hsu, M. G. (2008). Optimizing the information outsourcing practices of primary care medical organizations using entropy and TOPSIS. *Quality & Quantity, 42*(2), 181–201. doi:10.1007/s11135-006-9040-8

Huang, Z., Zavarsky, P., & Ruhl, R. (2009). An Efficient Framework for IT Controls of Bill 198 (Canada Sarbanes-Oxley) Compliance by Aligning COBIT 4.1, ITIL v3 and ISO/IEC 27002. *2009 International Conference on Computational Science and Engineering.* doi:10.1109/CSE.2009.336

Hunton, A., & Wright, S. (2001). *Business and audit risks associated with ERP systems: knowledge differences between information systems audit specialists and financial auditors.* Academic Press.

Hu, Q., Dinev, T., Hart, P., & Cooke, D. (2012). Managing employee compliance with information security policies: The critical role of top management and organizational culture. *Decision Sciences, 43*(4), 615–660. doi:10.1111/j.1540-5915.2012.00361.x

Hussain, S. J., & Siddiqui, M. S. (2005). Quantified Model of COBIT for Corporate IT Governance. *1st International Conference on Information and Communication technologies.* doi:10.1109/ICICT.2005.1598575

Hwang, C. L., & Yoon, K. (1981). *Multiple attributes decision making methods and applications.* Berlin: Springer. doi:10.1007/978-3-642-48318-9

IBM. (2010). *IBM Social Computing Guidelines.* Retrieved from https://www.ibm.com/blogs/zz/en/guidelines.html

Ibrahim, N. (2014). IT Audit 101. *Internal Auditor, 71*(3), 19–21.

IEC/FDIS. (2009). *Risk management — Risk assessment techniques. IEC/FDIS 31010.* Final Draft.

Ifinedo, P. (2012). Understanding information systems security policy compliance: An integration of the theory of planned behavior and the protection motivation theory. *Computers & Security, 31*(1), 83–95. doi:10.1016/j.cose.2011.10.007

Ifinedo, P. (2014). Information systems security policy compliance: An empirical study of the effects of socialisation, influence, and cognition. *Information & Management, 51*(1), 69–79. doi:10.1016/j.im.2013.10.001

Imgraben, J., Engelbrecht, A., & Choo, K. K. R. (2014). Always connected, but are smart mobile users getting more security savvy? A survey of smart mobile device users. *Behaviour & Information Technology, 33*(12), 1347–1360. doi:10.1080/0144929X.2014.934286

Information Technology and HIPAA. (n.d.). Retrieved from http://www.ct.gov/dph/lib/dph/ohca/hospitalstudy/it&hipaa.pdf

Intel. (n.d.). *Intel Social Media Guidelines*. Retrieved from http://www.intel.com/content/www/us/en/legal/intel-social-media-guidelines.html

ISACA. (2009). *The Risk IT frameworks, Principles Process Details Management Guidelines Maturity Models. Risk IT based on COBIT*. ISACA.

ISACA. (2010). *Social media: Business benefits and Security, governance and Assurance perspective*. Retrieved from: http://www.isaca.org/groups/professional-english/security-trend/groupdocuments/social-media-wh-paper-26-may10-research.pdf

ISO/FDIS ISO TMBWG on risk management. (2009). *Risk Management - Principles and guidelines, ISO/FDIS 31000:2009, ISO/FDIS*.

ISO/IEC JTC 1 IT SC 27. (2011). *Information technology – Security techniques - Information security risk management, ISO/IEC 27005:2011, ISO/IEC*.

ISO/IEC JTC 1 IT SC 27. (2014). *Information technology – Security techniques - Information security management systems – Overview and vocabulary, ISO/IEC 27000:2014, ISO/IEC*.

IT Governance Institute. (2008). Information security governance: guidance for information security managers. ITGI Publishing.

Jackson, R. (2012). Facing IT risk head - on. *Internal Auditor, 69*(4), 36–42.

Jacobson, W. S., & Tufts, S. H. (2013). To Post or Not to Post: Employee Rights and Social Media. *Review of Public Personnel Administration, 33*(1), 84–107. doi:10.1177/0734371X12443265

Jaeger, L., & Eckhardt, A. (2016). *A neurosecurity perspective on the formation of information security awareness–Proposing a multi-method approach*. Academic Press.

Jain, A. K., & Shanbhag, D. (2012). Addressing Security and Privacy Risks in Mobile Applications. *IT Professional, 14*(5), 28–33. doi:10.1109/MITP.2012.72

Jakoubi, S., Tjoa, S., Goluch, S., & Kitzler, G. (2010). Risk-Aware Business Process Management—Establishing the Link Between Business and Security. In *Book of Complex Intelligent Systems and Their Applications*. Springer Science+Business Media.

Jansson, K., & von Solms, R. (2013). Phishing for phishing awareness. *Behaviour & Information Technology, 32*(6), 584–593. doi:10.1080/0144929X.2011.632650

Jennings, S. E., Blount, J. R., & Gail Weatherly, M. (2014). Social Media – A Virtual Pandoras Box: Prevalence, Possible Legal Liabilities, and Policies. *Business and Professional Communication Quarterly, 77*(1), 96–113. doi:10.1177/2329490613517132

Jet. (2016). *5 terrific examples of Company social media policies* [Web post log]. Retrieved from http://blog.hirerabbit.com/5-terrific-examples-of-company-social-media-policies/

Jiang, J. J., & Klein, G. (1999). Risks to different aspects of system success. *Information & Management, 36*(5), 263–272. doi:10.1016/S0378-7206(99)00024-5

Jones, L. B. (2013, Mar 28). *Best practice example: GAP Social Media Policy.* Retrieved from http://oursocialtimes.com/best-practice-example-gaps-social-media-policy/

Jurison, J. (1995). The role of risk and return in information technology outsourcing decisions. *Journal of Information Technology, 10*(4), 239–247. doi:10.1057/jit.1995.27

Kadam, Y. (2011). Security Issues in Cloud Computing A Transparent View. *International Journal of Computer Science Emerging Technology, 2*(5), 316–322.

Kähkönen, T., Smolander, K., & Maglyas, A. (2016). Lack of integration governance in ERP development: a case study on causes and effects. *Enterprise Information Systems*, 1-34. doi:10 .1080/17517575.2016.1179347

Kallas, C. S., Pravasi, N. I., Sievel, M. E., & Tokarski, J. P. (2009). *U.S. Patent Application 12/648,525.* Retrieved online on 23rd January 2015 from https://www.google.com/patents/US20110161231

Kaplinsky, R., Chataway, J., Clark, N., Hanlin, R., Kale, D., Muraguri, L, Papaioannou, T., Robbins, P. and Wamae, W. (2009). Below the radar: what does innovation in emerging economies have to offer other low-income economies? *International Journal Technology Management Sustenance Development, 8*(3), 177–197.

Karabacaka, B., & Sogukpinarb, I. (2005). ISRAM: Information security risk analysis method. *International Journal of Computers & Security, 24*(2), 147–159. doi:10.1016/j.cose.2004.07.004

Kassner, M. (2014). *Breach Detection Systems take aim at targeted persistent attacks.* Retrieved on 10th November 2014 from http://www.techrepublic.com/blog/it-security/breach-detection-systems-take-aim-at-targeted-persistent-attacks/

Kaufman, L. M. (2009). Data security in the world of cloud computing. *IEEE Security and Privacy, 7*(4), 61–64. doi:10.1109/MSP.2009.87

Kaupins, G., & Park, S. (2011). Legal and Ethical Implications of Corporate Social Networks. *Employee Responsibilities and Rights Journal, 23*(2), 83–99. doi:10.1007/s10672-010-9149-8

Kaya, O. (2011). Outsourcing vs. in-house production: A comparison of supply chain contracts with effort dependent demand. *Omega, 39*(2), 168–178. doi:10.1016/j.omega.2010.06.002

Keil, M., Cule, P. E., Lyytinen, K., & Schmidt, R. C. (1998). A framework for identifying software project risks. *Communications of the ACM, 41*(11), 76–83. doi:10.1145/287831.287843

Kepes, B. (2016). *CloudVelox offers automated cloud network customizations.* Retrieved online on December 15, 2016 from http://www.networkworld.com/article/3142742/cloud-computing/cloudvelox-offers-automated-cloud-network-customizations.html

Kerr, D. S., & Murthy, U. S. (2013). *The importance of COBIT framework IT processes for effective internal control over financial reporting in organizations: An international survey. Information and Management Journal.*

Khanmohammadi, K., & Houmb, S. H. (2010). Business Process-based Information Security Risk Assessment. *Proceedings of the 4th International Conference on Network and System Security,* 199-206.

Kidd, R. (2008). Counting the cost of non-compliance with PCI DSS. *Computer Fraud & Security, 2008*(11), 13-14. Retrieved online on 23rd January 2015 from http://www.sciencedirect.com.gate.lib.buffalo.edu/science/article/pii/S1361372308701635

Kim, Y. J., Lee, J. M., Koo, C., & Nam, K. (2013). The role of governance effectiveness in explaining IT outsourcing performance. *International Journal of Information Management, 33*(5), 850–860. doi:10.1016/j.ijinfomgt.2013.07.003

King, W. R., & He, J. (2005). Understanding the Role and Methods of Meta-Analysis in IS Research. *Communications of the Association for Information Systems,* (16), 665–686.

Kirby & Raphan. (2014). The NLRB's Continued Regulation of Social Media in the Workplace. *Journal of Internet Law, 18*(2), 13–17.

Kirlappos, I., & Sasse, M. A. (2012). Security education against phishing: A modest proposal for a major rethink. *IEEE Security and Privacy Magazine, 10*(2), 24–32. doi:10.1109/MSP.2011.179

Ko, R. K., Jagadpramana, P., Mowbray, M., Pearson, S., Kirchberg, M., Liang, Q., & Lee, B. S. (2011, July). TrustCloud: A framework for accountability and trust in cloud computing. In *2011 IEEE World Congress on Services* (pp. 584-588). doi:10.1109/SERVICES.2011.91

Korpela, K. (2015). Improving cyber security awareness and training programs with data analytics. *Information Security Journal: A Global Perspective, 24*(1-3), 72-77.

Kotzanikolaou, P., Theoharidou, M., & Gritzalis, D. (2013). Interdependencies between Critical Infrastructures: Analyzing the Risk of Cascading Effects. *Proceedings of the CRITIS 2011,* 104–115. doi:10.1007/978-3-642-41476-3_9

Kou, Y.-C., & Lu, S.-T. (2013). Using fuzzy multiple criteria decision making approach to enhance risk assessment for metropolitan construction projects. *International Journal of Project Management, 31*(4), 602–614. doi:10.1016/j.ijproman.2012.10.003

Kraut, R., Patterson, M., Lundmark, V., Kiesler, S., Mukophadhyay, T., & Scherlis, W. (1998). Internet Paradox: A Social Technology That Reduces Social Involvement and Psychological Well-Being?. *American Psychologist, 53*(9), 1017.

Krebs on Security. (2014). *The Target Breach, By the Numbers*. Retrieved online on 10th November from http://krebsonsecurity.com/2014/05/the-target-breach-by-the-numbers/#more-25847

Krebs, B. (2012). *Global Payments Breach Window Expands*. Retrieved on 10th November 2014 from http://krebsonsecurity.com/tag/global-payments-breach/

Krebs, B. (2014a). *Home Depot Hit By Same Malware as Target*. Retrieved on 10th November 2014 from http://krebsonsecurity.com/tag/home-depot-breach/

Krebs, B. (2014b). *3 Million Customer Credit, Debit Cards Stolen in Michaels, Aaron Brothers Breaches*. Retrieved on 10th November 2014 from http://krebsonsecurity.com/2014/04/3-million-customer-credit-debit-cards-stolen-in-michaels-aaron-brothers-breaches/

Krebs, B. (2014c). *Breach at Goodwill Vendor Lasted 18 Months*. Retrieved online 10th October January from http://krebsonsecurity.com/2014/09/breach-at-goodwill-vendor-lasted-18-months/

Krebsonsecurity.com. (2014). *Staples: 6-Month Breach, 1.16 Million Cards*. Retrieved online on 22nd January from http://krebsonsecurity.com/2014/12/staples-6-month-breach-1-16-million-cards-

Kremzar, M. H., & Wallace, T. F. (2001). *ERP: Making It Happen: The Implementers' Guide to Success with Enterprise Resource Planning*. New York: John Wiley & Sons, Inc.

Kroes, N. (2014). *Making the cloud more transparent - a boost for secure, trustworthy services*. Retrieved online on December 15, 2016 from http://ec.europa.eu.gate.lib.buffalo.edu/commission_2010-2014/kroes/en/content/making-cloud-more-transparent-boost-secure-trustworthy-services

Krueger, C. (2002). Eliminating the adoption barrier. *IEEE Software*, *19*(4), 29–31. doi:10.1109/MS.2002.1020284

Kruger, H. A., & Kearney, W. D. (2006). A prototype for assessing information security awareness. *Computers & Security*, *25*(4), 289–296. doi:10.1016/j.cose.2006.02.008

Kumaraguru, P. (2007). Protecting people from phishing: the design and evaluation of an embedded training email system. In *Proceedings of the computer human interaction (CHI 2007)*. New York, NY: ACM Press. doi:10.1145/1240624.1240760

Kureva, G., Loock, M., & Kritzinger, E. (2014). *Towards addressing Information Security Awareness through Internet Service Providers*. Academic Press.

Kwang, T. W. (2016). *Cloud technology for public sector innovation*. Retrieved online on December 15, 2016 from http://www.enterpriseinnovation.net/article/cloud-technology-public-sector-innovation-2130602017

Labuschagne, W. A., & Eloff, M. (2014, July). The Effectiveness of Online Gaming as Part of a Security Awareness Program. *13th European Conference on Cyber Warfare and Security ECCWS-2014*, 125.

Lambert, J. H., Jennings, R. K., & Joshi, N. N. (2006). Integration of Risk Identification with Business Process Models. *International Journal of Systems Engineering, 9*(3), 187–198. doi:10.1002/sys.20054

Latifi, F., Ramin, N., & Mohsenzadeh, M. (2014). Enriched eTOM Framework in Service Deliver Operation through Alignment with some of COBIT5 Strategic Objectives. *International Journal of Digital Information and Wireless Communications, 4*(1), 35–42. doi:10.17781/P001081

Lauby, S. (2009, June 02). *10 Must-Haves for your social media policy* [Web post log]. Retrieved from: http://mashable.com/2009/06/02/social-media-policy-musts/#225temiNmaqO

Lau, L. (2003). Developing a successful implementation plan for ERP: Issues and challenges. *Proceedings of the International Association for Computer Information Systems*, 223-229.

Lee, J. N., & Kim, Y. G. (2005). Understanding outsourcing partnership: A comparison of three theoretical perspectives. *IEEE Transactions on Engineering Management, 52*(1), 43–57. doi:10.1109/TEM.2004.839958

Lee, M. C. (2014). Information Security Risk Analysis Methods and Research Trends: AHP and Fuzzy Comprehensive Method. *International Journal of Computer Science & Information Technology, 6*(1). doi:10.5121/ijcsit.2014.6103

Leinwand, A. (2016). *Transparency in the cloud or the lack of thereof*. Retrieved online on December 15, 2016 from http://cloudtweaks.com/2016/11/transparency-cloud/

Lemus, S. M., Pino, F. J., & Velthius, M. P. (2010). Towards a Model for Information Technology Governance applicable to the Banking Sector. *5th Iberian Conference on Information Systems and Technologies*.

Levinthal, D. A., & March, J. G. (1993). The myopia of learning. *Strategic Management Journal, 14*(S2), 95–112. doi:10.1002/smj.4250141009

Leyva, C. (2013, February 3). *HIPAA Omnibus Rule Summary*. Retrieved from http://www.hipaasurvivalguide.com/hipaa-omnibus-rule.php

Li, D.-F., & Wan, S.-P. (2014). Fuzzy heterogeneous multiattribute decision making method for outsourcing provider selection. *Expert Systems with Applications, 41*(6), 3047–3059. doi:10.1016/j.eswa.2013.10.036

Lieberman. (2016a). *Lieberman Software to Present Cloud Security Session at Gartner Identity and Access*. Retrieved online on December 15, 2016 from http://www.marketwired.com/press-release/lieberman-software-present-cloud-security-session-gartner-identity-access-management-2178865.htm

Lieberman. (2016b). *Enterprise Random Password Manager*. Retrieved online on December 15, 2016 from https://liebsoft.com/products/Enterprise_Random_Password_Manager/

Lin, C. J., & Wu, W. W. (2008). A causal analytical method for group decision-making under fuzzy environment. *Expert Systems with Applications, 34*(1), 205–213. doi:10.1016/j.eswa.2006.08.012

Lindell, M. K., & Whitney, D. J. (2001). Accounting for Common Method Variance in Cross-Sectional Research Designs. *Journal of Applied Psychology, 86*(1), 114.

Lindenbaum, J., Healton, E. B., Savage, D. G., Brust, J. C., Garrett, T. J., Podell, E. R., ... Allen, R. H. (1988). Neuropsychiatric Disorders Caused by Cobalamin Deficiency in the Absence of Anemia or Macrocytosis. *New England Journal of Medicine, 318*(26), 1720-1728.

Linder, J. G. (2004). *Outsourcing for radical change: A bold approach to enterprise transformation.* New York: AMACOM.

Lin, Y. T., Lin, C. L., Yu, H. C., & Tzeng, G. H. (2010). A novel hybrid MCDM approach for outsourcing vendor selection: A case study for a semiconductor company in Taiwan. *Expert Systems with Applications, 37*(7), 4796–4804. doi:10.1016/j.eswa.2009.12.036

Liou, J. J. H., & Chuang, Y.-T. (2010). Developing a hybrid multi-criteria model for selection of outsourcing providers. *Expert Systems with Applications, 37*(5), 3755–3761. doi:10.1016/j.eswa.2009.11.048

Lo, C., & Chen, W. (2012). A hybrid information security risk assessment procedure considering interdependences between controls. *International Journal of Expert Systems with Applications, 39*(1), 247–257. doi:10.1016/j.eswa.2011.07.015

Lovrić, Z. (2012). *Model of Simplified Implementation of PCI DSS by Using ISO 27001 Standard.* Retrieved online on 23rd January 2015 from http://www.ceciis.foi.hr/app/public/conferences/1/papers2012/iss8.pdf

Mabert, V. A., Soni, A., & Venkataramanan, M. (2001). Enterprise resource planning: Common myths versus evolving reality. *Business Horizons, 44*(3), 69–76. doi:10.1016/S0007-6813(01)80037-9

MacCarthy, M. (2011). Information security policy in the US retail payments industry. *Stan. Tech. L. Rev., 2011,* 3-12. Retrieved online on 23rd January 2015 from http://www18.georgetown.edu/data/people/maccartm/publication-66522.pdf

Mahnic, V., & Zabkar, N. (2008). *Using COBIT indicators for measuring scrum-based software development.* 12th WSEAS International Conference on Computers, Heraklion, Greece.

Mangalraj, G., Singh, A., & Taneja, A. (2014). *IT Governance Frameworks and COBIT - A Literature Review.* Academic Press.

Manzo, J. (2003). Agile Development Methods, the Myths, and the Reality: A user perspective. *Proceedings, USC-CSE Agile Methods Workshop.* Retrieved from http://sunset.usc.edu/events/past

Margulis, S. T. (1977). Conceptions of Privacy: Current Status and Next Steps. *Journal of Social Issues, 33*(3), 5-21.

Marken, G. A. (2007). Social Media . . . The Hunted can Become the Hunter. *Public Relations Quarterly, 52*(4), 9–12.

Marrone, M., Hoffmann, L., & Kolbe, L. M. (2010). *IT Executives' Perception of COBIT: Satisfaction, Business-IT Alignment and Benefits. 16th Americas Conference on Information Systems.* AMICS.

Marston, S., Li, Z., Bandyopadhyay, S., Zhang, J., & Ghalsasi, A. (2011). Cloud computing – the business perspective. *Decision Support Systems, 51*(1), 176–189. doi:10.1016/j.dss.2010.12.006

Massonet, P., Naqvi, S., Ponsard, C., Latanicki, J., Rochwerger, B., & Villari, M. (2011, May). A monitoring and audit logging architecture for data location compliance in federated cloud infrastructures. In *Parallel and Distributed Processing Workshops and Phd Forum (IPDPSW), 2011 IEEE International Symposium on* (pp. 1510-1517). IEEE. doi:10.1109/IPDPS.2011.304

Mataracioglu, T., & Ozkan, S. (2011). *Governing information security in conjunction with COBIT and ISO 27001.* Researchgate article.

Mayer, N., & Heymans, P. (2007). Design of a Modeling Language for Information System Security Risk Management. *Proceedings of the First International Conference on Research Challenges in Information Science.*

Mayfield, A. (2006). *What is Social Media?.* Retrieved from http://www.spannerworks.com/fileadmin/uploads/eBooks/What_is_ Social_Media.pdf

Mayhorn, C. B., & Nyeste, P. G. (2012). Training users to counteract phishing. *Work (Reading, Mass.), 41*(Supplement 1), 3549–3552. PMID:22317259

McCart, J. A., Padmanabhan, B., & Berndt, D. J. (2013). Goal Attainment on Long Tail Web Sites: An Information Foraging Approach. *Decision Support Systems, 55*(1), 235-246.

McCarthy, I., & Anagroustou, A. (2004). The impact of outsourcing on the transaction costs and boundaries of manufacturing. *International Journal of Production Economics, 88*(1), 61–71. doi:10.1016/S0925-5273(03)00183-X

McCay Solicitors. (2015). *Employees' use and misuse of social media.* Retrieved from http://www.mccaysolicitors.co.uk/employees-use-misuse-of-social-media/

McCormac, A., Zwaans, T., Parsons, K., Calic, D., Butavicius, M., & Pattinson, M. (2016). Individual differences and Information Security Awareness. *Computers in Human Behavior.*

McCrohan, K. F., Engel, K., & Harvey, J. W. (2010). Influence of awareness and training on cyber security. *Journal of Internet Commerce, 9*(1), 23–41. doi:10.1080/15332861.2010.487415

McDonough, S. (n.d.). *How the use of social media can affect your employment.* Retrieved from http://www.md-solicitors.co.uk/how-the-use-of-social-media-can-affect-your-employment/

McKendrick, J. (2016). For healthcare: cloud computing comes in measured doses. *Forbes.* Retrieved online on December 15, 2016 from http://www.forbes.com/sites/joemckendrick/2016/11/27/for-healthcare-cloud-computing-comes-in-measured-doses/#62b6087d6894

MEHARI. (2010). *Risk analysis and treatment Guide.* Available at: http://46.227.81.250/fr/production/ouvrages/pdf/MEHARI-2010-Risk-Analysis-and-Treatment-Guide.pdf

Mejias, R. J., & Balthazard, P. A. (2014). A model of information security awareness for assessing information security risk for emerging technologies. *Journal of Information Privacy and Security, 10*(4), 160–185. doi:10.1080/15536548.2014.974407

Mell, P., & Grance, T. (2011). *The NIST definition of cloud computing: Recommendations of the 33666 Institute of Standards and Technology.* Retrieved online on January 6 from http://csrc.nist.gov/publications/nistpubs/800-145/SP800-145.pdf

Menlo. (2016). *Half of the Web is Vulnerable to Malware.* Retrieved online on December 15, 2016 from http://www.prnewswire.com/news-releases/half-of-the-web-is-vulnerable-to-malware-300376971.html

Merrill, T., Latham, K., Santalesa, D., & Navetta, D. (2011, April). *Social media: The business benefits may be enormous, but can the risks – reputational, legal, operational- be mitigated?* Retrieved from http://www.acegroup.com/us-en/news-room/wp-social-media-the-business-benefits-may-be-enormous-but-can-the-risks-reputational-legal-operational-be-mitigated.aspx?frmmob=tr

Microsoft. (2016). *Cloud Security Alliance.* Retrieved online on December 15, 2016 from https://www.microsoft.com/en-us/trustcenter/Compliance/CSA

Mihailescu, V. L. (2012). Risk analysis and risk management using MEHARI. *International Journal of Applied Business Information Systems., 3*(4), 143–162.

Miller, H. S., Fleet, M. R., Celenza, B. J., & Shust, D. (2012). *U.S. Patent Application 13/417,883.* Retrieved online on 23rd January 2015 from http://www.google.com/patents/US20110161231

Miller, G. (2001). *The Characteristics of Agile Software Processes.* IEEE Computer Society.

Moeller, B., Erek, K., Loeser, F., & Zarnekow, R. (2013). *How Sustainable is COBIT 5? Insights from Theoretical Analysis and Empirical Survey Data. 19th Americas Conference on Information Systems.* Chicago: AMICS.

Moe, N. B., Dingsøyr, T., & Dybå, T. (2010). A teamwork model for understanding an agile team: A case study of a Scrum project. *Information and Software Technology, 52*(5), 480–491. doi:10.1016/j.infsof.2009.11.004

Molenaar, K., Anderson, S., & Schexnader, C. (2010). Guide to Planning Phase: Guidebook on Risk Analysis Tools and Management to Control Transportation Project Cost. The National Academies of Science, Engineering and Medicine.

Montesdioca, G. P. Z., & Maçada, A. C. G. (2015). Measuring user satisfaction with information security practices. *Computers & Security, 48,* 267–280. doi:10.1016/j.cose.2014.10.015

Mooney, J. A. (2013). Locked Out on LinkedIn: LinkedIn Account Belongs to Employee, Not Employer. *Intellectual Property & Technology Law Journal, 25*(6), 16–18.

Morales, J. (2014). 6 Tips for implementing IT governance with COBIT 5. *COBIT Focus, 3*, 7-8. Retrieved online on January 30, 2017 from http://www.isaca.org

Morgan, S. (2016). IBM's new cyberframe is the world's most secure server for datacenters, cloud and mobile. *Forbes*. Retrieved online on December 15, 2016 from http://www.forbes.com/sites/stevemorgan/2016/02/16/ibms-new-cyberframe-is-the-worlds-most-secure-server/#e0781e868fa6

Morimoto, S. (2009). Application of COBIT to Security Management. *International Conference on Frontier of Computer Science and Technology*.

Morse, E. A., & Raval, V. (2008). PCI DSS: Payment card industry data security standards in context. *Computer Law & Security Review, 24*(6), 540-554. Retrieved Online on January 22, 2015 from http://www.sciencedirect.com/science/article/pii/S0267364908000976

MW. (2016). *Dictionary Definition of Social Media*. Retrieved from http://www.merriam-webster.com/dictionary/social%20media

Nadkarni, A., & Hofmann, S. G. (2012). Why do people use Facebook? *Personality and Individual Differences, 52*(3), 243–249. doi:10.1016/j.paid.2011.11.007 PMID:22544987

Nastase, P., Nastase, F., & Ionescu, C. (2010). *Challenges Generated By the Implementation of the IT Standards COBIT 4.1, ITIL V3 and ISO/IEC 27002 in Enterprises*. Academic Press.

Nelson, R. R., & Winter, S. G. (1982). *An evolutionary theory of economic change*. Cambridge, MA: Belknap Press/Harvard University Press.

Nicho, M., & MBA, M. (2011). *Effectiveness of the PCI DSS 2.0 on Preventing Security Breaches: A Holistic perspective*. Retrieved online on 23rd January from http://www.sc2labs.com/public/uploaded/Effectiveness-of-PCI-DSS.pdf

Nicho, M., Fakhry, H., & Haiber, C. (2011). An Integrated Security Governance Framework for Effective PCI DSS Implementation. *International Journal of Information Security and Privacy (IJISP), 5*(3), 50-67. Retrieved online on 23rd January 2015 from http://www.igi-global.com/article/integrated-security-governance-framework-effective/58982

Ni, S., Zhuang, Y., Gu, J., & Huo, Y. (2016). A formal model and risk assessment method for security-critical real-time embedded systems. *International Journal of Computers & Security, 58*, 199–215. doi:10.1016/j.cose.2016.01.005

Norton, E. C., Wang, H., & Ai, C. (2004). Computing Interaction Effects and Standard Errors in Logit and Probit Models. *The Stata Journal*, (4): 154–167.

NSNA. (n.d.). *Recommendations For: Social Media Usage and Maintaining Privacy, Confidentiality and Professionalism*. Retrieved from: http://www.nsna.org/Portals/0/Skins/NSNA/pdf/NSNA_Social_Media_Recommendations.pdf

Nugroho, H. (2014). Conceptual Model Of It Governance For Higher Education Based On COBIT 5 Framework. *Journal of Theoretical and Applied Information Technology*.

Nwafor, C. I., Zavarsky, P., Ruhl, R., & Lindskog, D. (2012). A COBIT and NIST-Based Conceptual Framework for Enterprise User Account Lifecycle Management. *World Congress on Internet Security (WorldCIS)*.

Nyfjord, J., & Mattsson, M. (2008). *Degree of Agility in Pre- Implementation Process Phases*. Academic Press.

Nyfjord, J., & Kajko-Mattsson, M. (2007). Commonalities in Risk Management and Agile Process Models. *International Conference on Software Engineering Advances (ICSEA 2007)*. doi:10.1109/ICSEA.2007.22

OCEG. (2016). *GRC capability model: Red Book 2.0*. Retrieved from http://www.oceg.com

Ogutcu, G., Testik, Ö. M., & Chouseinoglou, O. (2016). Analysis of personal information security behavior and awareness. *Computers & Security*, *56*, 83–93. doi:10.1016/j.cose.2015.10.002

Olajide, P., Zavarsky, P., Ruhl, R., & Lindskog, D. (n.d.). *PCI DSS Compliance Validation of Different Levels of Merchants in a Multi-tenant Private Cloud*. Retrieved online on 23rd January 2015 from http://infosec.concordia.ab.ca/files/2013/02/OlajideP.pdf

Olavsrud, T. (2016). *IBM Buiding blockchain ecosystem*. Retrieved online on December 15, 2016. http://www.cio.com/article/3147358/it-industry/ibm-building-blockchain-ecosystem.html

Oliver, D., & Lainhart, J. (2011). Delivering Business Benefits With COBIT: An Introduction to COBIT 5. *COBIT Focus Journal*.

Oliver, D., & Lainhart, J. (2012). *COBIT 5: Adding Value Through Effective GEIT: EDPACS: The Edp Audit. Control, And Security Newsletter*.

Onwubiko, C. (2010). Security issues to cloud computing. In *Cloud Computing* (pp. 271–288). Springer London. doi:10.1007/978-1-84996-241-4_16

Ophoff, J., & Robinson, M. (2014, August). Exploring end-user smartphone security awareness within a South African context. In *2014 Information Security for South Africa* (pp. 1-7). IEEE.

Opricovic, S. (1998). *Multicriteria optimization of civil engineering systems*. Belgrade: Faculty of Civil Engineering.

Opricovic, S., & Tzeng, G. H. (2004). Compromise solution by MCDM methods: A comparative analysis of VIKOR and TOPSIS. *European Journal of Operational Research*, *156*(2), 445–455. doi:10.1016/S0377-2217(03)00020-1

Oracle Primavera. (2011). *The Yin and Yang of Enterprise Project Portfolio Management and Agile Software Development: Combining Creativity and Governance*. Academic Press.

Othman, M. Ahmad, M. N., Suliman, A. Arshad, N. H., & Maidin, S. S. (2014). COBIT principles to govern flood management. *International Journal of Disaster Risk Reduction*.

OWASP. (2010). *Cloud-10 Multi Tenancy and Physical Security*. Retrieved online on December 15, 2016 from https://www.owasp.org/index.php/Cloud-10_Multi_Tenancy_and_Physical_Security

Owen, M., & Dixon, C. (2007). A new baseline for cardholder security. *Network Security, 6.* Retrieved online on 23rd January 2015 from http://www.sciencedirect.com.gate.lib.buffalo.edu/science/article/pii/S1353485807700545

Parker, D., & Mobey, A. (2004). Action research to explore perceptions of risk in project management. *International Journal of Productivity and Performance Management, 53*(1), 18–32. doi:10.1108/17410400410509932

Parker, F., Ophoff, J., Van Belle, J. P., & Karia, R. (2015, November). Security awareness and adoption of security controls by smartphone users. In *2015 Second International Conference on Information Security and Cyber Forensics (InfoSec)* (pp. 99-104). IEEE. doi:10.1109/InfoSec.2015.7435513

Parsons, K., McCormac, A., Butavicius, M., Pattinson, M., & Jerram, C. (2014). Determining employee awareness using the human aspects of information security questionnaire (HAIS-Q). *Computers & Security, 42*, 165-176.

Pasquini, A., & Galie, E. (2013). COBIT 5 and the Process Capability Model Improvements Provided for IT Governance Process. *Symposium for Young Researchers.*

PCI DSS Compliance Blog. (2013). *SRED Requirements for Point-of-Interaction Devices.* Retrieved Online on January 23rd 2015 from http://blog.elementps.com/element_payment_solutions/2013/01/sred-requirements-for-point-of-interaction-devices.html

PCI Security Standards Council, LLC. (n.d.a). Retrieved on 10th November 2014 from https://www.pcisecuritystandards.org/documents/PCI_DSS_v3.pdf

PCI Security Standards Council, LLC. (n.d.b). Retrieved on 10th November 2014 from https://www.pcisecuritystandards.org/documents/pci_dss_v2_summary_of_changes.pdf

PCI-SSC. (2014). *Security Standards Council, LLC.* Retrieved on 10th October 2014 from https://www.pcisecuritystandards.org/organization_info/index.php

Peltier, T. R. (2005). *Information security risk analysis.* Auerbach Pub. doi:10.1201/9781420031195

Peltier, T. R. (2010). *Information Security Risk Analysis* (3rd ed.). Auerbach Publications.

Peña, J. J. S., Fernández Vicente, E., & Ocaña, A. M. (2013). ITIL, COBIT and EFQM: Can They Work Together?. *International Journal of Combinatorial Optimization Problems and Informatics, 4*(1).

Peretti, K. K. (2008). Data breaches: what the underground world of carding reveals. *Santa Clara Computer & High Tech. LJ, 25*, 375. Retrieved online on 23rd January 2015 from http://digitalcommons.law.scu.edu/cgi/viewcontent.cgi?article=1472&context=chtlj&sei-redir=1&referer=http%3A%2F%2Fscholar.google.com%2Fscholar%3Fq%3Dpoint%2Bof%2Bsale%2Bdata%2Bbreach%2Bpci%2Bdss%26btnG%3D%26hl%3Den%26as_sdt%3D0%252C33%26authuser%3D1#search=%22point%20sale%20data%20breach%20pci%20dss%22

Pesek, G. (2016). *Bringing cloud security innovations to the enterprise.* Retrieved online on December 15, 2016 from http://siliconangle.com/blog/2016/12/02/bringing-cloud-security-innovations-enterprise-reinvent/

Peterson, G. (2010). From auditor-centric to architecture-centric: SDLC for PCI DSS. *Information Security Technical Report, 15*(4), 150-153. Retrieved online on 23rd January 2015 from http://www.sciencedirect.com/science/article/pii/S1363412711000148

Petter, S., & McLean, E. R. (2009). A Meta-analytic Assessment of the Delone and Mclean IS Success Model: An Examination of IS Success at the Individual Level. *Information & Management, 3*(46), 159–166. doi:10.1016/j.im.2008.12.006

Pettigrew, K. E., Durrance, J. C., & Unruh, K. T. (2002). Facilitating Community Information Seeking Using the Internet: Findings from Three Public Library–Community Network Systems. *Journal of the American Society for Information Science and Technology, 53*(11), 894-903.

Pew Research Center. (2014). *Mobile Technology Fact Sheet.* Retrieved October, 2014, from http://www.pewinternet.org/fact-sheets/mobile-technology-fact-sheet/

Pirolli, P., & Card, S. (1999). Information Foraging. *Psychological Review, 106*(4), 643.

Pirolli, P. (2007). *Information Foraging Theory: Adaptive Interaction with Information.* Oxford University Press. doi:10.1093/acprof:oso/9780195173321.001.0001

Pirolli, P. (2009). An Elementary Social Information Foraging Model. *Proceedings of the SIGCHI Conference on Human Factors in Computing Systems,* 605-614.

Podsakoff, P. M., MacKenzie, S. B., Lee, J.-Y., & Podsakoff, N. P. (2003). Common Method Biases in Behavioral Research: A Critical Review of the Literature and Recommended Remedies. *Journal of Applied Psychology, 88*(5), 879.

Ponemon. (2011). *2011 PCI DSS Compliance Trends Study, Survey of IT & IT security practitioners in the U.S.* Retrieved on 10th October 2014 from http://www.imperva.com/docs/AP_Ponemon_2011_PCI_DSS_Compliance_Trends_Study.pdf

Poolsappasit, N., Dewri, R., & Ray, I. (2012). Dynamic Security Risk Management Using Bayesian Attack Graphs. *International Journal of IEEE Transactions on Dependable and Secure Computing, 9*(1), 61–74. doi:10.1109/TDSC.2011.34

Portny, S. E. (2013). Venturing with Unknown: Dealing with Risk. In Project Management for Dummies (4th ed.). Academic Press.

Prafull. (2012). *5 great corporate social media policy examples* [Web post log]. Retrieved from http://blog.hirerabbit.com/5-great-corporate-social-media-policy-examples/

Prahalad, C. K. (2009). In volatile times, agility rules. *Business Week, 80*(September), 21.

Pretorius, E., & Solms, B. v. (2005). *Information Security Governance using ISO 17799 and COBIT.* KPMG Study. doi:10.1109/AMS.2008.145

Prisco, G. (2016). *IBM Launches Blockchain Cloud Services on High Security Server*. Retrieved online on December 15, 2016 from https://bitcoinmagazine.com/articles/ibm-launches-blockchain-cloud-services-on-high-security-server-linuxone-1469043762

Privacilla.org. (2003, April). *The HIPAA Privacy Regulation — Troubled Process, Troubling Results*. Retrieved from http://www.privacilla.org/releases/HIPAA_Report.html

Privacy Rights Clearing House. (2014). *Chronology of Data Breaches*. Retrieved on 10th November 2014 from https://www.privacyrights.org/data-breach/new

Privacy Rights Clearinghouse. (n.d.). Retrieved on January 22, 2015 from https://www.privacyrights.org/

PRMS. (2012). Protecting your practice from social media misadventures. *Rx for Risk, 20*(4).

Project Management Institute. (2013). A guide to the project management body of knowledge. In PMBOK(R) Guide (5th ed.). Author.

Proskauer, D. (2014, July 5). *Employee access to social media in the workplace decreases*. Retrieved from http://www.danpontefract.com/employee-access-to-social-media-in-the-workplace-decreases/

Proskauer. (2014). *Social media in the workplace around the world*. Retrieved from http://www.proskauer.com/files/uploads/social-media-in-the-workplace-2014.pdf

ProtectWise. (2016). *ProtectWise Achieves Advanced Partner Status in the Amazon Web Services Partner Network*. Retrieved online on December 15, 2016 from http://www.businesswire.com/news/home/20161201005006/en/ProtectWise-Achieves-Advanced-Partner-Status-Amazon-Web

Qi, W., Liu, X., Zhang, J., & Yuan, W. (2010). Dynamic Assessment and VaR-based Quantification of Information Security Risk. *Proceedings of the 2nd International Conference on e-Business and Information System Security (EBISS 10)*, 1 – 4. Doi:10.1109/EBISS.2010.5473537

Quinn, J., & Hilmer, F. (1994). Strategic outsourcing. *Sloan Management Review*, (Summer), 43–55.

Radovanović, D., Radojević, T., Lučić, D., & Šarac, M. (2010). *IT audit in accordance with COBIT standard*. IEEE xplore.

Radovanović, D., Lučić, D., Radojević, T., & Šarac, M. (2011). *Information technology governance – COBIT Model*. MIPRO.

Raisch, S., & Birkinshaw, J. (2008). Organizational ambidexterity: Antecedents, outcomes, and moderators. *Journal of Management, 34*(3), 375–409. doi:10.1177/0149206308316058

Rasheed, H. (2011). *Auditing for standards compliance in the cloud: Challenges and directions*. Academic Press.

Rashmi, M. S., & Sahoo, G. (2012). A five-phased approach for the cloud migration. *Int J Emerg Technol Adv Eng, 2*(4), 286–291.

Rayner, J. (2003). *Managing Reputational Risk: Curbing Threats, Leveraging Opportunities.* Chichester, UK: John Wiley & Sons.

Rees, J. (2010). The challenges of PCI DSS compliance. *Computer Fraud & Security, 2010*(12), 14-16. Retrieved online on 23rd January 2015 from http://www.sciencedirect.com/science/article/pii/S1361372310701561

Reinholt, M., Pedersen, T., & Foss, N. J. (2011). Why a Central Network Position Isn't Enough: The Role of Motivation and Ability for Knowledge Sharing in Employee Networks. *Academy of Management Journal, 54*(6), 1277-1297.

Ren, K., Wang, C., & Wang, Q. (2012, January-February). Security Challenges for the Public Cloud. *IEEE Internet Computing, 16*(1), 69–73. doi:10.1109/MIC.2012.14

Ribeiro, J., & Gomes, R. (2009). IT Governance using COBIT implemented in a High Public Educational Institution – A Case Study. *3rd International Conference on European Computing.*

Richard, A. (2007). *Introducing OCTAVE Allegro: Improving the Information Security Risk Assessment Process.* Software Engineering Institute Technical Report CMU/SEI-2007-TR-012 ESC-TR-2007-012. Retrieved from ftp://ftp.sei.cmu.edu/pub/documents/07.reports/07tr012.pdf

Rico, D. F. (2008). What is the Return on Investment (ROI) of agile methods? *Methods (San Diego, Calif.),* 1–7.

Ridley, G., Young, J., & Carroll, P. (2005). COBIT and its Utilization: A framework from the literature. *Proceedings of the 37th Hawaii International Conference on System Sciences.*

Rogers, M. (1998). *The Definition and Measurement of Innovation* (Working paper no. 9/ 98). Melbourne Institute of Applied Economic and Social Research. Retrieved online on January 6, 2017 from http://melbourneinstitute.com/downloads/working_paper_series/ wp1998n09.pdf

Rose, R. (2012, August 15). *HIPAA/HITECH Risk Assessments: Are the Standards Being Met?* Retrieved from http://www.beckershospitalreview.com/healthcare-information-technology/hipaahitech-risk-assessments-are-the-standards-being-met.html

Ross, J. W., & Weill, P. (2002). Six IT decisions your IT people shouldn't make. *Harvard Business Review, 80*(11), 84–95.

Rowlingson, R., & Winsborrow, R. (2006). A comparison of the Payment Card Industry data security standard with ISO17799. *Computer Fraud & Security, 2006*(3), 16-19. Retrieved online January 22, 2015 from http://www.sciencedirect.com/science/article/pii/S1361372306703232

Rubino, M., & Vitolla, F. (2014). Corporate governance and the information system: How a framework for IT governance supports ERM. *Corporate Governance, 14*(3), 320–338. doi:10.1108/CG-06-2013-0067

Rusu, L., & Hudosi, G. (2011). Assessing the risk exposure in IT outsourcing for large companies. *International Journal of Information Technology and Management, 10*(1), 24–44. doi:10.1504/IJITM.2011.037760

Ryoo, J., Rizvi, S., Aiken, W., & Kissell, J. (2013). Cloud Security Auditing: Challenges and Emerging Approaches. *IEEE Security & Privacy, 12*(6), 68-74. doi: 10.1109/MSP.2013.132

Saaty, T. L. (1996). *Decision making with dependence and feedback: Analytic network process.* Pittsburgh, PA: RWS Publications.

Sabherwal, R., Jeyaraj, A., & Chowa, C. (2006). Information System Success: Individual and Organizational Determinants. *Management Science, 12*(52), 1849–1864. doi:10.1287/mnsc.1060.0583

Safa, N. S., Von Solms, R., & Furnell, S. (2016). Information security policy compliance model in organizations. *Computers & Security, 56,* 70-82.

Safa, N. S., Sookhak, M., Von Solms, R., Furnell, S., Ghani, N. A., & Herawan, T. (2015). Information security conscious care behaviour formation in organizations. *Computers & Security, 53,* 65–78. doi:10.1016/j.cose.2015.05.012

Safa, N. S., & Von Solms, R. (2016). An information security knowledge sharing model in organizations. *Computers in Human Behavior, 57,* 442–451. doi:10.1016/j.chb.2015.12.037

Sahibudin, S., Sharifi, M., & Ayat, M. (2008). Combining ITIL, COBIT and ISO/IEC 27002 in Order to Design a Comprehensive IT Framework in Organizations. *Second Asia International Conference on Modelling & Simulation.*

Salle, M., & Rosenthal, S. (2005). Formulating and Implementing an HP IT program strategy using COBITT and HP ITSM. *Proceedings of the 38th Hawaii International Conference on System Sciences.* doi:10.1109/HICSS.2005.276

Saltmarsh, T. J., & Browne, P. S. (1983). Data Processing – Risk Assessment. In M. M. Wofsey (Ed.), *Advances in Computer Security Management* (Vol. 2, pp. 93–116). John Wiley and Sons Ltd.

Samantra, D., Datta, S., & Mahapatra, S. S. (2014). Risk assessment in IT outsourcing using fuzzy decision-making approach: An Indian perspective. *Expert Systems with Applications, 41*(8), 4010–4022. doi:10.1016/j.eswa.2013.12.024

Sanidas, E. (2004). Technology, technical and organizational innovations, economic and societal growth. *Technology in Society, 26*(1), 67–84. doi:10.1016/j.techsoc.2003.10.006

Sarukkai, S. (2015). *How Data Science And Machine Learning Is Enabling Cloud Threat Protection.* Retrieved online on December 15, 2016 from http://cloudtweaks.com/2015/12/data-science-machine-learning/

Schlienger, T., & Teufel, S. (2003). Information security culture – From analysis to change. *3rd annual information security South Africa conference, information security South Africa – Proceedings of ISSA 2003.*

Schwartz, M. J. (2014). *Michaels Data Breach Response: 7 Facts.* Retrieved on 10th November 2014 from http://www.darkreading.com/attacks-breaches/michaels-data-breach-response-7-facts/d/d-id/1204630

Scutt, M. (2013, Sept). *Misuse of Social media by Employees*. Retrieved from http://www.infolaw. co.uk/newsletter/2013/09/misuse-of-social-media-by-employees/

Semer, L. J. (2012). Evaluating the employee security awareness program: Regular audits of IT safeguards can reveal whether staff members are doing their part to protect the organization's data and networks. *Internal Auditor, 69*(6), 53–57.

Senft, S., Gallegos, F., & Davis, A. (2012). *Information technology control and audit*. Auerbach Publications.

Shackleford, D. (n.d.). *How to overcome unique cloud-based patch management challenges* Retrieved online on December 15, 2016 from http://searchcloudsecurity.techtarget.com/tip/ How-to-overcome-unique-cloud-based-patch-management-challenges

Shaw, A. (2009). Data breach: from notification to prevention using PCI DSS. *Column. JL & Soc. Probs., 43*, 517. Retrieved Online on January 22, 2015 from http://www.columbia.edu/cu/ jlsp/pdf/Summer%202010/Shaw.JLSP.43.4.pdf

Shaw, R. S., Chen, C. C., Harris, A. L., & Huang, H. J. (2009). The impact of information richness on information security awareness training effectiveness. *Computers & Education, 52*(1), 92–100. doi:10.1016/j.compedu.2008.06.011

Shedden, P., Smith, W., & Ahmad, A. (2010). Information Security Risk Assessment: Towards a Business Practice Perspective. *Proceedings of the 8th Australian Information Security Management Conference.*

Sheldon, K. M., Abad, N., & Hinsch, C. (2011). A two-process view of Facebook use and relatedness need-satisfaction: Disconnection drives use, and connection rewards it. *Journal of Personality and Social Psychology, 100*(4), 766–775. doi:10.1037/a0022407 PMID:21280967

Shivashankarappa, A. N., Dharmalingam, R., Smalov, L., & Anbazhagan, N. (2012). Implementing it Governance Using Cobit: A Case Study Focusing on Critical Success Factors. *World Congress on Internet Security (WorldCIS-2012).*

Shi, X. J., Tsuji, H., & Zhang, S. M. (2011). Eliciting experts perceived risk of software offshore outsourcing incorporating individual heterogeneity. *Expert Systems with Applications, 38*(3), 2283–2291. doi:10.1016/j.eswa.2010.08.016

Shrivastava, S., & Rathod, U. (2015). Categorization of risk factors for distributed agile projects. *Information and Software Technology, 58*(February), 373–387. doi:10.1016/j.infsof.2014.07.007

Shukla, N., & Kumar, S (2012). A Comparative Study on Information Security Risk Analysis Practices. *International Journal of Computer Applications.*

Shullich, R. (2011, December 5). *Risk assessment of Social Media*. Retrieved from https://www. sans.org/reading-room/whitepapers/privacy/risk-assessment-social-media-33940

Silic, M., & Back, A. (2016). The dark side of social networking sites: Understanding phishing risks. *Computers in Human Behavior, 60*, 35–43. doi:10.1016/j.chb.2016.02.050

Simonsson, M., & Johnson, P. (2006). Assessment of IT Governance - A Prioritization of COBIT. *Conference on Engineering Systems Research.*

Singleton, T. (2014). The Core of IT Auditing. *ISACA Journal, 6.* Retrieved from https://www. isaca.org/Journal/archives/2014/Volume-6/Pages/The-Core-of-IT-Auditing.aspx

Siponen, M., Baskerville, R., & Kuivalainen, T. (2005, January). Integrating security into agile development methods. In *Proceedings of the 38th Annual Hawaii International Conference on System Sciences, HICSS'05* (pp. 185a-185a). IEEE.

Siponen, M., Mahmood, M. A., & Pahnila, S. (2014). Employees adherence to information security policies: An exploratory field study. *Information & Management, 51*(2), 217–224. doi:10.1016/j.im.2013.08.006

SkyHigh. (2016). *What is a cloud access security broker.* Academic Press.

Smith, A. (2011, November 14). *Why Americans use social media.* Pew Research Center.

Smith, P. G., & Merritt, G. M. (2002). *Proactive risk management.* New York: Productivity Press.

Smith, P., & Pichler, R. (2005). *Agile Risks/Agile Rewards.* Software Development.

Sobol, M., & Apte, U. (1995). Domestic and global outsourcing practices of Americas most effective IS users. *Journal of Information Technology, 10*(4), 269–280. doi:10.1057/jit.1995.30

Solove, D. J. (2003, April). HIPAA Turns 10: Analyzing the Past, Present and Future Impact. *Journal of American Health Information Management Association, 84*(4).

Son, J. Y. (2011). Out of fear or desire? Toward a better understanding of employees motivation to follow IS security policies. *Information & Management, 48*(7), 296–302. doi:10.1016/j.im.2011.07.002

Spagnoletti, P. (Ed.). (2011). Information Technology and Innovation Trends in Organizations: A Business Aware Information Security Risk Analysis Method. Physica-Verlag. Doi:10.1007/978-3-7908-2632-6_51

Srinivasan, V., & Shocker, A. D. (1973). Linear programming techniques for multidimensional analysis of preference. *Psychometrica, 38*(3), 337–342. doi:10.1007/BF02291658

Stapleton, J. (1997). DSDM: Dynamic Systems Development Method. *Proceedings Technology of Object-Oriented Languages and Systems. TOOLS 29* (Cat. No.PR00275).

State of Software Risk Management Practice. (2008). *Software Engineering.*

Stekhoven, A. (2012). Active Software Escrow's Usefulness for Companies Embracing COBIT 5. *COBIT Focus Journal.*

Stephens, D. W., & Krebs, J. R. (1986). *Foraging Theory.* Princeton University Press.

Stewart, G., & Lacey, D. (2012). Death by a thousand facts: Criticising the technocratic approach to information security awareness. *Information Management & Computer Security, 20*(1), 29–38. doi:10.1108/09685221211219182

Stoica, M., Mircea, M., & Ghilic-Micu, B. (2013). Software Development: Agile vs. Traditional. *Informatica Economica, 17*(4), 64-76. doi:10.12948/issn14531305/17.4.2013.06

Stoneburner, G., Goguen, A., & Feringa, A. (2002). Risk management guide for information technology systems. National Institute of Standards and Technology. doi:10.6028/NIST.SP.800-30

Stoneburner, G., Goguen, A., & Feringa, A. (2002). *Risk Management Guide for Information Technology Systems, NIST Special Publication 800-30*. Gaithersburg, MD: NIST.

Strauss, A., & Corbin, J. (1997). *Grounded Theory in Practice*. London: Sage Publications.

Subashini, S., & Kavitha, V. (2011). A survey on security issues in service delivery models of cloud computing. *Journal of Network and Computer Applications, 34*(1), 1–11. doi:10.1016/j.jnca.2010.07.006

Suh, B., & Han, I. (2003). The IS risk analysis based on a business model. *International Journal of Information Management, 41*(2), 149–158. doi:10.1016/S0378-7206(03)00044-2

Sullivan, R. (2010, May). The Changing Nature of US Card Payment Fraud: Issues for Industry and Public Policy. In *WEIS*. Retrieved Online on January 22, 2015 from http://weis2010.econinfosec.org/papers/panel/weis2010_sullivan.pdf

Summary of the HIPAA Privacy Rule. (n.d.). Retrieved from https://www.hhs.gov/hipaa/for-professionals/privacy/laws-regulations/index.html?language=es

Sun, B. L., Srivastava, R. P., & Mock, T. J. (2006). An Information Systems Security Risk Assessment Model under Dempster-Shafer Theory of Belief Functions. *International Journal of Management Information Systems, 22*(4), 109–142. doi:10.2753/MIS0742-1222220405

Suryanarayana, G., Sharma, T., & Samarthyam, G. (2015). Software Process versus Design Quality: Tug of War? *IEEE Software, 32*(4), 7–11. doi:10.1109/MS.2015.87

Susanto, H., Almunawar, M. N., & Tuan, Y. C. (2011). *Information security management system standards: A comparative study of the big five*. Academic Press.

Susanto, H., Almunawar, M. N., & Tuan, Y. C. (2011). Information Security Management System Standards: A Comparative Study of the Big Five. *International Journal of Electrical & Computer Sciences, 11*(5).

Sussman, B. (2008). Mastering the Payment Card Industry Standard: Private Framework Seeks to Shield Credit and Debit Card Account Information. *Journal of Accountancy, 205*(1), 50. Retrieved online on 23rd January 2015 from https://www.questia.com/read/1G1-173922998/mastering-the-payment-card-industry-standard-private

Svata, V. (2009). *IS Audit Considerations in Respect of Current Economic Environment.* International Auditing and Assurance Standards Board.

Symons, C. (2006). *COBIT Versus Other Frameworks: A Road Map to Comprehensive IT Governance. Trends Journal.*

Taft, D. (2016a). *IBM takes the power of mainframe to cloud.* Retrieved online on December 15, 2016 from http://www.eweek.com/cloud/ibm-takes-the-power-of-the-mainframe-to-the-cloud.html

Taft, D. (2016b). *IBM Delivers Secure Blockchain Services in the Cloud.* Retrieved online on December 15, 2016 from http://www.eweek.com/cloud/ibm-delivers-secure-blockchain-services-in-the-cloud.html

Taylor, J., Jr. (2013). *Risk Management: Keeping track of risk and utilizing risk manager.* Bright Hub Project Management.

Taylor, A., & Helfat, C. E. (2009). Organizational Linkages for Surviving Technological Change: Complementary Assets, Middle Management, and Ambidexterity. *Organization Science, 20*(4), 718–739. doi:10.1287/orsc.1090.0429

Taylor, L. (2014). FedRAMP: History and Future Direction. *IEEE Cloud Computing, 1*(3), 10–14. doi:10.1109/MCC.2014.54

TeachBeacon. (2016). *Survey: Is agile the new norm?* Retrieved from https://techbeacon.com/survey-agile-new-norm

Techopedia. (2016). Retrieved from https://www.techopedia.com/definition/25836/it-risk-management

Teilans, A., Romanovs, A., Merkuryer, Y., Kleins, A., Dorogovs, P., & Krastas, O. (2011). Functional modelling of IT risks assessment support system. *Economics & Management, 16*, 1061–1068.

Teneyuca, D. (2011). Internet cloud security: The illusion of inclusion. *Information Security Technical Report, 16*(3).

The HIPAA Privacy Rule's Right of Access and Health Information Technology. (n.d.). Retrieved from https://www.hhs.gov/sites/default/files/ocr/privacy/hipaa/understanding/special/healthit/eaccess.pdf

The History of HIPAA & the Consequences of A HIPAA Violation. (n.d.). Retrieved from https://www.recordnations.com/articles/history-hipaa/

Thompson, T., Jr., Hertzberg, J., & Sullivan, M. (2011). *Social media and its associated risks.* Retrieved from https://www.grantthornton.ca/resources/insights/white_papers/ social%20media_whitepaper%20CDN%20-%20FINAL.pdf

Thouin, M. F., Hoffman, J. J., & Ford, E. W. (2009). IT outsourcing and firm-level performance: A transaction cost perspective. *Information & Management, 46*(8), 463–469. doi:10.1016/j.im.2009.08.006

Times. (2009). *Times updates social media guidelines.* Retrieved from http://latimesblogs.latimes.com/readers/2009/11/updated-social-media-guidelines.html

Tipton, H. F., & Krause, M. (2007). *Information security management handbook.* Auerbach Publications.

Tjoa, S. (2011). A Formal Approach Enabling Risk-Aware Business Process Modeling and Simulation. *International Journal of IEEE Transactions On Services Computing, IEEE., 4*(2), 153–166. doi:10.1109/TSC.2010.17

Tobias, S. (2014). *2014: The Year in Cyberattacks.* Retrieved on 10th January 2015 from http://www.newsweek.com/2014-year-cyber-attacks-295876

Trendmicro.com. (n.d.). *Anatomy of a Data Breach by Hipolito. J.* Retrieved on February 15th 2015 from http://www.trendmicro.com/vinfo/us/threat-encyclopedia/web-attack/110/anatomy-of-a-data-breach

Tsai, J. Y., Egelman, S., Cranor, L., & Acquisti, A. (2011). The Effect of Online Privacy Information on Purchasing Behavior: An Experimental Study. *Information Systems Research, 22*(2), 254-268.

Tsohou, A., Karyda, M., & Kokolakis, S. (2015). Analyzing the role of cognitive and cultural biases in the internalization of information security policies: Recommendations for information security awareness programs. *Computers & Security, 52*, 128–141. doi:10.1016/j.cose.2015.04.006

Tushman, M. L., & Anderson, P. C. (1986). Technological discontinuities and organizational environments. *Administrative Science Quarterly, 31*(3), 439–465. doi:10.2307/2392832

Tuttle, B., & Vandervelde, S. D. (2007). An empirical examination of COBIT as an internal control framework for IT. *International Journal of Accounting Information Systems.* doi:10.1016/j.accinf.2007.09.001

Tutton, J. (2010). Incident response and compliance: A case study of the recent attacks. *Information Security Technical Report, 15*(4), 145-149. Retrieved online on 23rd January 2015 from http://www.sciencedirect.com/science/article/pii/S1363412711000124

United States Computer Emergency Readiness Team Alert (TA14-212A), Backoff Point-of-Sale Malware. (2014). Retrieved on February 15th 2015 from https://www.us-cert.gov/ncas/alerts/TA14-212A

Vaast, E., & Kaganer, E. (2013). Social Media Affordances and Governance in the Workplace: An Examination of Organizational Policies. *Journal of Computer-Mediated Communication, 19*(1), 78–101. doi:10.1111/jcc4.12032

Valentine, J. A. (2006). Enhancing the employee security awareness model. *Computer Fraud & Security, 2006*(6), 17–19. doi:10.1016/S1361-3723(06)70370-0

Van Haren Publishing. (2012). *COBIT 5 - A Management Guide*. Author.

Vance, A., & Siponen, M. T. (2012). IS security policy violations: A rational choice perspective. *Journal of Organizational and End User Computing, 24*(1), 21–41. doi:10.4018/joeuc.2012010102

Vance, A., Siponen, M., & Pahnila, S. (2012). Motivating IS security compliance: Insights from habit and protection motivation theory. *Information & Management, 49*(3), 190–198. doi:10.1016/j.im.2012.04.002

Varhol, P. (2016, November 21). *The complete history of agile software development*. Retrieved from https://techbeacon.com/agility-beyond-history%E2%80%94-legacy%E2%80%94-agile-development

Vaultive. (2016). *Vaultive and Gemalto Team Up to Deliver Increased Cloud Data Security Control for SaaS Applications*. Retrieved online on December 15, 2016 from http://www.prnewswire.com/news-releases/vaultive-and-gemalto-team-up-to-deliver-increased-cloud-data-security-control-for-saas-applications-300342211.html

Verizon Communication. (2014). Retrieved on November 4, 2014 from http://www.verizonenterprise.com/pcireport/2014/

Verizon. (2013). *Verizon Data Breach Investigations Report*. Retrieved on 10th October 2014 from http://www.verizonenterprise.com/resources/reports/rp_data-breach-investigations-report-2013_en_xg.pdf

Vijayan, J. (2016). *Google Initiates Customer-Supplied Cloud Data Encryption Keys*. Retrieved online on December 15, 2016 from http://www.eweek.com/cloud/google-initiates-customer-supplied-cloud-data-encryption-keys.html

VISA Inc. (n.d.a). Retrieved online 10th January 2015 from http://usa.visa.com/merchants/protect-your-business/cisp/service-providers.jsp

VISA Inc. (n.d.b). Retrieved on 10th January 2015 from http://usa.visa.com/merchants/protect-your-business/cisp/merchant-pci-dss-compliance.jsp

von Solms, B. (2005). *Information Security governance: COBIT or ISO 17799 or both? Computers & Security Journal*.

Walker, A., McBride, T., Basson, G., & Oakley, R. (2012). ISO/IEC 15504 measurement applied to COBIT process maturity". Benchmarking. *International Journal (Toronto, Ont.), 19*(2), 159–176.

Wang, J. (2013, October 30). *How do I become HIPAA compliant? (A checklist)*. Retrieved from https://www.truevault.com/blog/how-do-i-become-hipaa-compliant.html

Wang, J., Chaudhury, A., & Rao, H. R. (2008). A Value-at-Risk Approach to Information Security Investment. *International Journal of Information Systems Research, 19*(1), 106–120. doi:10.1287/isre.1070.0143

Watt, A. (2014). *Project Management: Risk Management Planning*. BC Open Textbook.

Weber, R. P. (1990). *Basic content analysis*. Beverly Hills, CA: Sage. doi:10.4135/9781412983488

Webster, J., & Watson, R. T. (2002). Analyzing the Past to Prepare for the Future: Writing a Literature Review. *Management Information Systems Quarterly*, 2(26), iii–xiii.

Welles, K. (2008, Dec 4). *Online Comments lead to privacy complaint*. Retrieved from http://www.databreaches.net/online-comments-lead-to-privacy-complaint/

Why Is the HIPAA Privacy Rule Needed? (n.d.). Retrieved from https://www.hhs.gov/hipaa/for-professionals/faq/188/why-is-the-privacy-rule-needed/index.html

Widerman, R. M. (1992). *Project and program risk management: A guide to managing project risks*. Academic Press.

Wieder, B., Booth, P., Matolcsy, Z. P., & Ossimitz, M. (2006). The impact of ERP systems on firm and business process performance. *Journal of Enterprise Information Management*, 19(1), 13–29. doi:10.1108/17410390610636850

Wijnand, I., de Kort, Y., Midden, C., & van den Hoven, E. (2006). Persuasive Technology for Human Well-Being: Setting the Scene. Persuasive Technology, 1-5.

Wikipedia. (2016). Retrieved information from https://en.wikipedia.org/wiki/Risk_analysis

Wikipedia: The Free Encyclopedia. (2014, December 19). Retrieved on November 4, 2014, from http://www.wikipedia.org

Wilkin, C., Campbell, J., Moore, S., & Van Grembergen, W. (2013). Co-Creating Value from IT in a Contracted Public Sector Service Environment: Perspectives on COBIT and Val IT. *Journal of Information Systems, 27*.

Williams & Ayobami. (2013). Relationship between Information Security Awareness and Information Security Threat. *International Journal of Research in Commerce, IT & Management, 3*(8).

Williams, P. (2008). *In a 'trusting' environment, everyone is responsible for information security*. Elsevier Information Security Technical Report 13.

Winkler, T., & Rinner, B. (2012). User-centric privacy awareness in video surveillance. *Multimedia Systems, 18*(2), 99–121. doi:10.1007/s00530-011-0241-1

Wipawayangkool & Villafranca. (2015). Exploring Millennials' Malware Awareness and Intention to Comply with Information Security Policy. *Review of Integrative Business and Economics Research, 4*(3), 153.

Wisconsin Writing Centre. (2016). *Learn how to write a review of literature*. Retrieved online on January 10 from http://writing.wisc.edu/Handbook/ReviewofLiterature.html#what

Wolfswinkel, Furtmueller, & Wilderom. (2011). Using Grounded Theory as a Method for Rigorously Reviewing Literature. *European Journal of Information Systems*. doi: 10.1057/ejis.2011.51

Wood, T., Cecchet, E., Ramakrishnan, K. K., Shenoy, P. J., van der Merwe, J. E., & Venkataramani, A. (2010). Disaster Recovery as a Cloud Service: Economic Benefits & Deployment Challenges. *HotCloud*, *10*, 8–15.

Wright, C. (2014). Agile Project need Agile Controls and Audit. *ISACA Ireland Conference GRC 2.0 - Breaking Down The Silos Conference*.

Wright, C. (2014). *Agile governance and audit: an overview for auditors and agile teams*. Cambridge, UK: IT Governance.

Wu, W. W., & Lee, Y. T. (2007). Developing global managers competencies using the fuzzy DEMATEL method. *Expert Systems with Applications*, *32*(2), 499–507. doi:10.1016/j.eswa.2005.12.005

Xiao, X., Califf, C.B., Sarker, S., & Sarker, S. (2013). ICT innovation in emerging economies: a review of the existing literature and a framework for future research. *Journal Information Technology*, *28*(4), 264–278.

Xifra, J., & Ordeix, E. (2009). Managing reputational risk in an economic downturn: The case of Banco Santander. *Public Relations Review*, *35*(4), 353–360. doi:10.1016/j.pubrev.2009.08.004

Yang, C. Y., & Huang, J. B. (2000). A decision model for IS outsourcing. *International Journal of Information Management*, *20*(3), 225–239. doi:10.1016/S0268-4012(00)00007-4

Yang, D. H., Kim, S., Nam, C., & Min, J. W. (2007). Developing a decision model for business process outsourcing. *Computers & Operations Research*, *34*(12), 3769–3778. doi:10.1016/j.cor.2006.01.012

Yath v. Fairview Clinics, N. P. (2009). Retrieved from http://www.casebriefs.com/blog/law/health-law/health-law-keyed-to-furrow/the-professional-patient-relationship/yath-v-fairview-clinics-n-p/

Yazar, Z. (2002). *Qualitative Risk Analysis and Management Tool – CRAMM, (GSEC, Version 1.3)*. SANS Institute.

Younkins, L. R. (2013). #IHateMyBoss: Rethinking the NLRB's Approach to Social Media Policies. *Brooklyn Journal of Corporate, Financial & Commercial Law*, *8*(1), 222–252.

Yu, S., Wang, C., Ren, K., & Lou, W. (2010). Achieving Secure, Scalable, and Fine-grained Data Access Control in Cloud Computing. *Proceedings IEEE INFOCOM*. doi:10.1109/INFCOM.2010.5462174

Zech, P. (2011, March). Risk-based security testing in cloud computing environments. In *2011 Fourth IEEE International Conference on Software Testing, Verification and Validation* (pp. 411-414). doi:10.1109/ICST.2011.23

Zeltser, L. (2011). *Learning to live with social networks: risk and rewards*. Retrieved from: https://zeltser.com/media/docs/social-networking-risks-rewards.pdf

Zeng, Y. (2010). *Risk management for enterprise resource planning system implementations in project-based firms* (Doctoral dissertation).

Zhao, D. M., Liu, J. X., & Zhang, Z. H. (2009). Method of risk evaluation of information security based on neural networks. *Proceedings of the International Conference on Machine Learning and Cybernetics*, 1127-1132. Doi:10.1109/ICMLC.2009.5212464

Zscaler. (2016). *Zscaler Private Access—Remote Access without the Security Risks of VPNs*. Retrieved online on December 15, 2016 from https://www.zscaler.com/press/zscaler-private-access/remote-access-without-security-risks-vpns

About the Contributors

Manish Gupta is Manager of Information Risk Assurance at BlueCross BlueShield of Western New York and Adjunct Assistant Professor at State University of New York at Buffalo. He has more than 15 years of leadership experience in cybersecurity and IT risk management. Prior to his current role, he was VP of cybersercurity at one of the 15 largest banks in the US. Over the years, he has established, led and governed programs for corporate security awareness, threat and vulnerability management, regulatory and compliance, risk management and governance, security architecture and cybersecurity capabilities. He has authored or coauthored more than 70 research articles that are published in journals, books and conference proceedings. His research has won best paper awards and has been published in MISQ, DSS, ACM Transactions, JOEUC amongst others. He has edited or co-edited 7 books in the area of information assurance, cybersecurity and risk management. He holds several professional designations including CISSP, CISM, CISA, CRISC, CFE and PMP. He teaches graduate level courses in IT Auditing and IT Risk Management at SUNY Buffalo. He received PhD (Management/MIS) and MBA from State University of New York at Buffalo in 2011 and 2003, respectively and a bachelors degree in Mechanical Engineering from IET Lucknow, India in 1998.

* * *

Priyadarsini Kannan Krishnamachariar is a MIS graduate student at University at Buffalo, New York. She is an ISTQB Certified Business & Quality Analyst, trained Agile/Scrum practitioner having over four years of experience in the field of Quality Assurance, Risk Management and Business Process Improvement. Her latest job was with Entertainment Partners, United States and prior to that she worked for Oracle and Cognizant India. She has worked on various business domains which includes Oracle Primavera, US Payroll, Financial services and Insurance. Her areas of specialization include IS audit, IT Risk, Business Analysis & Quality Assurance. She has extensive experience in requirements engineering, auditing, testing & certification of IT systems and project management. She has received accolades for her proven analytical and problem solving skills from her employers. She has recently passed Certified Information Systems Auditor (CISA) examination, a globally recognized certification for IS Auditors and she is a student member of Information Systems Audit and Control Association (ISACA).

Salim Lahmiri is full professor at ESCA School of Management, Casablanca, Morocco. He graduated from Concordia University, Montreal, Canada; received the master of engineering degree within the department of electrical engineering of the École de Technologie Supérieure, Montreal, Canada; and the Ph.D. degree in cognitive informatics from the department of computer science of the University of Quebec at Montreal (UQAM), Montreal, Canada. His research interests include intelligent systems and decision support systems.

Amrita Nanda has over 5 and half years' experience in the IT industry and has worked as a business analyst consultant at various consulting organization (SDLC partners, PWC, Infosys Limited). She has played key roles in requirement gathering, project management, business process improvement, IT strategy & planning and acted as a consultant for release and delivery of many applications. She has obtained her master's degree in Management Information systems from State university of New York, Buffalo. Her areas of concentration were Risk management, advanced risk management, Information assurance and Digital Forensics.

Priyal Popat has over 4 years of experience in the IT industry and has contributed her expertise in Business Analysis and Information Security & Compliance consulting to various organizations over her tenure. She has extensively worked in Healthcare payer and provider domain and has played key roles in requirement gathering, data analysis, Medical device security and risk assessment and IT project implementation. She has obtained her master's degree in Management Information Systems from State university of New York, Buffalo. Her areas of concentration were IT Risk management, Information assurance, System Analysis and Design and Digital Forensics.

Niranjali Suresh has over three and a half years of experience in the IT industry and has worked as a software configuration management consultant at Intellect Design Arena Ltd. (A PolarisFT group company). She has played key roles in defining, implementing and auditing configuration management processes and has also built cross-platform continuous integration systems for several applications. She is currently pursuing her Master's degree in Management Information Systems from University at Buffalo, New York. Her areas of concentration include IT audit, risk and information assurance. She has recently written and passed the Certified Information Systems Auditor (CISA) exam, which is a world renowned standard of achievement in IT auditing.

Kaushik Swaminathan is currently pursuing Master's degree in Management Information Systems at University at Buffalo, New York. Prior to this, he has over three and a half years of experience as a QA Analyst at Tata Consultancy Services, India, working for telecom clients such as Rogers, Canada and Telia Sonera, Sweden. His areas of interests are IT audit, risk management and information assurance. He has also passed the highly reputed Certified Information Systems Auditor (CISA) examination.

Index

A

agile 59, 268-288, 292, 294-295
AHP 220, 222, 227
ANP 220, 222, 227
asset-based risk 3, 8-9
auditing 12, 58-59, 143, 160, 162, 218, 229-232, 237-238, 241, 244-245, 257, 268, 270-273, 277-279, 283-285, 288-289, 292-295

B

breaches 12, 23, 83, 90, 99-104, 106, 120-121, 124, 130-134, 142, 144, 176, 179-184, 188-189, 209-210, 238, 243
business process-based risk 4, 12

C

cell phone 104, 302
cell phone industry 302
challenges 2, 23, 80, 99-100, 110, 117, 119, 144, 231, 270, 273, 276-277, 280, 290
cloud computing 104, 146, 148, 229-233, 235, 237-239, 241-246, 249-250, 259
Cloud Security 229, 231, 237, 239, 242-244, 250, 253
COBIT 13, 48-61, 63-64, 104-105, 108, 238
compliance 21, 39, 45, 54, 71, 77-79, 81-82, 85, 91, 93-94, 99, 101-109, 111-113, 115-121, 123, 134, 143-144, 148, 150-154, 157-158, 160, 164, 178, 181, 200, 229, 232-234, 237, 241, 243-244, 251, 253, 256-257, 273, 286, 288, 293

D

Data Precision Ranking 36, 47
Decision-Tree-Analysis 47
DEMATEL 217, 220, 222, 227

F

financial institutions 99-100, 103, 119
fuzzy PROMETHEE 220, 222
fuzzy set 9, 218, 220, 222-223

G

governance of Enterprise IT 51

H

health insurance 71-75, 87, 244
HIPAA law 74, 76, 95

I

information leakage 177-179, 182-183
information security 1-5, 7, 9, 12, 53, 58, 102-105, 107-108, 143-144, 150-156, 158-160, 162, 164, 167, 220, 222, 241-242
Information Security Risk Management 1-3
integrated framework 52, 104, 108
IT audit 237, 268, 273
IT Governance 48-49, 52, 57, 105, 144
IT management 49, 54, 123, 291

L

LINMAP 221, 223, 227

M

MADM 220, 222, 227
MCDM 220, 222, 227
medical care 72
medical records 71-73, 75-76, 95
merchant 105, 109, 112-113, 115, 118, 120
Monte Carlo Simulation 47

N

networking sites 163, 166, 303, 306, 308, 312

O

operating systems 252, 301-302, 309

P

patient's information 76, 78
PCI DSS 99-112, 115-121, 124, 130, 132-134
personal computers 157, 302
phishing 151, 156-158, 163, 165-166, 255
project management 26, 59, 105, 273-274, 278, 294
PROMETHEE 220, 223, 227

Q

QFD 220, 223, 228
qualitative risk 7, 34, 36, 218
quantitative risk 3, 36, 282

R

Responsibility Assignment Matrix 32, 47
risk 1-9, 11-16, 21-31, 34-36, 38-45, 47, 50, 53, 55, 59, 73, 88, 91, 102-103, 105-108, 112, 142-144, 152, 155-156, 159-161, 165, 167, 176-177, 179-182, 184, 189, 214-218, 220-223, 229-230, 232, 234-237, 239, 241-243, 245-246, 254, 257, 268, 270-271, 273, 276-277,

280-284, 289-290, 292, 295, 305, 309
risk assessment 2-9, 11-16, 29, 91, 103, 106, 155, 182, 216-218, 222, 229-230, 232, 241, 280, 282, 284
Risk Audit 47
Risk Breakdown Structure 27, 47
risk management 1-5, 7, 11-14, 16, 21-26, 28-29, 34, 36, 38, 43-45, 88, 108, 182, 216, 237, 243, 276-277, 280-283, 292, 295
Risk Profile Report 44, 47

S

search engines 301-304, 306-309, 312
security awareness 142-146, 148, 150-152, 155-165, 167, 218
security training 143, 154, 157, 160, 166
seeking information 301-305, 307-309, 312
service provider 109, 114-116, 123, 160, 230, 233, 235-240, 242, 244, 252
smartphone users 164, 302, 312
social engineering 150-151, 155, 162-166
social media 151, 162, 176-184, 188-189, 195, 199-201, 203, 206, 208-211
social media policies 178, 180, 183, 188, 195
social networking 163, 166, 181-182, 250, 303, 306, 308, 312
software development 59, 268-276, 295

T

tax benefit, 72
technology innovation 229, 302
TOPSIS 220-222, 228
training sessions 188, 291

V

Variance and Trend Analysis 47
versions 60, 99, 108-109, 309
VIKOR 220, 222, 228

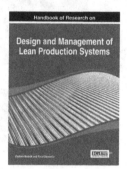
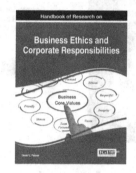

Printed in the United States
By Bookmasters